A Devil and Her Love Song

Story & Art by
Miyoshi Tomori

Volume 11

A Devil and Her Love Song

Volume 11
CONTENTS

The devil makes me LOVELY!!!

STORY THUS FAR

A disagreement between Maria and Shin causes them to fight. After that, Maria starts to suffer from hallucinations. During one particular episode, Shin hugs Maria to try and calm her down. Unfortunately, the embrace makes Maria recall her painful past, and she loses her voice. At the same time, Shin suffers a serious injury to his right hand. But even in the face of all of these difficulties, Maria and Shin's feelings only grow, and they are finally able to confirm their love for one another.

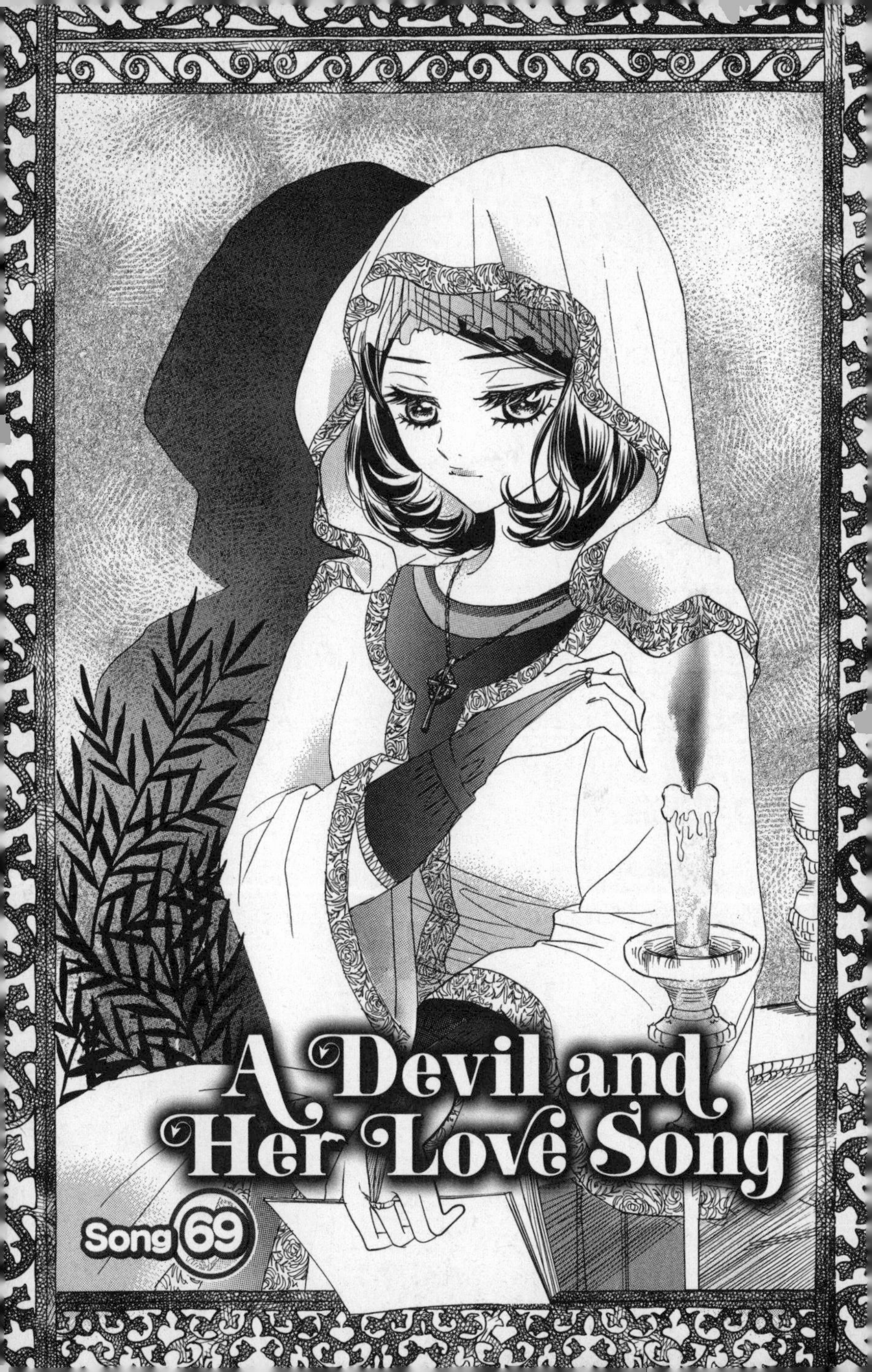
A Devil and Her Love Song
Song 69

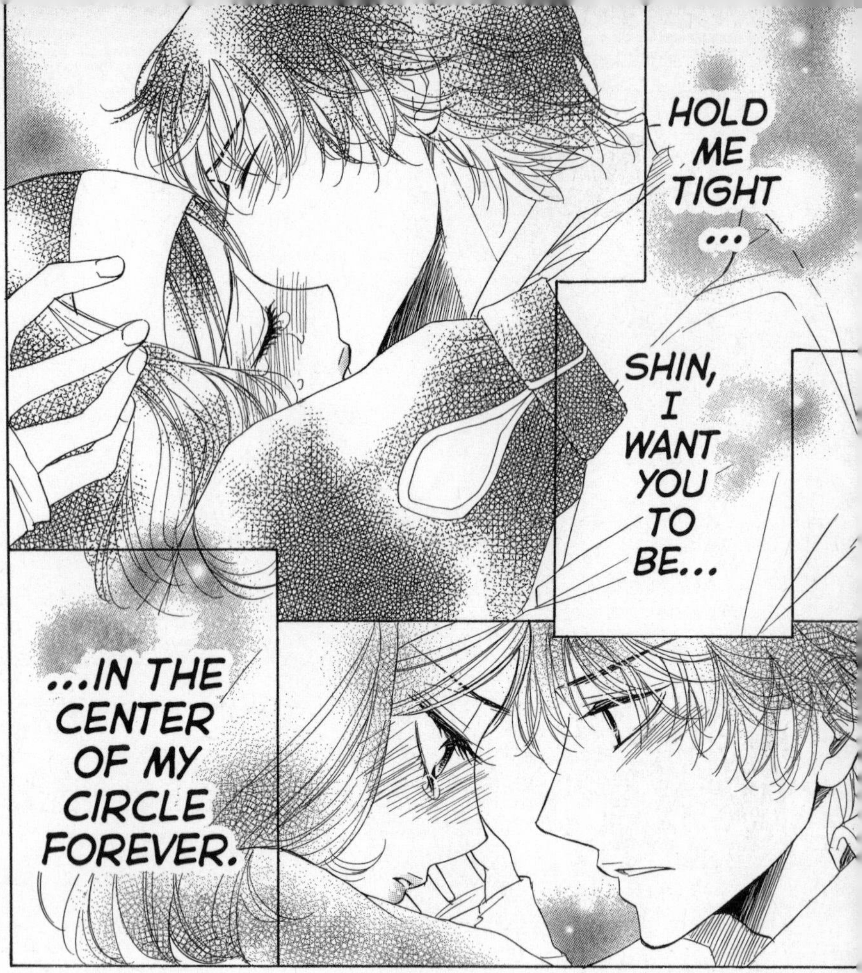
HOLD ME TIGHT...
SHIN, I WANT YOU TO BE...
...IN THE CENTER OF MY CIRCLE FOREVER.

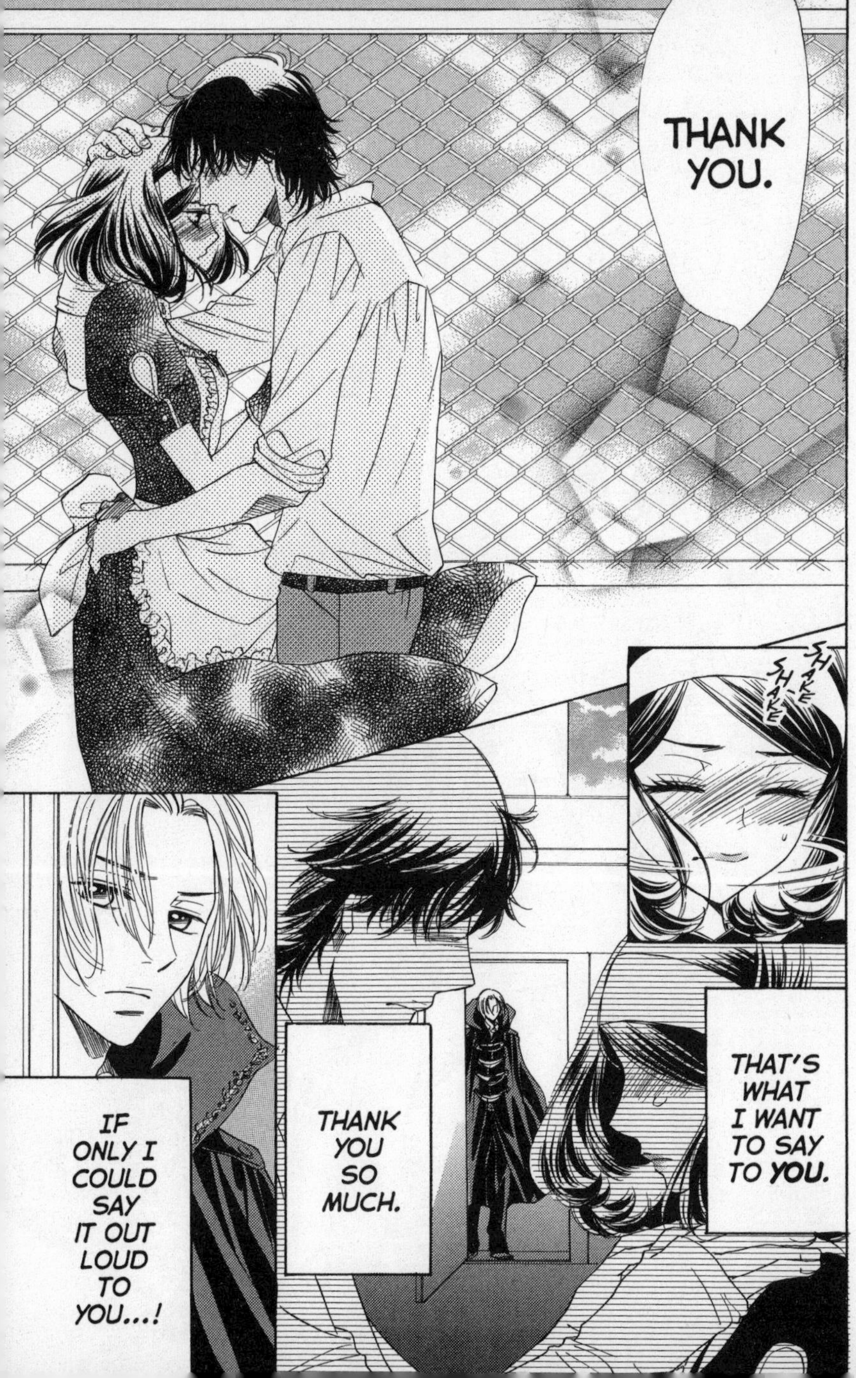
THANK YOU.
SHAKE SHAKE
THAT'S WHAT I WANT TO SAY TO **YOU**.
THANK YOU SO MUCH.
IF ONLY I COULD SAY IT OUT LOUD TO YOU...!

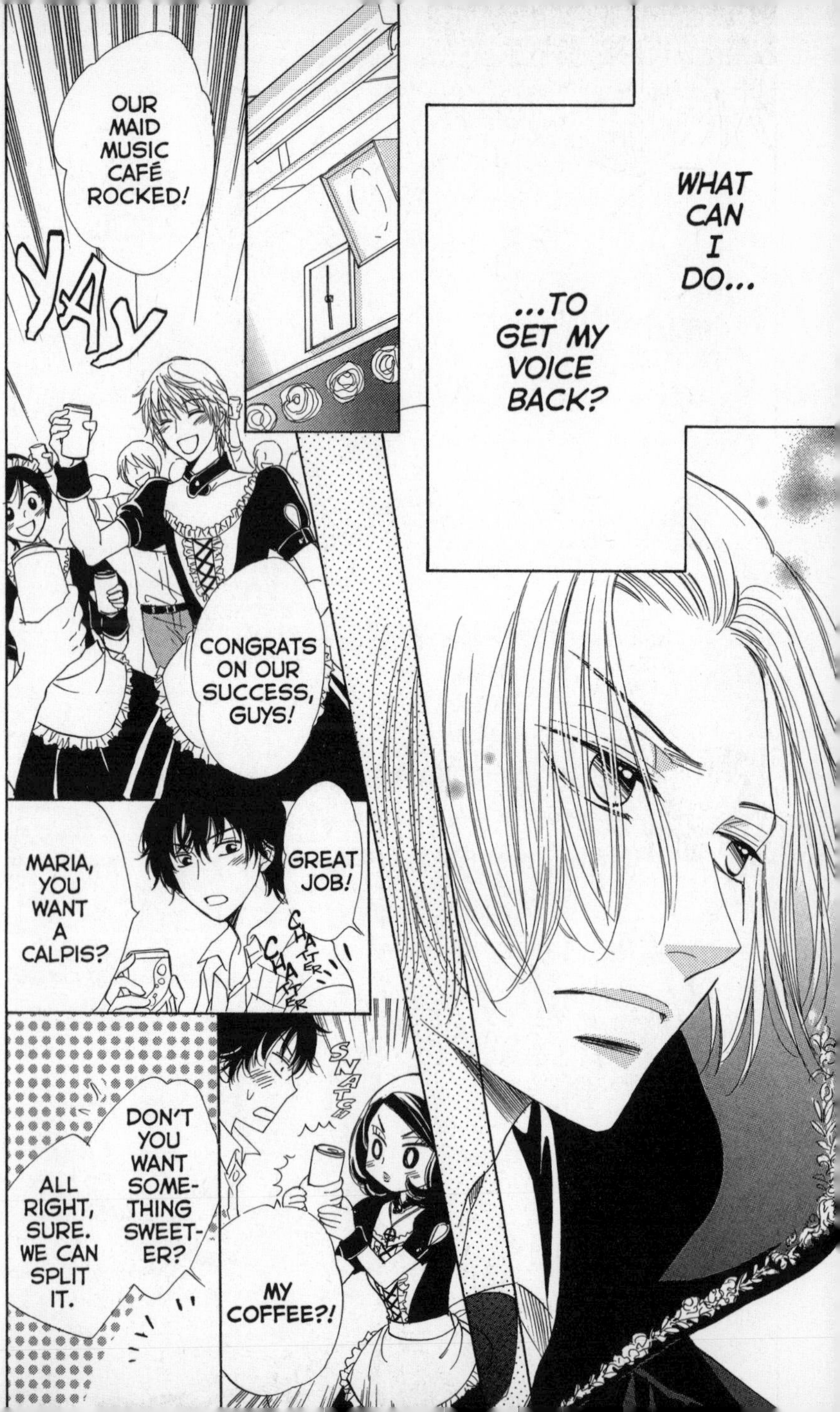
WHAT CAN I DO...
...TO GET MY VOICE BACK?
OUR MAID MUSIC CAFÉ ROCKED!
YAY
CONGRATS ON OUR SUCCESS, GUYS!
GREAT JOB!
MARIA, YOU WANT A CALPIS?
CHATTER CHATTER
SNATCH
MY COFFEE?!
DON'T YOU WANT SOME-THING SWEET-ER?
ALL RIGHT, SURE. WE CAN SPLIT IT.

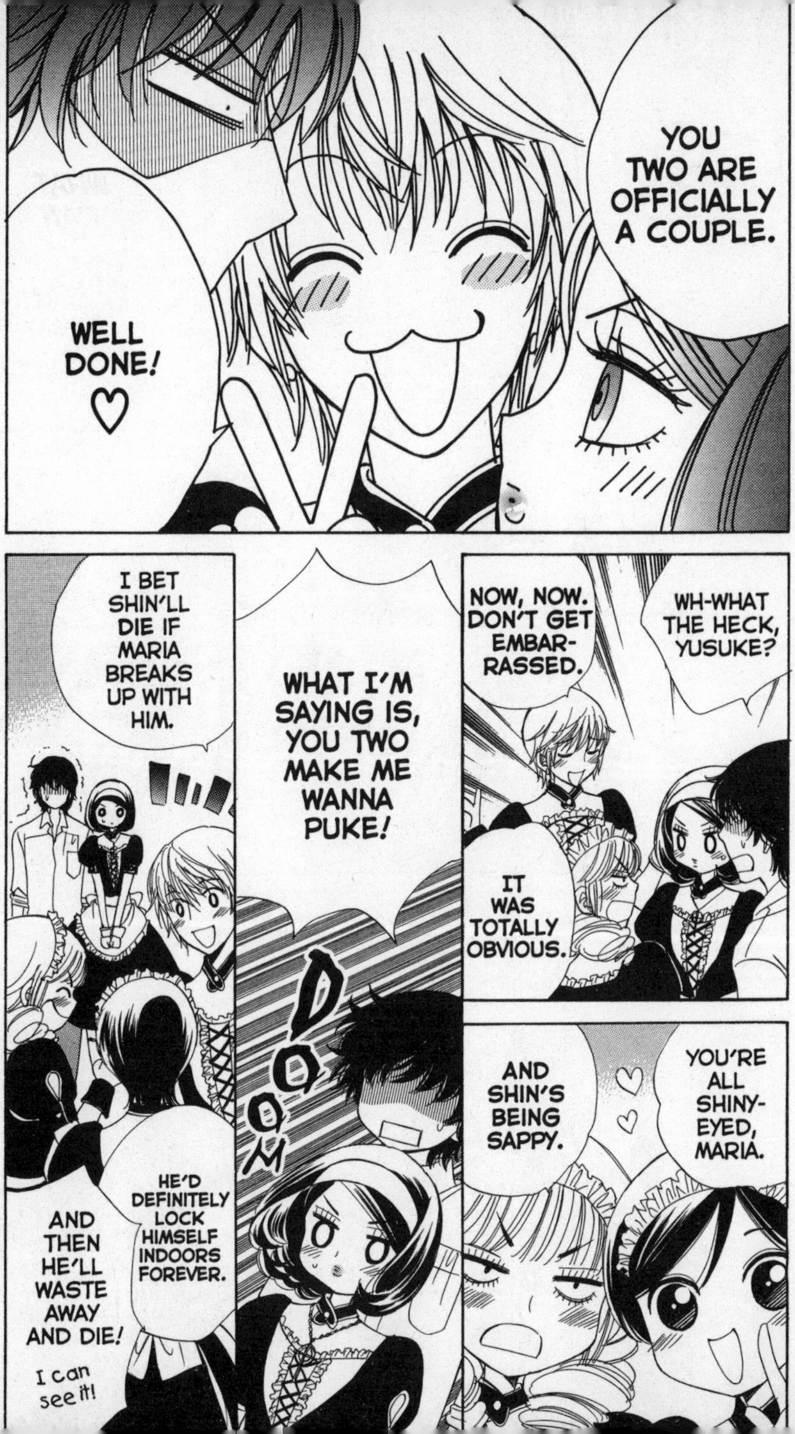
YOU TWO ARE OFFICIALLY A COUPLE.
WELL DONE! ♡
WH-WHAT THE HECK, YUSUKE?
NOW, NOW. DON'T GET EMBARRASSED.
IT WAS TOTALLY OBVIOUS.
YOU'RE ALL SHINY-EYED, MARIA.
AND SHIN'S BEING SAPPY.
WHAT I'M SAYING IS, YOU TWO MAKE ME WANNA PUKE!
DOOOM
I BET SHIN'LL DIE IF MARIA BREAKS UP WITH HIM.
HE'D DEFINITELY LOCK HIMSELF INDOORS FOREVER.
AND THEN HE'LL WASTE AWAY AND DIE!
I can see it!

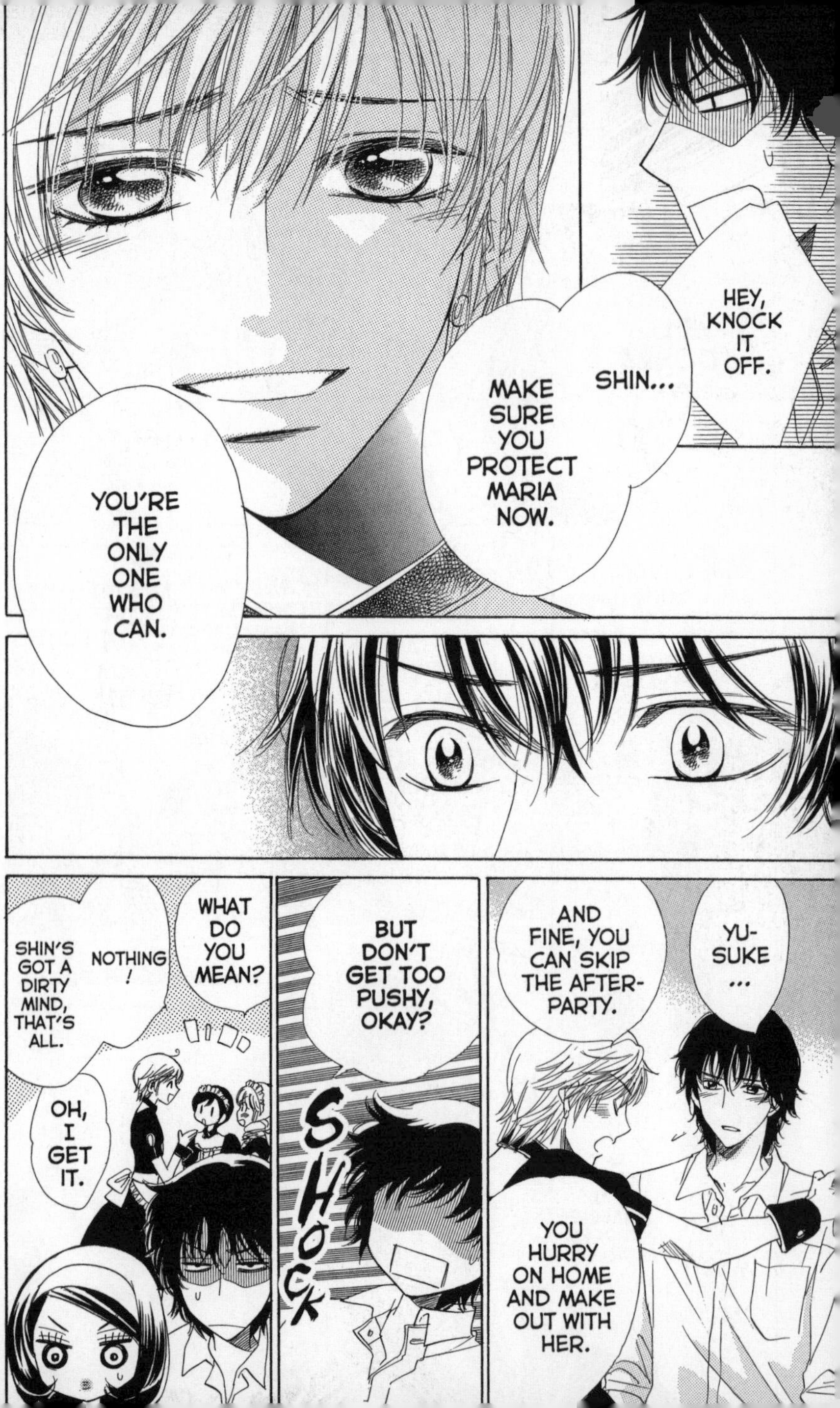
HEY, KNOCK IT OFF.
SHIN...
MAKE SURE YOU PROTECT MARIA NOW.
YOU'RE THE ONLY ONE WHO CAN.
YU-SUKE...
AND FINE, YOU CAN SKIP THE AFTER-PARTY.
YOU HURRY ON HOME AND MAKE OUT WITH HER.
BUT DON'T GET TOO PUSHY, OKAY?
SHOCK
WHAT DO YOU MEAN?
NOTHING!
SHIN'S GOT A DIRTY MIND, THAT'S ALL.
OH, I GET IT.

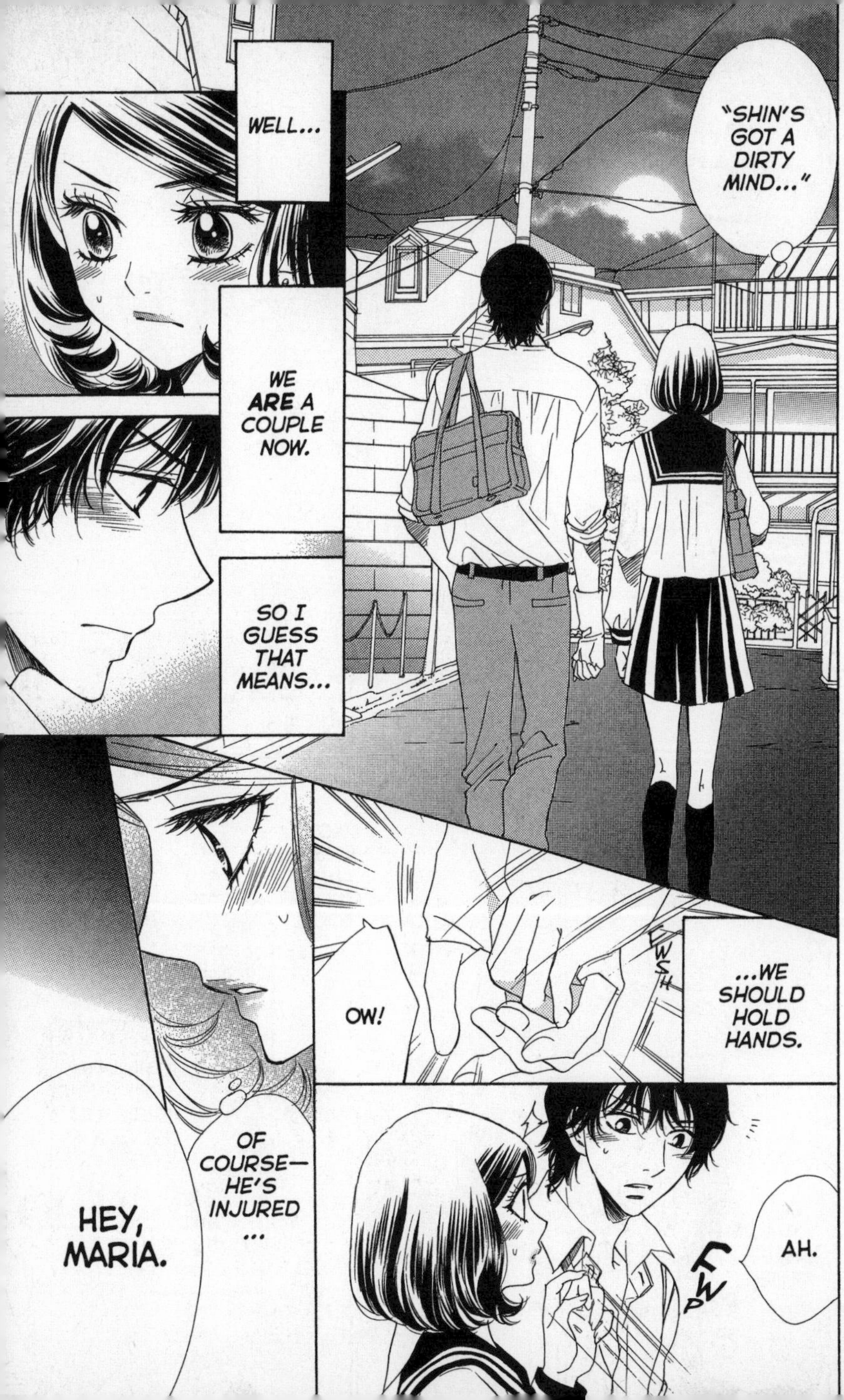

"SHIN'S GOT A DIRTY MIND..."
WELL...
WE **ARE** A COUPLE NOW.
SO I GUESS THAT MEANS...
...WE SHOULD HOLD HANDS.
FWSH
OW!
AH.
FWP
OF COURSE—HE'S INJURED...
HEY, MARIA.

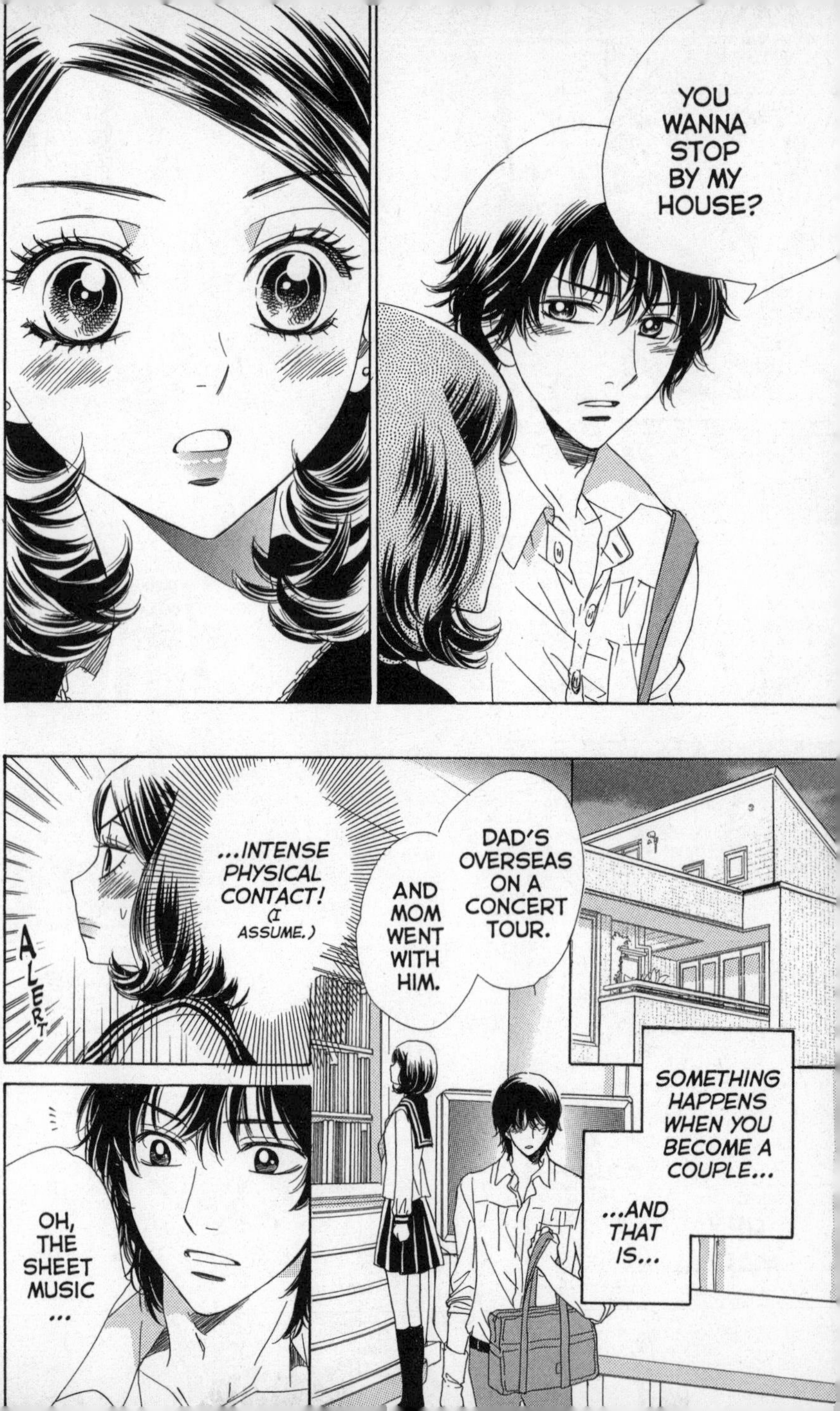

YOU WANNA STOP BY MY HOUSE?
DAD'S OVERSEAS ON A CONCERT TOUR.
AND MOM WENT WITH HIM.
SOMETHING HAPPENS WHEN YOU BECOME A COUPLE...
...AND THAT IS...
...INTENSE PHYSICAL CONTACT!
(I ASSUME.)
ALERT
OH, THE SHEET MUSIC...

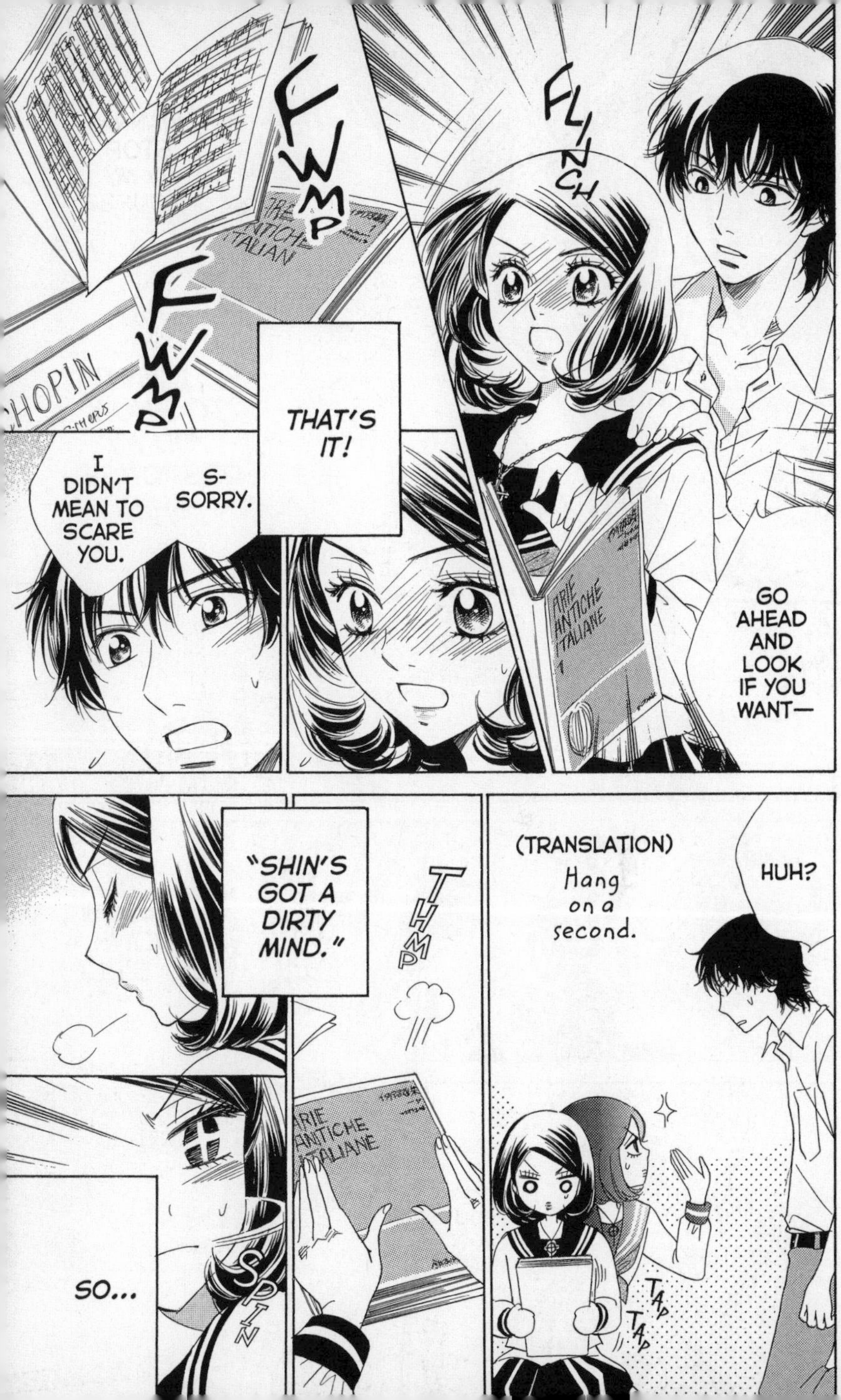
FLINCH
GO AHEAD AND LOOK IF YOU WANT—
FWMP
FWMP
ARIE ANTICHE ITALIANE
CHOPIN
THAT'S IT!
S-SORRY.
I DIDN'T MEAN TO SCARE YOU.
HUH?
(TRANSLATION)
Hang on a second.
TAP TAP
"SHIN'S GOT A DIRTY MIND."
THUMP
SO...
SPIN

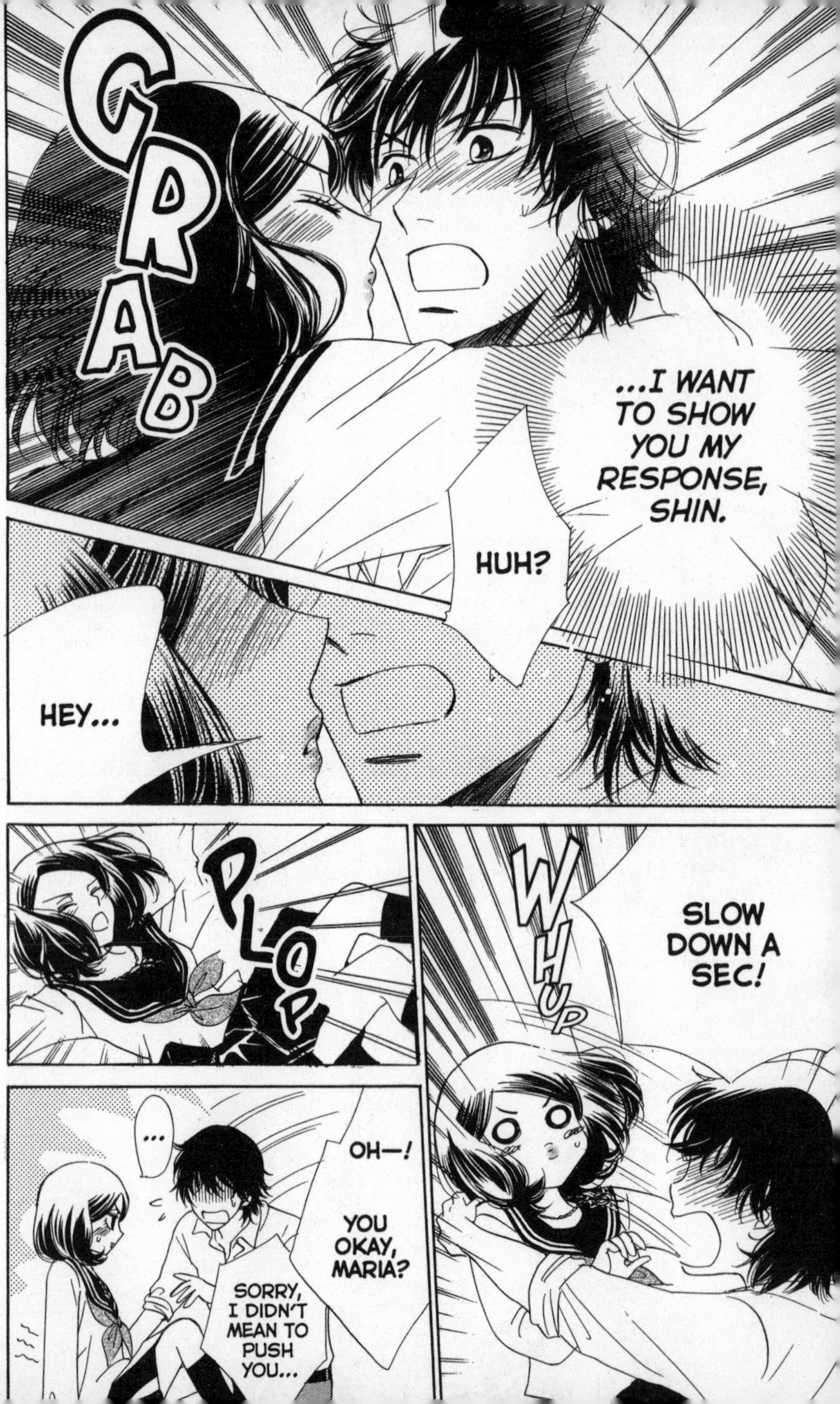
...I WANT TO SHOW YOU MY RESPONSE, SHIN.
GRAB
HUH?
HEY...
SLOW DOWN A SEC!
WHUP
PLOP
OH—!
YOU OKAY, MARIA?
SORRY, I DIDN'T MEAN TO PUSH YOU...
...

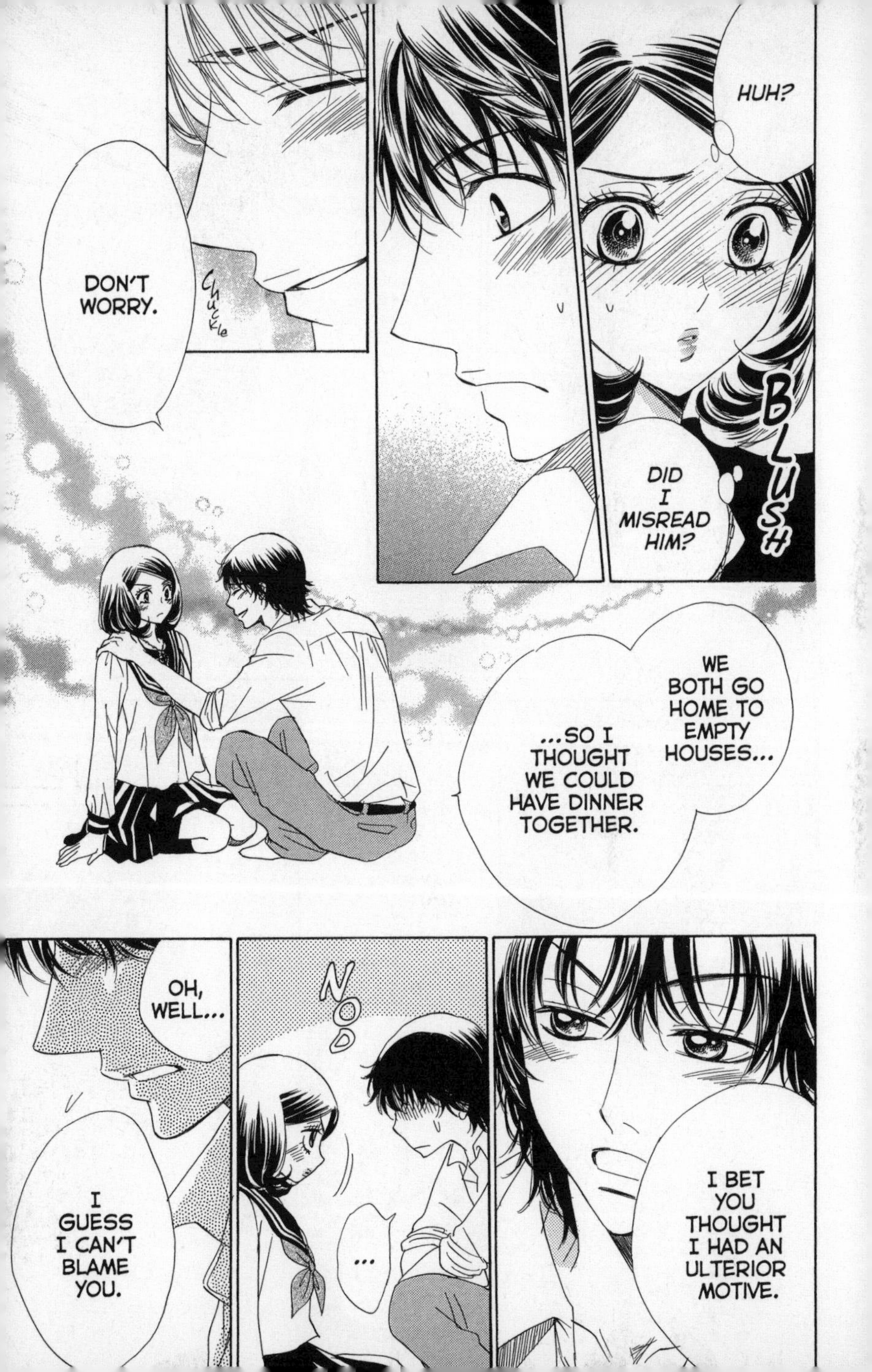
HUH?
DID I MISREAD HIM?
BLUSH
DON'T WORRY.
Chuckle
WE BOTH GO HOME TO EMPTY HOUSES...
...SO I THOUGHT WE COULD HAVE DINNER TOGETHER.
I BET YOU THOUGHT I HAD AN ULTERIOR MOTIVE.
NOD
...
OH, WELL...
I GUESS I CAN'T BLAME YOU.

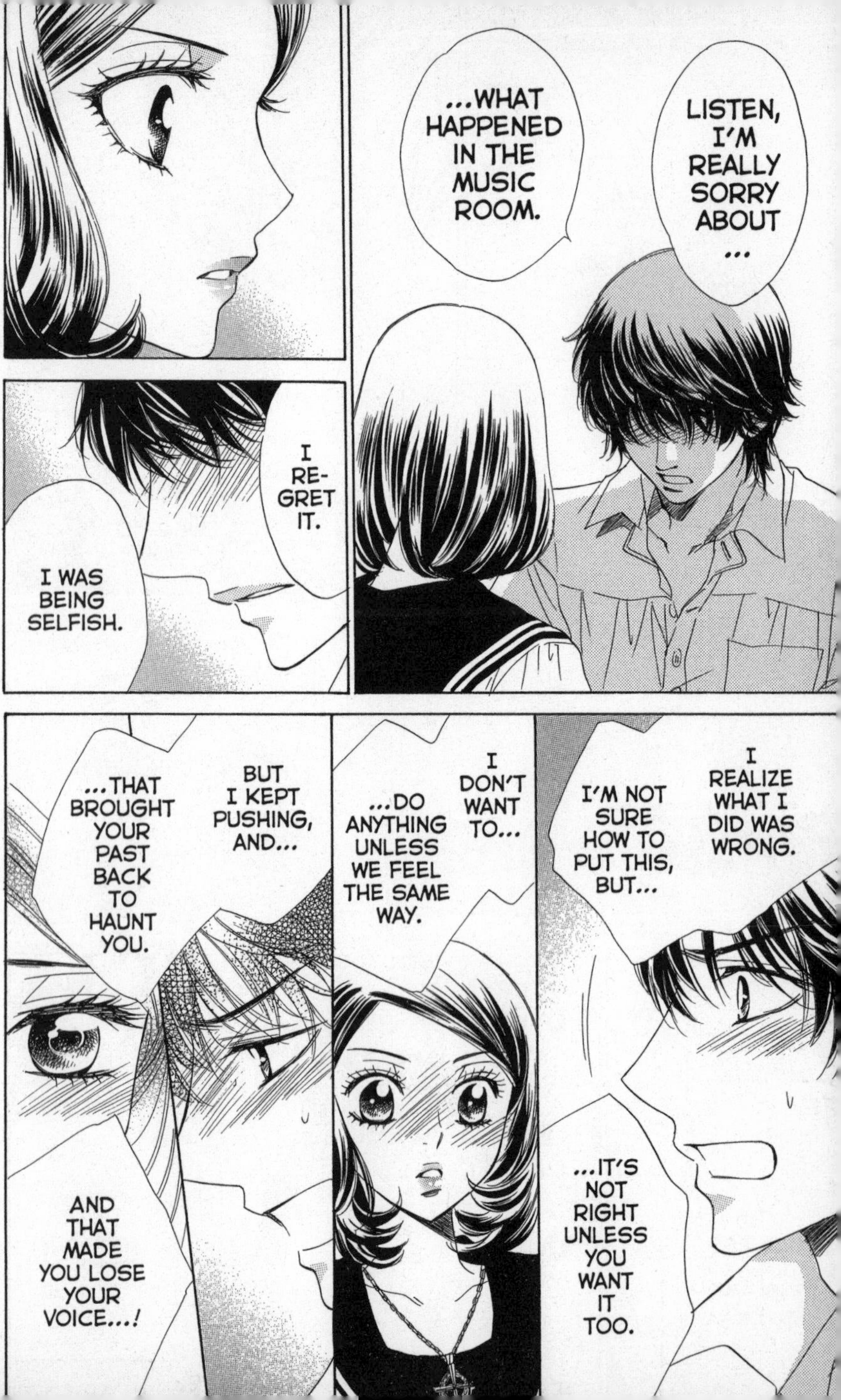
LISTEN, I'M REALLY SORRY ABOUT ...
...WHAT HAPPENED IN THE MUSIC ROOM.
I RE-GRET IT.
I WAS BEING SELFISH.
I REALIZE WHAT I DID WAS WRONG.
I'M NOT SURE HOW TO PUT THIS, BUT...
...IT'S NOT RIGHT UNLESS YOU WANT IT TOO.
I DON'T WANT TO...
...DO ANYTHING UNLESS WE FEEL THE SAME WAY.
BUT I KEPT PUSHING, AND...
...THAT BROUGHT YOUR PAST BACK TO HAUNT YOU.
AND THAT MADE YOU LOSE YOUR VOICE...!

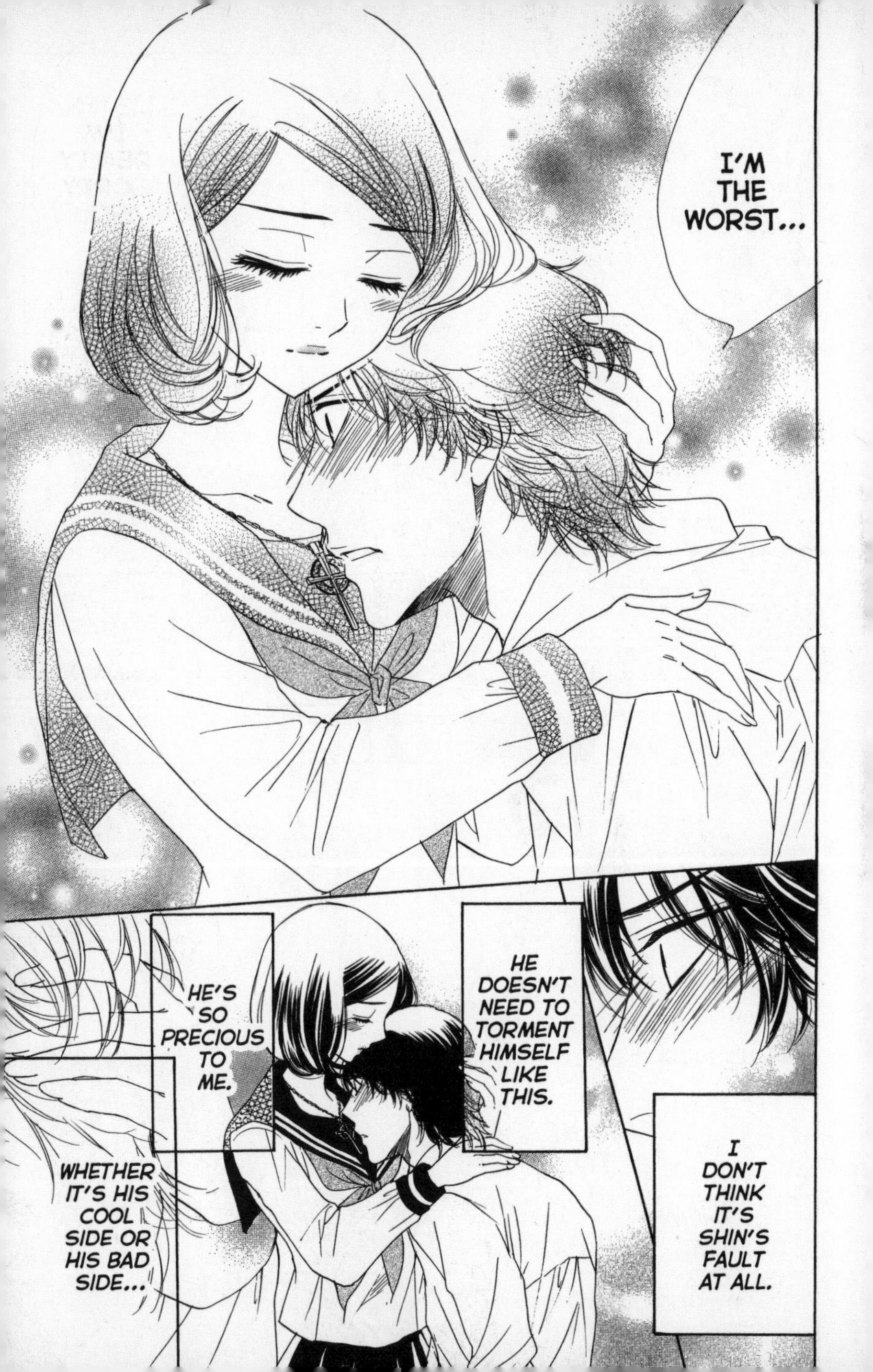
I'M THE WORST...
I DON'T THINK IT'S SHIN'S FAULT AT ALL.
HE DOESN'T NEED TO TORMENT HIMSELF LIKE THIS.
HE'S SO PRECIOUS TO ME.
WHETHER IT'S HIS COOL SIDE OR HIS BAD SIDE...

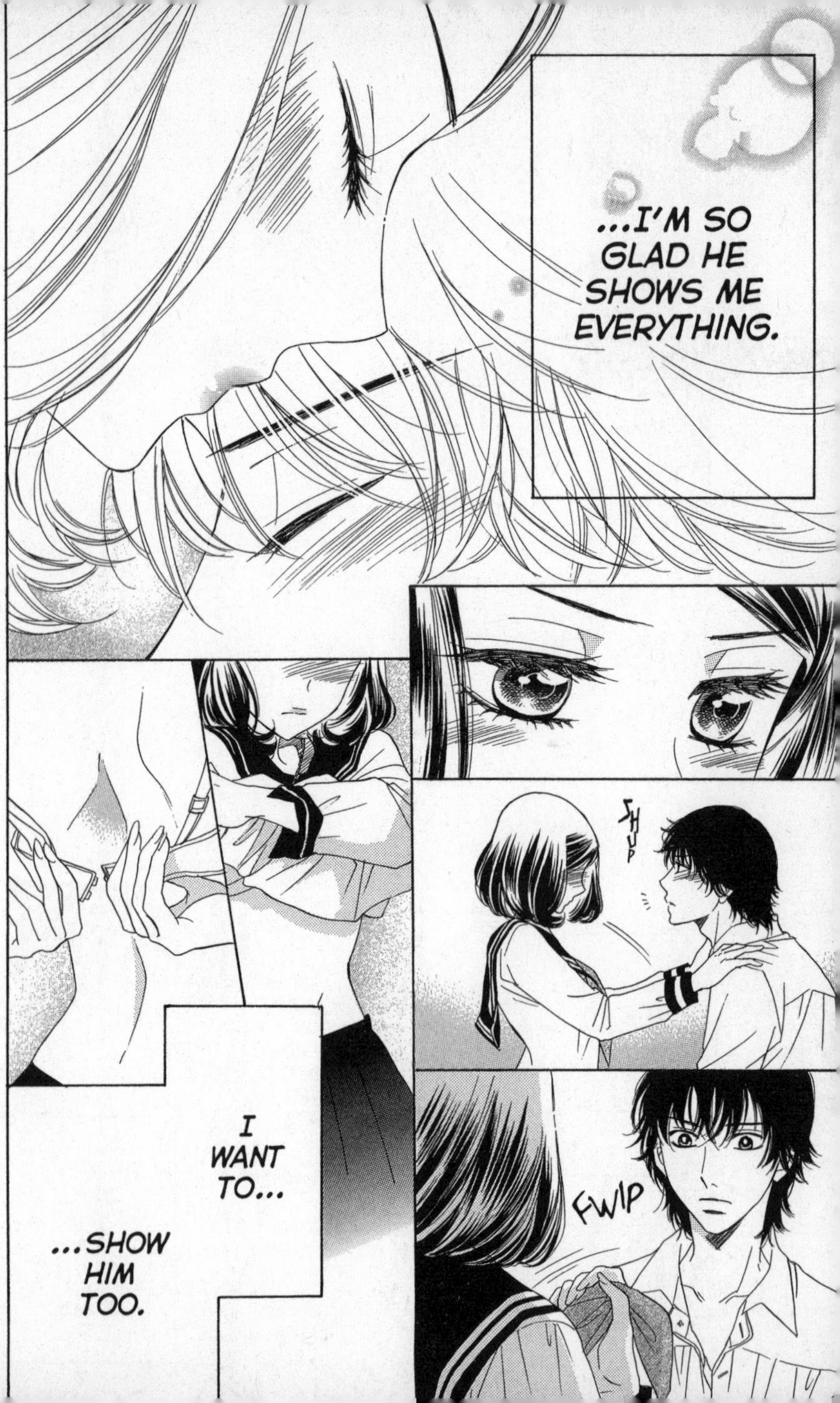
...I'M SO GLAD HE SHOWS ME EVERYTHING.
SHUP
FWIP
I WANT TO...
...SHOW HIM TOO.

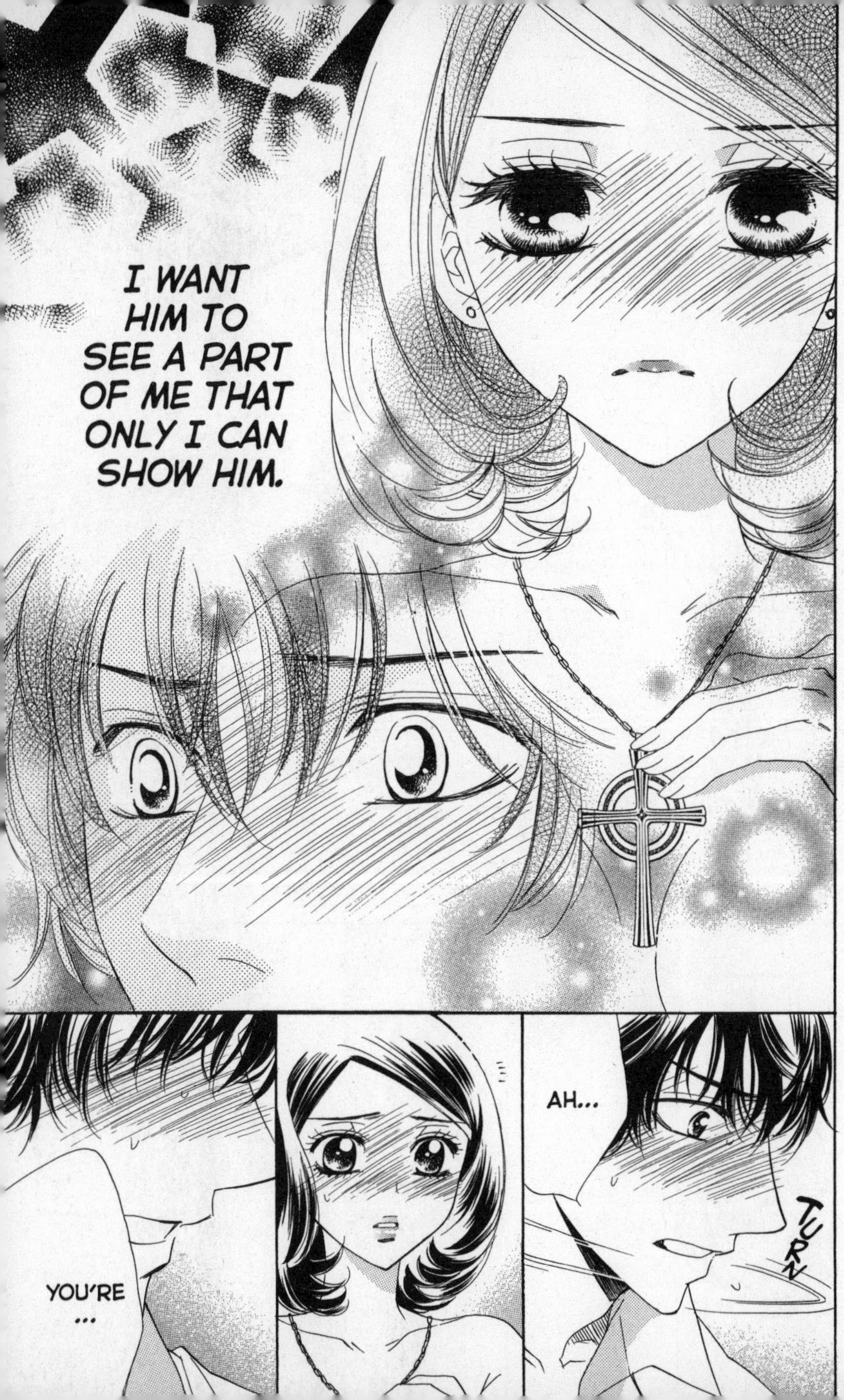
I WANT HIM TO SEE A PART OF ME THAT ONLY I CAN SHOW HIM.
AH...
TURN
YOU'RE ...

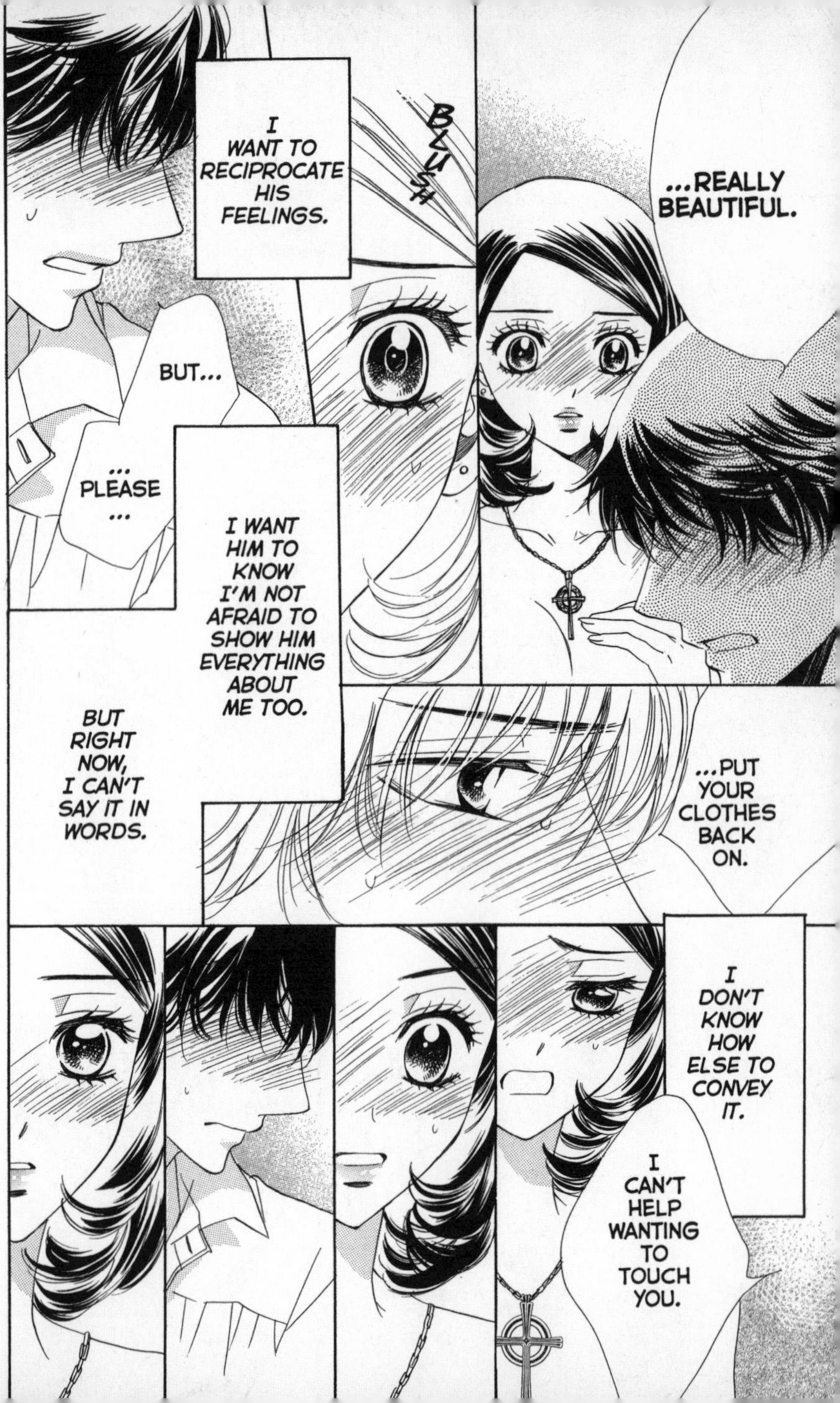
...REALLY BEAUTIFUL.
BLUSH
I WANT TO RECIPROCATE HIS FEELINGS.
BUT...
...PLEASE...
...PUT YOUR CLOTHES BACK ON.
I WANT HIM TO KNOW I'M NOT AFRAID TO SHOW HIM EVERYTHING ABOUT ME TOO.
BUT RIGHT NOW, I CAN'T SAY IT IN WORDS.
I DON'T KNOW HOW ELSE TO CONVEY IT.
I CAN'T HELP WANTING TO TOUCH YOU.

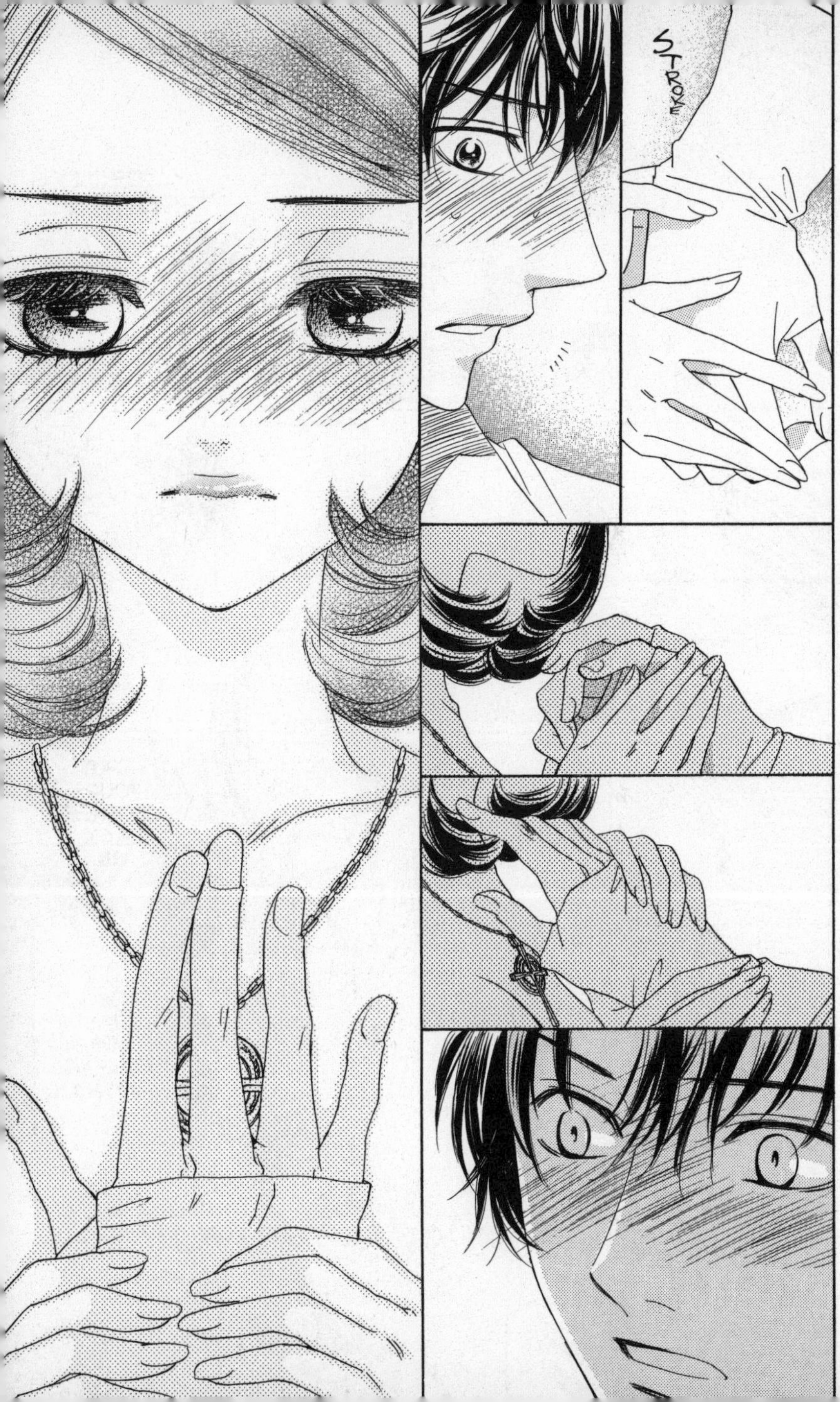
STROKE

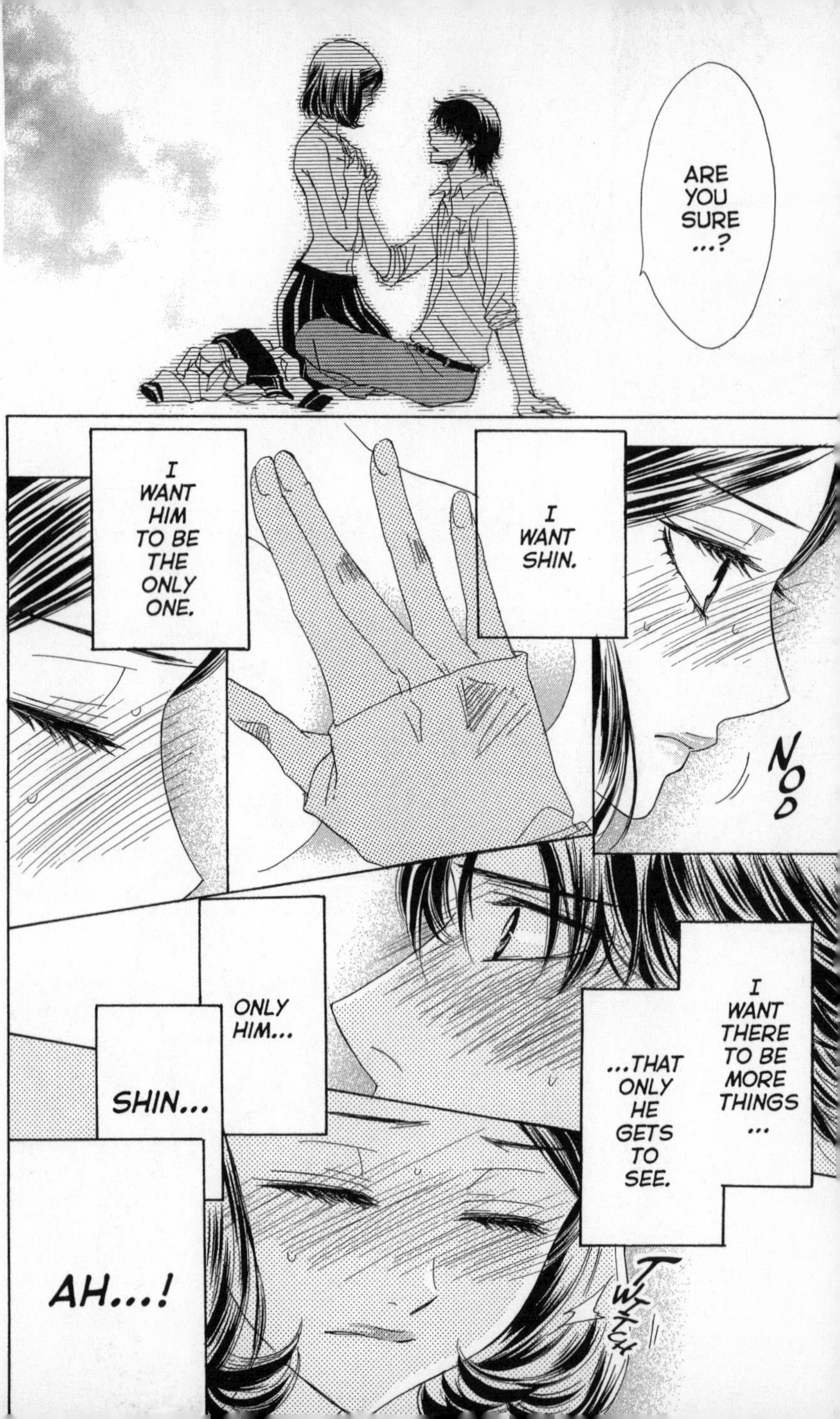
ARE YOU SURE ...?
I WANT SHIN.
NOD
I WANT HIM TO BE THE ONLY ONE.
I WANT THERE TO BE MORE THINGS ...
...THAT ONLY HE GETS TO SEE.
ONLY HIM...
SHIN...
TWITCH
AH...!

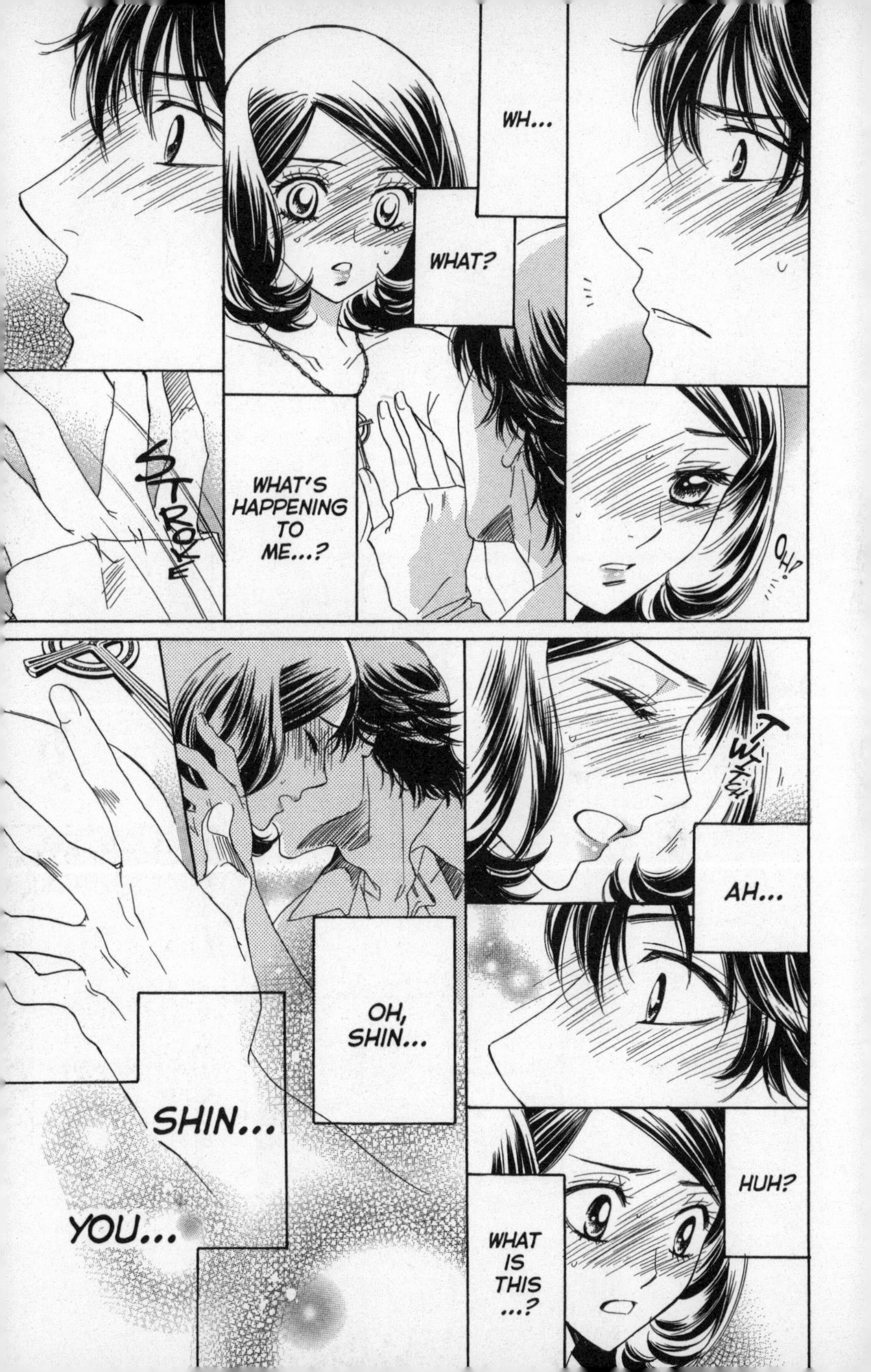
OH!
WH...
WHAT?
WHAT'S HAPPENING TO ME...?
STROKE
TWITCH
AH...
HUH?
WHAT IS THIS ...?
OH, SHIN...
SHIN...
YOU...

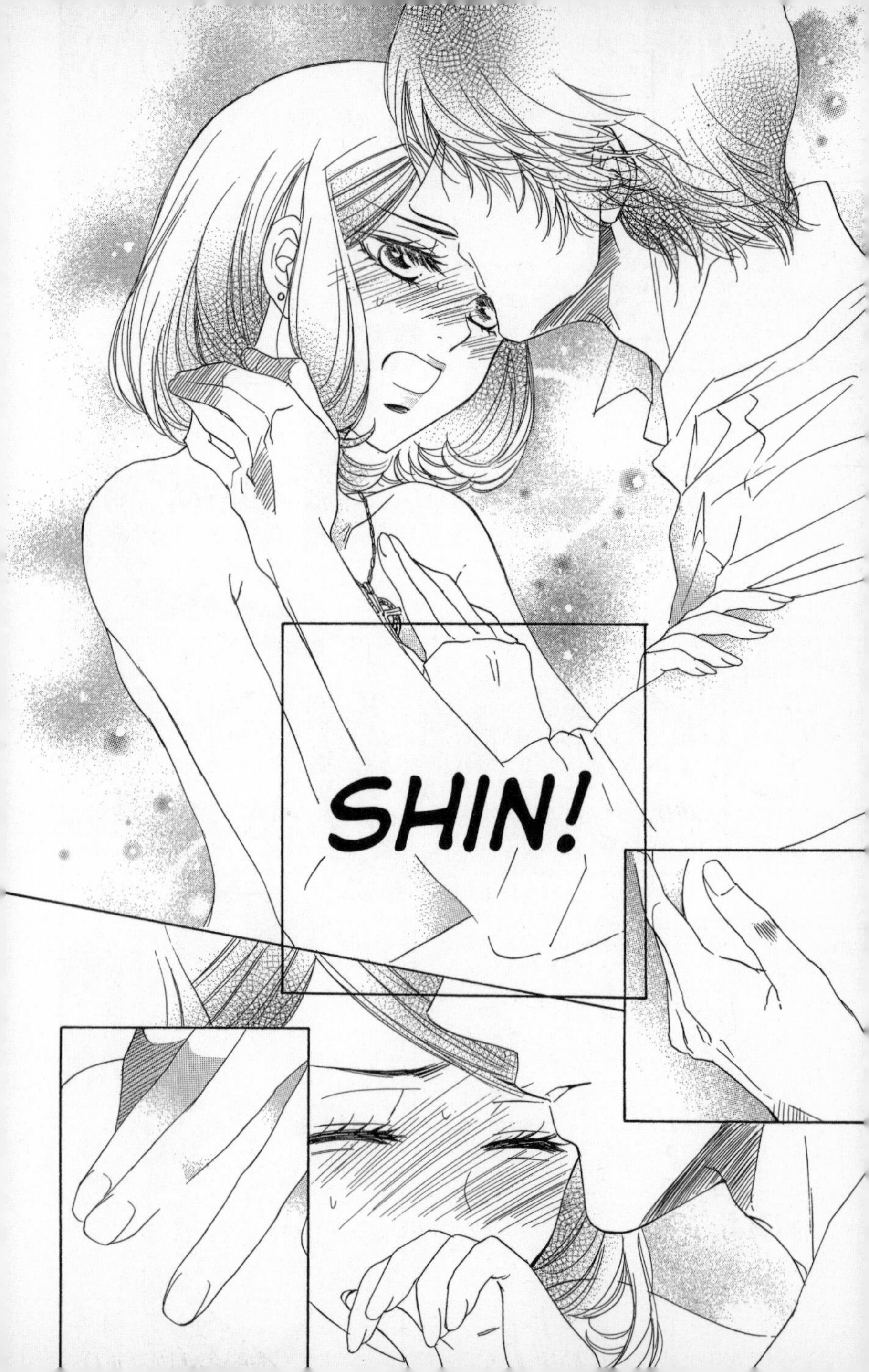
SHIN!

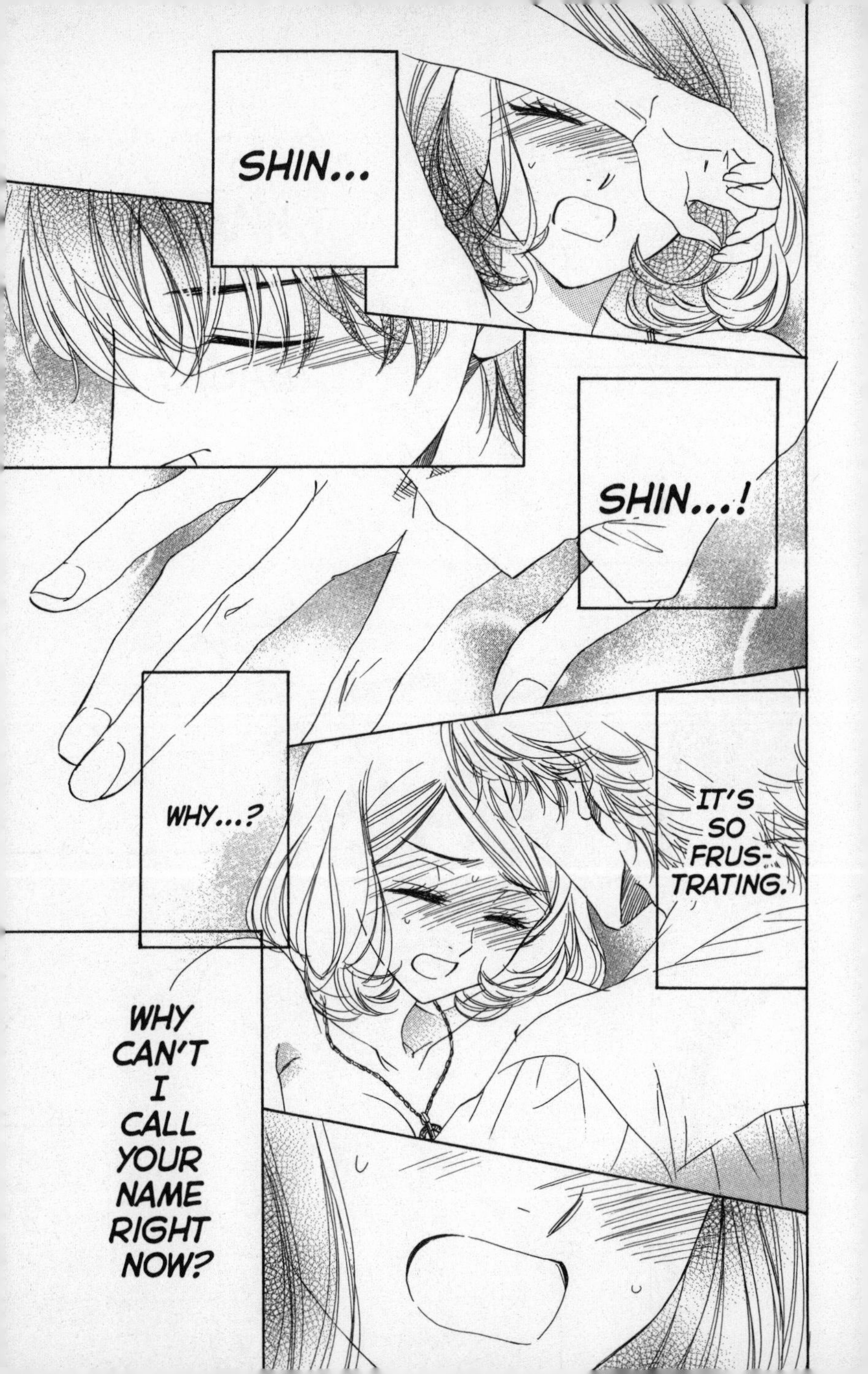
SHIN...
SHIN...!
IT'S SO FRUS-TRATING.
WHY...?
WHY CAN'T I CALL YOUR NAME RIGHT NOW?

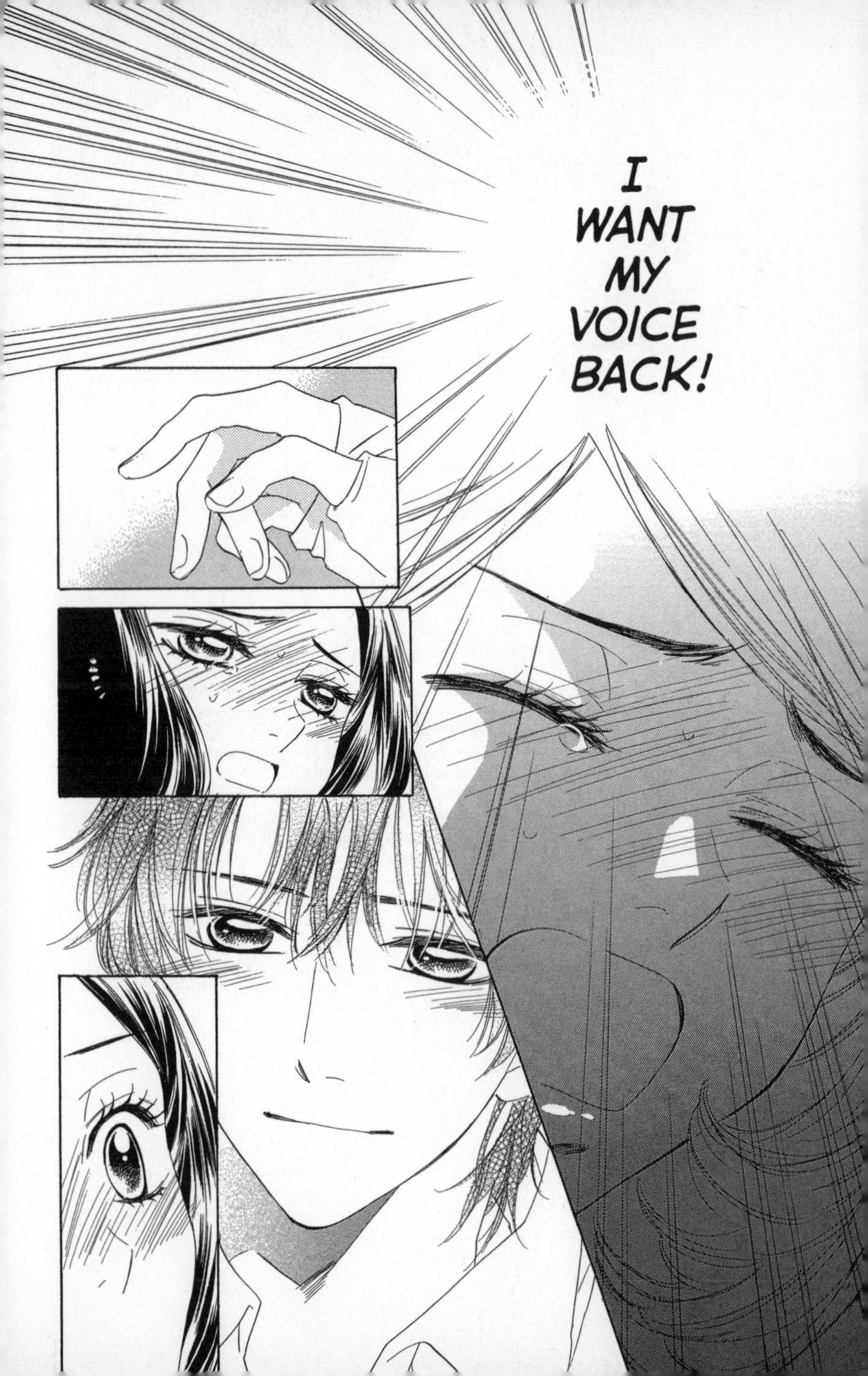
I WANT MY VOICE BACK!

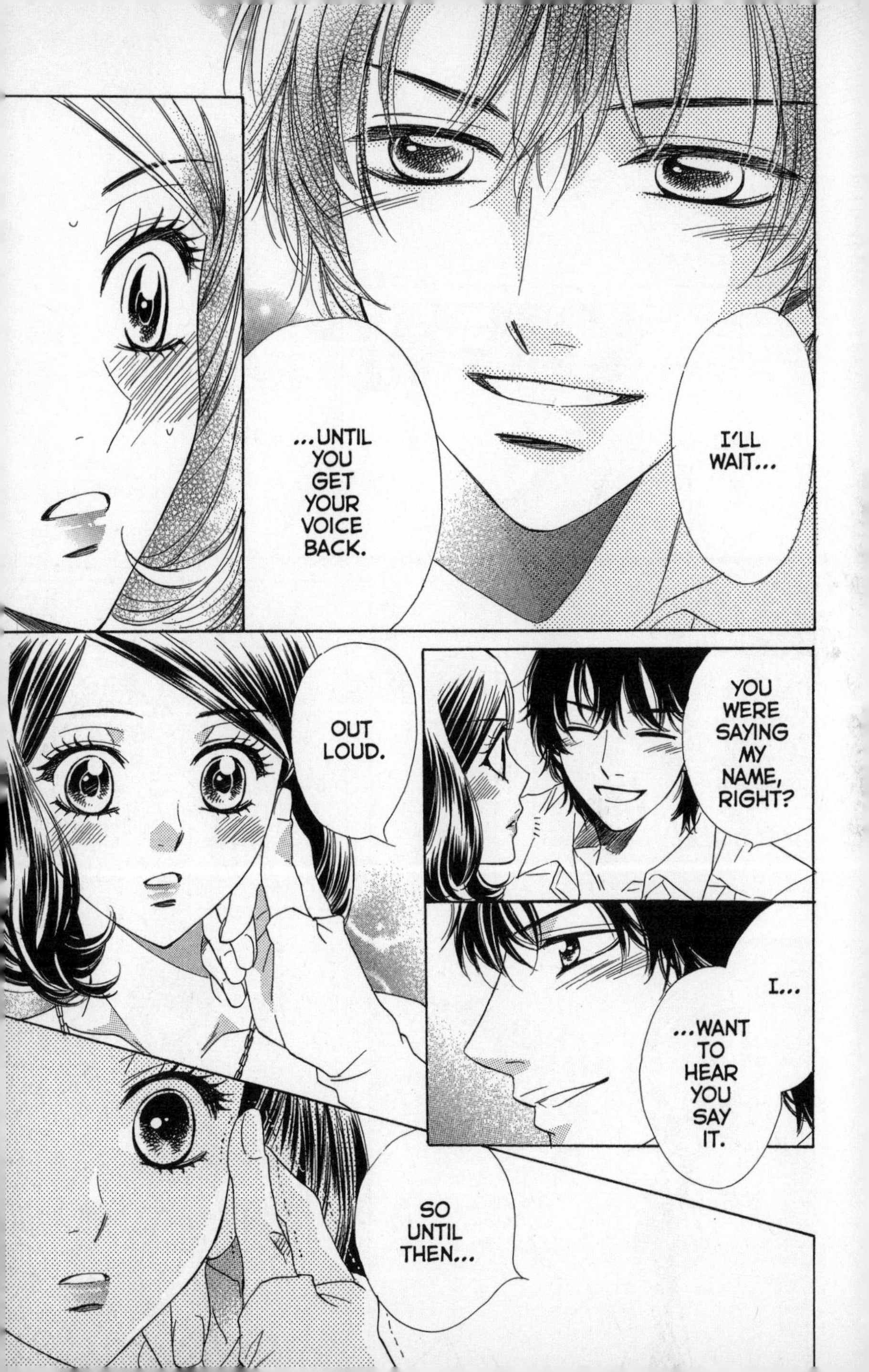
I'LL WAIT...
...UNTIL YOU GET YOUR VOICE BACK.
YOU WERE SAYING MY NAME, RIGHT?
I...
...WANT TO HEAR YOU SAY IT.
OUT LOUD.
SO UNTIL THEN...

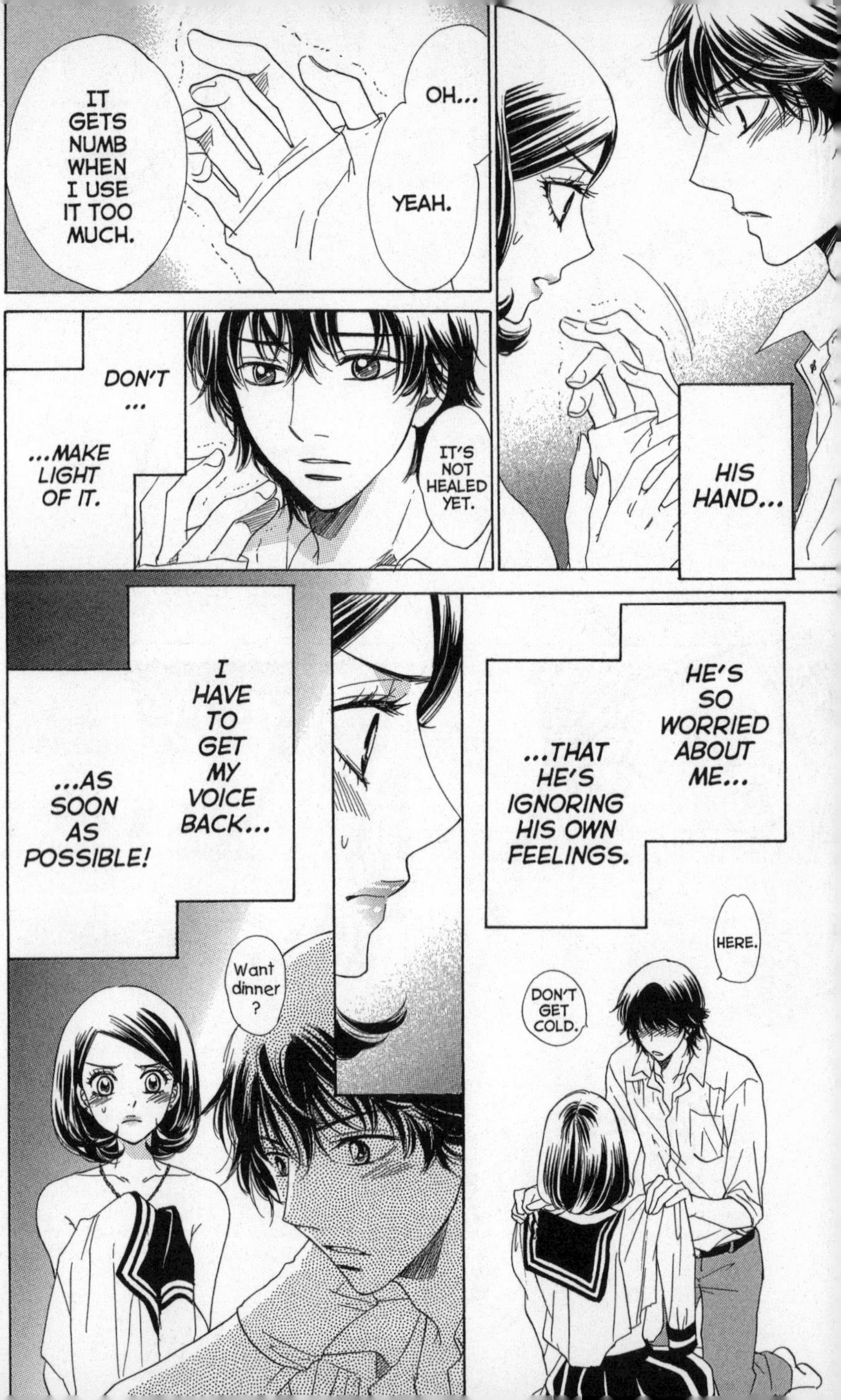
HIS HAND...
OH...
YEAH.
IT GETS NUMB WHEN I USE IT TOO MUCH.
IT'S NOT HEALED YET.
DON'T ...
...MAKE LIGHT OF IT.
HE'S SO WORRIED ABOUT ME...
...THAT HE'S IGNORING HIS OWN FEELINGS.
HERE.
DON'T GET COLD.
I HAVE TO GET MY VOICE BACK...
...AS SOON AS POSSIBLE!
Want dinner?

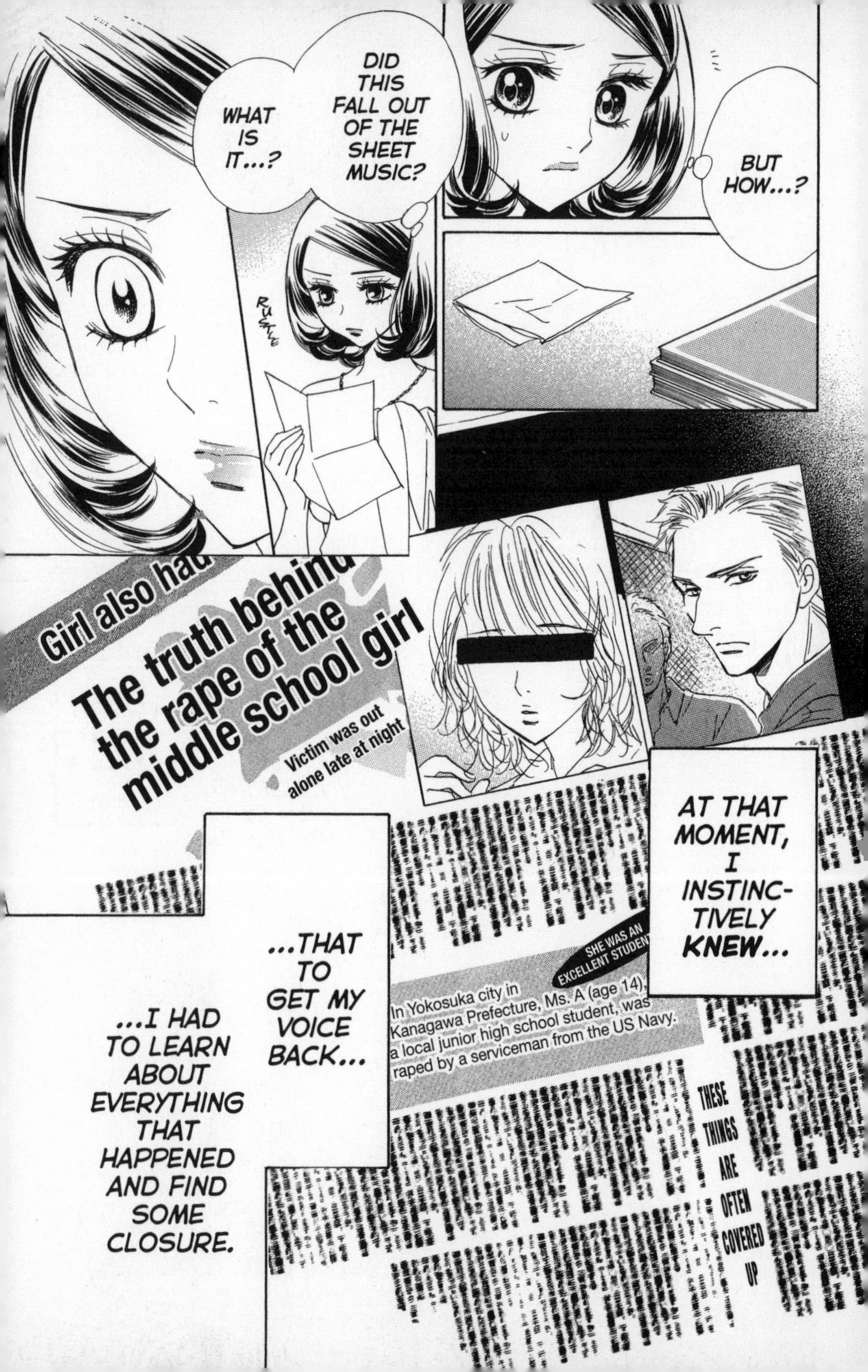
BUT HOW...?
DID THIS FALL OUT OF THE SHEET MUSIC?
WHAT IS IT...?
RUSTLE
Girl also had
The truth behind the rape of the middle school girl
Victim was out alone late at night
AT THAT MOMENT, I INSTINCTIVELY KNEW...
SHE WAS AN EXCELLENT STUDENT
In Yokosuka city in Kanagawa Prefecture, Ms. A (age 14), a local junior high school student, was raped by a serviceman from the US Navy.
THESE THINGS ARE OFTEN COVERED UP
...THAT TO GET MY VOICE BACK...
...I HAD TO LEARN ABOUT EVERYTHING THAT HAPPENED AND FIND SOME CLOSURE.

A Devil and
Her Love Song

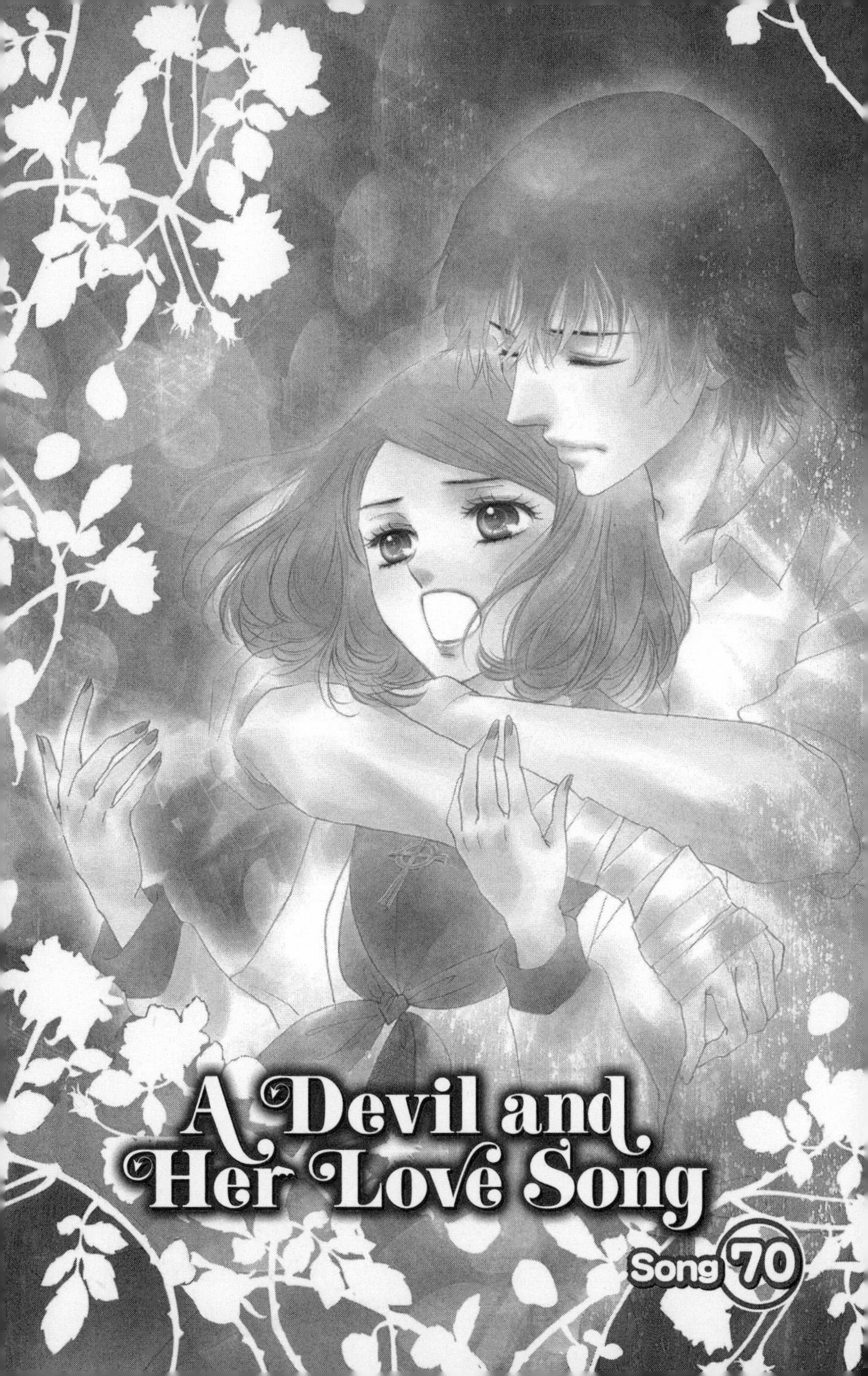
A Devil and
Her Love Song
Song 70

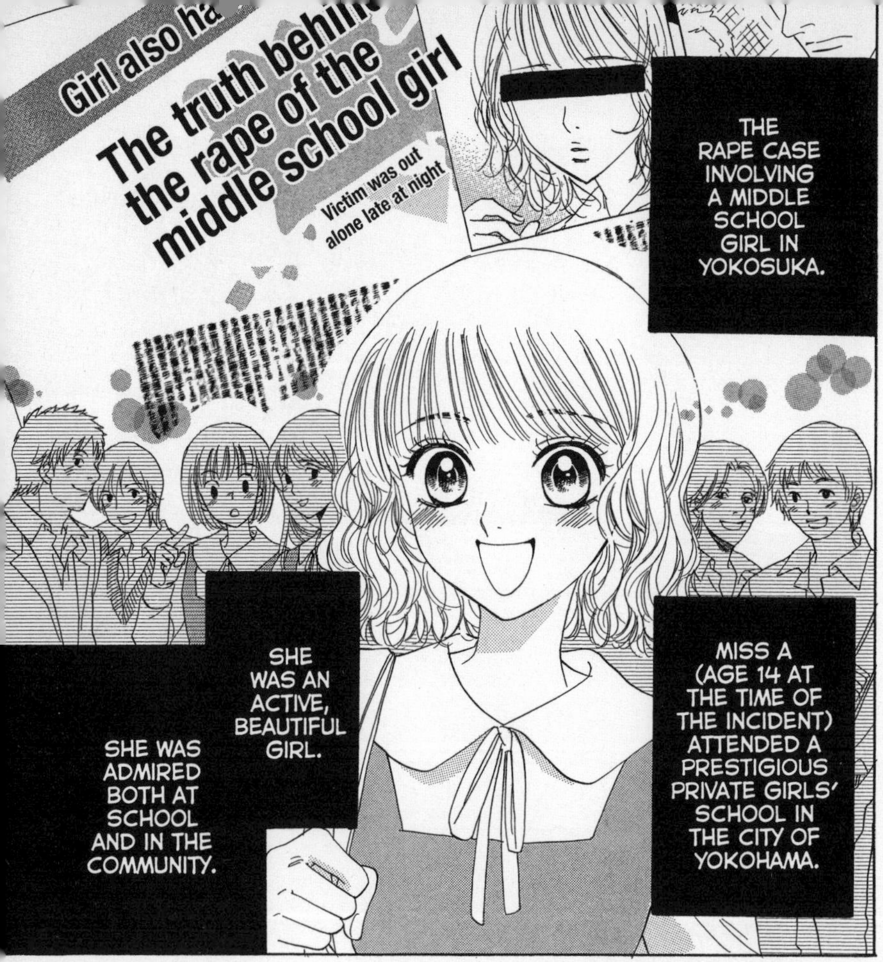
THE RAPE CASE INVOLVING A MIDDLE SCHOOL GIRL IN YOKOSUKA.
Girl also ha
The truth behin
the rape of the middle school girl
Victim was out alone late at night
MISS A (AGE 14 AT THE TIME OF THE INCIDENT) ATTENDED A PRESTIGIOUS PRIVATE GIRLS' SCHOOL IN THE CITY OF YOKOHAMA.
SHE WAS AN ACTIVE, BEAUTIFUL GIRL.
SHE WAS ADMIRED BOTH AT SCHOOL AND IN THE COMMUNITY.

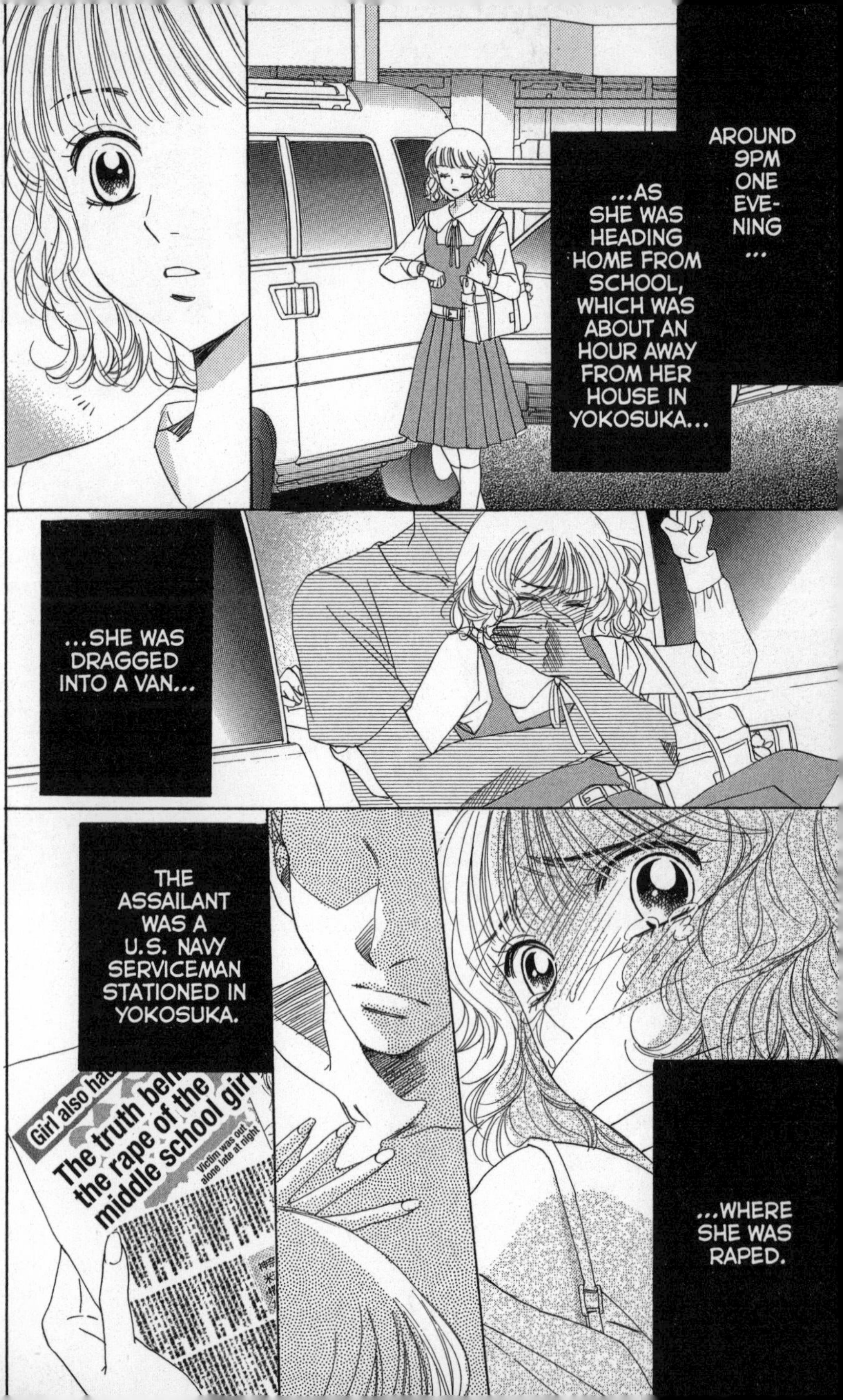
AROUND 9PM ONE EVE-NING...
...AS SHE WAS HEADING HOME FROM SCHOOL, WHICH WAS ABOUT AN HOUR AWAY FROM HER HOUSE IN YOKOSUKA...
...SHE WAS DRAGGED INTO A VAN...
...WHERE SHE WAS RAPED.
THE ASSAILANT WAS A U.S. NAVY SERVICEMAN STATIONED IN YOKOSUKA.
Girl also ha
The truth beh
the rape of the
middle school gir
Victim was out alone late at night

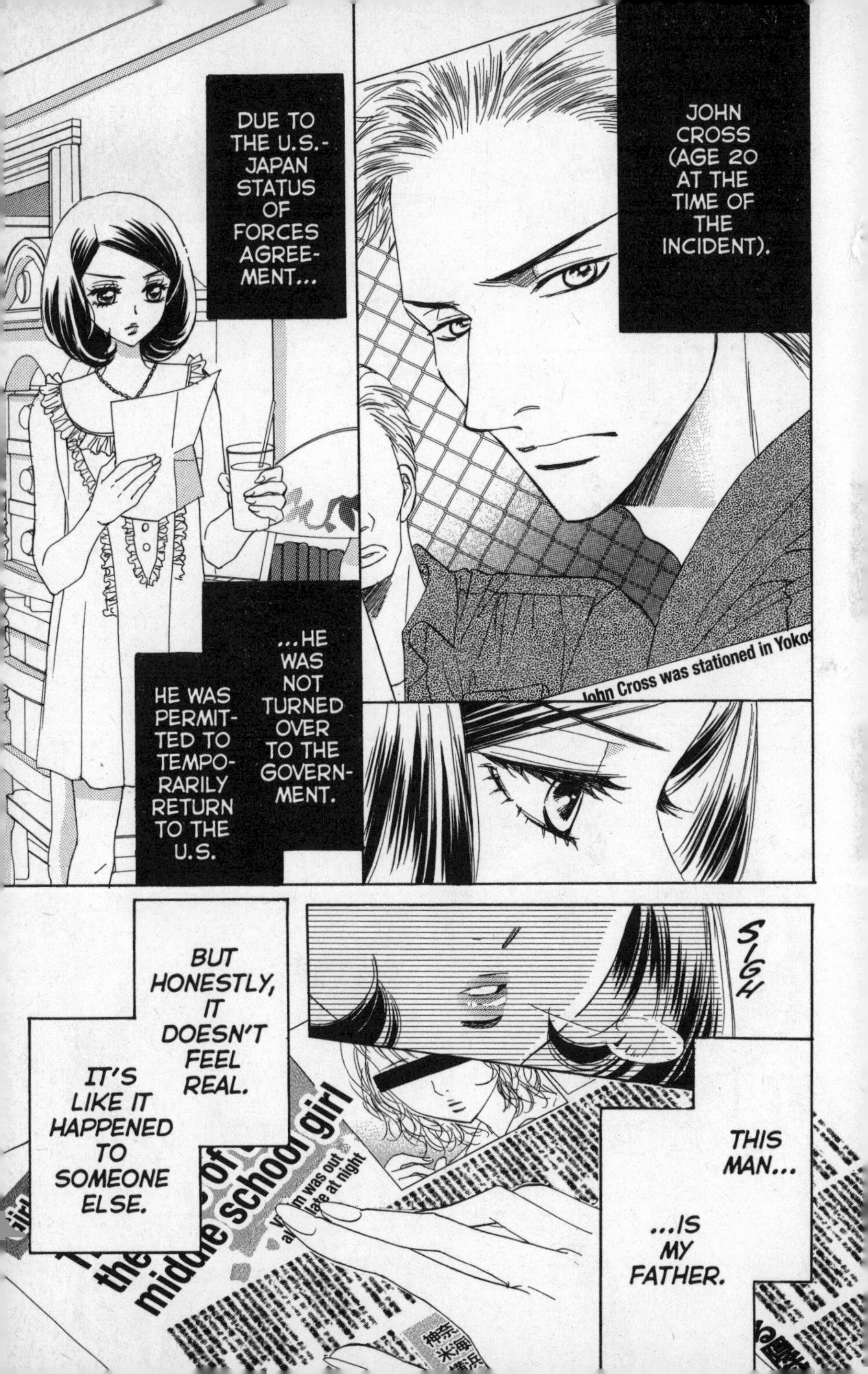
JOHN CROSS (AGE 20 AT THE TIME OF THE INCIDENT).
John Cross was stationed in Yokos
DUE TO THE U.S.-JAPAN STATUS OF FORCES AGREEMENT...
...HE WAS NOT TURNED OVER TO THE GOVERNMENT.
HE WAS PERMITTED TO TEMPORARILY RETURN TO THE U.S.
SIGH
THIS MAN...
...IS MY FATHER.
BUT HONESTLY, IT DOESN'T FEEL REAL.
IT'S LIKE IT HAPPENED TO SOMEONE ELSE.
middle school girl
late at night

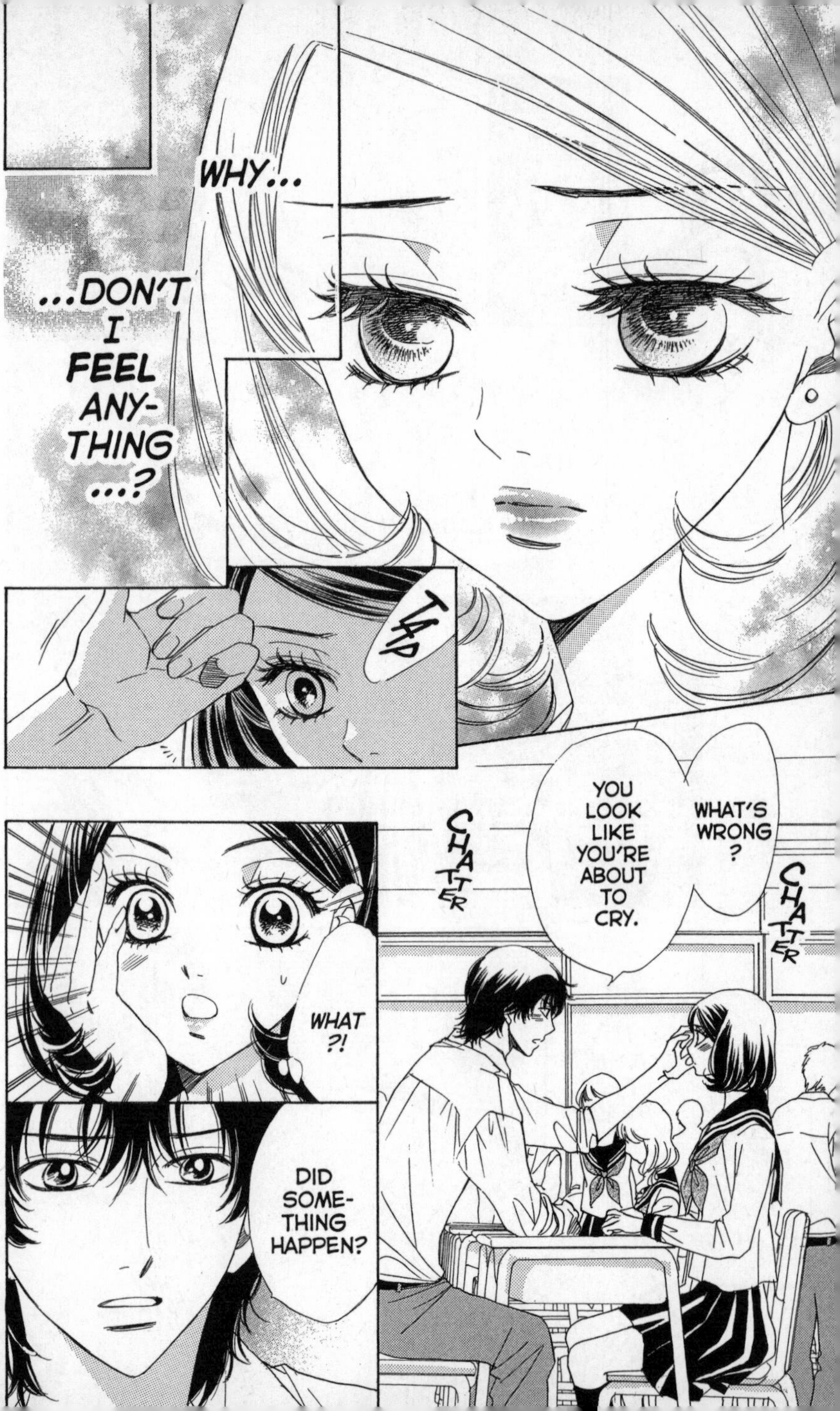
WHY...
...DON'T I FEEL ANYTHING...?
TAP
WHAT'S WRONG?
YOU LOOK LIKE YOU'RE ABOUT TO CRY.
CHATTER
CHATTER
WHAT?!
DID SOMETHING HAPPEN?

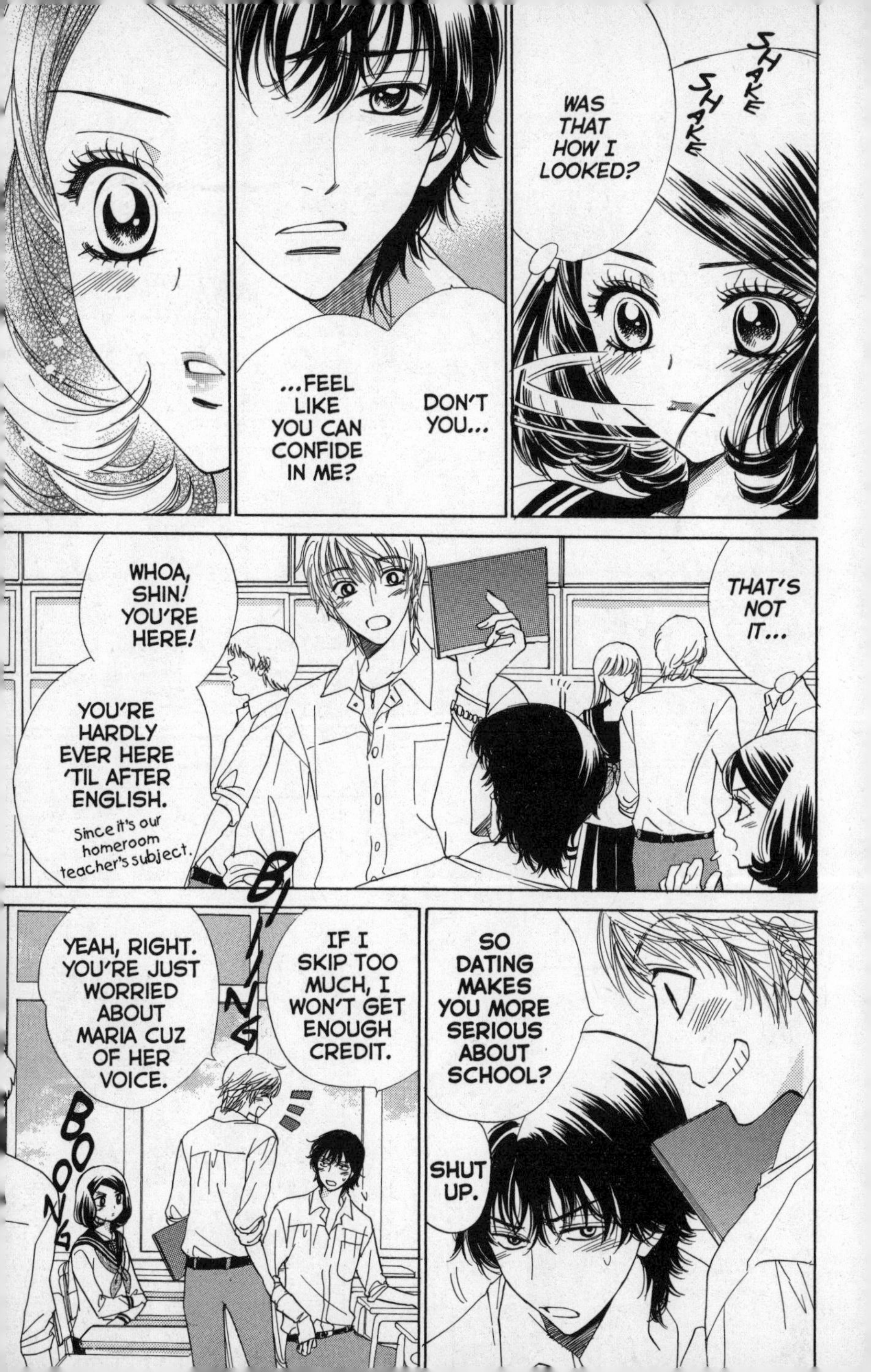
SHAKE SHAKE
WAS THAT HOW I LOOKED?
DON'T YOU...
...FEEL LIKE YOU CAN CONFIDE IN ME?
THAT'S NOT IT...
WHOA, SHIN! YOU'RE HERE!
YOU'RE HARDLY EVER HERE 'TIL AFTER ENGLISH.
Since it's our homeroom teacher's subject.
SO DATING MAKES YOU MORE SERIOUS ABOUT SCHOOL?
SHUT UP.
IF I SKIP TOO MUCH, I WON'T GET ENOUGH CREDIT.
YEAH, RIGHT. YOU'RE JUST WORRIED ABOUT MARIA CUZ OF HER VOICE.
BIIING
BOONG

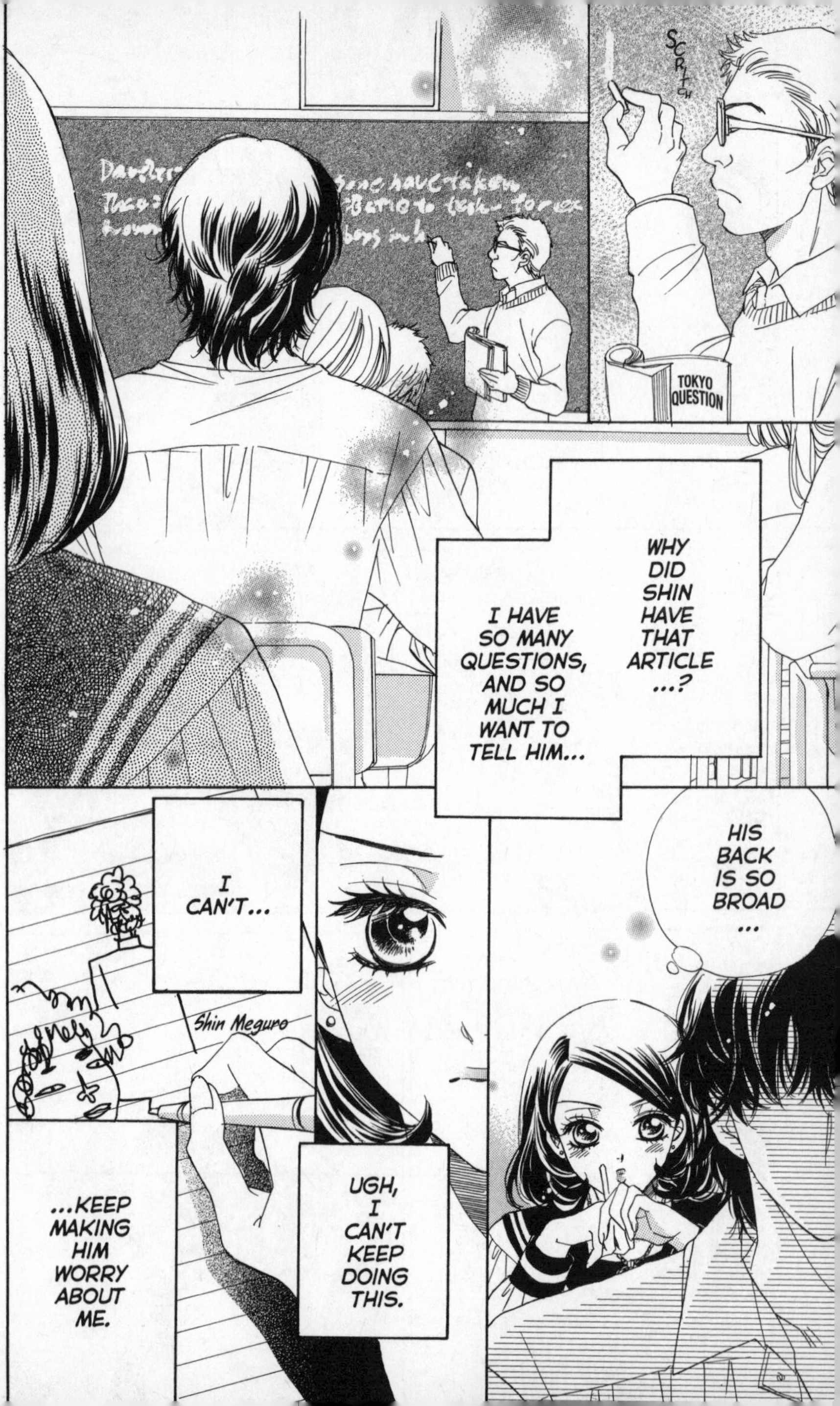
SCRITCH
TOKYO QUESTION
WHY DID SHIN HAVE THAT ARTICLE ...?
I HAVE SO MANY QUESTIONS, AND SO MUCH I WANT TO TELL HIM...
HIS BACK IS SO BROAD ...
UGH, I CAN'T KEEP DOING THIS.
I CAN'T...
Shin Meguro
...KEEP MAKING HIM WORRY ABOUT ME.

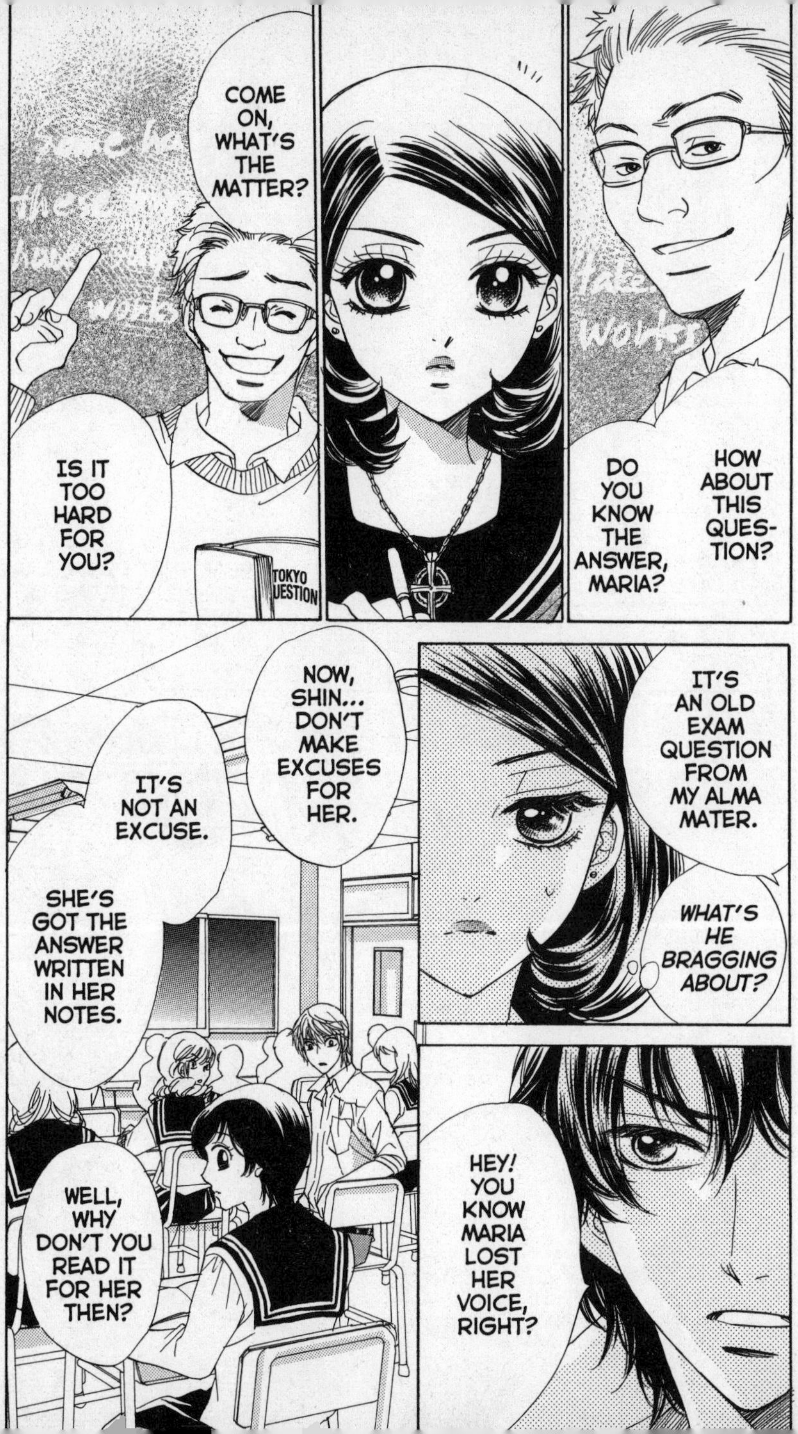
HOW ABOUT THIS QUESTION?
DO YOU KNOW THE ANSWER, MARIA?
COME ON, WHAT'S THE MATTER?
IS IT TOO HARD FOR YOU?
TOKYO UESTION
IT'S AN OLD EXAM QUESTION FROM MY ALMA MATER.
WHAT'S HE BRAGGING ABOUT?
HEY! YOU KNOW MARIA LOST HER VOICE, RIGHT?
NOW, SHIN... DON'T MAKE EXCUSES FOR HER.
IT'S NOT AN EXCUSE.
SHE'S GOT THE ANSWER WRITTEN IN HER NOTES.
WELL, WHY DON'T YOU READ IT FOR HER THEN?

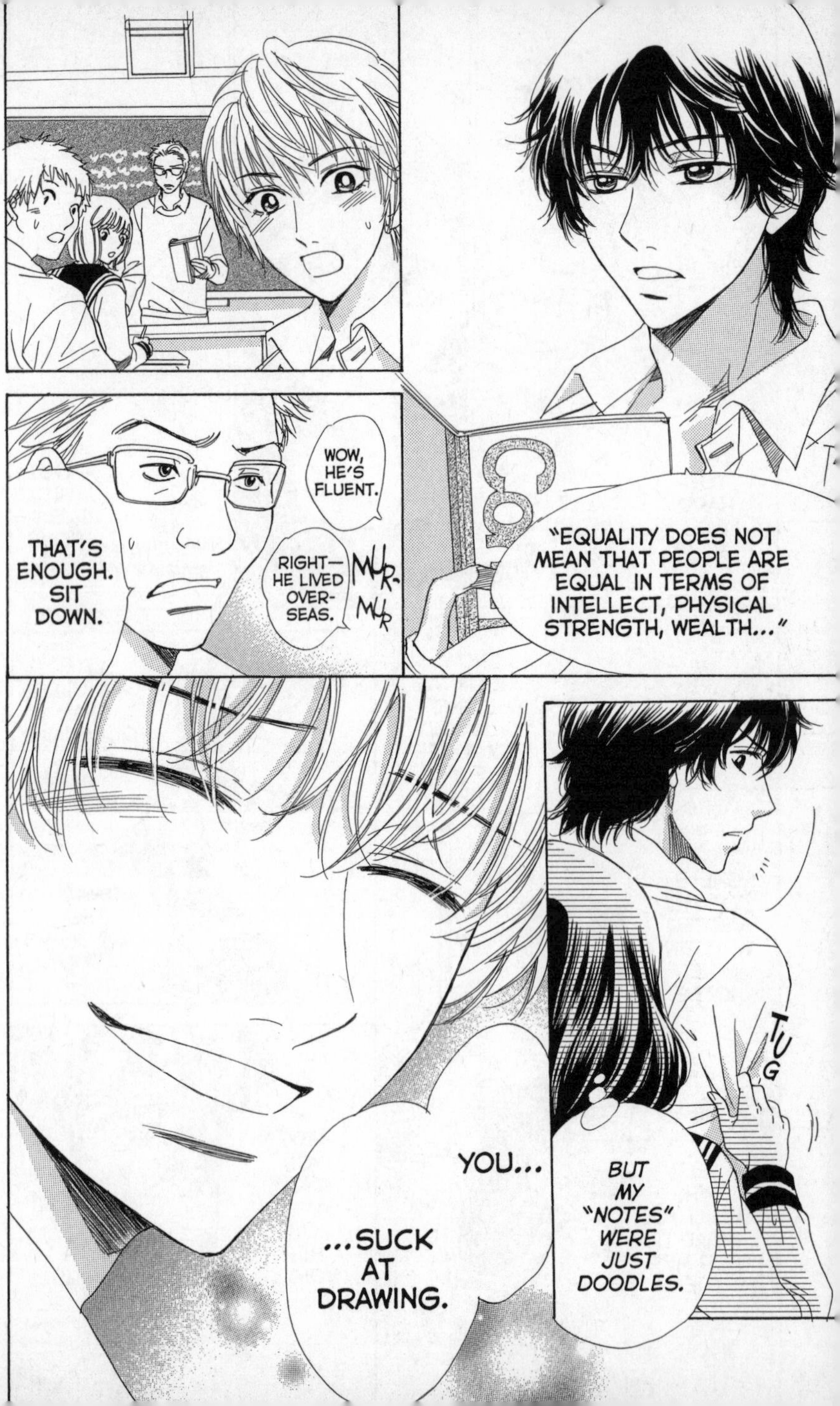
"EQUALITY DOES NOT MEAN THAT PEOPLE ARE EQUAL IN TERMS OF INTELLECT, PHYSICAL STRENGTH, WEALTH..."
WOW, HE'S FLUENT.
MUR-MUR
RIGHT—HE LIVED OVERSEAS.
THAT'S ENOUGH. SIT DOWN.
TUG
BUT MY "NOTES" WERE JUST DOODLES.
YOU...
...SUCK AT DRAWING.

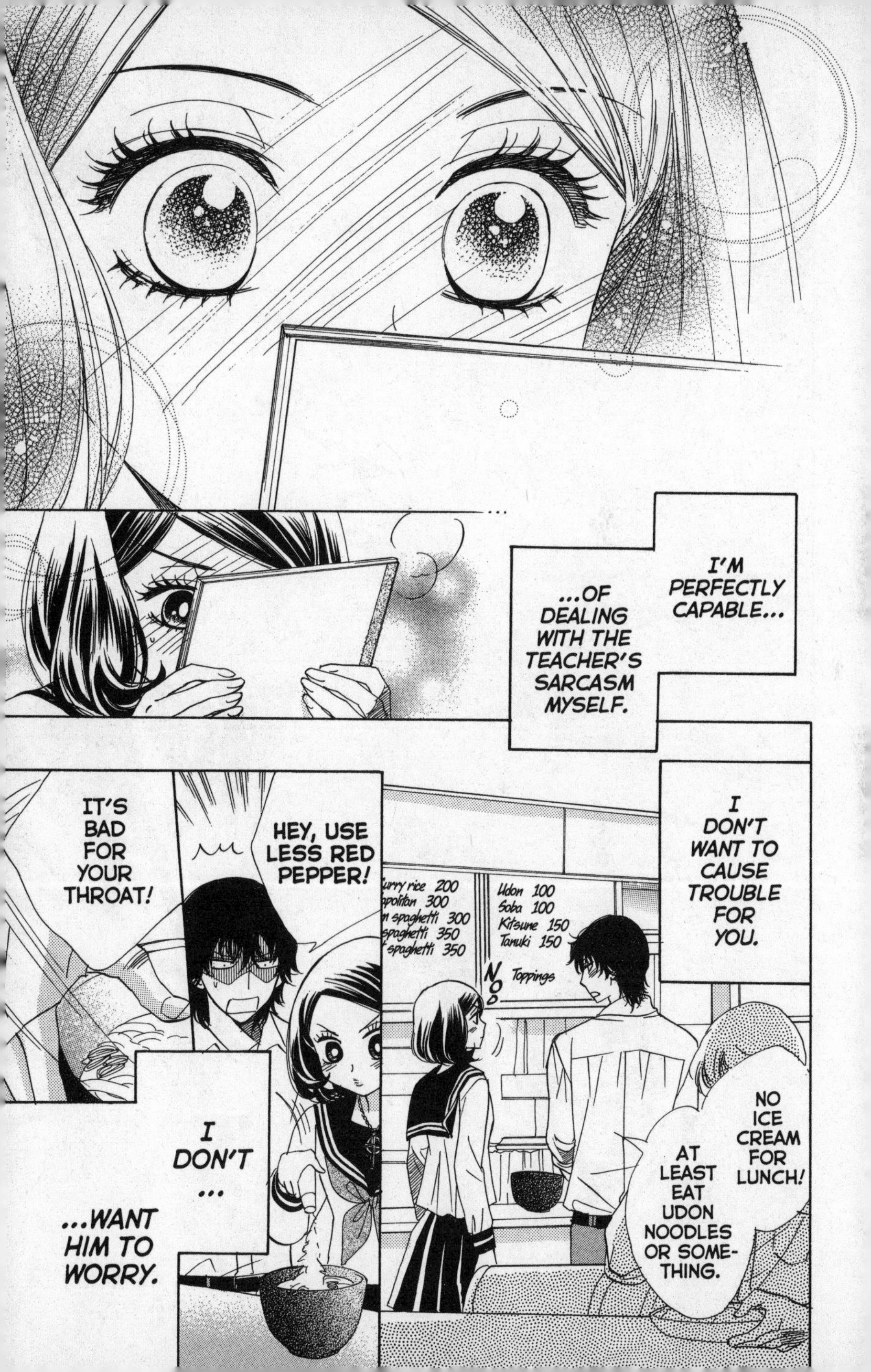
...
I'M PERFECTLY CAPABLE...
...OF DEALING WITH THE TEACHER'S SARCASM MYSELF.
I DON'T WANT TO CAUSE TROUBLE FOR YOU.
Udon 100
Soba 100
Kitsune 150
Tanuki 150
Toppings
NO ICE CREAM FOR LUNCH!
AT LEAST EAT UDON NOODLES OR SOME-THING.
HEY, USE LESS RED PEPPER!
IT'S BAD FOR YOUR THROAT!
I DON'T...
...WANT HIM TO WORRY.

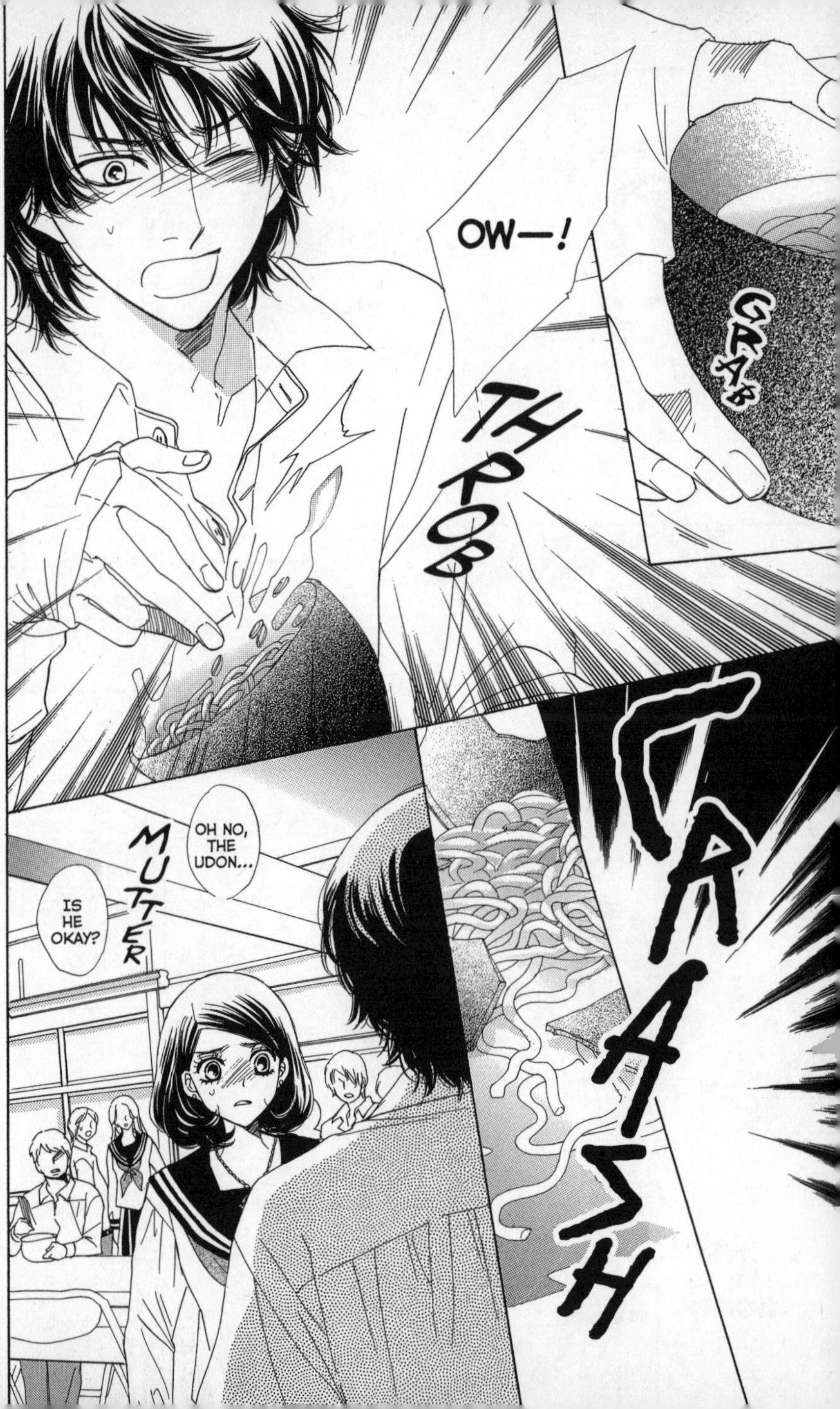
GRAB
OW—!
THROB
CRASH
OH NO, THE UDON...
MUTTER
IS HE OKAY?

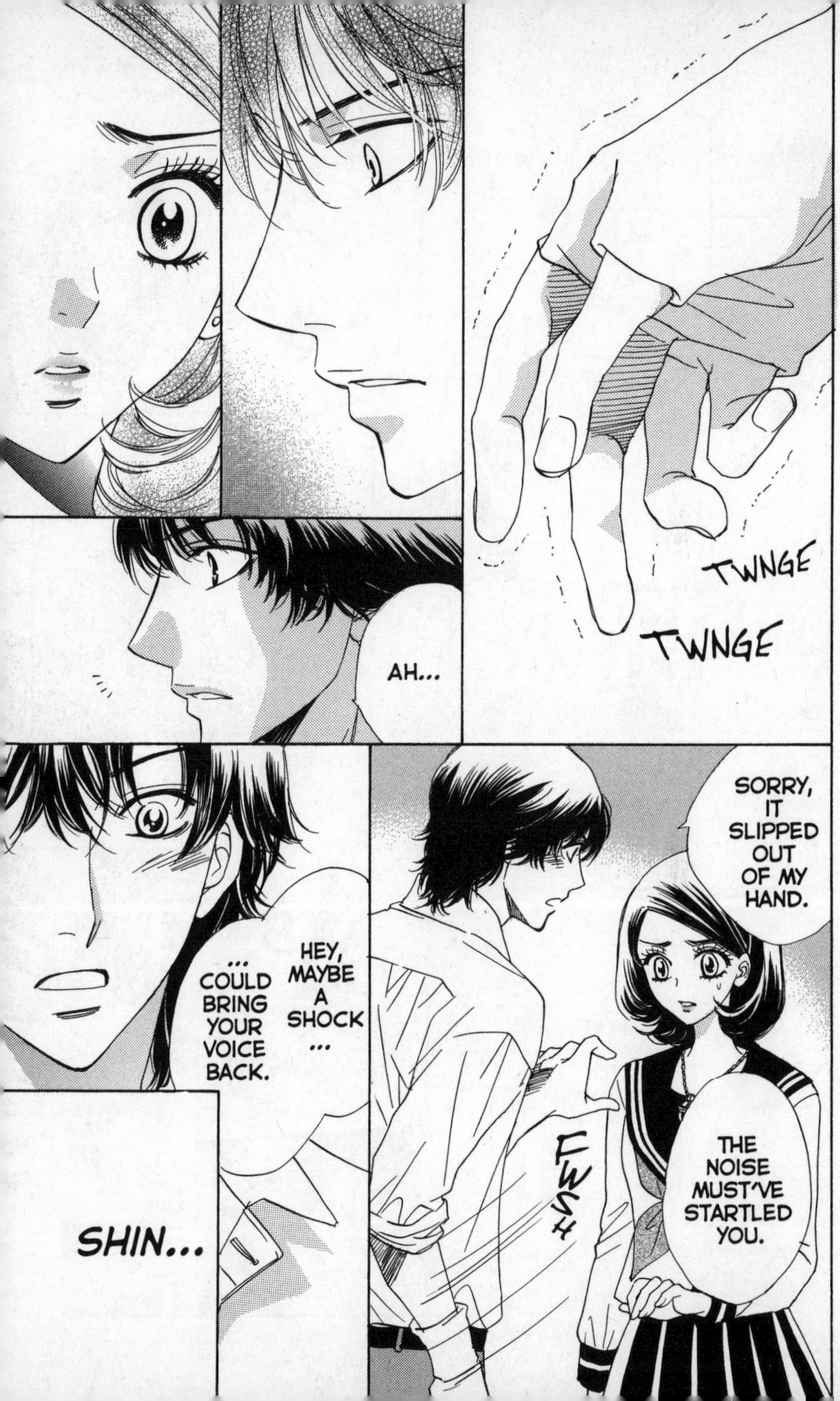
TWNGE
TWNGE
AH...
SORRY, IT SLIPPED OUT OF MY HAND.
THE NOISE MUST'VE STARTLED YOU.
FWSH
HEY, MAYBE A SHOCK...
...COULD BRING YOUR VOICE BACK.
SHIN...

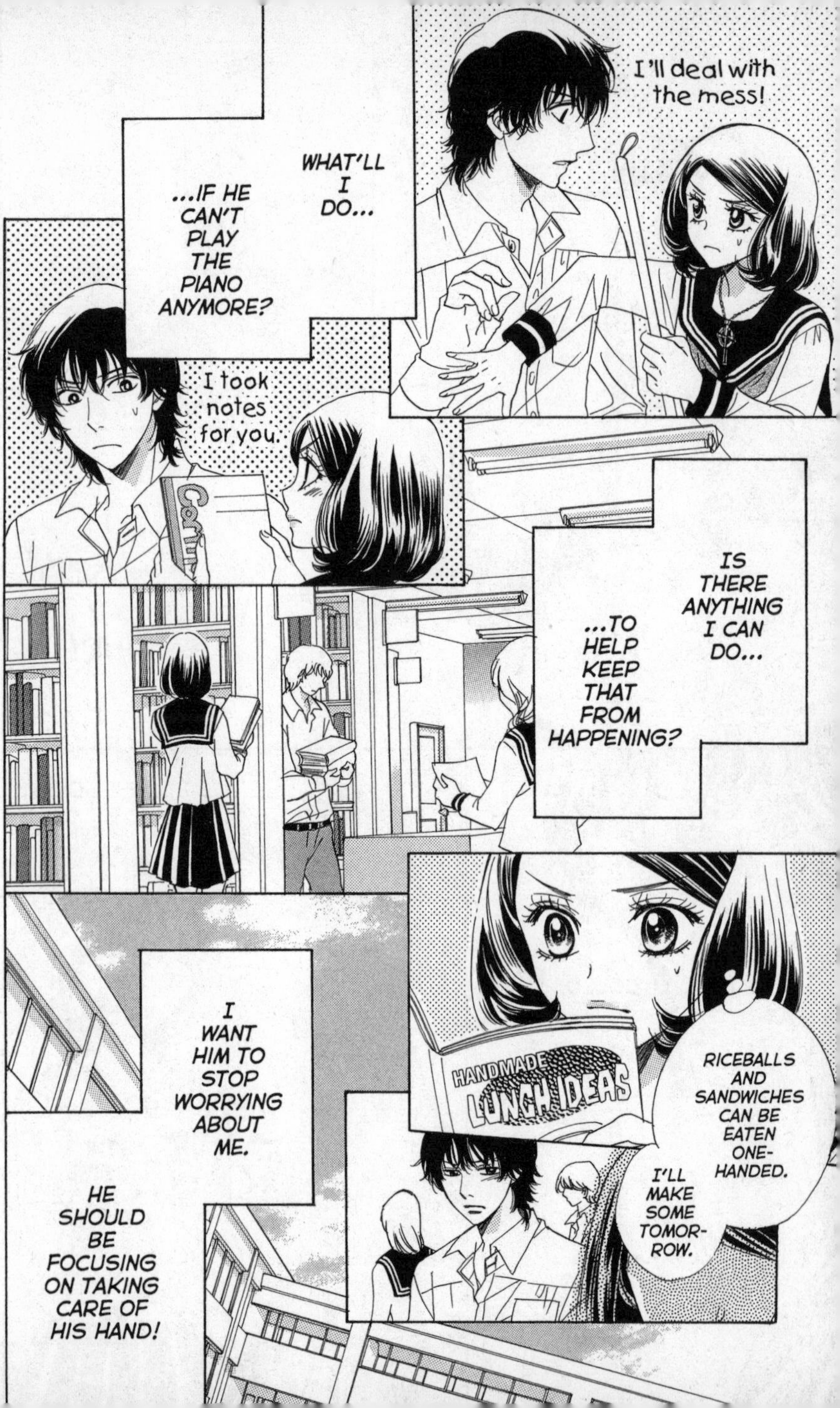
I'll deal with the mess!
WHAT'LL I DO...
...IF HE CAN'T PLAY THE PIANO ANYMORE?
I took notes for you.
IS THERE ANYTHING I CAN DO...
...TO HELP KEEP THAT FROM HAPPENING?
HANDMADE LUNCH IDEAS
RICEBALLS AND SANDWICHES CAN BE EATEN ONE-HANDED.
I'LL MAKE SOME TOMOR-ROW.
I WANT HIM TO STOP WORRYING ABOUT ME.
HE SHOULD BE FOCUSING ON TAKING CARE OF HIS HAND!

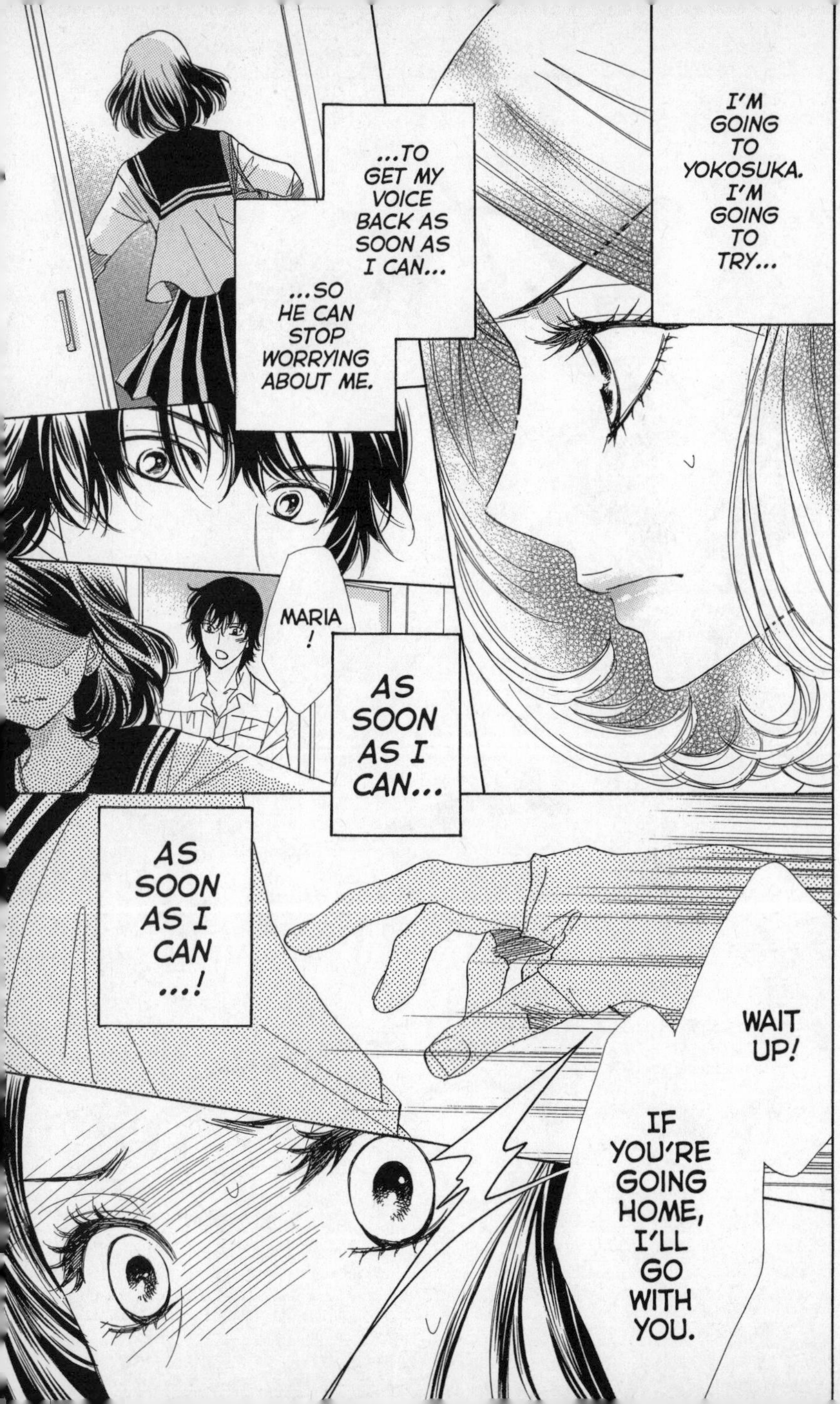
I'M GOING TO YOKOSUKA. I'M GOING TO TRY...
...TO GET MY VOICE BACK AS SOON AS I CAN...
...SO HE CAN STOP WORRYING ABOUT ME.
MARIA!
AS SOON AS I CAN...
AS SOON AS I CAN...!
WAIT UP!
IF YOU'RE GOING HOME, I'LL GO WITH YOU.

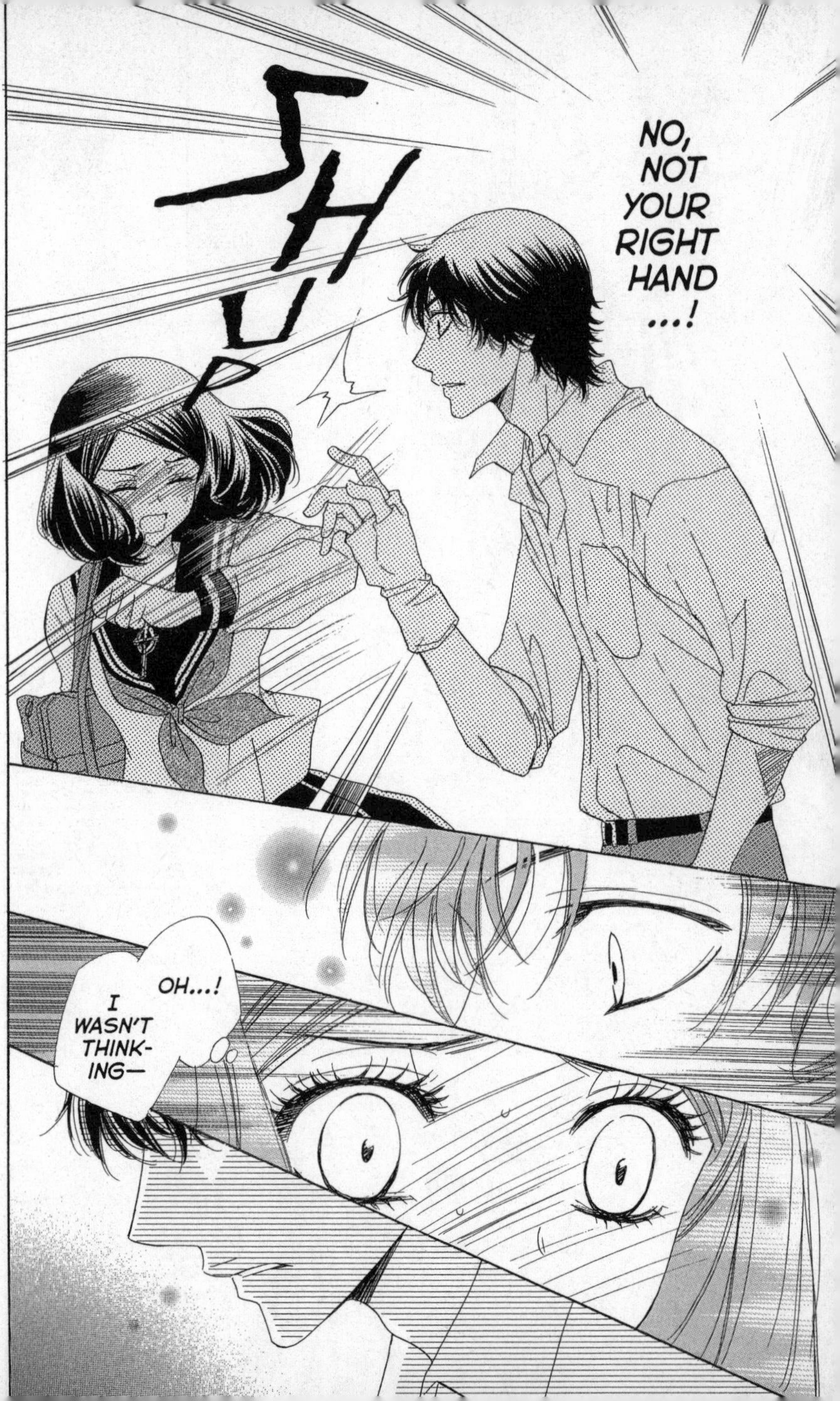
NO, NOT YOUR RIGHT HAND ...!
SHLUP
OH...! I WASN'T THINKING—

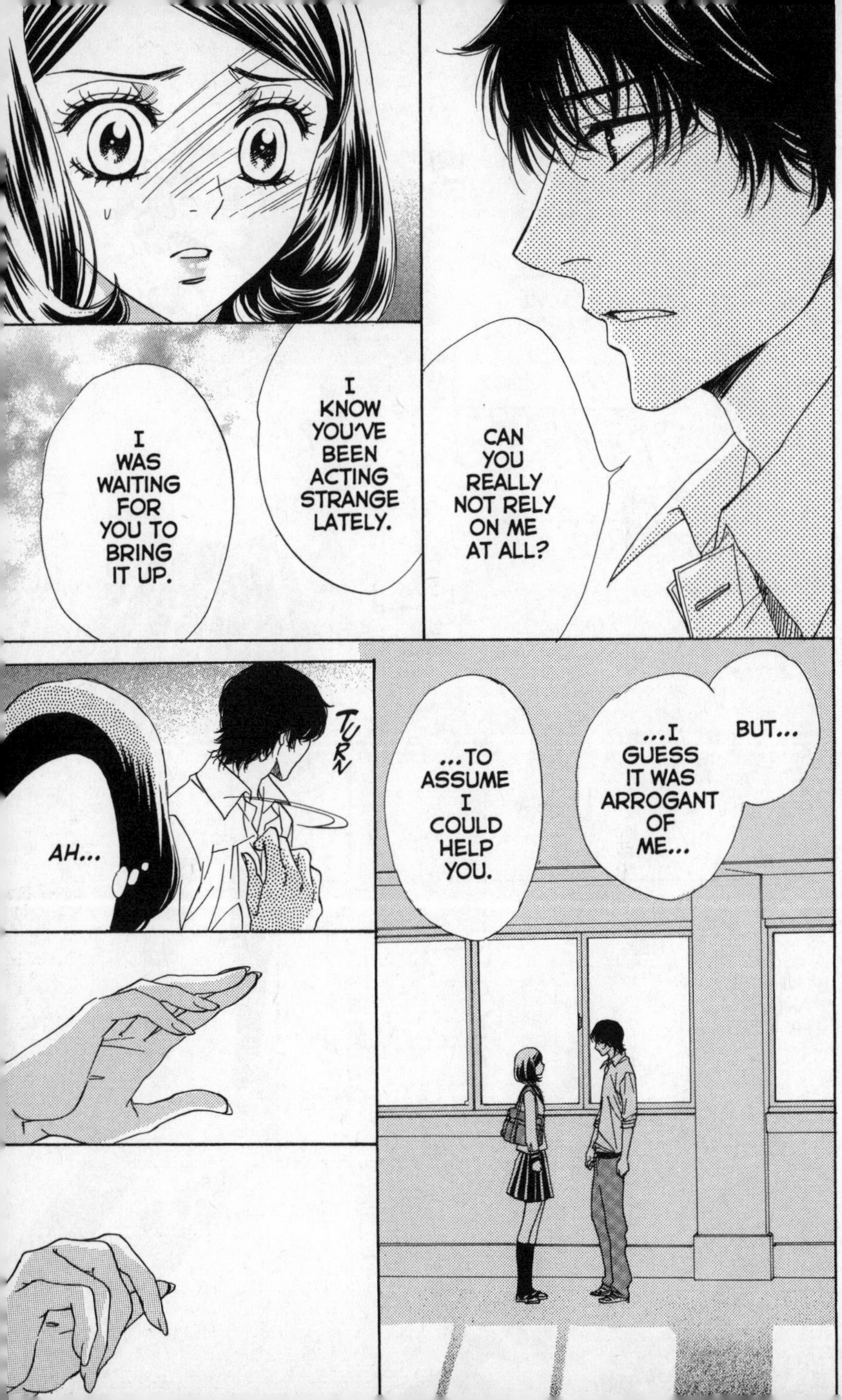
CAN YOU REALLY NOT RELY ON ME AT ALL?
I KNOW YOU'VE BEEN ACTING STRANGE LATELY.
I WAS WAITING FOR YOU TO BRING IT UP.
BUT...
...I GUESS IT WAS ARROGANT OF ME...
...TO ASSUME I COULD HELP YOU.
TURN
AH...

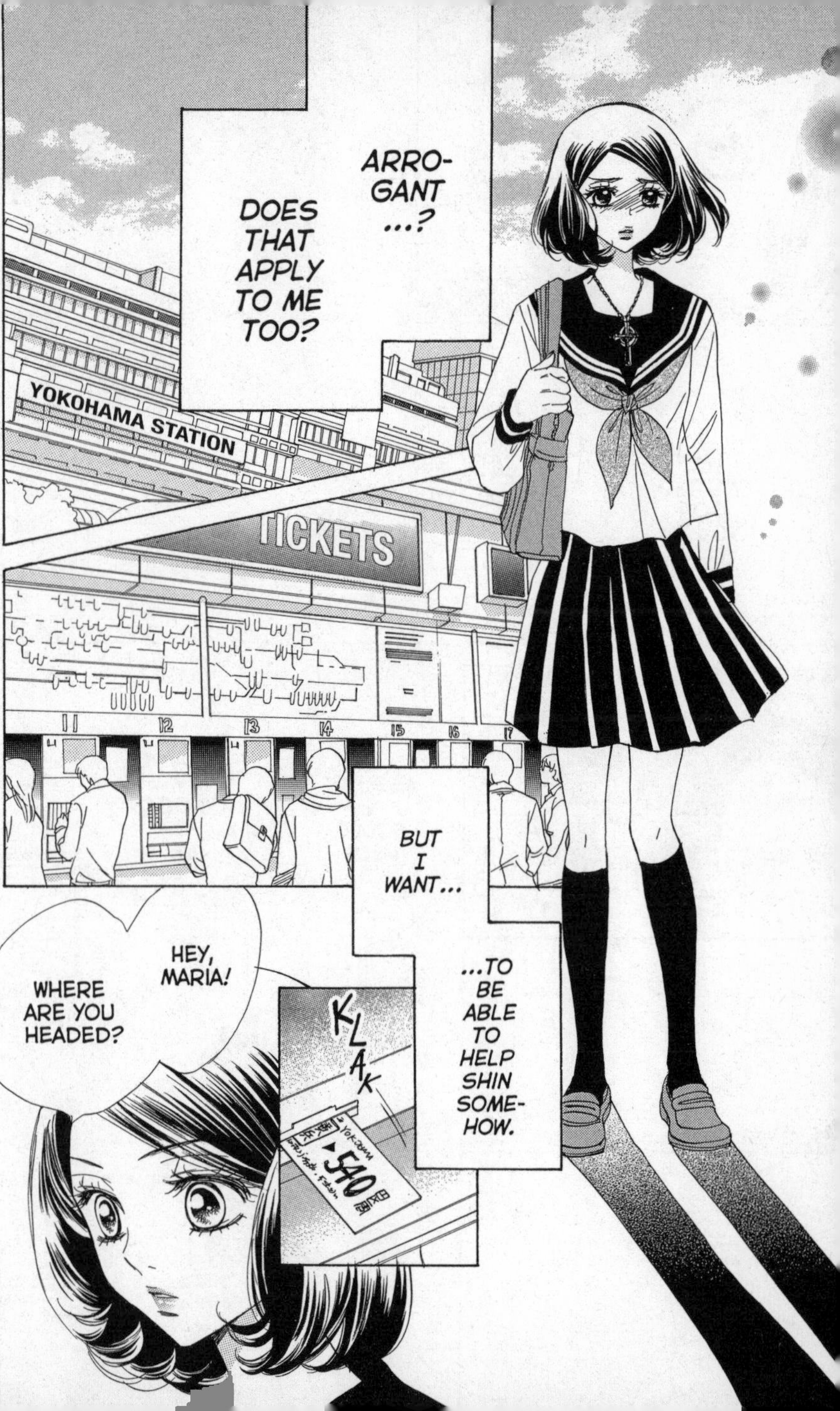
ARRO-GANT ...?
DOES THAT APPLY TO ME TOO?
YOKOHAMA STATION
TICKETS
BUT I WANT...
...TO BE ABLE TO HELP SHIN SOME-HOW.
KLAK
540
HEY, MARIA!
WHERE ARE YOU HEADED?

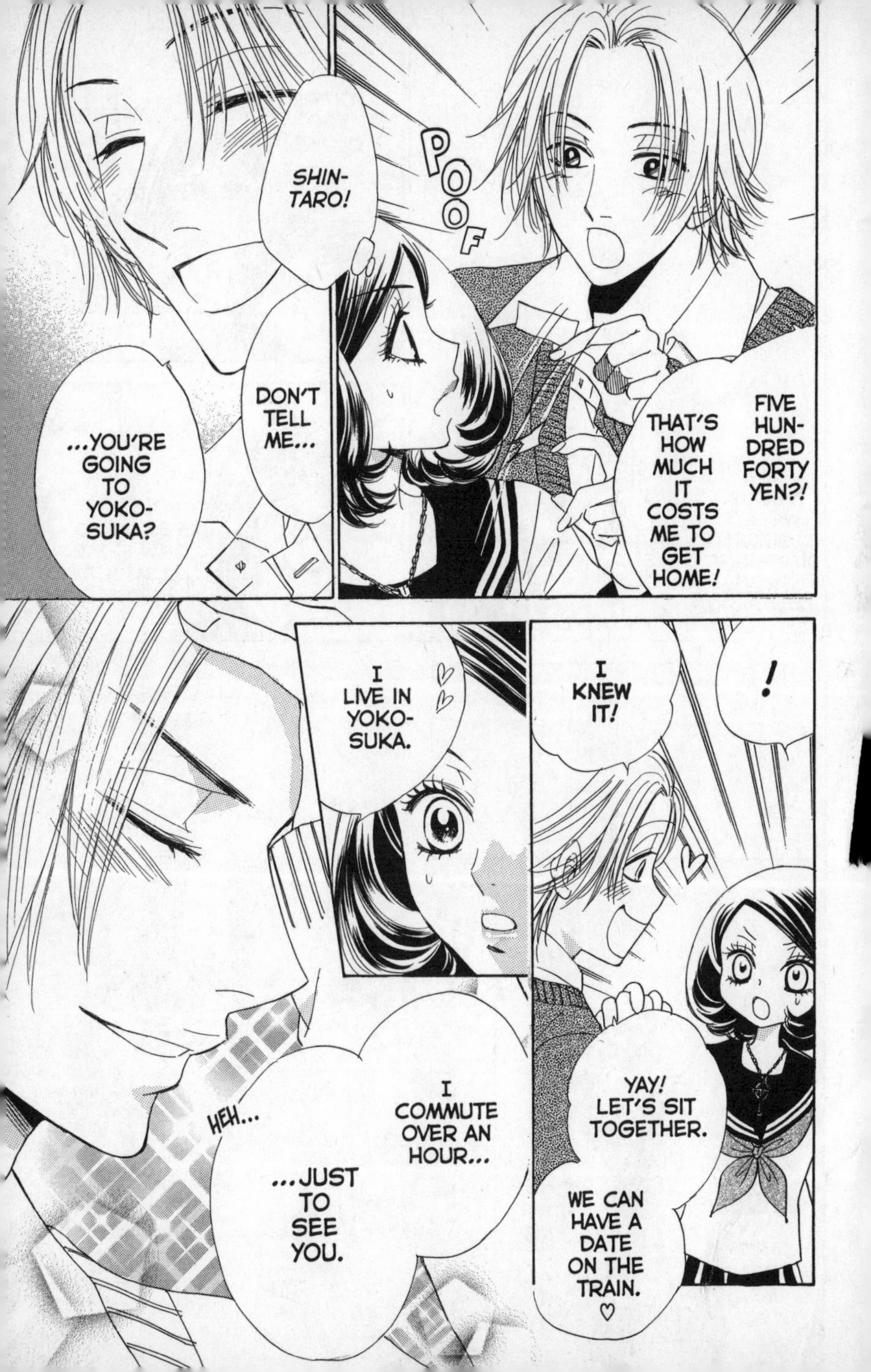
FIVE HUNDRED FORTY YEN?!
THAT'S HOW MUCH IT COSTS ME TO GET HOME!
POOF
SHIN-TARO!
DON'T TELL ME...
...YOU'RE GOING TO YOKO-SUKA?
!
I KNEW IT!
YAY! LET'S SIT TOGETHER.
WE CAN HAVE A DATE ON THE TRAIN. ♡
I LIVE IN YOKO-SUKA. ♡♡
HEH...
I COMMUTE OVER AN HOUR...
...JUST TO SEE YOU.

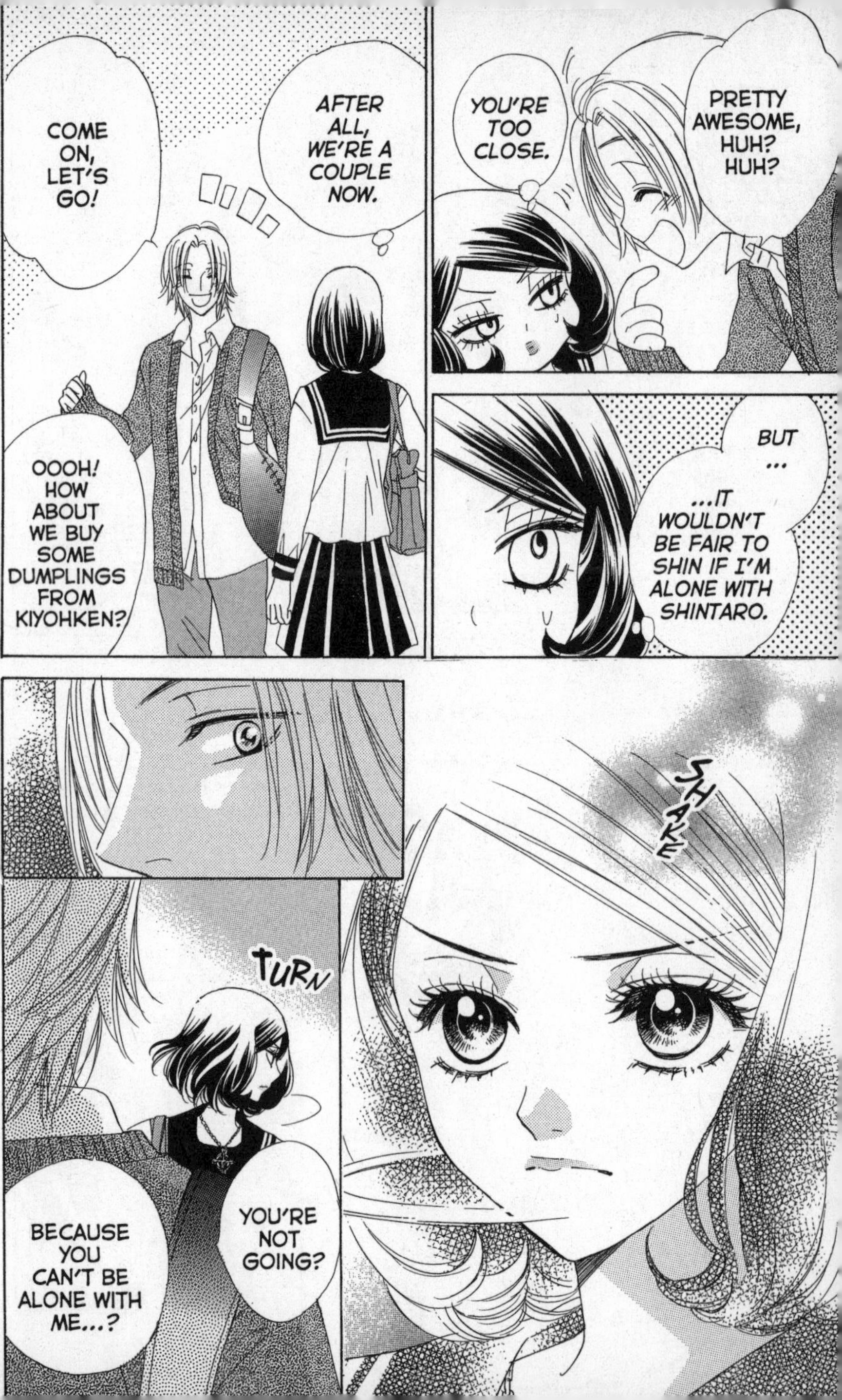
PRETTY AWESOME, HUH? HUH?
YOU'RE TOO CLOSE.
BUT...
...IT WOULDN'T BE FAIR TO SHIN IF I'M ALONE WITH SHINTARO.
AFTER ALL, WE'RE A COUPLE NOW.
COME ON, LET'S GO!
OOOH! HOW ABOUT WE BUY SOME DUMPLINGS FROM KIYOHKEN?
SHAKE
TURN
YOU'RE NOT GOING?
BECAUSE YOU CAN'T BE ALONE WITH ME...?

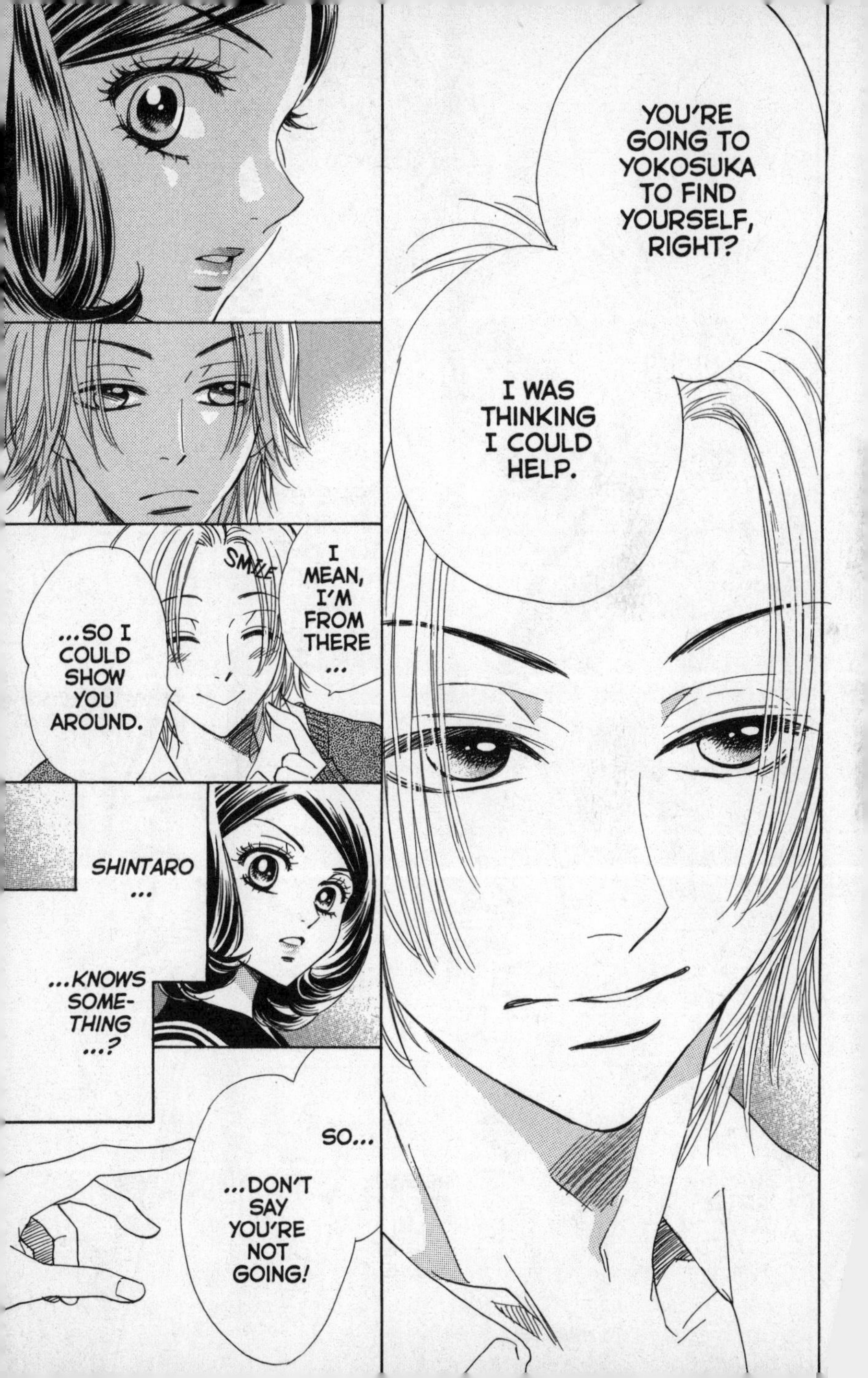
YOU'RE GOING TO YOKOSUKA TO FIND YOURSELF, RIGHT?
I WAS THINKING I COULD HELP.
I MEAN, I'M FROM THERE...
SMILE
...SO I COULD SHOW YOU AROUND.
SHINTARO...
...KNOWS SOMETHING...?
SO...
...DON'T SAY YOU'RE NOT GOING!

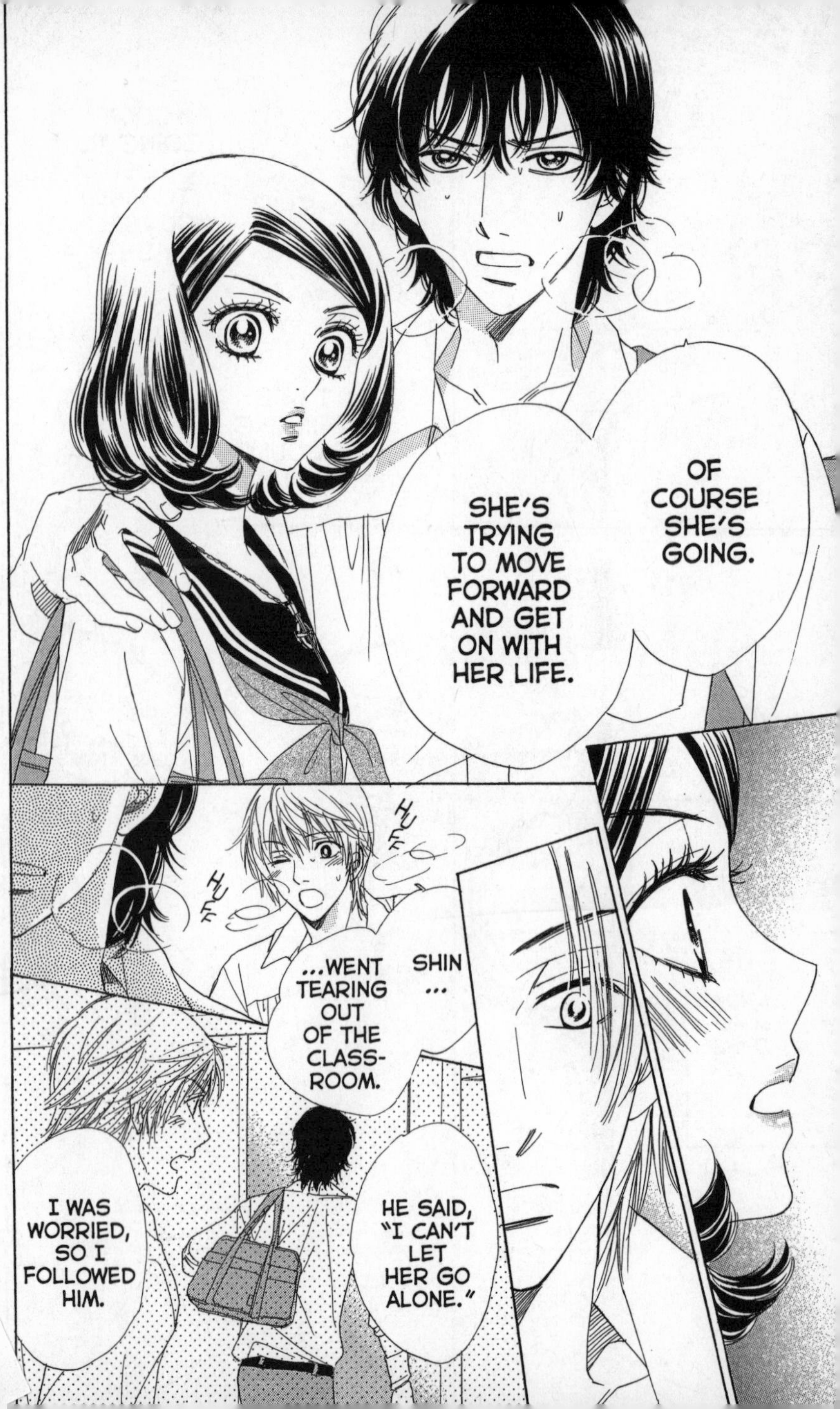
OF COURSE SHE'S GOING.
SHE'S TRYING TO MOVE FORWARD AND GET ON WITH HER LIFE.
HUFF
HUFF
SHIN...
...WENT TEARING OUT OF THE CLASS-ROOM.
HE SAID, "I CAN'T LET HER GO ALONE."
I WAS WORRIED, SO I FOLLOWED HIM.

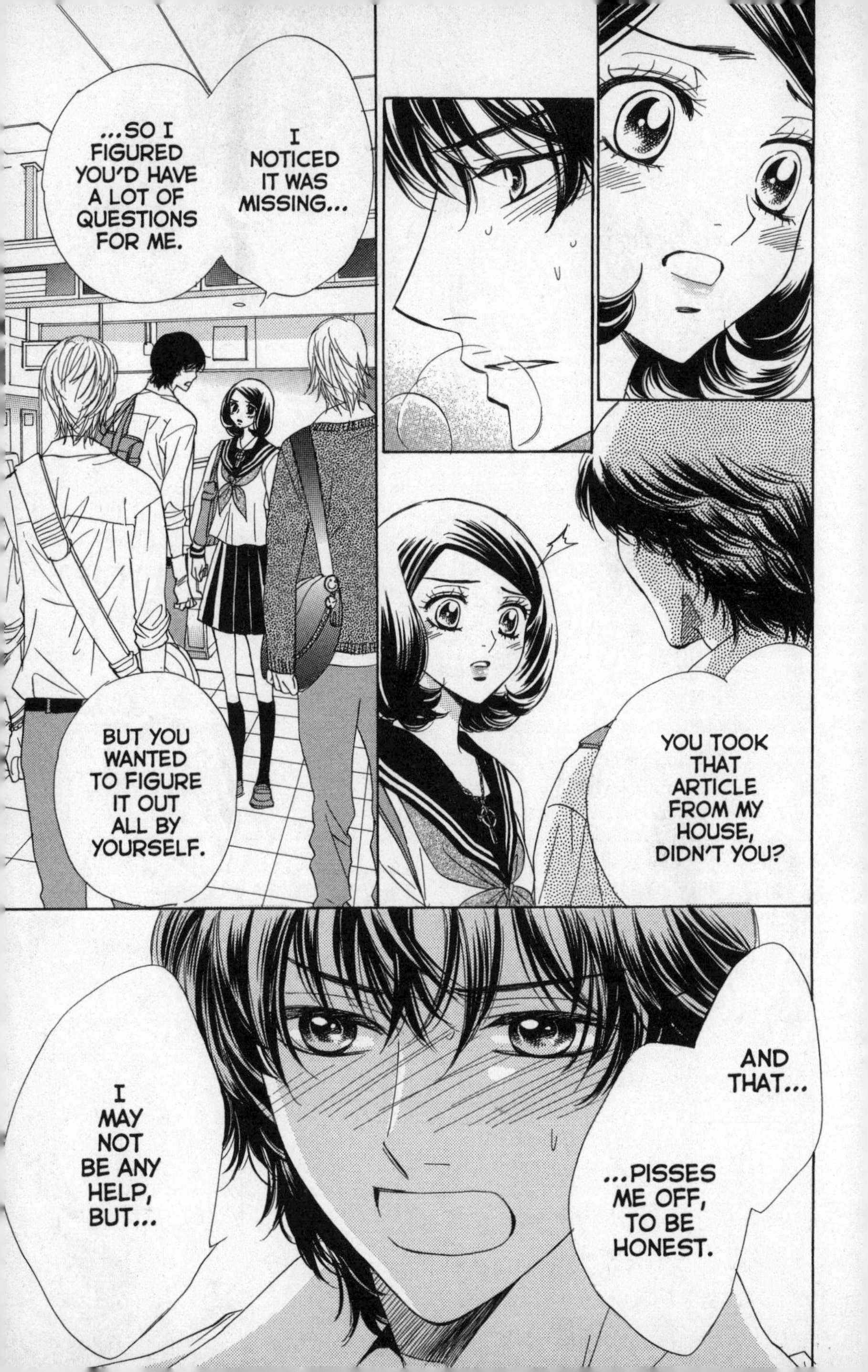
YOU TOOK THAT ARTICLE FROM MY HOUSE, DIDN'T YOU?
I NOTICED IT WAS MISSING...
...SO I FIGURED YOU'D HAVE A LOT OF QUESTIONS FOR ME.
BUT YOU WANTED TO FIGURE IT OUT ALL BY YOURSELF.
AND THAT...
...PISSES ME OFF, TO BE HONEST.
I MAY NOT BE ANY HELP, BUT...

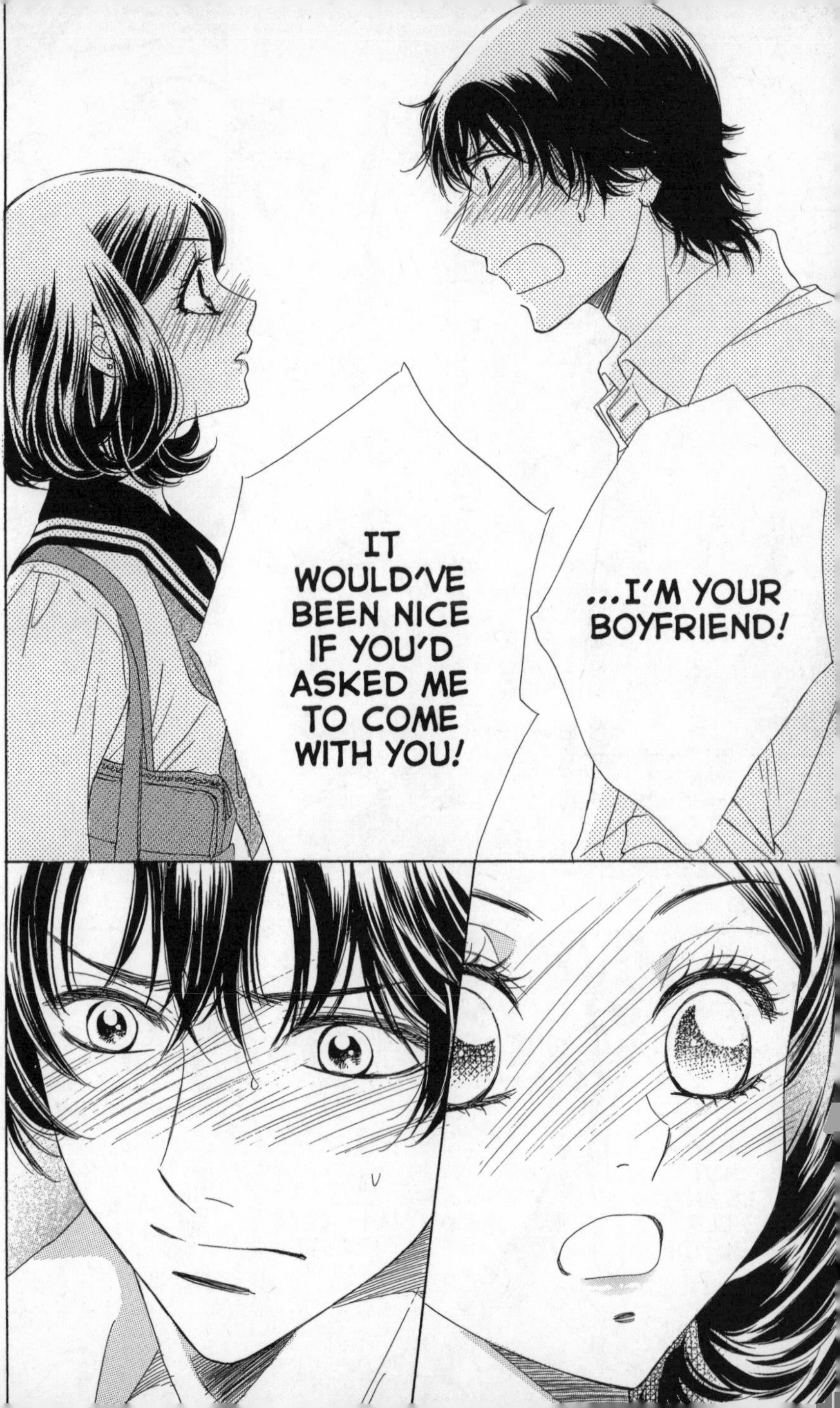
...I'M YOUR BOYFRIEND!
IT WOULD'VE BEEN NICE IF YOU'D ASKED ME TO COME WITH YOU!

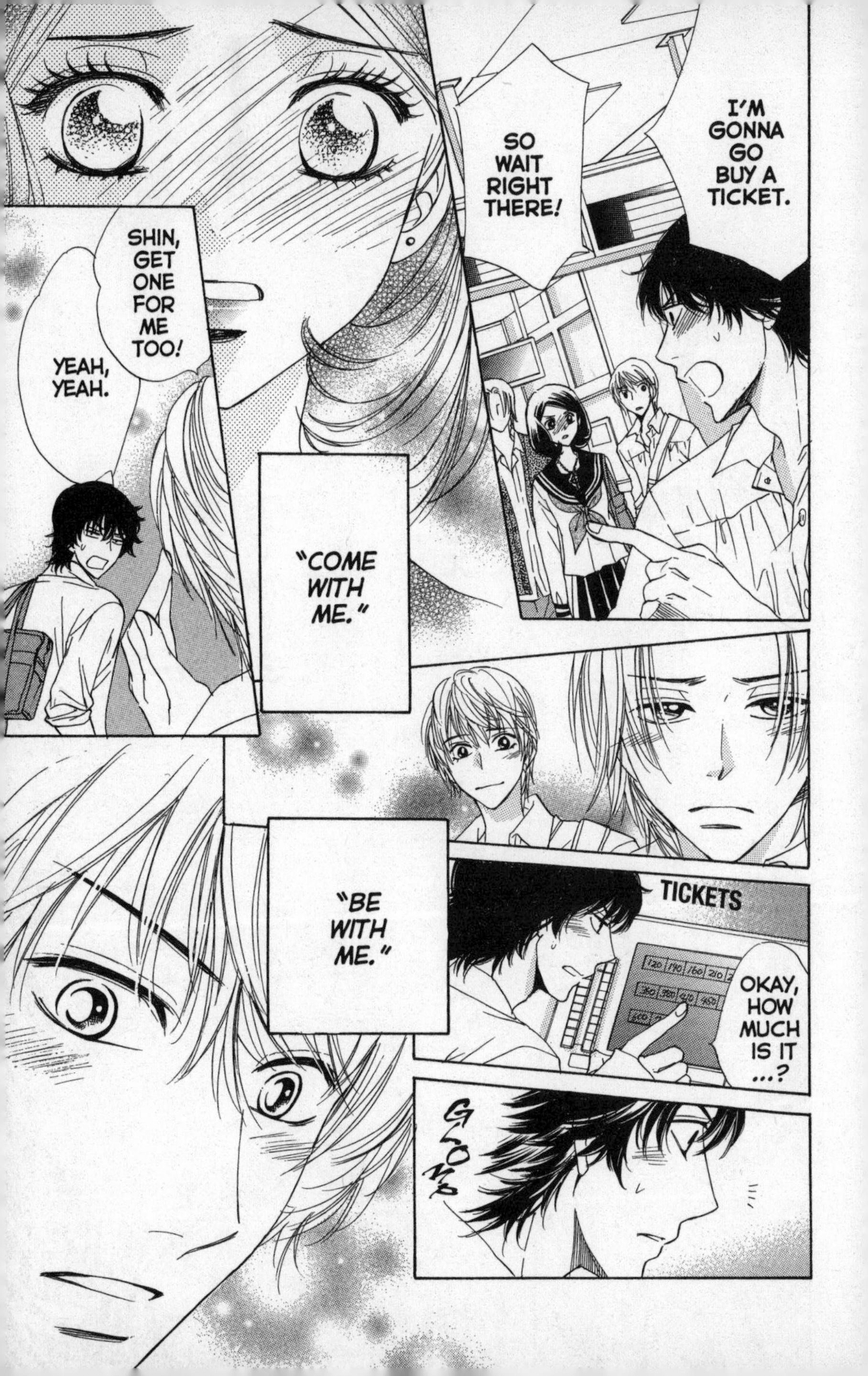
I'M GONNA GO BUY A TICKET.
SO WAIT RIGHT THERE!
SHIN, GET ONE FOR ME TOO!
YEAH, YEAH.
"COME WITH ME."
TICKETS
OKAY, HOW MUCH IS IT ...?
"BE WITH ME."
GLOMP

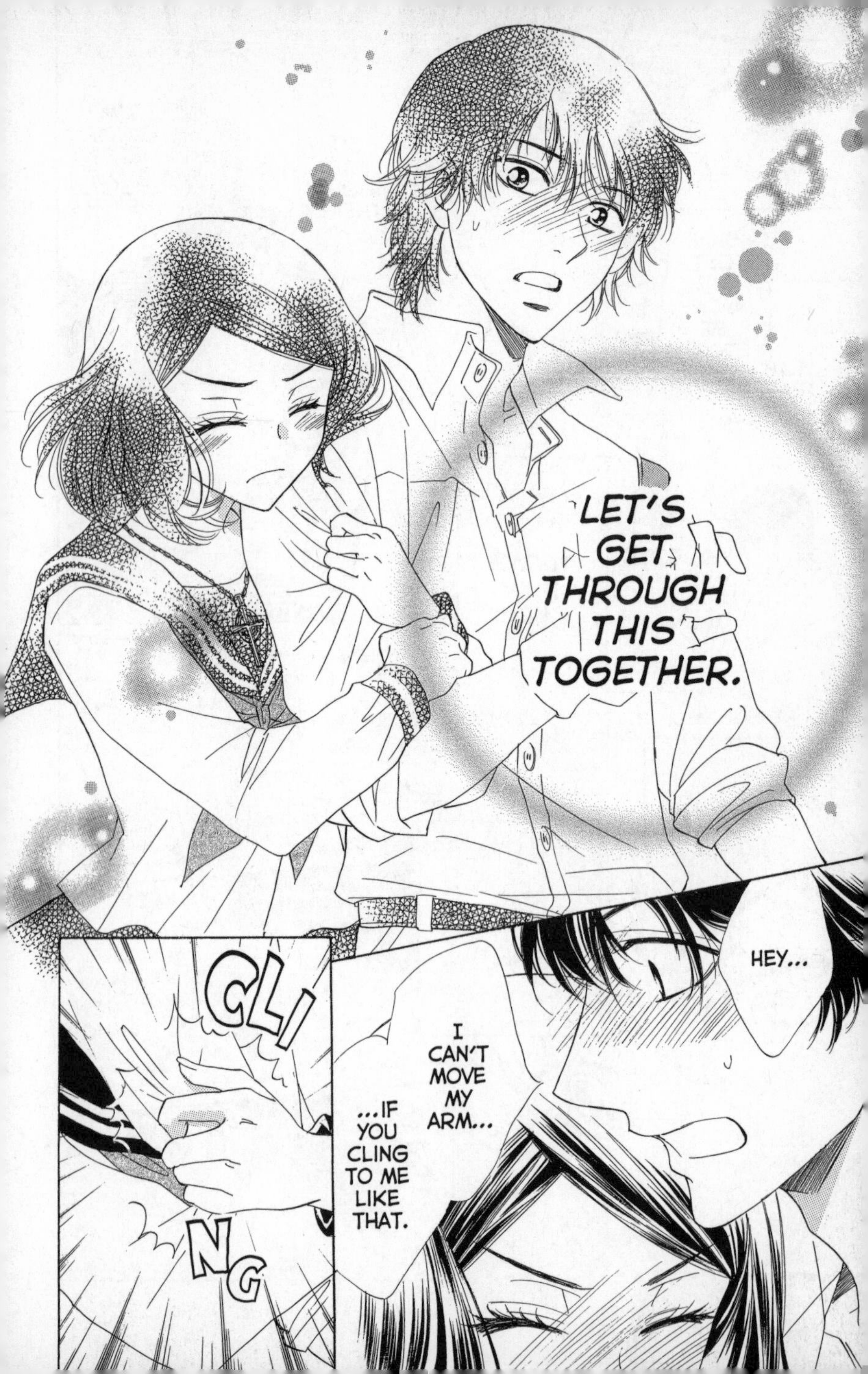
LET'S GET THROUGH THIS TOGETHER.
HEY...
I CAN'T MOVE MY ARM...
...IF YOU CLING TO ME LIKE THAT.
CLING

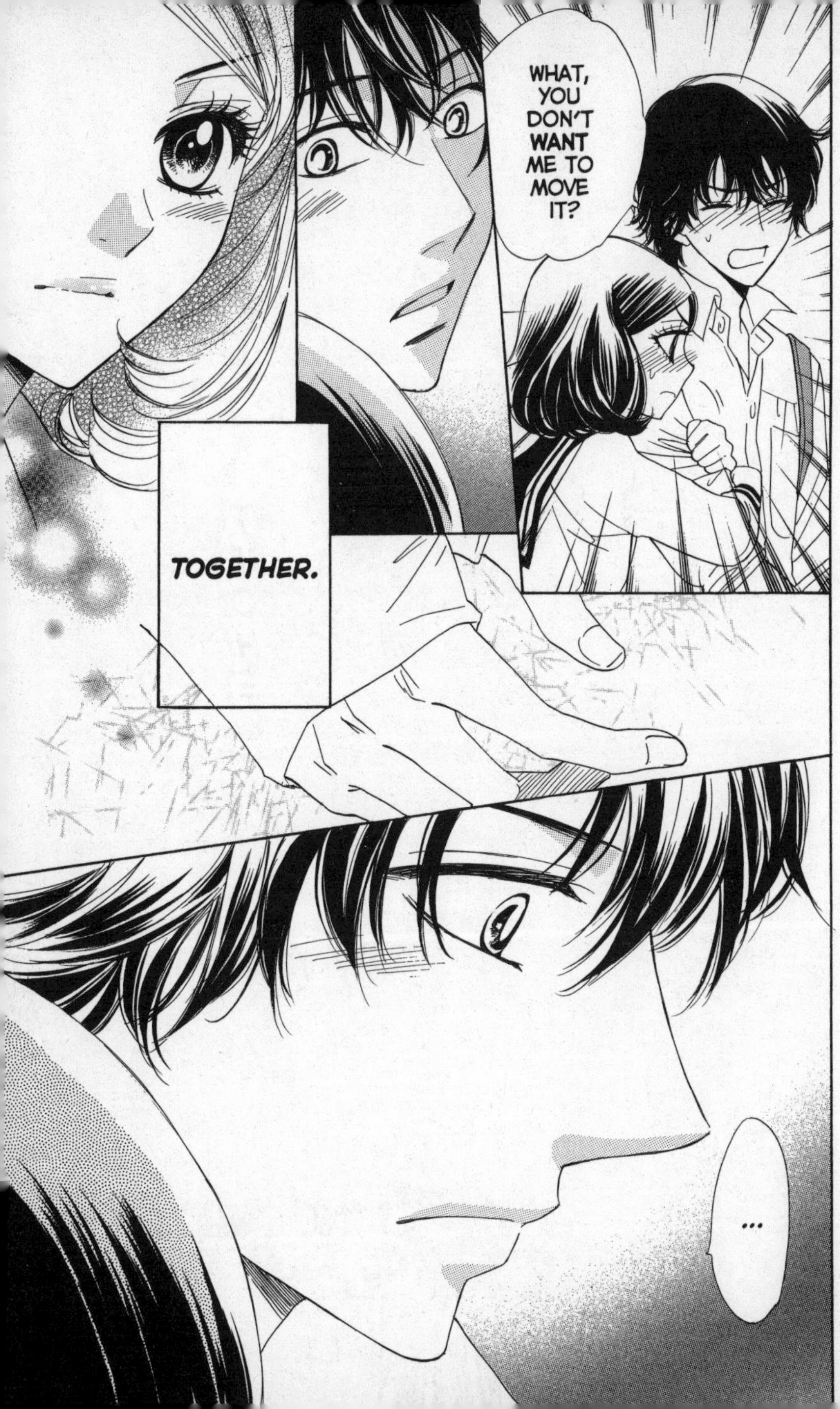
WHAT, YOU DON'T WANT ME TO MOVE IT?
TOGETHER.
...

A Devil and
Her Love Song

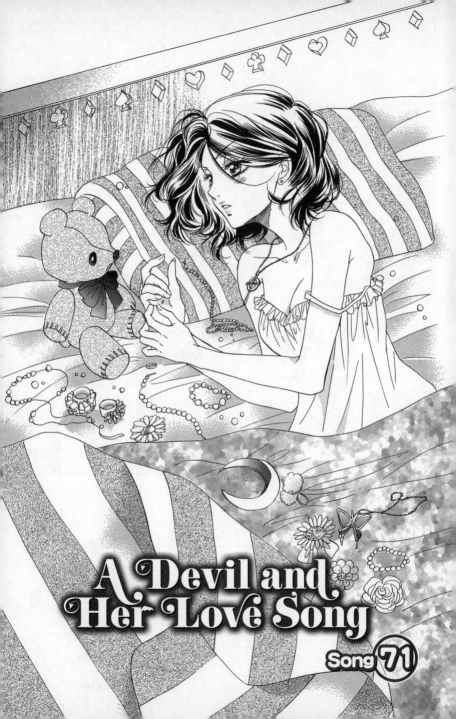

A Devil and Her Love Song

Song 71

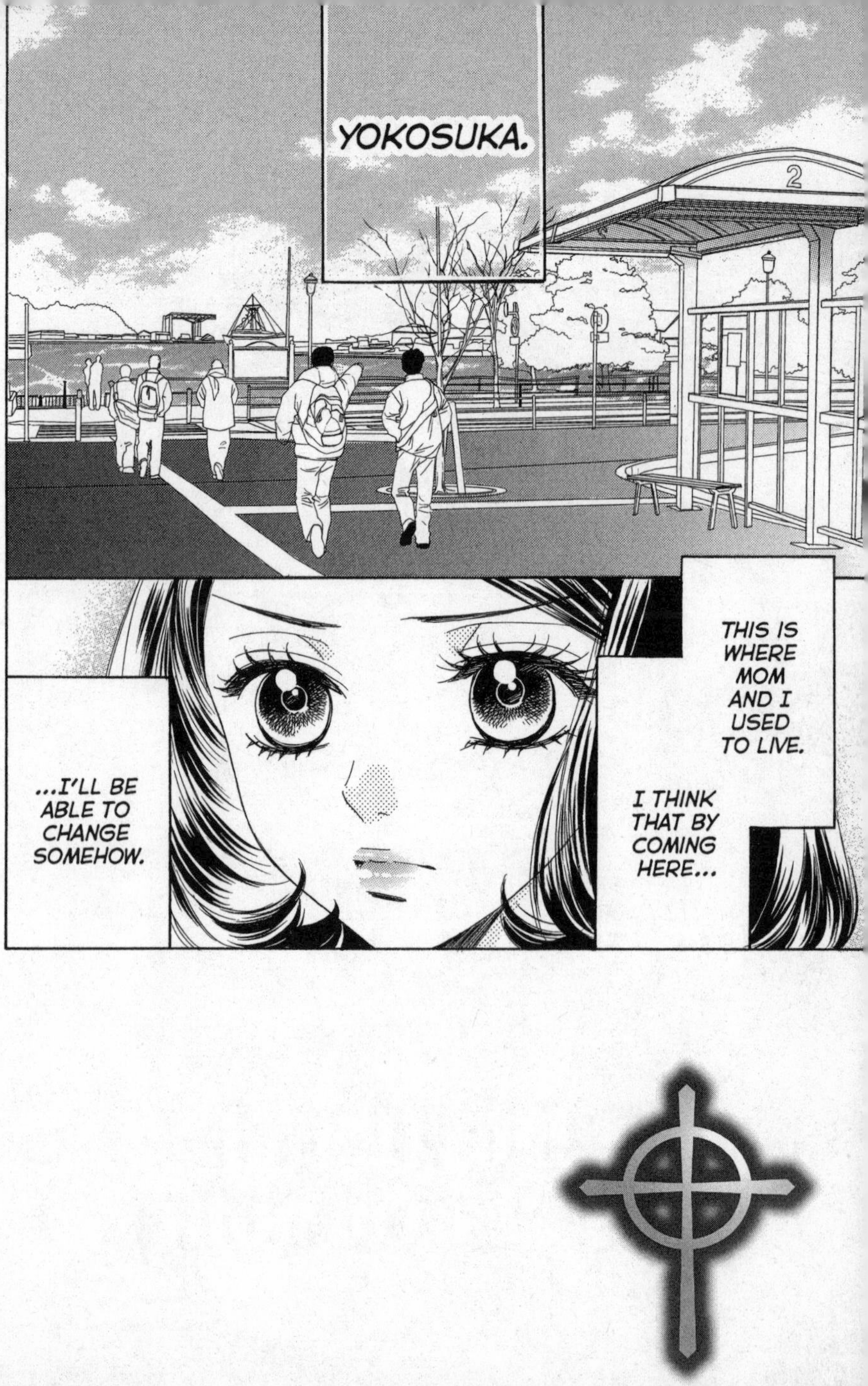
YOKOSUKA.
THIS IS WHERE MOM AND I USED TO LIVE.
I THINK THAT BY COMING HERE...
...I'LL BE ABLE TO CHANGE SOMEHOW.

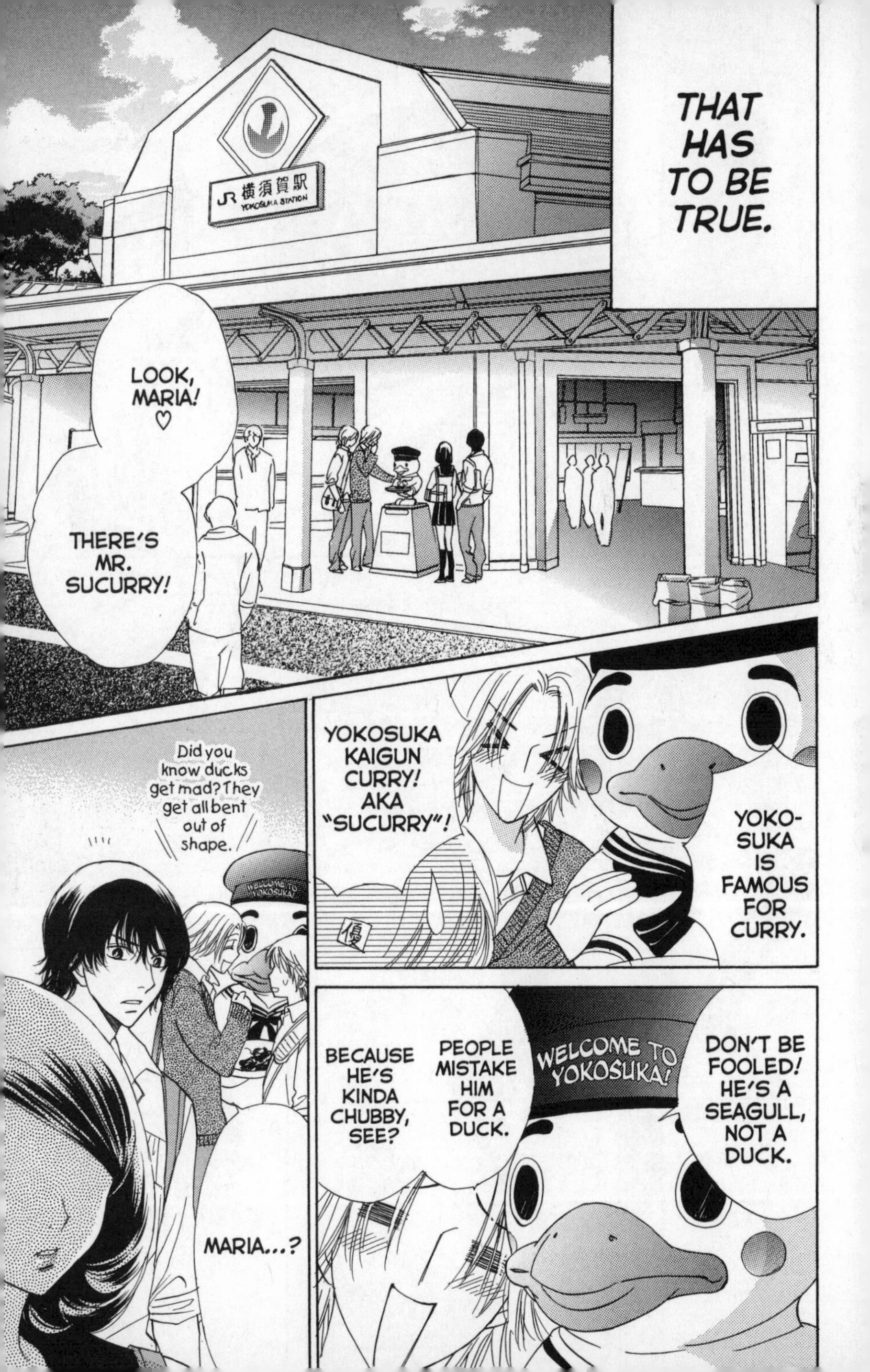
THAT HAS TO BE TRUE.
JR 横須賀駅
YOKOSUKA STATION
LOOK, MARIA! ♡
THERE'S MR. SUCURRY!
YOKO-SUKA IS FAMOUS FOR CURRY.
YOKOSUKA KAIGUN CURRY! AKA "SUCURRY"!
DON'T BE FOOLED! HE'S A SEAGULL, NOT A DUCK.
WELCOME TO YOKOSUKA!
PEOPLE MISTAKE HIM FOR A DUCK.
BECAUSE HE'S KINDA CHUBBY, SEE?
Did you know ducks get mad? They get all bent out of shape.
WELCOME TO YOKOSUKA!
MARIA...?

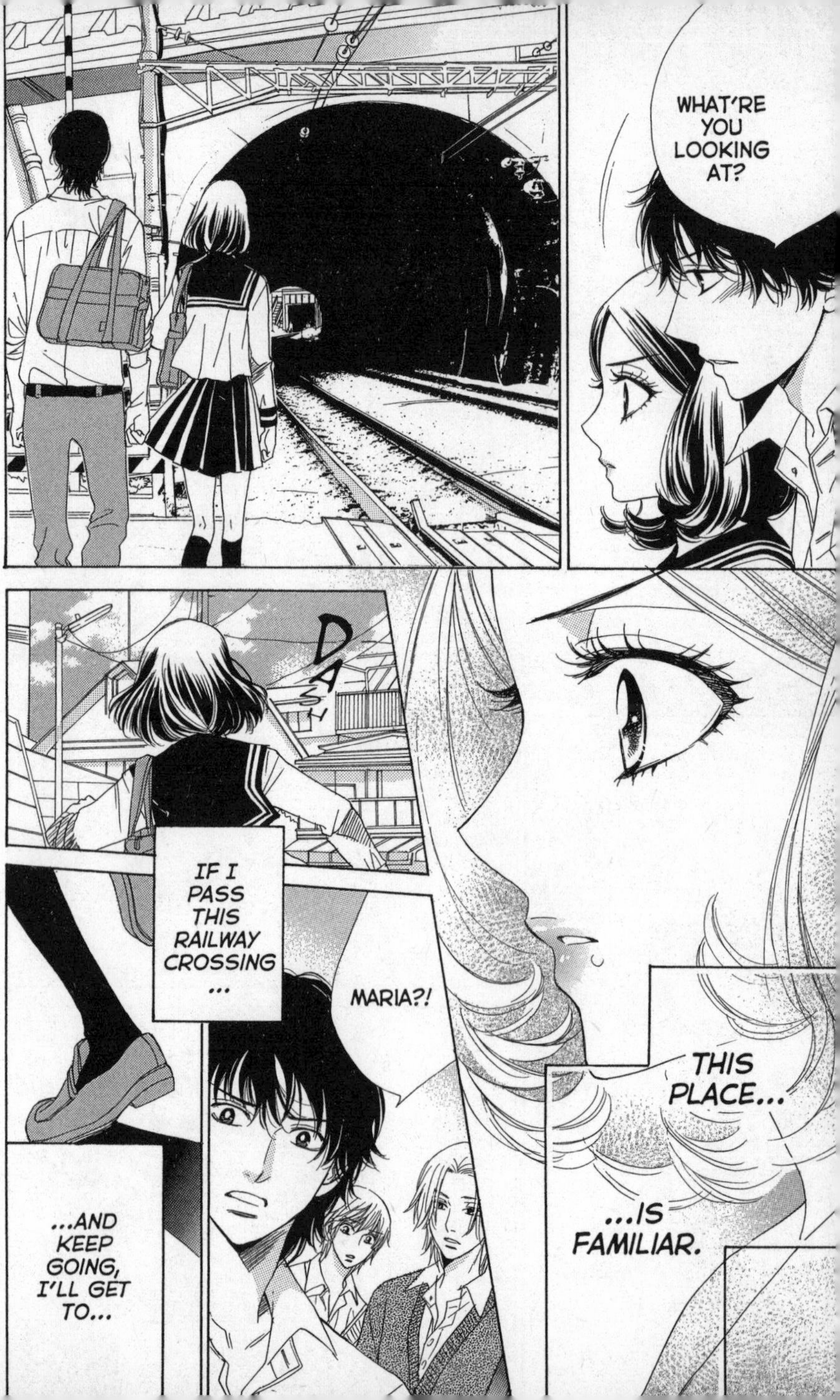
WHAT'RE YOU LOOKING AT?
THIS PLACE...
...IS FAMILIAR.
DASH
IF I PASS THIS RAILWAY CROSSING...
MARIA?!
...AND KEEP GOING, I'LL GET TO...

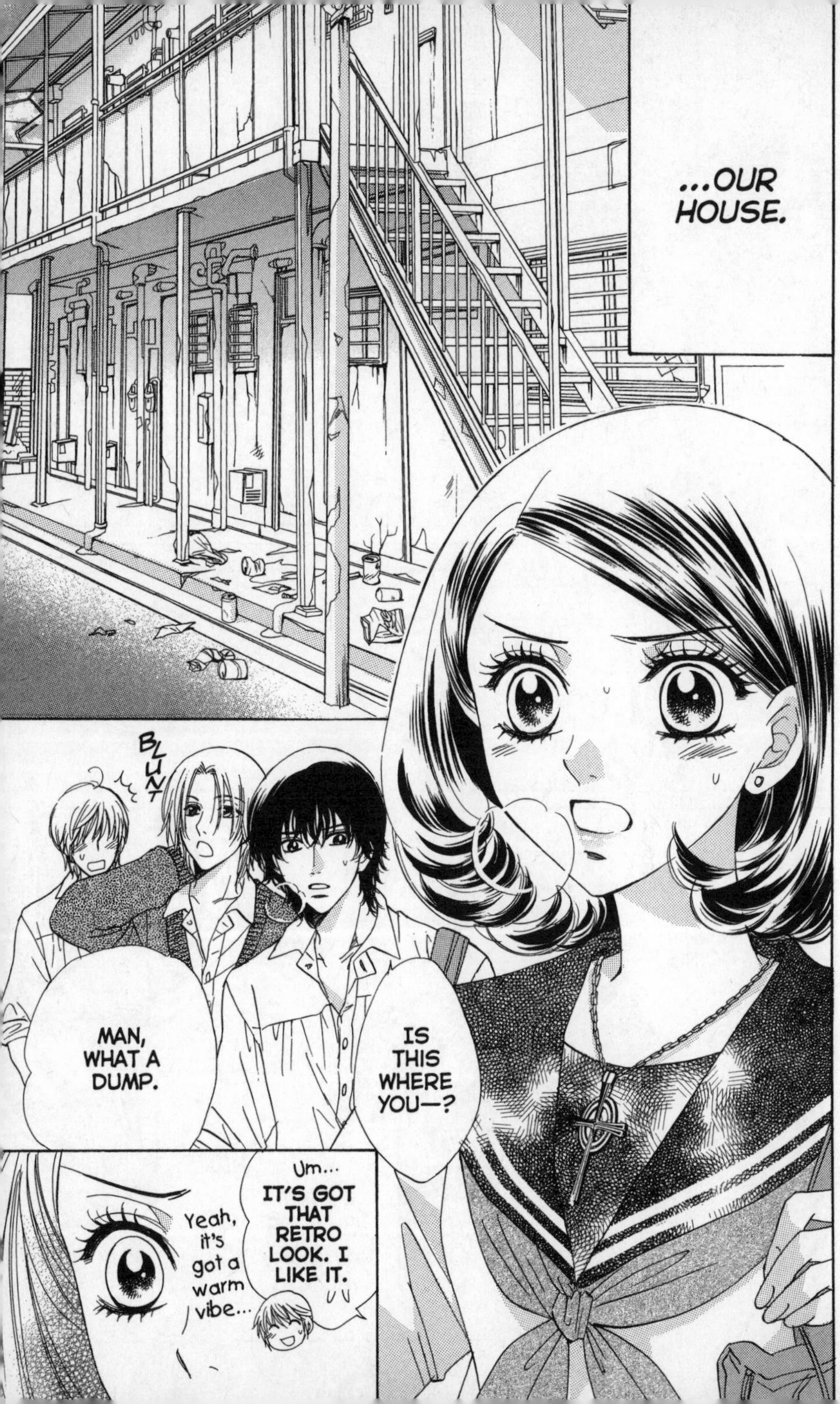
...OUR HOUSE.
IS THIS WHERE YOU—?
BLUNT
MAN, WHAT A DUMP.
Um... IT'S GOT THAT RETRO LOOK. I LIKE IT.
Yeah, it's got a warm vibe...

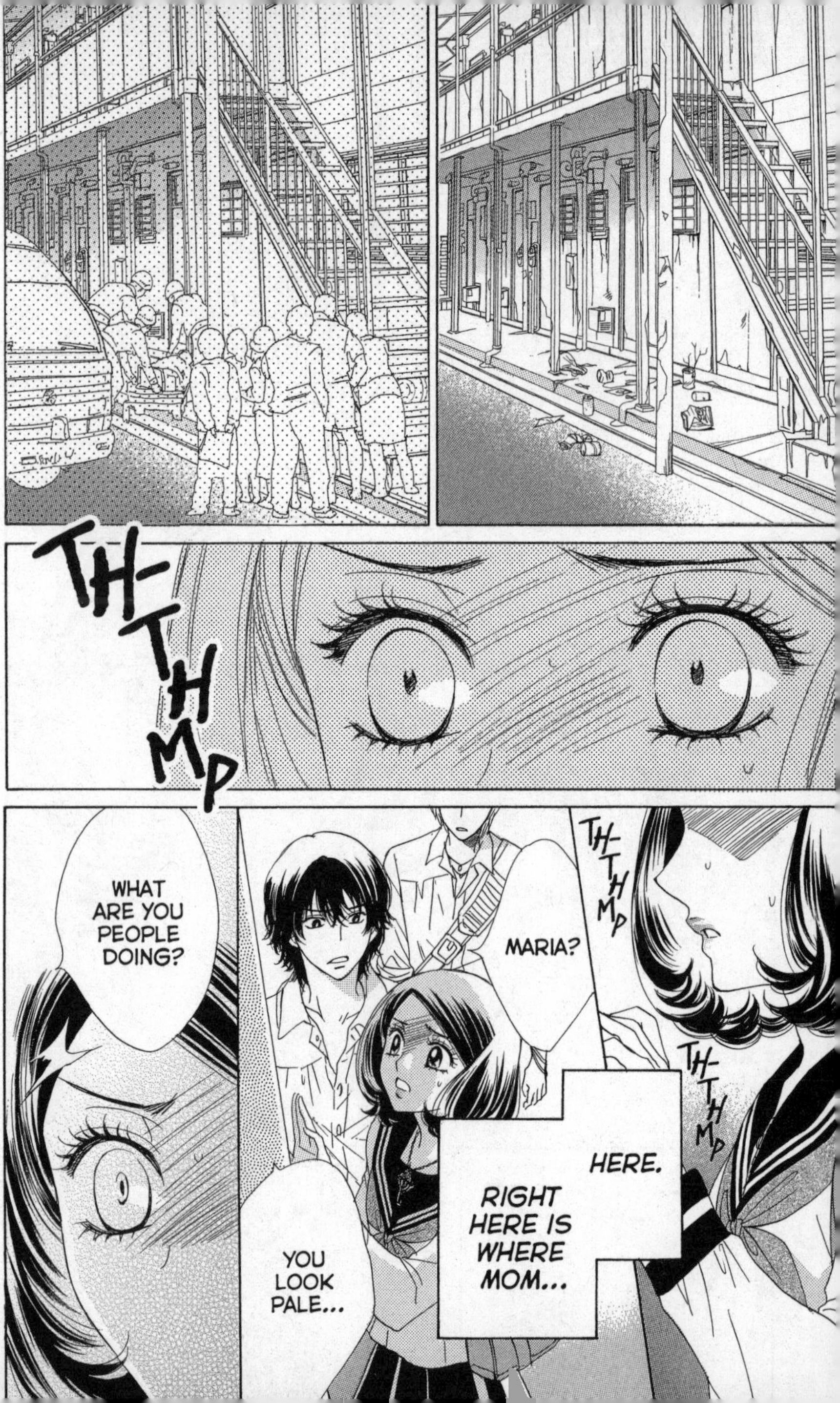
TH-THMP
TH-THMP
TH-THMP
HERE.
RIGHT HERE IS WHERE MOM...
MARIA?
YOU LOOK PALE...
WHAT ARE YOU PEOPLE DOING?

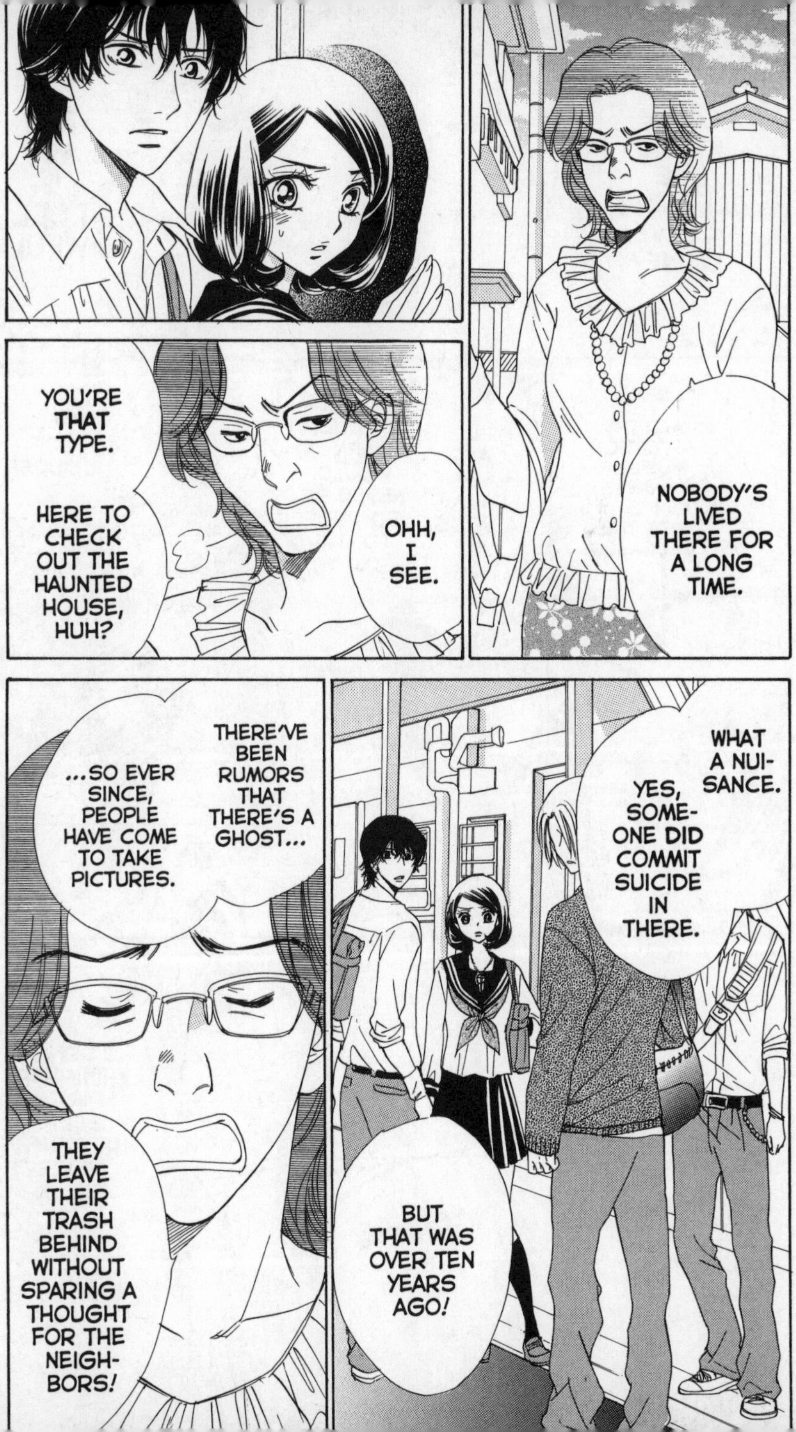
NOBODY'S LIVED THERE FOR A LONG TIME.
OHH, I SEE.
YOU'RE THAT TYPE.
HERE TO CHECK OUT THE HAUNTED HOUSE, HUH?
WHAT A NUISANCE.
YES, SOMEONE DID COMMIT SUICIDE IN THERE.
BUT THAT WAS OVER TEN YEARS AGO!
THERE'VE BEEN RUMORS THAT THERE'S A GHOST...
...SO EVER SINCE, PEOPLE HAVE COME TO TAKE PICTURES.
THEY LEAVE THEIR TRASH BEHIND WITHOUT SPARING A THOUGHT FOR THE NEIGHBORS!

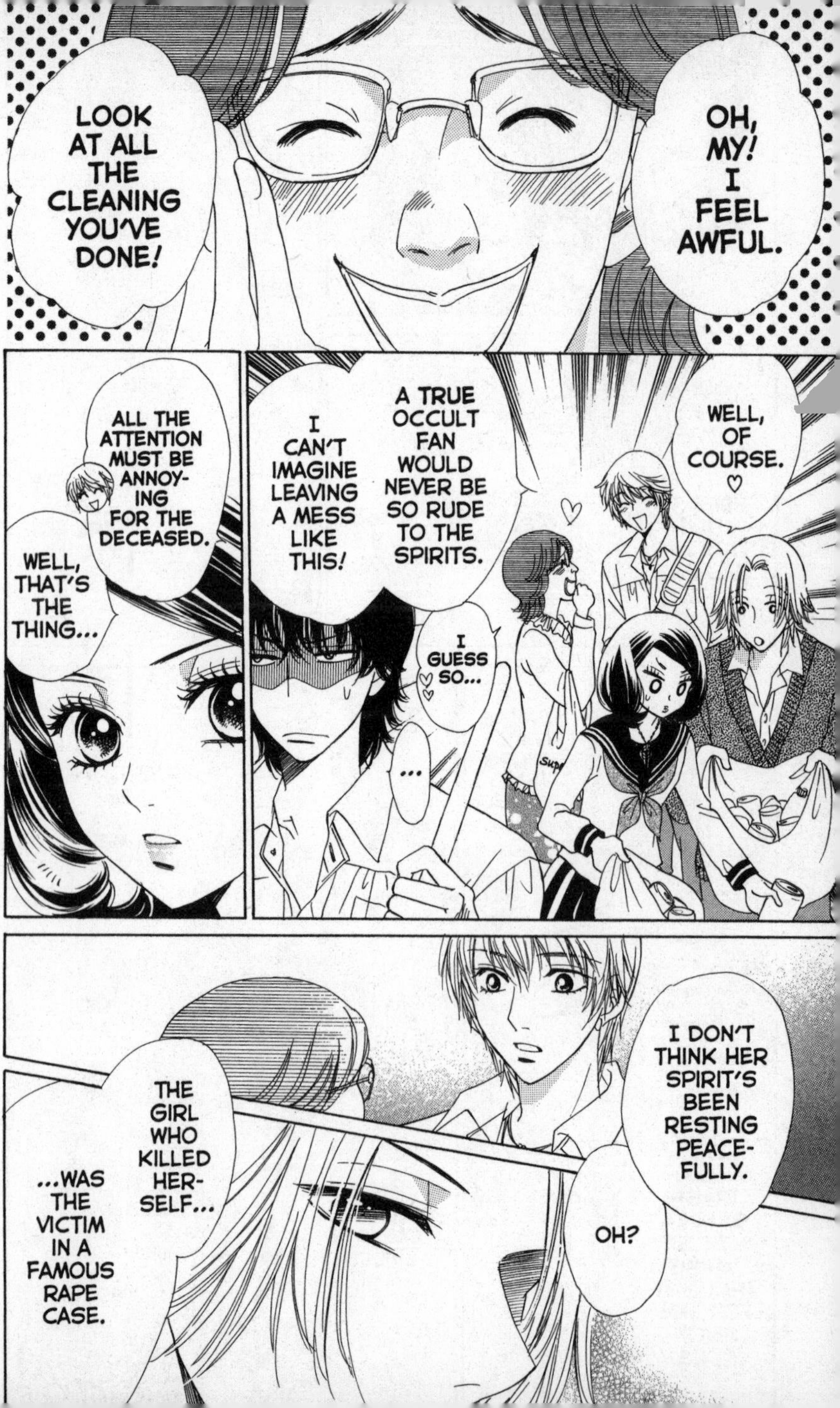
OH, MY! I FEEL AWFUL.
LOOK AT ALL THE CLEANING YOU'VE DONE!
WELL, OF COURSE. ♡
A TRUE OCCULT FAN WOULD NEVER BE SO RUDE TO THE SPIRITS.
I CAN'T IMAGINE LEAVING A MESS LIKE THIS!
I GUESS SO... ♡♡
...
ALL THE ATTENTION MUST BE ANNOYING FOR THE DECEASED.
WELL, THAT'S THE THING...
I DON'T THINK HER SPIRIT'S BEEN RESTING PEACEFULLY.
OH?
THE GIRL WHO KILLED HERSELF...
...WAS THE VICTIM IN A FAMOUS RAPE CASE.

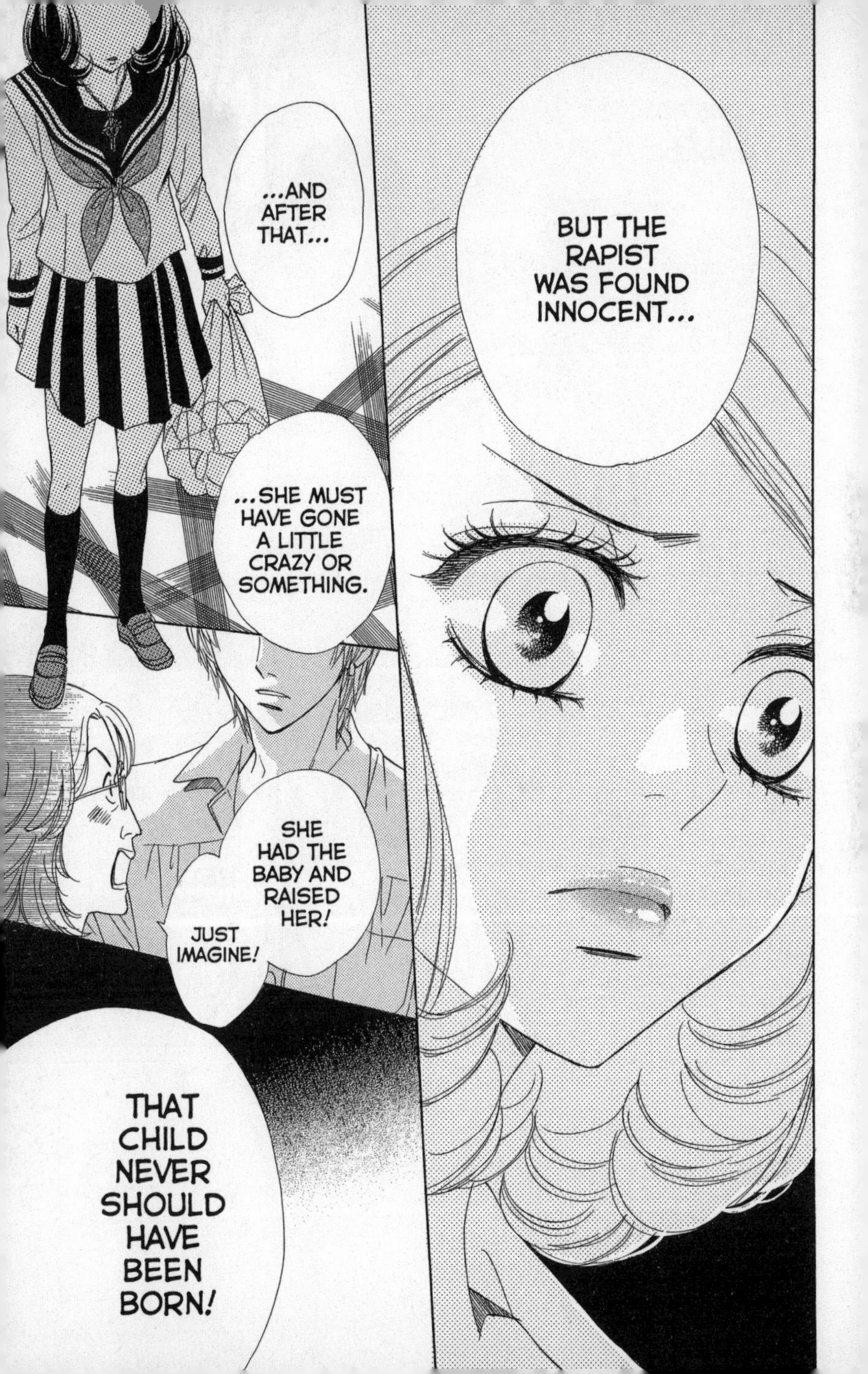
BUT THE RAPIST WAS FOUND INNOCENT...
...AND AFTER THAT...
...SHE MUST HAVE GONE A LITTLE CRAZY OR SOMETHING.
SHE HAD THE BABY AND RAISED HER!
JUST IMAGINE!
THAT CHILD NEVER SHOULD HAVE BEEN BORN!

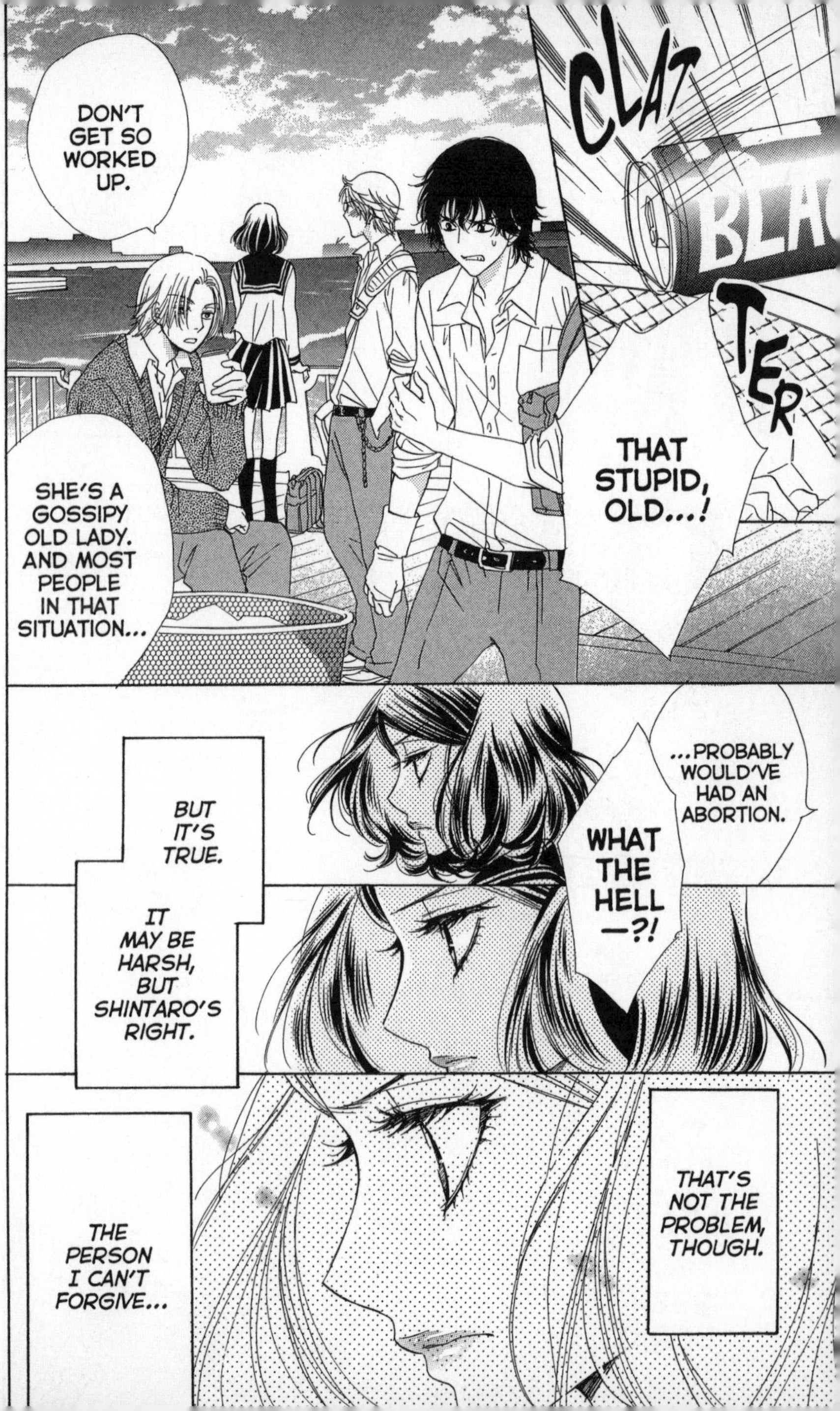
CLATTER
THAT STUPID, OLD...!
DON'T GET SO WORKED UP.
SHE'S A GOSSIPY OLD LADY. AND MOST PEOPLE IN THAT SITUATION...
...PROBABLY WOULD'VE HAD AN ABORTION.
WHAT THE HELL—?!
BUT IT'S TRUE.
IT MAY BE HARSH, BUT SHINTARO'S RIGHT.
THAT'S NOT THE PROBLEM, THOUGH.
THE PERSON I CAN'T FORGIVE...

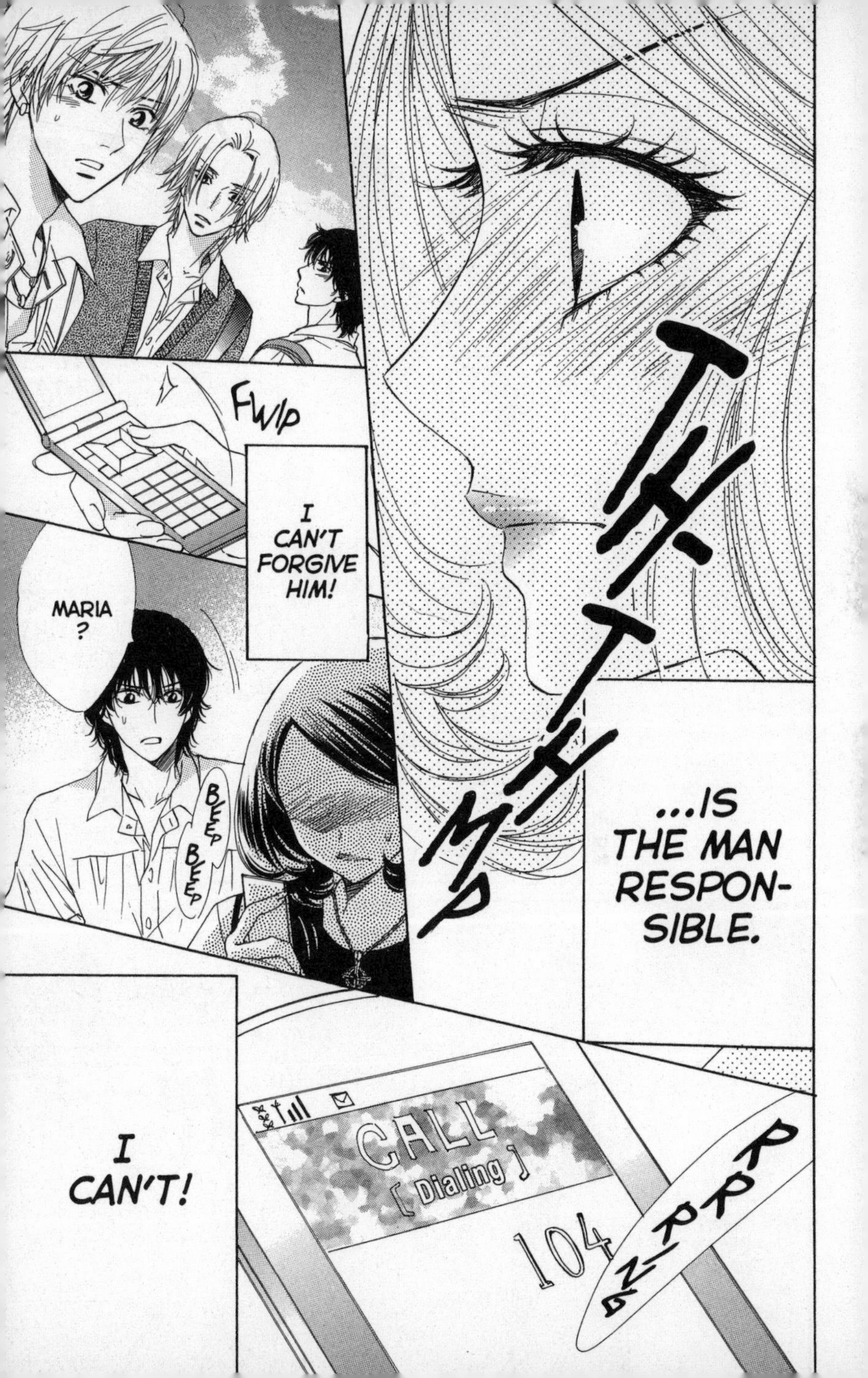
THTHMP
...IS THE MAN RESPONSIBLE.
FWIP
I CAN'T FORGIVE HIM!
MARIA?
BEEP BEEP
CALL
[Dialing]
104
RRRING
I CAN'T!

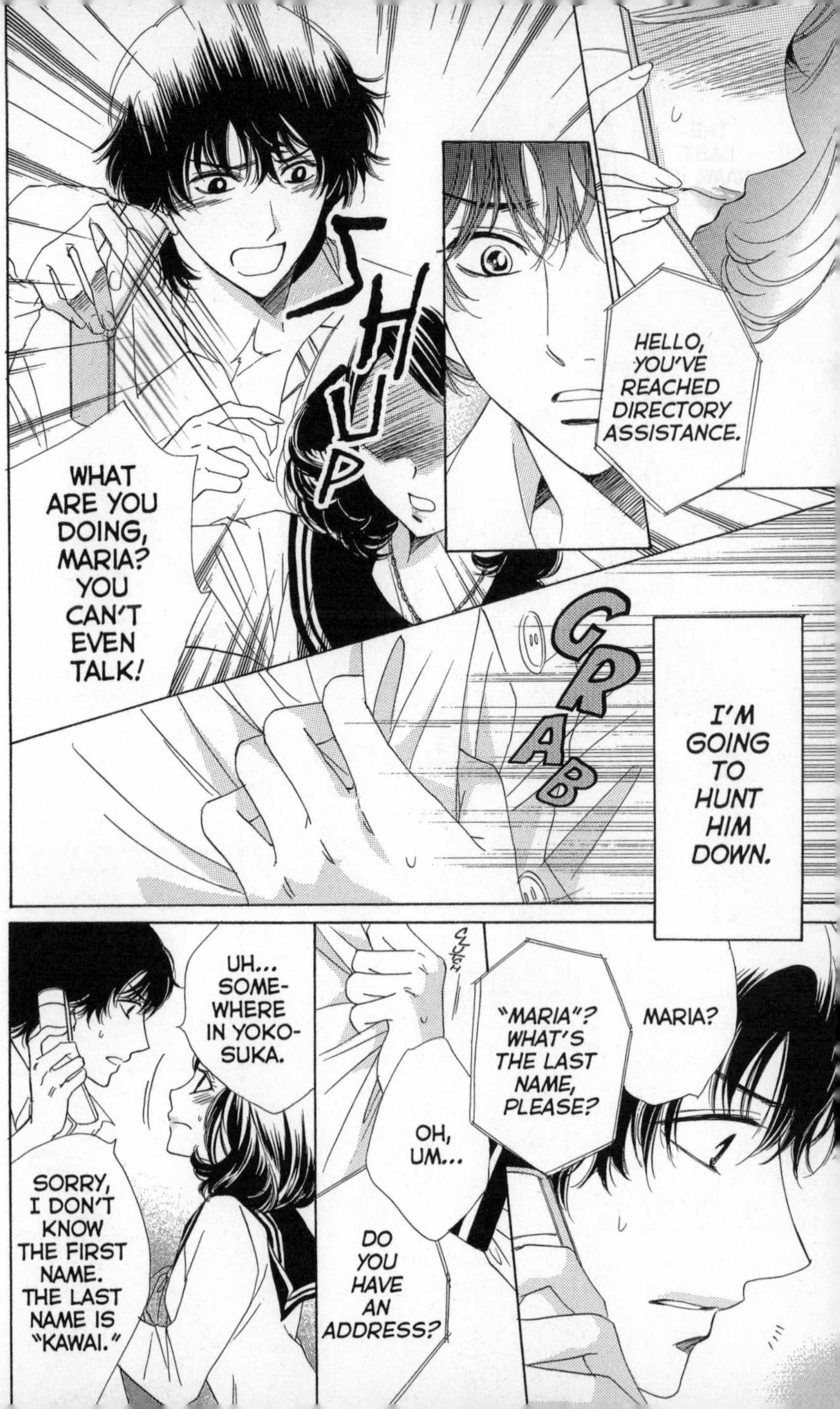
HELLO, YOU'VE REACHED DIRECTORY ASSISTANCE.
SHUP
WHAT ARE YOU DOING, MARIA? YOU CAN'T EVEN TALK!
I'M GOING TO HUNT HIM DOWN.
GRAB
MARIA?
"MARIA"? WHAT'S THE LAST NAME, PLEASE?
OH, UM...
DO YOU HAVE AN ADDRESS?
UH... SOME-WHERE IN YOKO-SUKA.
SORRY, I DON'T KNOW THE FIRST NAME. THE LAST NAME IS "KAWAI."

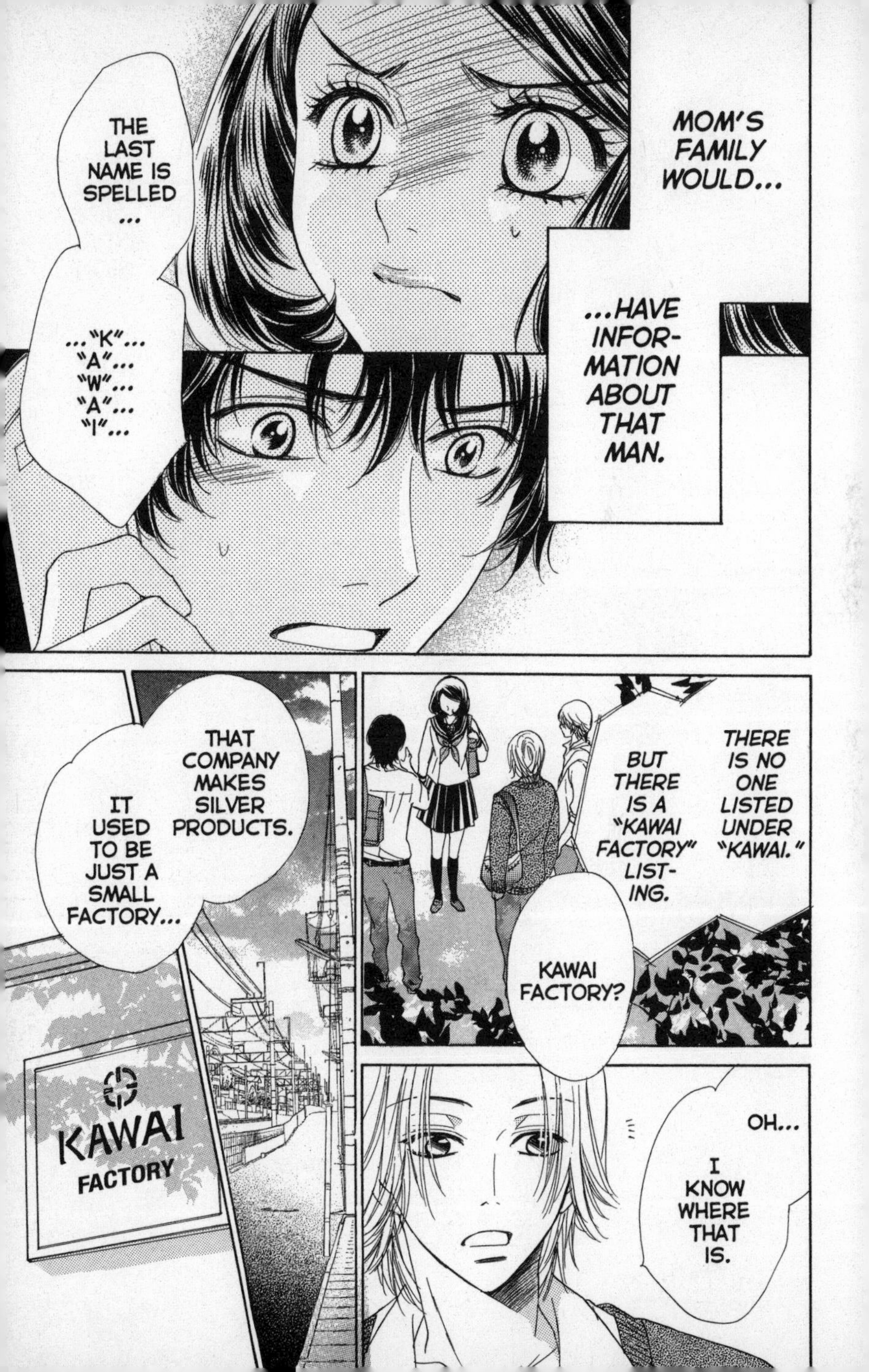
MOM'S FAMILY WOULD...
THE LAST NAME IS SPELLED ...
...HAVE INFORMATION ABOUT THAT MAN.
..."K"... "A"... "W"... "A"... "I"...
THERE IS NO ONE LISTED UNDER "KAWAI."
BUT THERE IS A "KAWAI FACTORY" LISTING.
KAWAI FACTORY?
OH...
I KNOW WHERE THAT IS.
THAT COMPANY MAKES SILVER PRODUCTS.
IT USED TO BE JUST A SMALL FACTORY...
KAWAI FACTORY

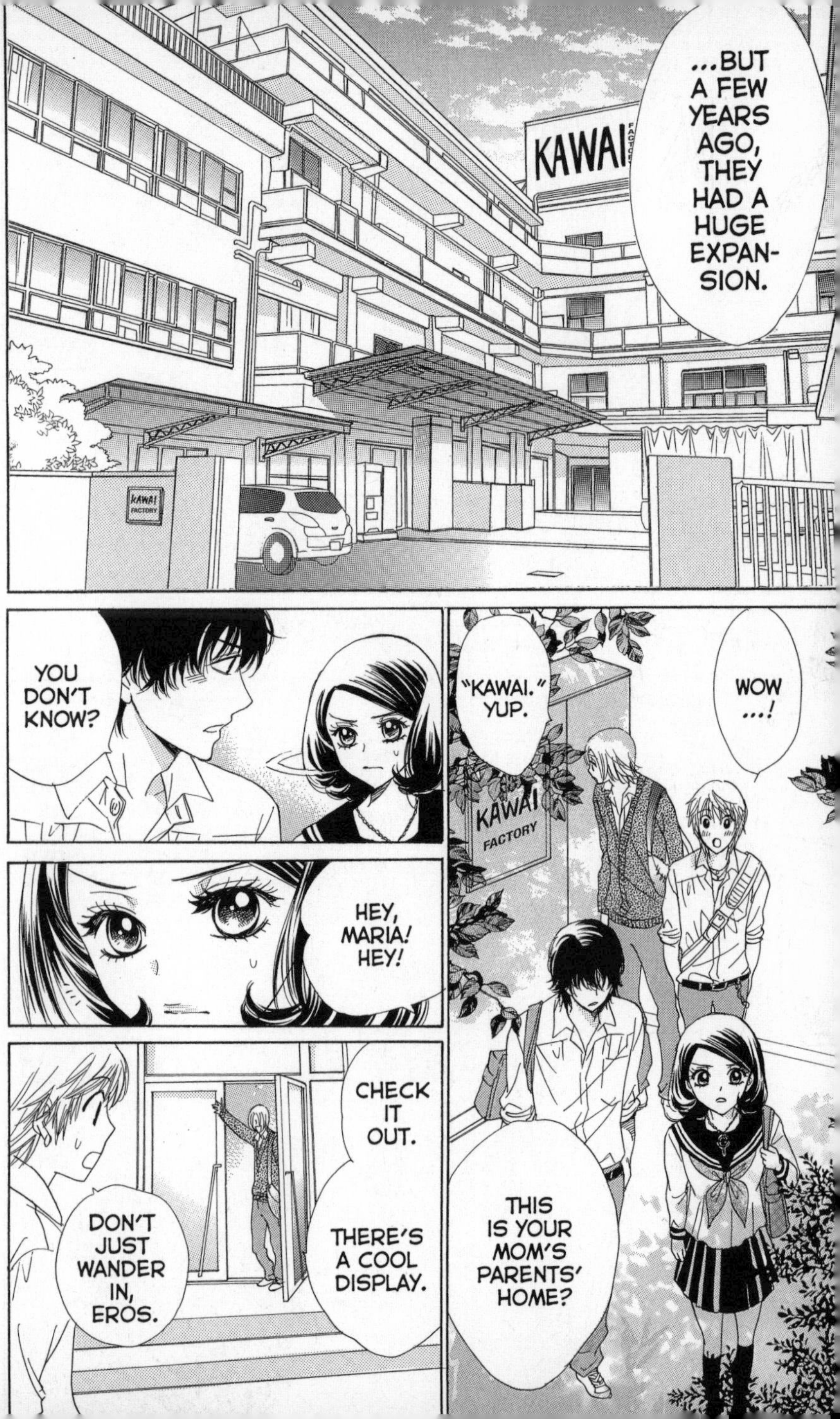
...BUT A FEW YEARS AGO, THEY HAD A HUGE EXPANSION.
KAWAI
KAWAI FACTORY
WOW ...!
"KAWAI." YUP.
KAWAI FACTORY
THIS IS YOUR MOM'S PARENTS' HOME?
YOU DON'T KNOW?
HEY, MARIA! HEY!
CHECK IT OUT.
THERE'S A COOL DISPLAY.
DON'T JUST WANDER IN, EROS.

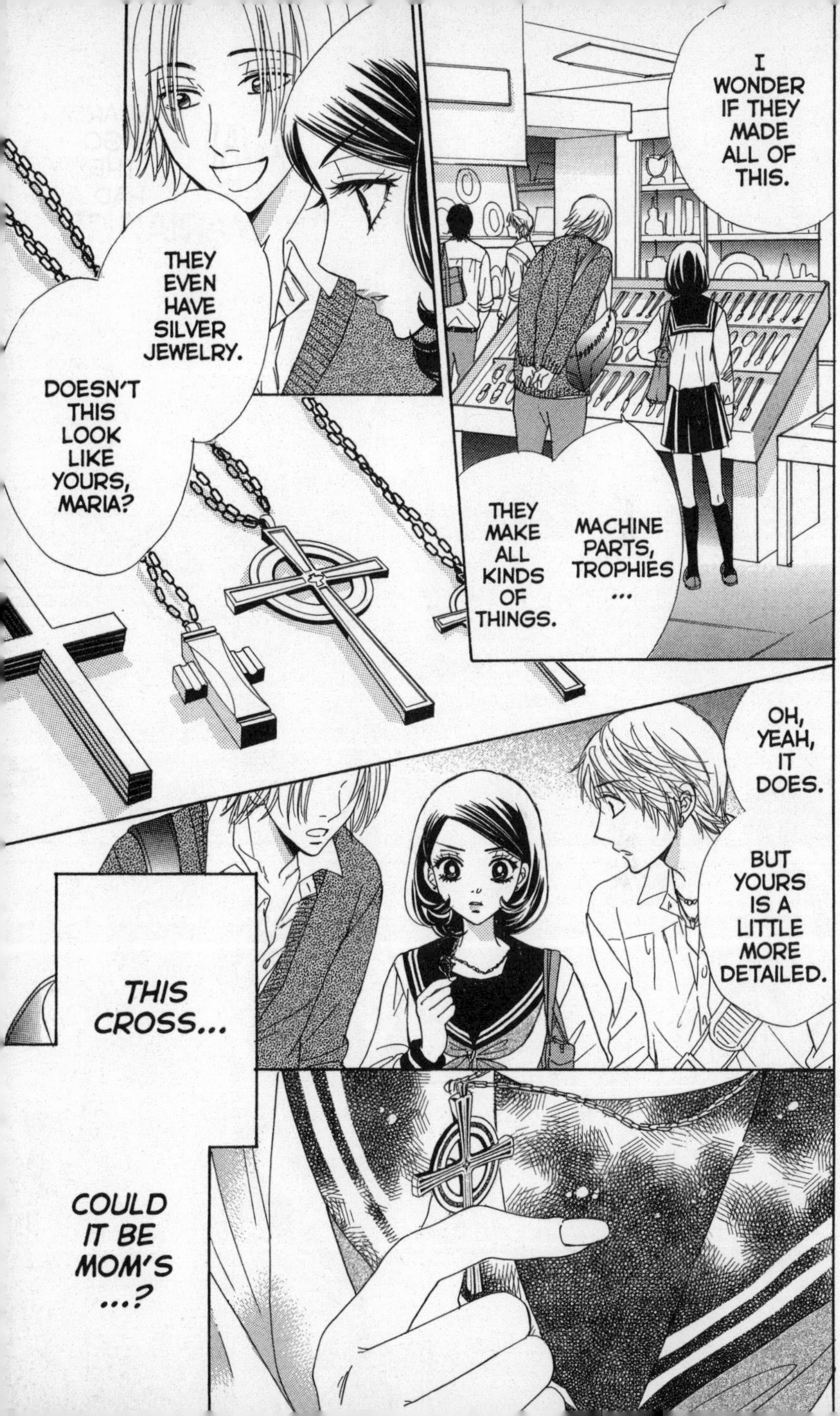
I WONDER IF THEY MADE ALL OF THIS.
MACHINE PARTS, TROPHIES...
THEY MAKE ALL KINDS OF THINGS.
THEY EVEN HAVE SILVER JEWELRY.
DOESN'T THIS LOOK LIKE YOURS, MARIA?
OH, YEAH, IT DOES.
BUT YOURS IS A LITTLE MORE DETAILED.
THIS CROSS...
COULD IT BE MOM'S ...?

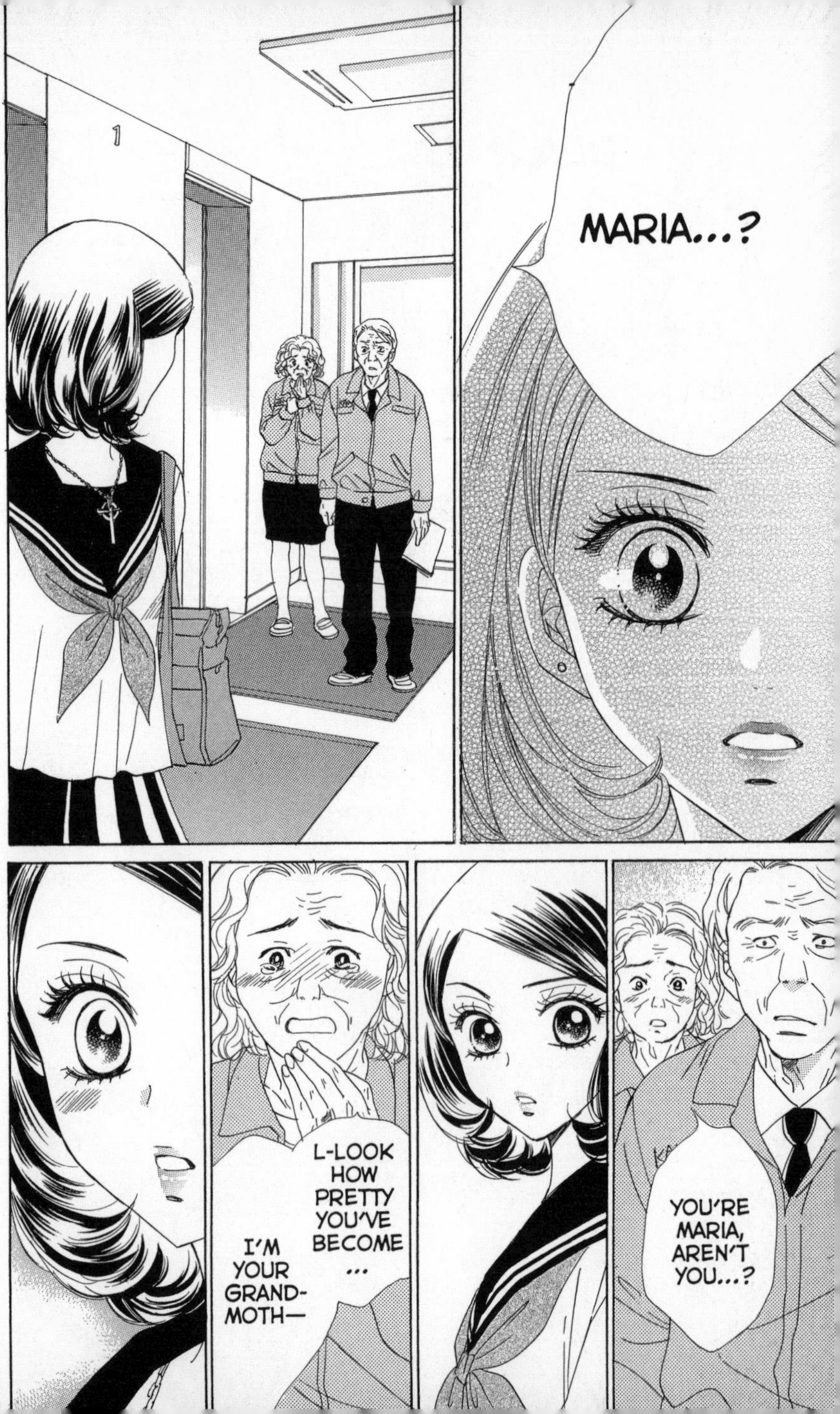
MARIA...?
1
YOU'RE MARIA, AREN'T YOU...?
L-LOOK HOW PRETTY YOU'VE BECOME...
I'M YOUR GRANDMOTH—

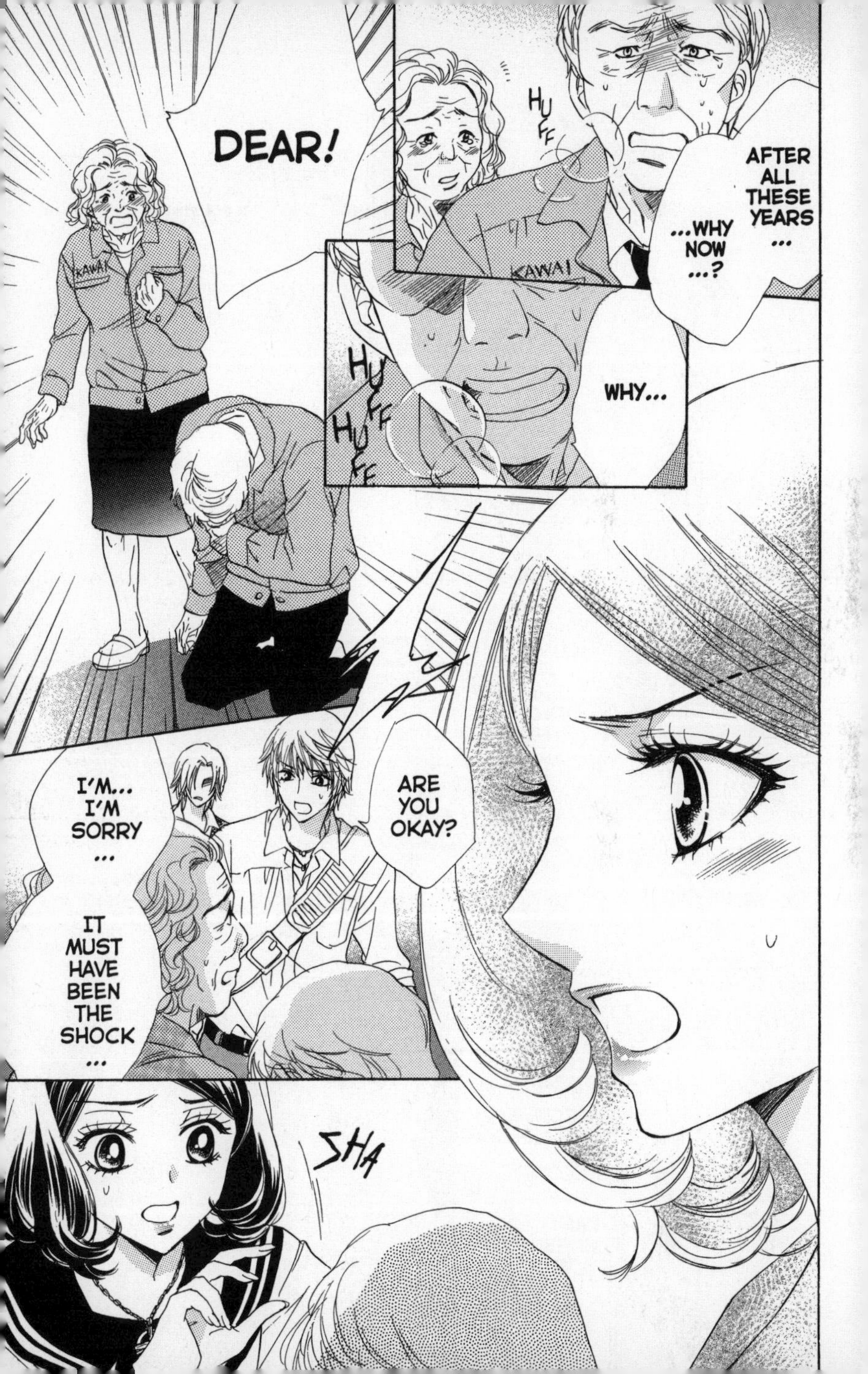
AFTER ALL THESE YEARS ...
...WHY NOW ...?
HUFF
WHY...
HUFF HUFF
DEAR!
ARE YOU OKAY?
I'M... I'M SORRY ...
IT MUST HAVE BEEN THE SHOCK ...
SHA

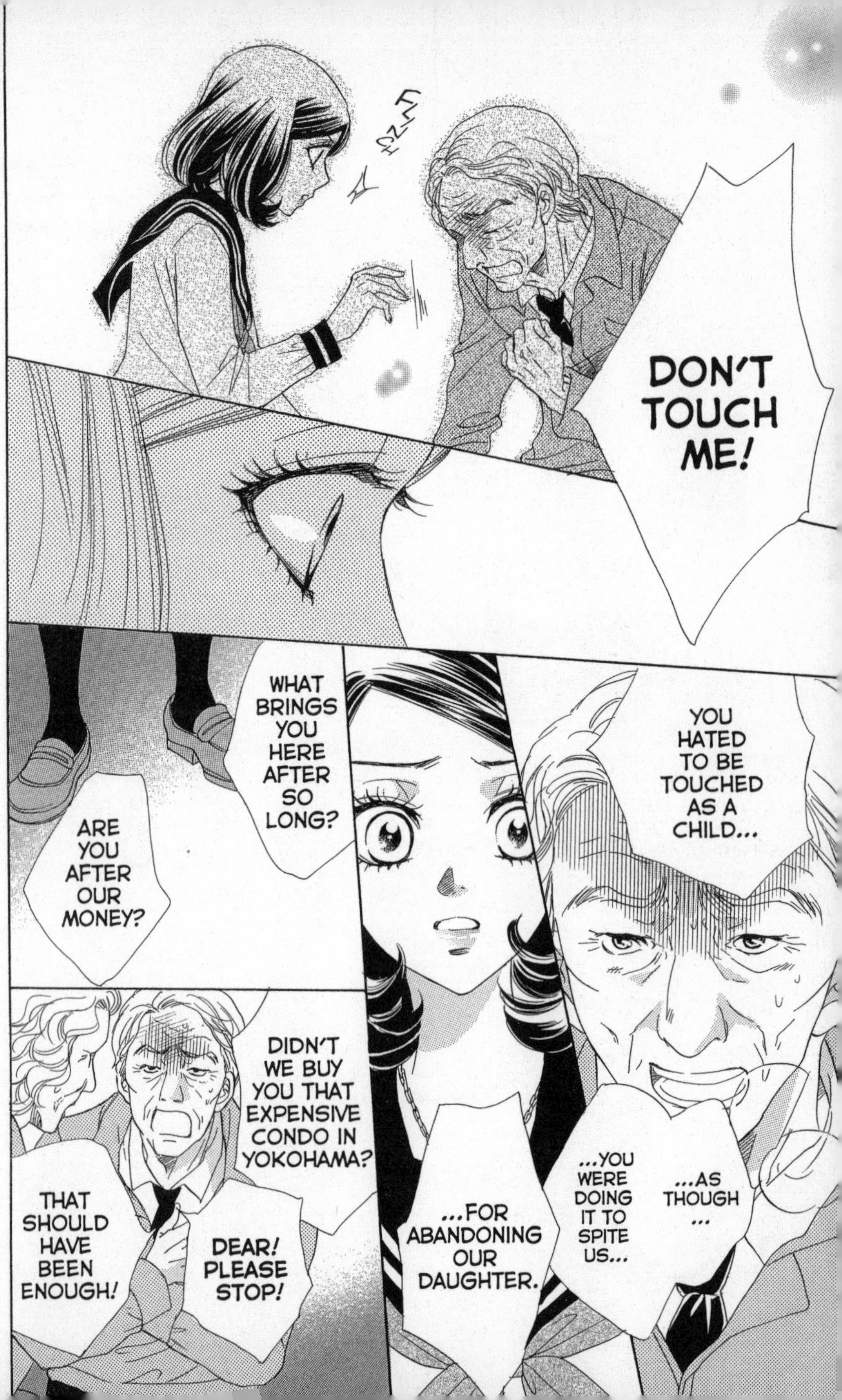
DON'T TOUCH ME!
YOU HATED TO BE TOUCHED AS A CHILD...
...AS THOUGH...
...YOU WERE DOING IT TO SPITE US...
...FOR ABANDONING OUR DAUGHTER.
WHAT BRINGS YOU HERE AFTER SO LONG?
ARE YOU AFTER OUR MONEY?
DIDN'T WE BUY YOU THAT EXPENSIVE CONDO IN YOKOHAMA?
DEAR! PLEASE STOP!
THAT SHOULD HAVE BEEN ENOUGH!

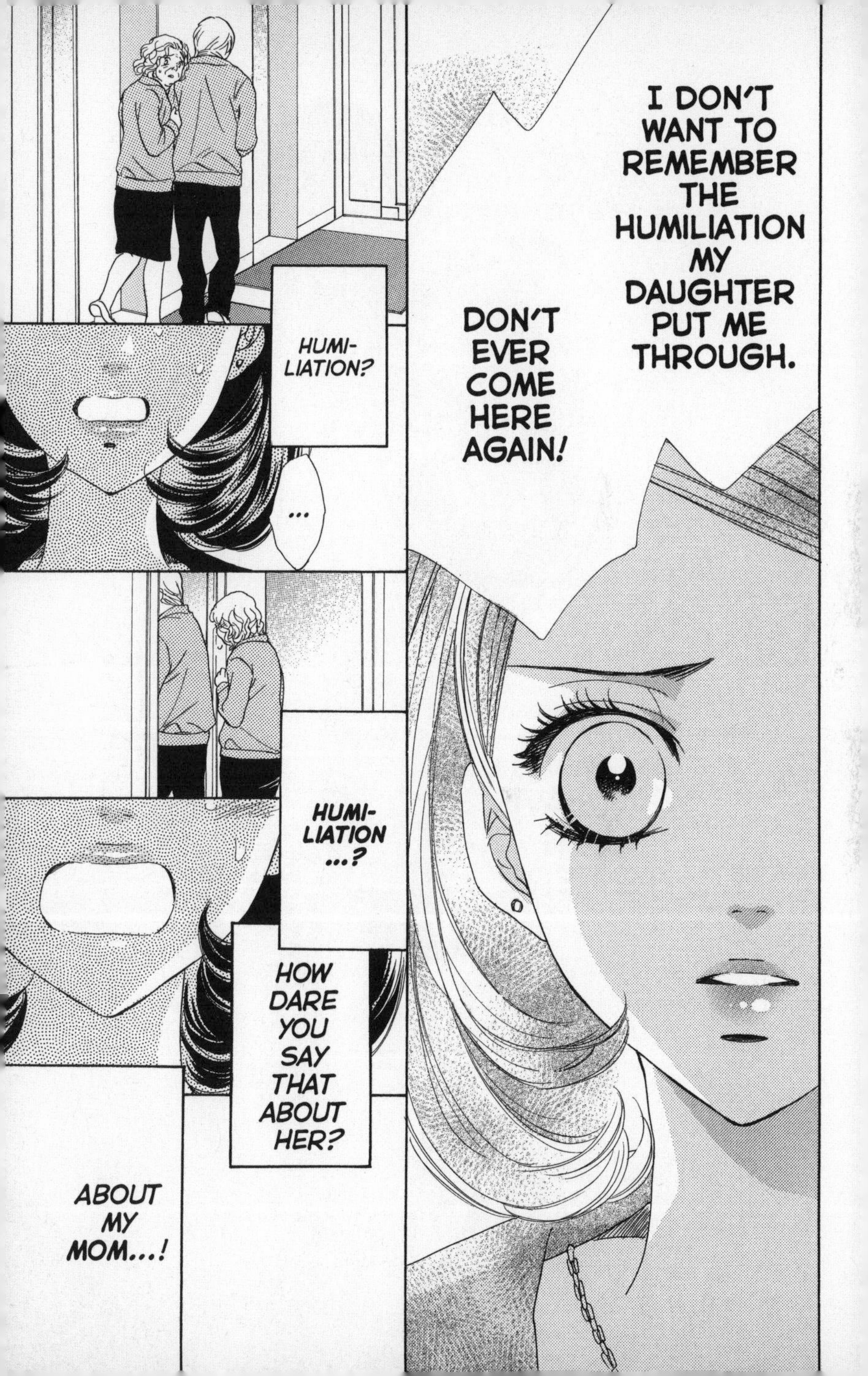
I DON'T WANT TO REMEMBER THE HUMILIATION MY DAUGHTER PUT ME THROUGH.
DON'T EVER COME HERE AGAIN!
HUMI-LIATION?
...
HUMI-LIATION...?
HOW DARE YOU SAY THAT ABOUT HER?
ABOUT MY MOM...!

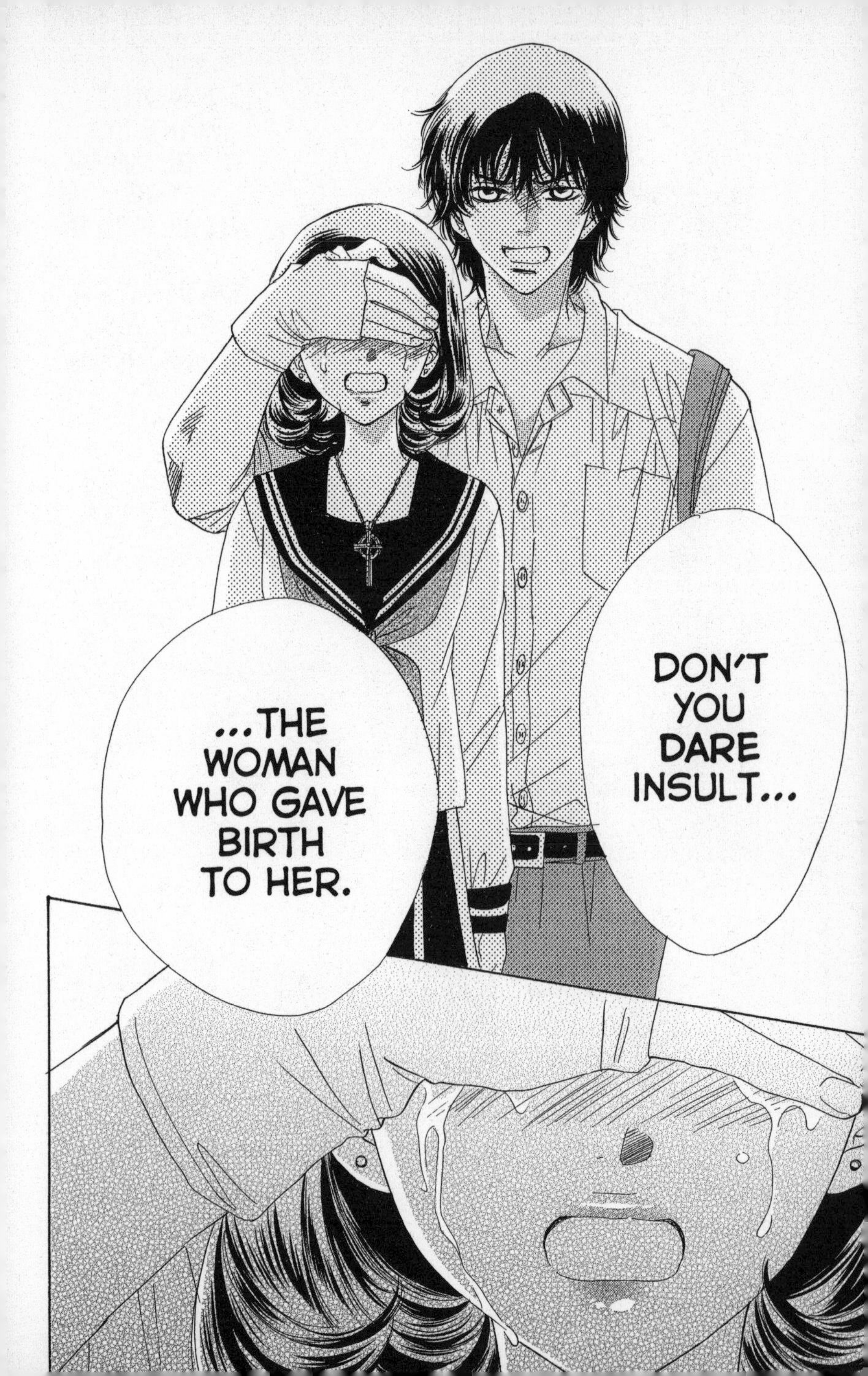
DON'T YOU DARE INSULT...
...THE WOMAN WHO GAVE BIRTH TO HER.

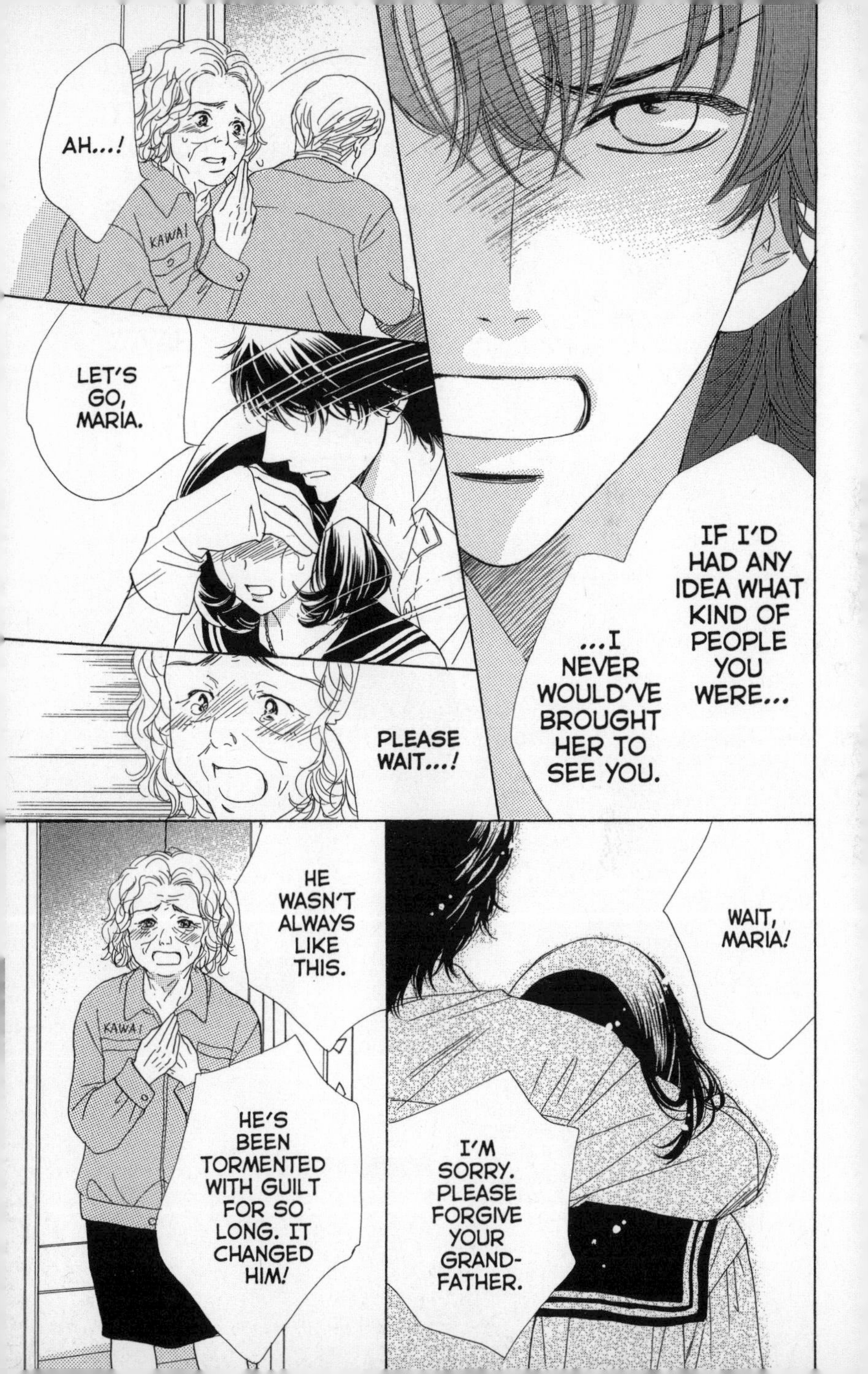
IF I'D HAD ANY IDEA WHAT KIND OF PEOPLE YOU WERE...
...I NEVER WOULD'VE BROUGHT HER TO SEE YOU.
AH...!
KAWAI
LET'S GO, MARIA.
PLEASE WAIT...!
WAIT, MARIA!
I'M SORRY. PLEASE FORGIVE YOUR GRANDFATHER.
HE WASN'T ALWAYS LIKE THIS.
KAWAI
HE'S BEEN TORMENTED WITH GUILT FOR SO LONG. IT CHANGED HIM!

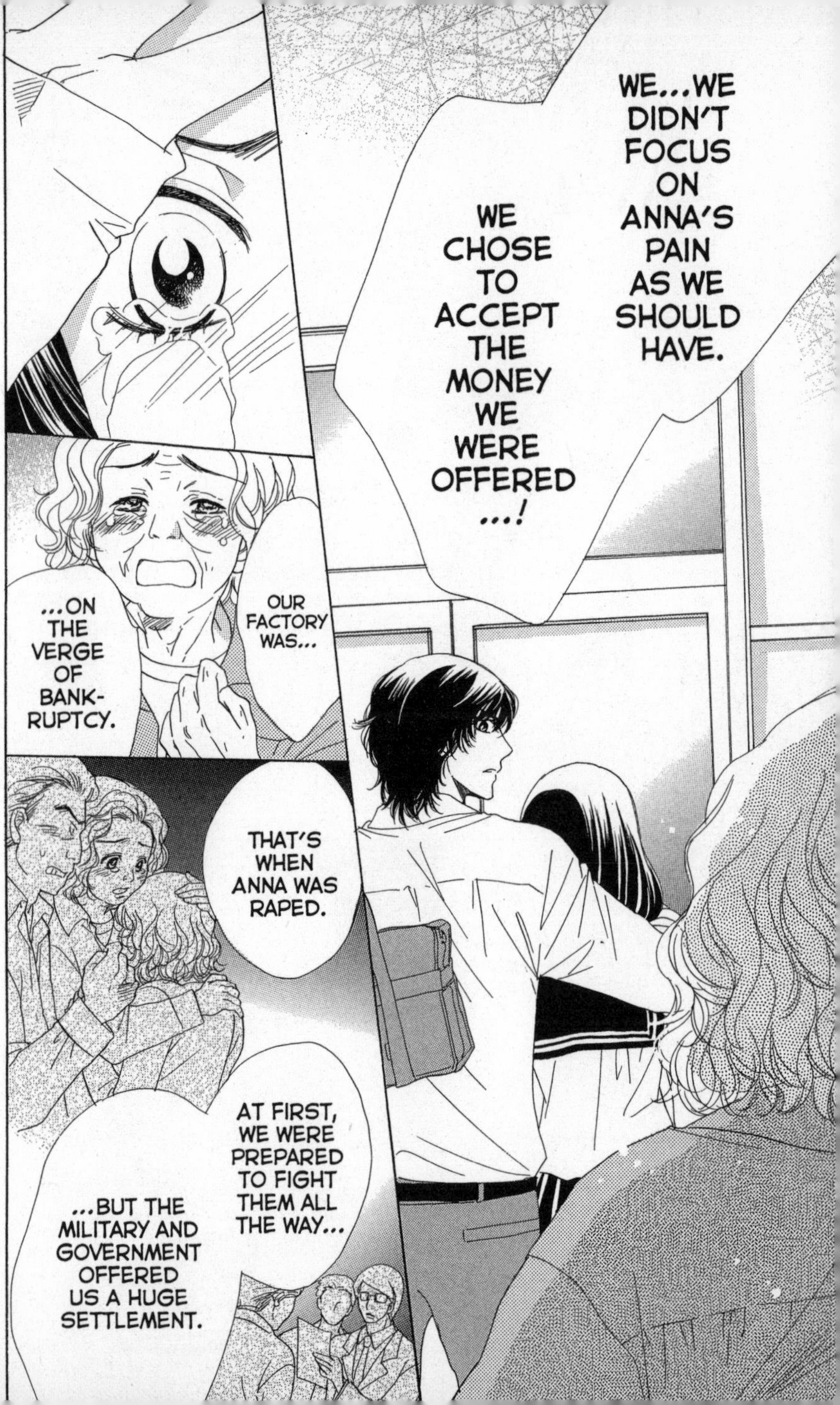
WE...WE DIDN'T FOCUS ON ANNA'S PAIN AS WE SHOULD HAVE.
WE CHOSE TO ACCEPT THE MONEY WE WERE OFFERED ...!
OUR FACTORY WAS...
...ON THE VERGE OF BANK-RUPTCY.
THAT'S WHEN ANNA WAS RAPED.
AT FIRST, WE WERE PREPARED TO FIGHT THEM ALL THE WAY...
...BUT THE MILITARY AND GOVERNMENT OFFERED US A HUGE SETTLEMENT.

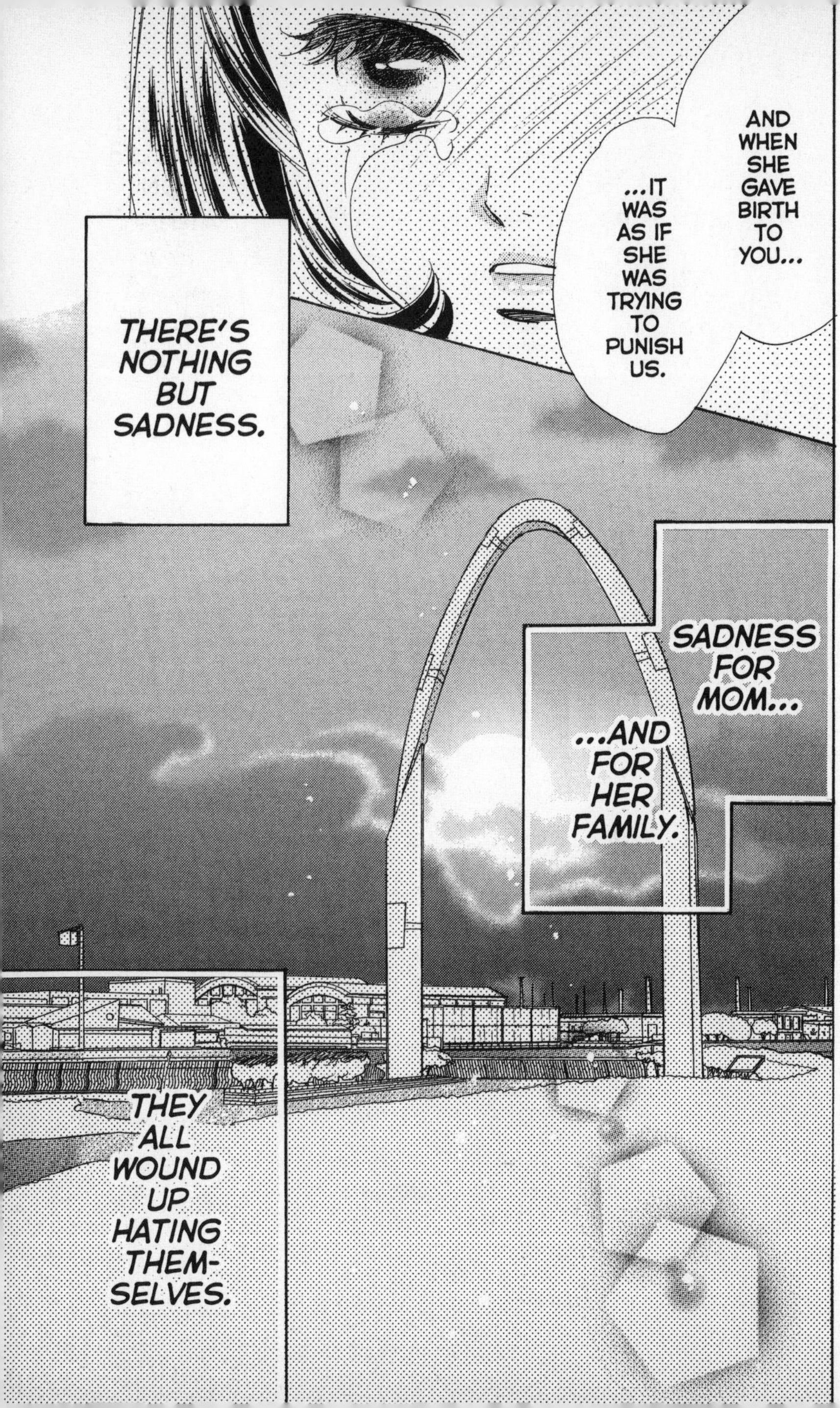
AND WHEN SHE GAVE BIRTH TO YOU...
...IT WAS AS IF SHE WAS TRYING TO PUNISH US.
THERE'S NOTHING BUT SADNESS.
SADNESS FOR MOM...
...AND FOR HER FAMILY.
THEY ALL WOUND UP HATING THEM-SELVES.

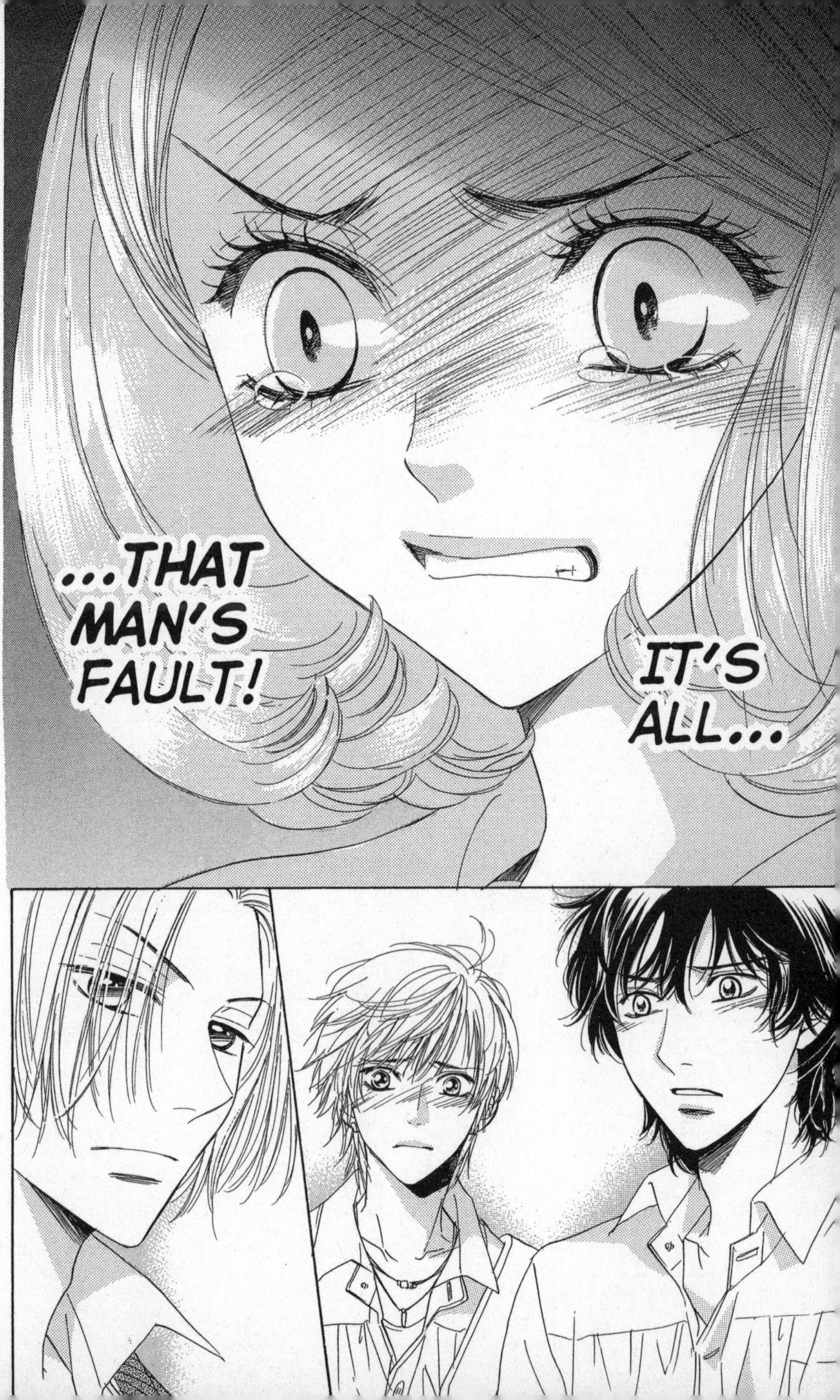
IT'S ALL...
...THAT MAN'S FAULT!

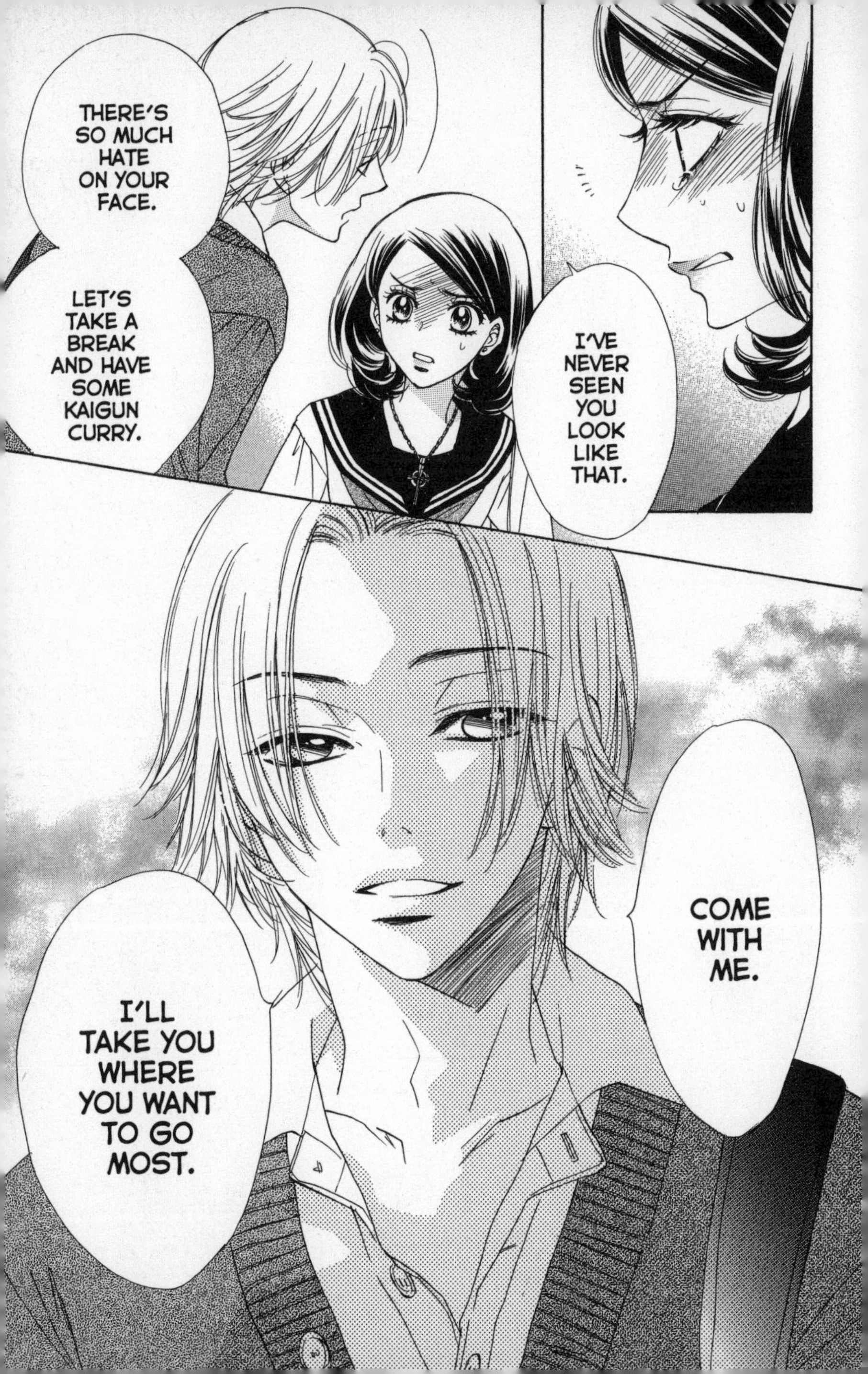
I'VE NEVER SEEN YOU LOOK LIKE THAT.
THERE'S SO MUCH HATE ON YOUR FACE.
LET'S TAKE A BREAK AND HAVE SOME KAIGUN CURRY.
COME WITH ME.
I'LL TAKE YOU WHERE YOU WANT TO GO MOST.

A Devil and
Her Love Song

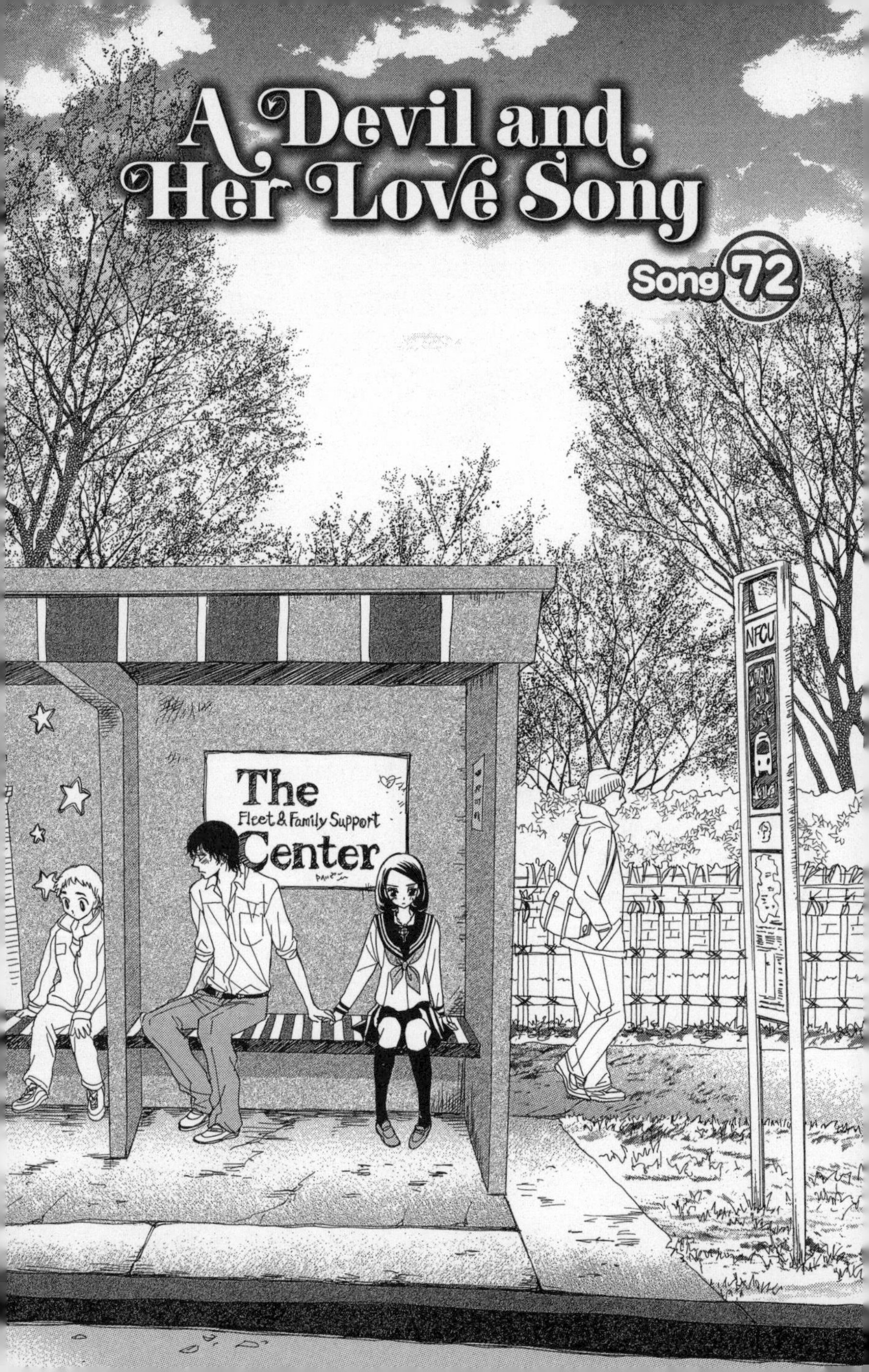
A Devil and Her Love Song
Song 72
The
Fleet & Family Support
Center
NFCU

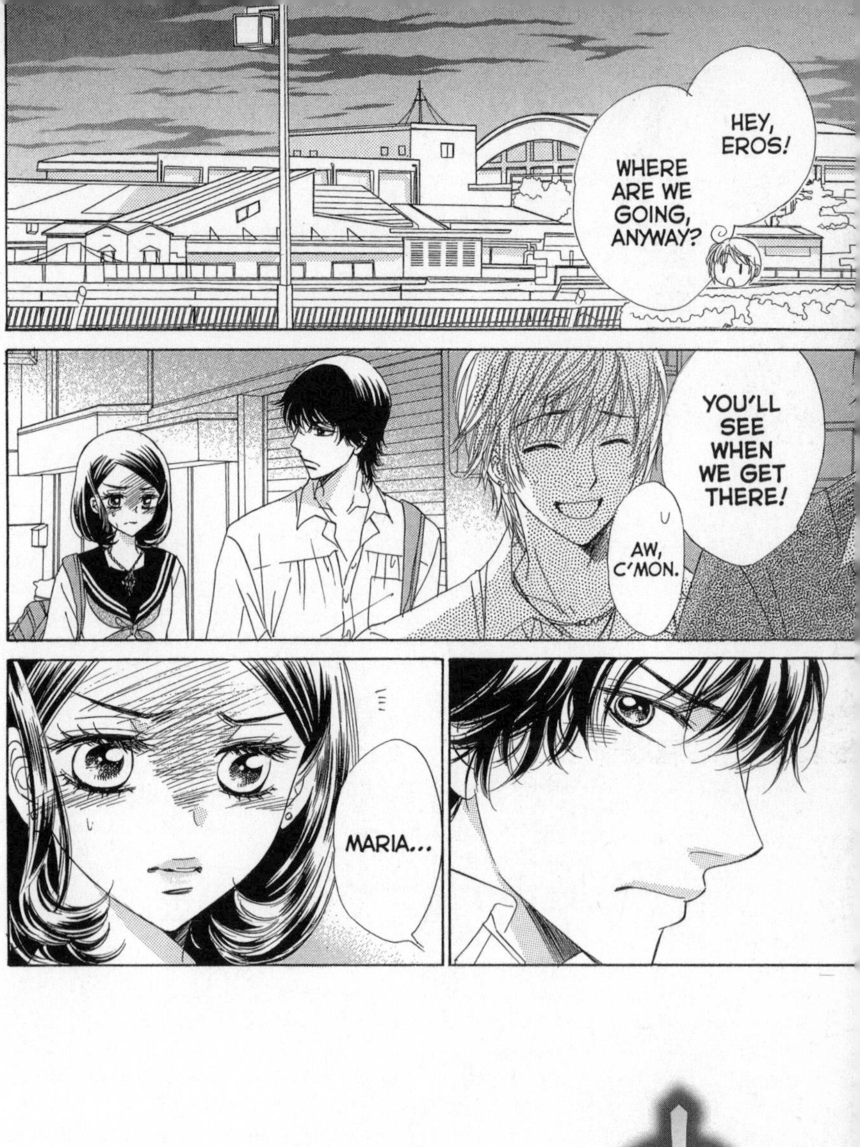
HEY, EROS!
WHERE ARE WE GOING, ANYWAY?
YOU'LL SEE WHEN WE GET THERE!
AW, C'MON.
MARIA...

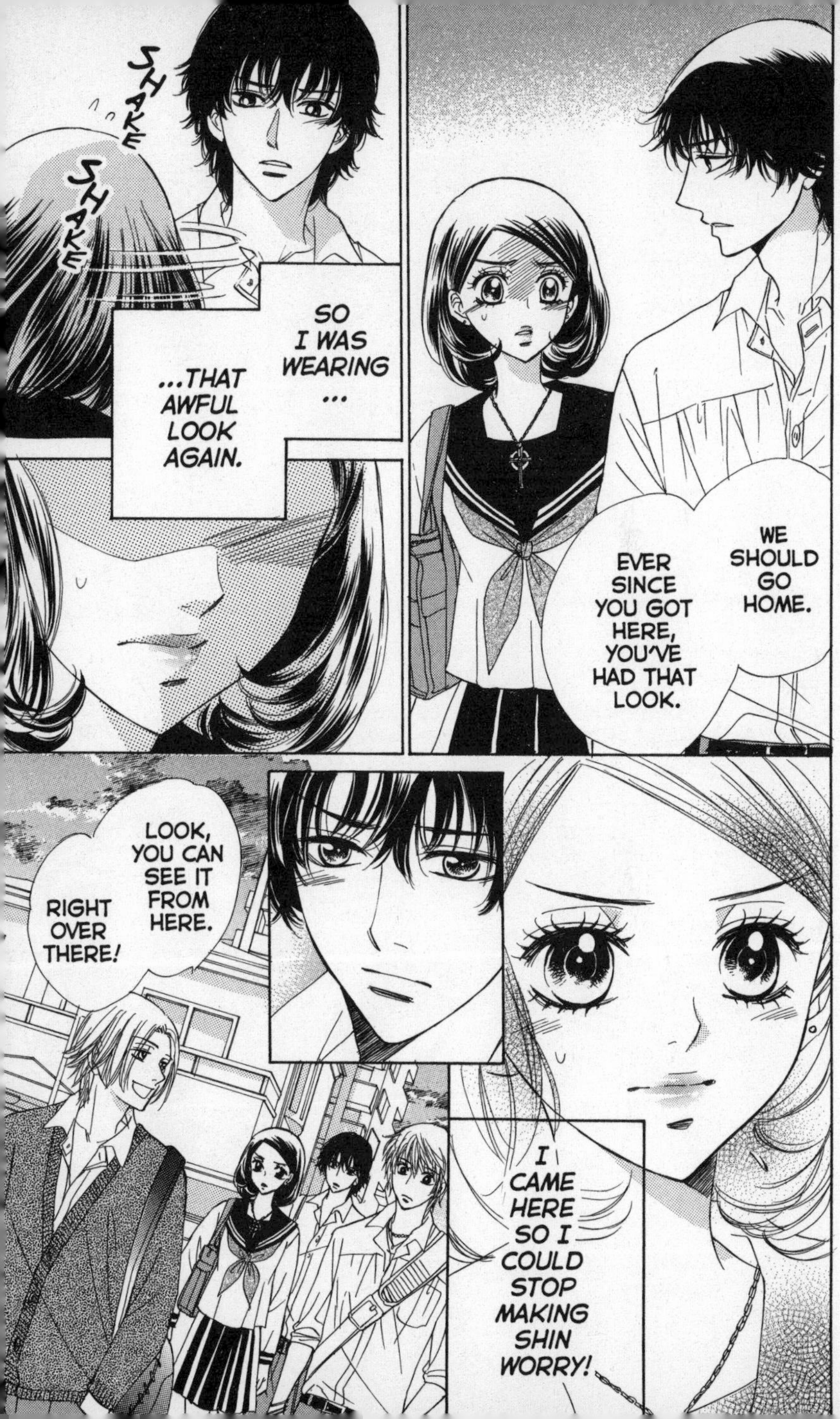
WE SHOULD GO HOME.
EVER SINCE YOU GOT HERE, YOU'VE HAD THAT LOOK.
SHAKE SHAKE
SO I WAS WEARING ...
...THAT AWFUL LOOK AGAIN.
I CAME HERE SO I COULD STOP MAKING SHIN WORRY!
LOOK, YOU CAN SEE IT FROM HERE.
RIGHT OVER THERE!

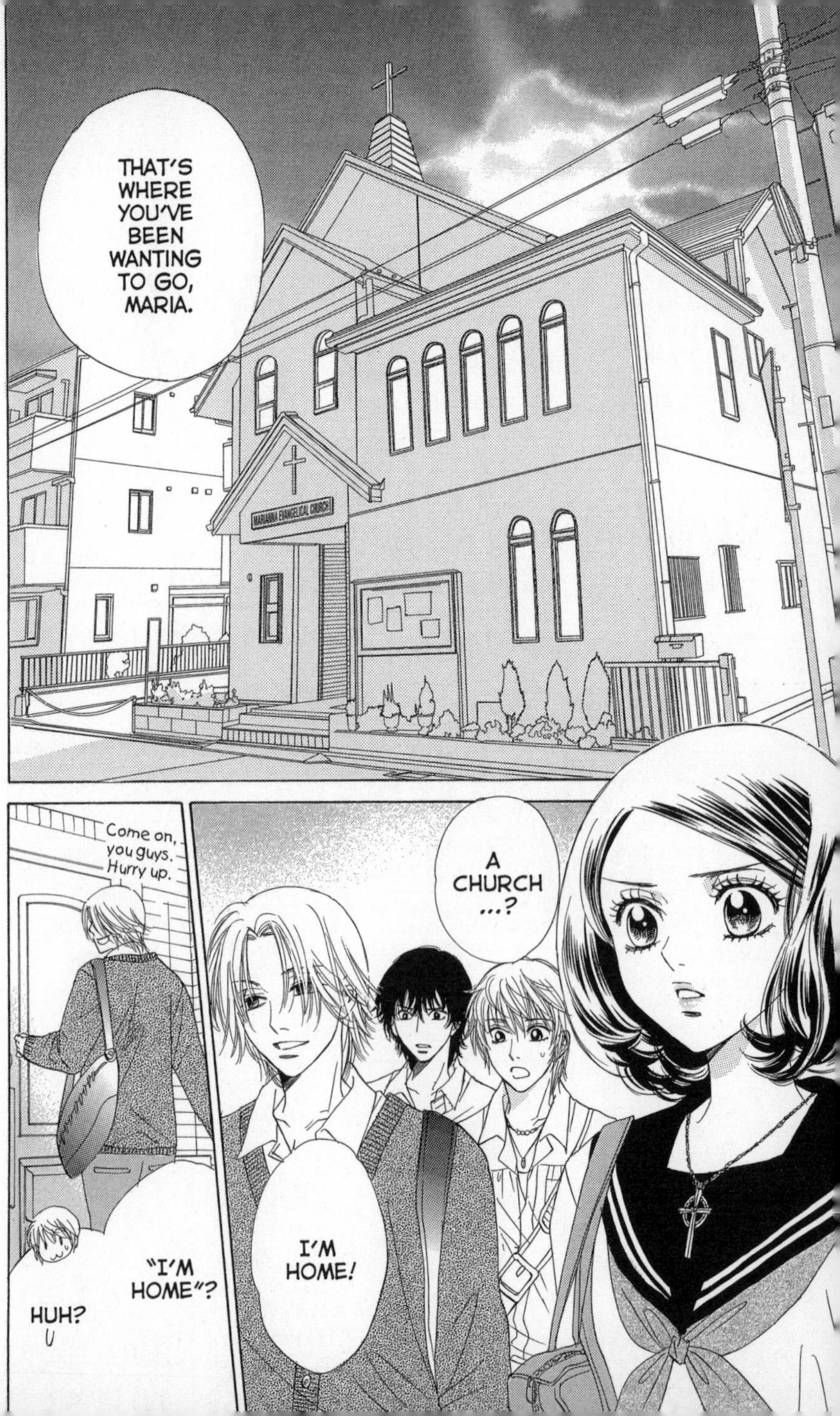
THAT'S WHERE YOU'VE BEEN WANTING TO GO, MARIA.
MARIANNA EVANGELICAL CHURCH
A CHURCH ...?
I'M HOME!
"I'M HOME"?
Come on, you guys. Hurry up.
HUH?

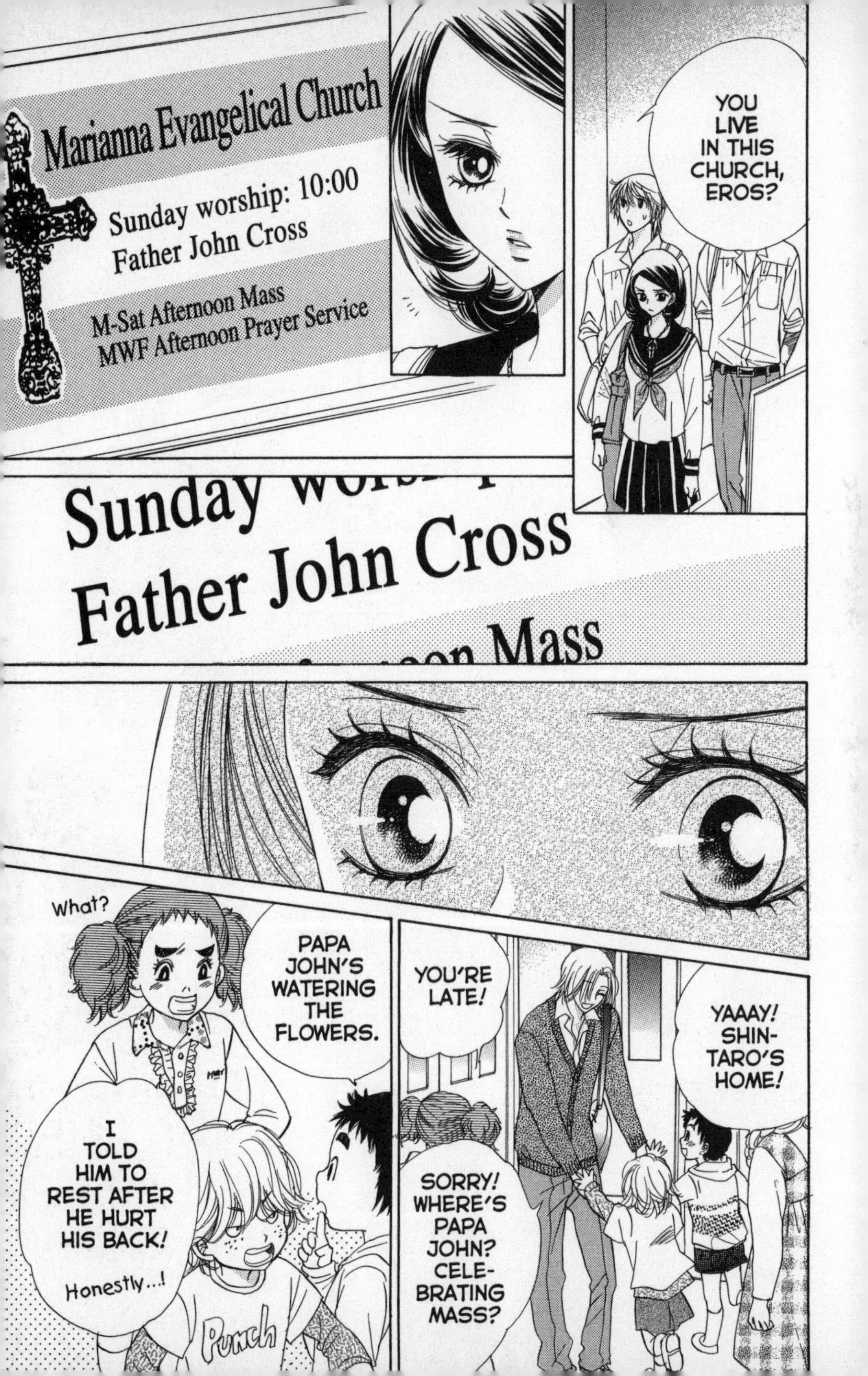
YOU LIVE IN THIS CHURCH, EROS?
Marianna Evangelical Church
Sunday worship: 10:00
Father John Cross
M-Sat Afternoon Mass
MWF Afternoon Prayer Service
Sunday
Father John Cross
Mass
YAAAY! SHIN-TARO'S HOME!
YOU'RE LATE!
SORRY! WHERE'S PAPA JOHN? CELE-BRATING MASS?
PAPA JOHN'S WATERING THE FLOWERS.
What?
I TOLD HIM TO REST AFTER HE HURT HIS BACK!
Honestly...!
Punch

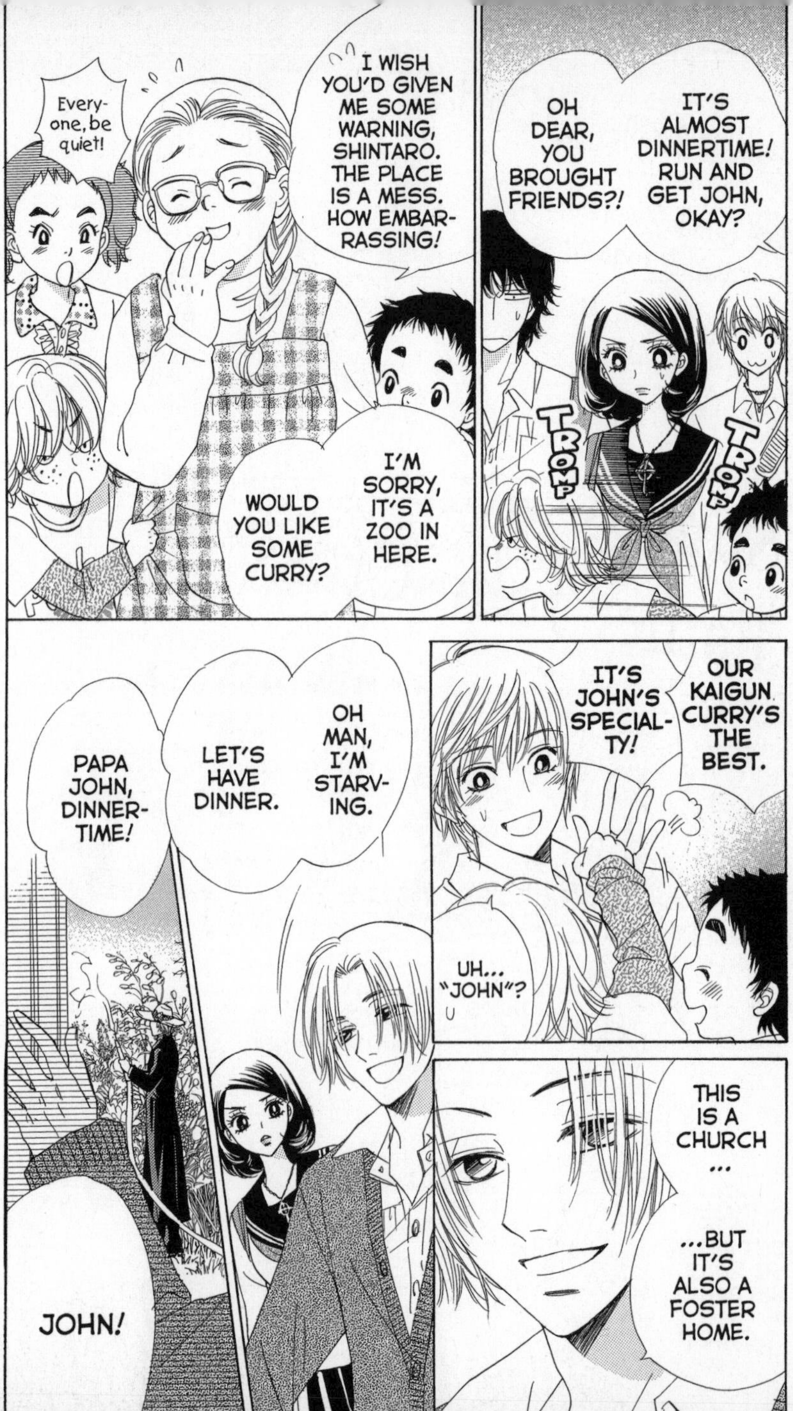
IT'S ALMOST DINNERTIME! RUN AND GET JOHN, OKAY?
OH DEAR, YOU BROUGHT FRIENDS?!
TROMP
TROMP
I WISH YOU'D GIVEN ME SOME WARNING, SHINTARO. THE PLACE IS A MESS. HOW EMBARRASSING!
Everyone, be quiet!
I'M SORRY, IT'S A ZOO IN HERE.
WOULD YOU LIKE SOME CURRY?
OUR KAIGUN CURRY'S THE BEST.
IT'S JOHN'S SPECIALTY!
UH... "JOHN"?
THIS IS A CHURCH...
...BUT IT'S ALSO A FOSTER HOME.
OH MAN, I'M STARVING.
LET'S HAVE DINNER.
PAPA JOHN, DINNERTIME!
JOHN!

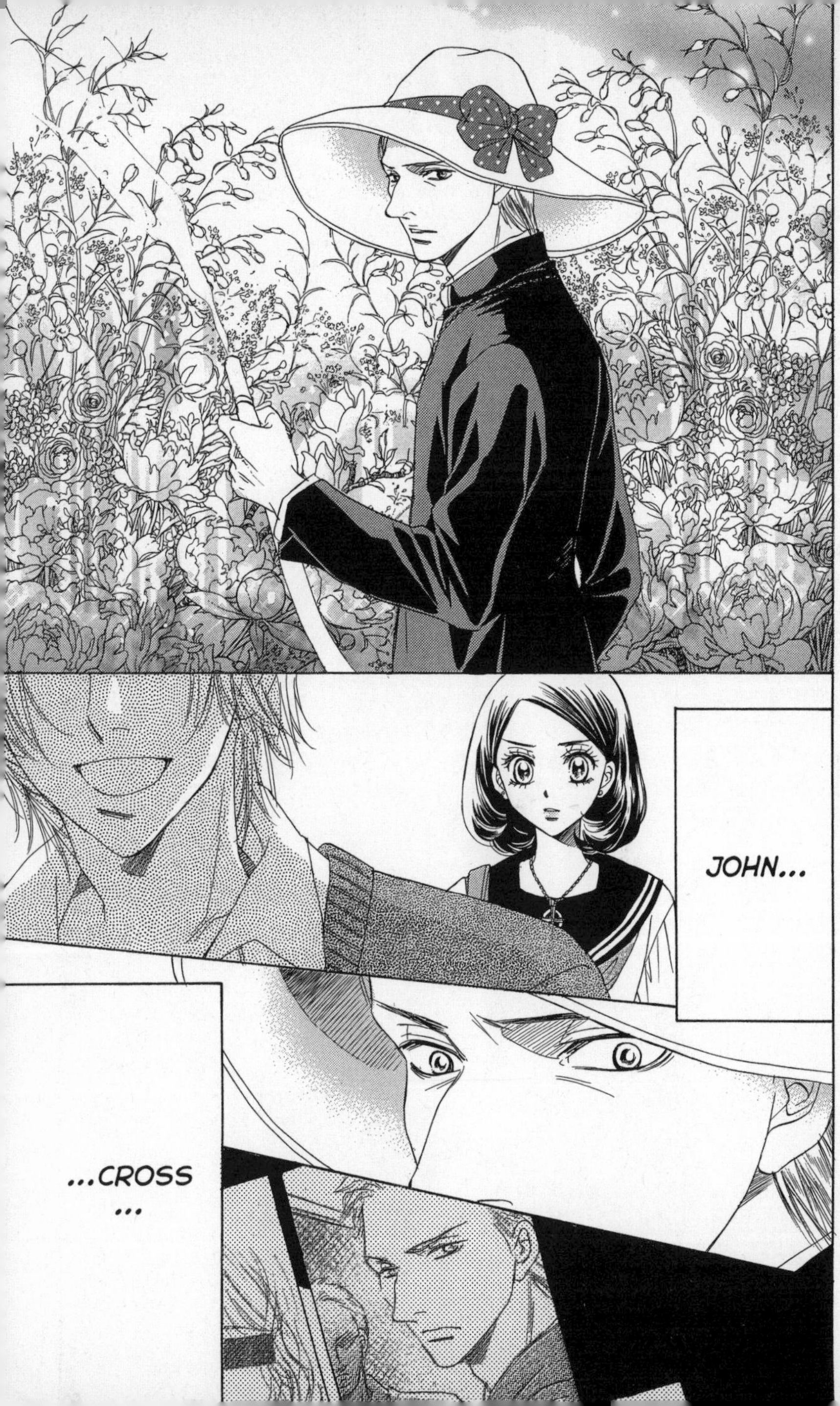
JOHN...
...CROSS
...

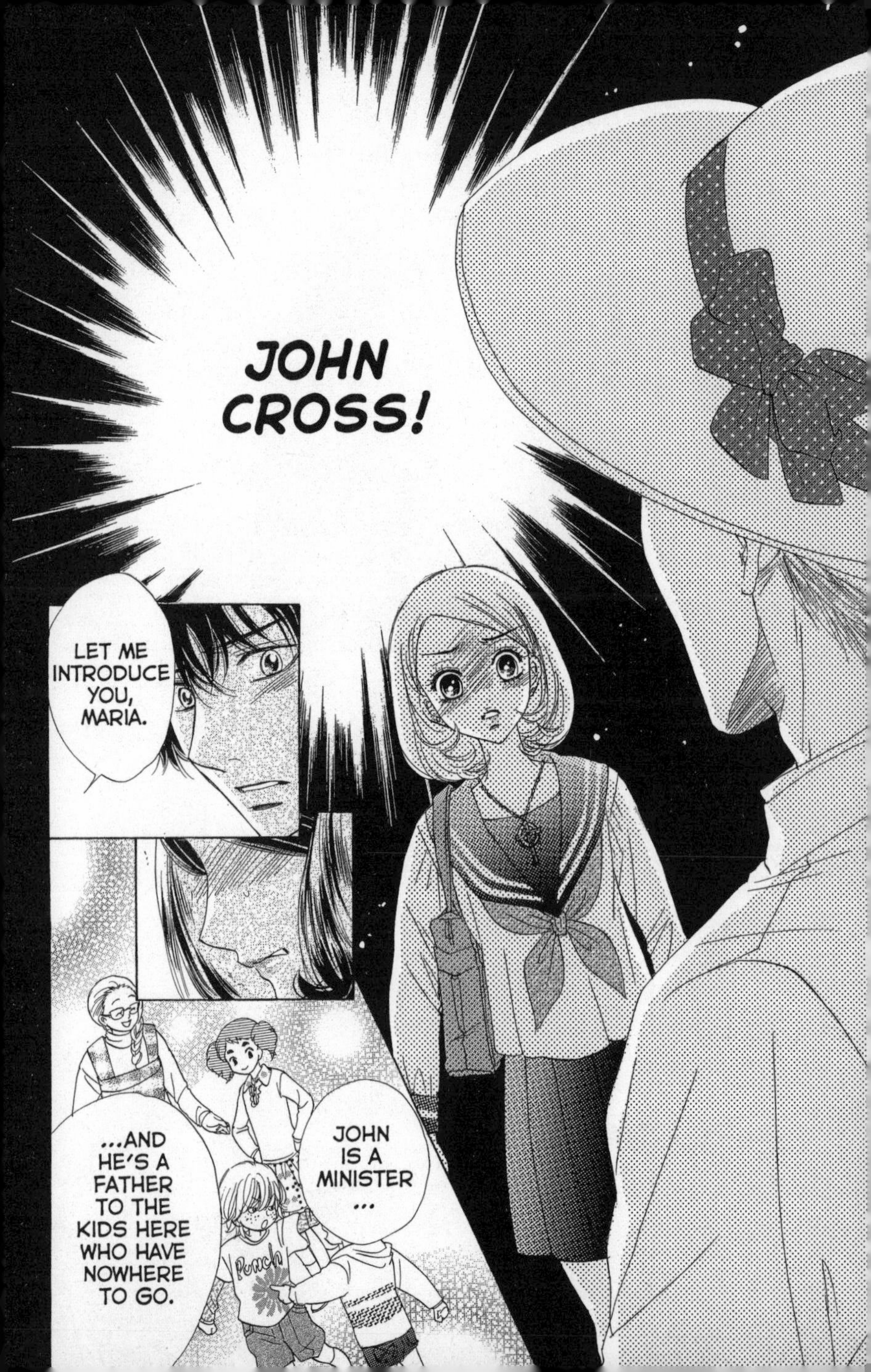
JOHN CROSS!
LET ME INTRODUCE YOU, MARIA.
JOHN IS A MINISTER ...
...AND HE'S A FATHER TO THE KIDS HERE WHO HAVE NOWHERE TO GO.

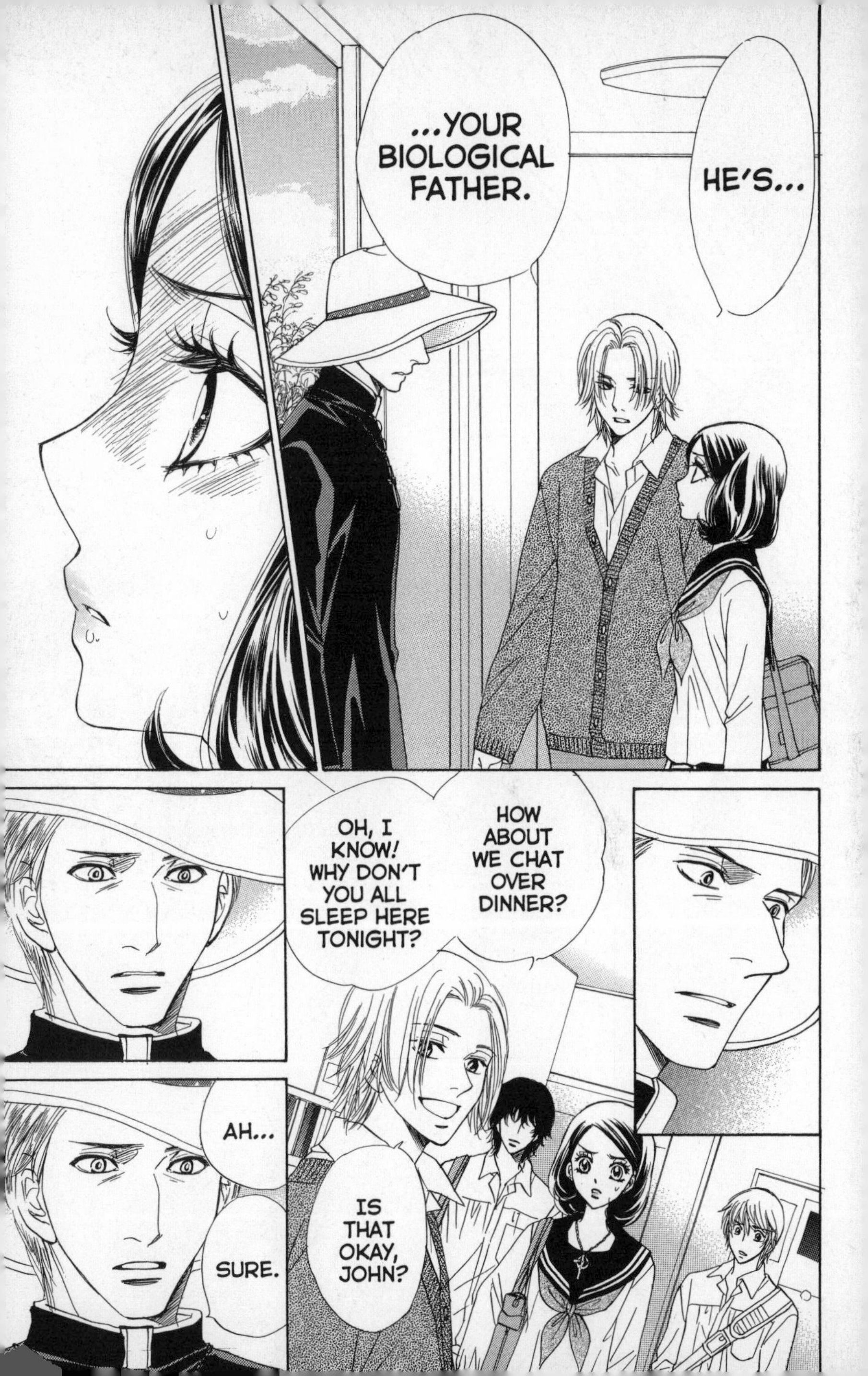
HE'S...
...YOUR BIOLOGICAL FATHER.
HOW ABOUT WE CHAT OVER DINNER?
OH, I KNOW! WHY DON'T YOU ALL SLEEP HERE TONIGHT?
IS THAT OKAY, JOHN?
AH...
SURE.

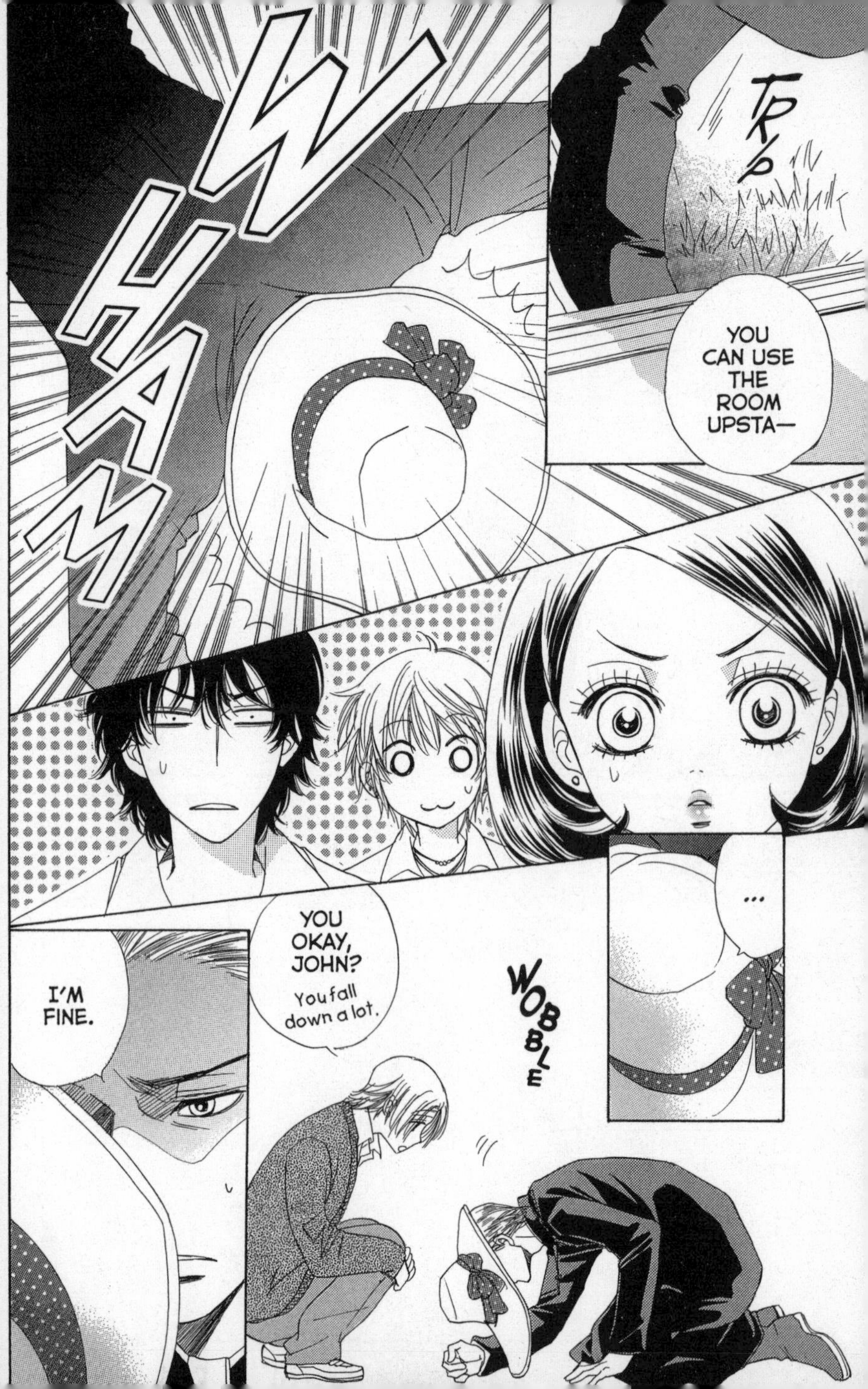
TRIP
YOU CAN USE THE ROOM UPSTA—
WHAM
...
WOBBLE
YOU OKAY, JOHN?
You fall down a lot.
I'M FINE.

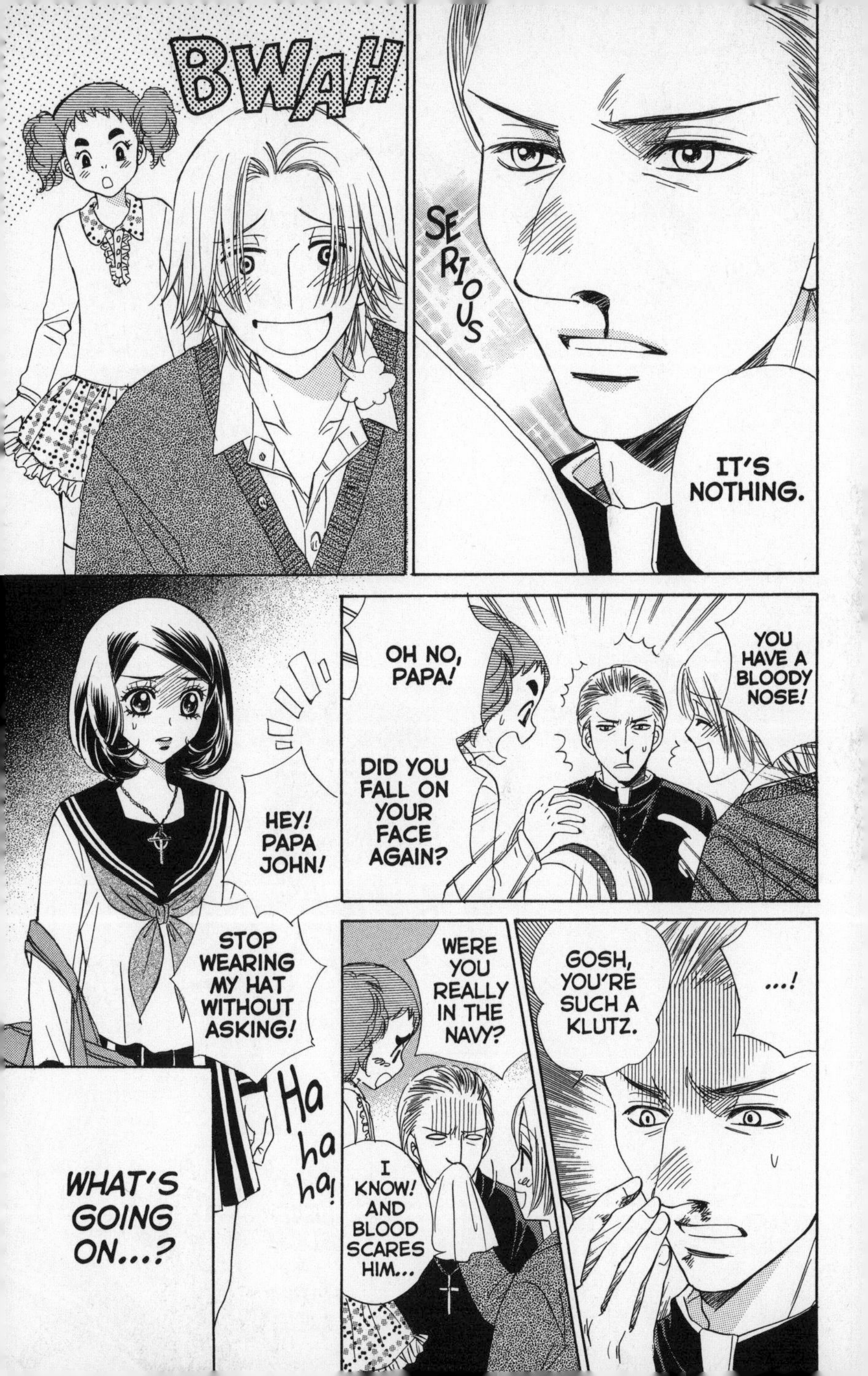
SERIOUS
IT'S NOTHING.
BWAH
YOU HAVE A BLOODY NOSE!
OH NO, PAPA!
DID YOU FALL ON YOUR FACE AGAIN?
...!
GOSH, YOU'RE SUCH A KLUTZ.
WERE YOU REALLY IN THE NAVY?
I KNOW! AND BLOOD SCARES HIM...
Ha ha ha!
HEY! PAPA JOHN!
STOP WEARING MY HAT WITHOUT ASKING!
WHAT'S GOING ON...?

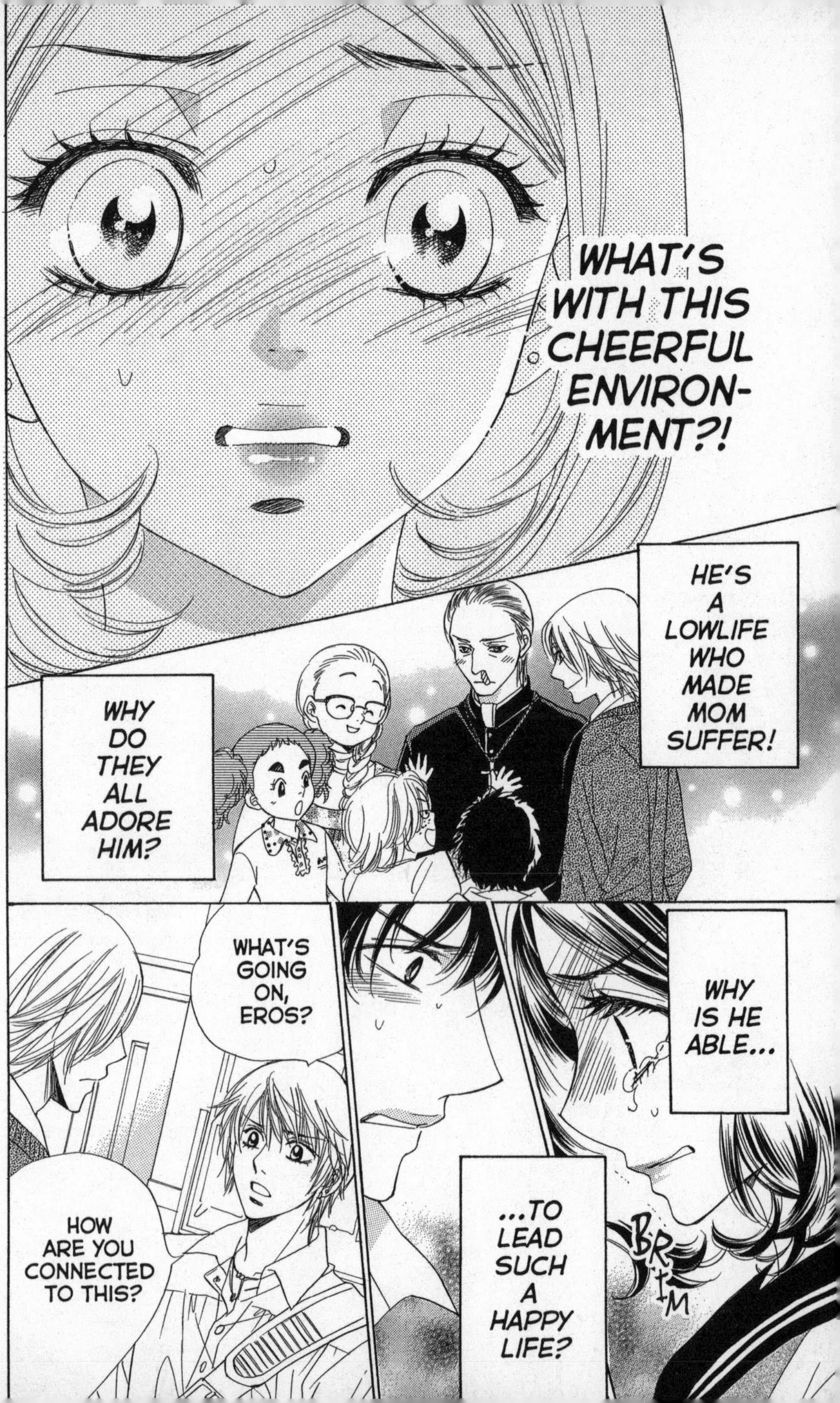
WHAT'S WITH THIS CHEERFUL ENVIRON-MENT?!
HE'S A LOWLIFE WHO MADE MOM SUFFER!
WHY DO THEY ALL ADORE HIM?
WHY IS HE ABLE...
...TO LEAD SUCH A HAPPY LIFE?
BRIM
WHAT'S GOING ON, EROS?
HOW ARE YOU CONNECTED TO THIS?

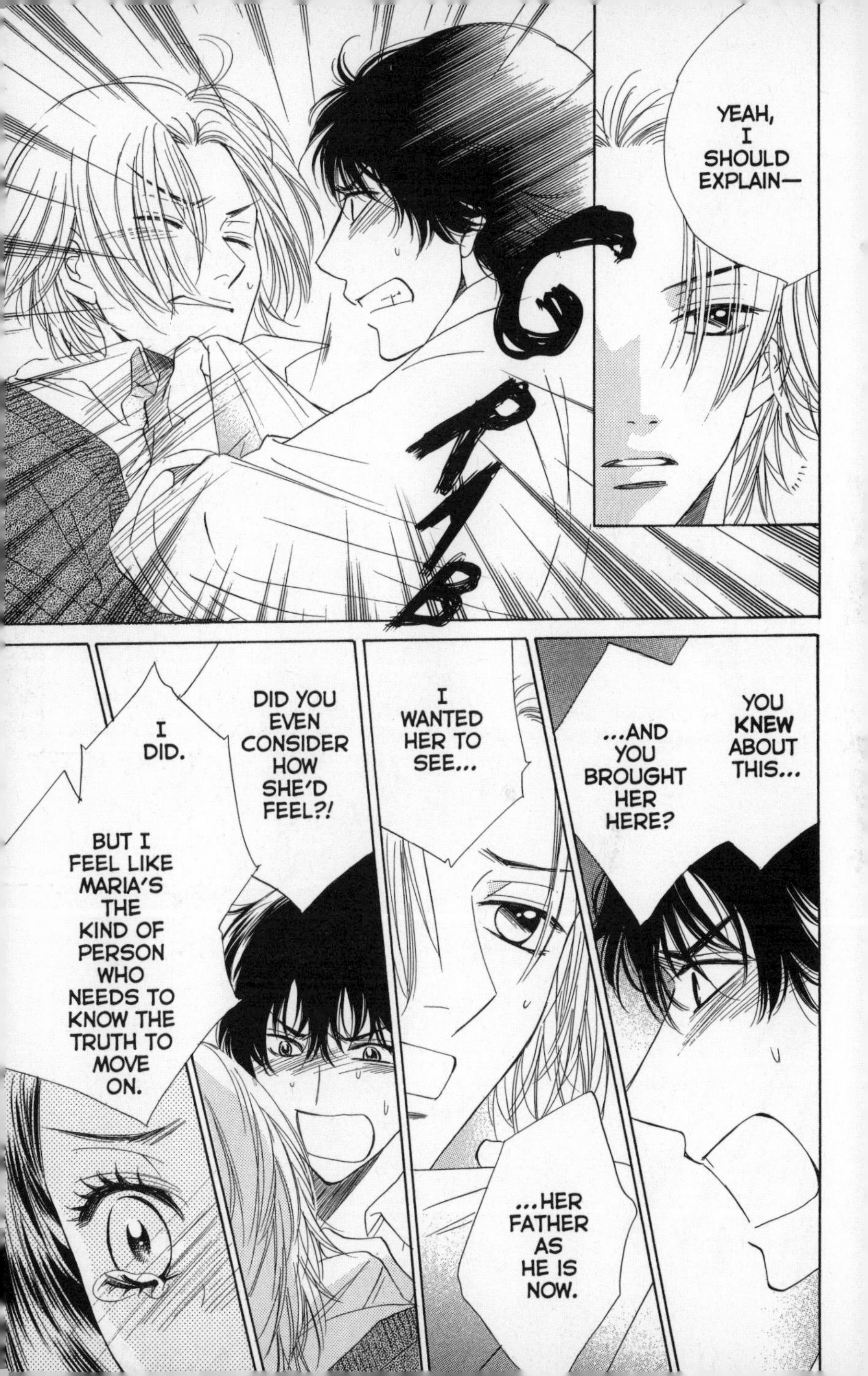
YEAH, I SHOULD EXPLAIN—
GRAB
YOU KNEW ABOUT THIS...
...AND YOU BROUGHT HER HERE?
I WANTED HER TO SEE...
...HER FATHER AS HE IS NOW.
DID YOU EVEN CONSIDER HOW SHE'D FEEL?!
I DID.
BUT I FEEL LIKE MARIA'S THE KIND OF PERSON WHO NEEDS TO KNOW THE TRUTH TO MOVE ON.

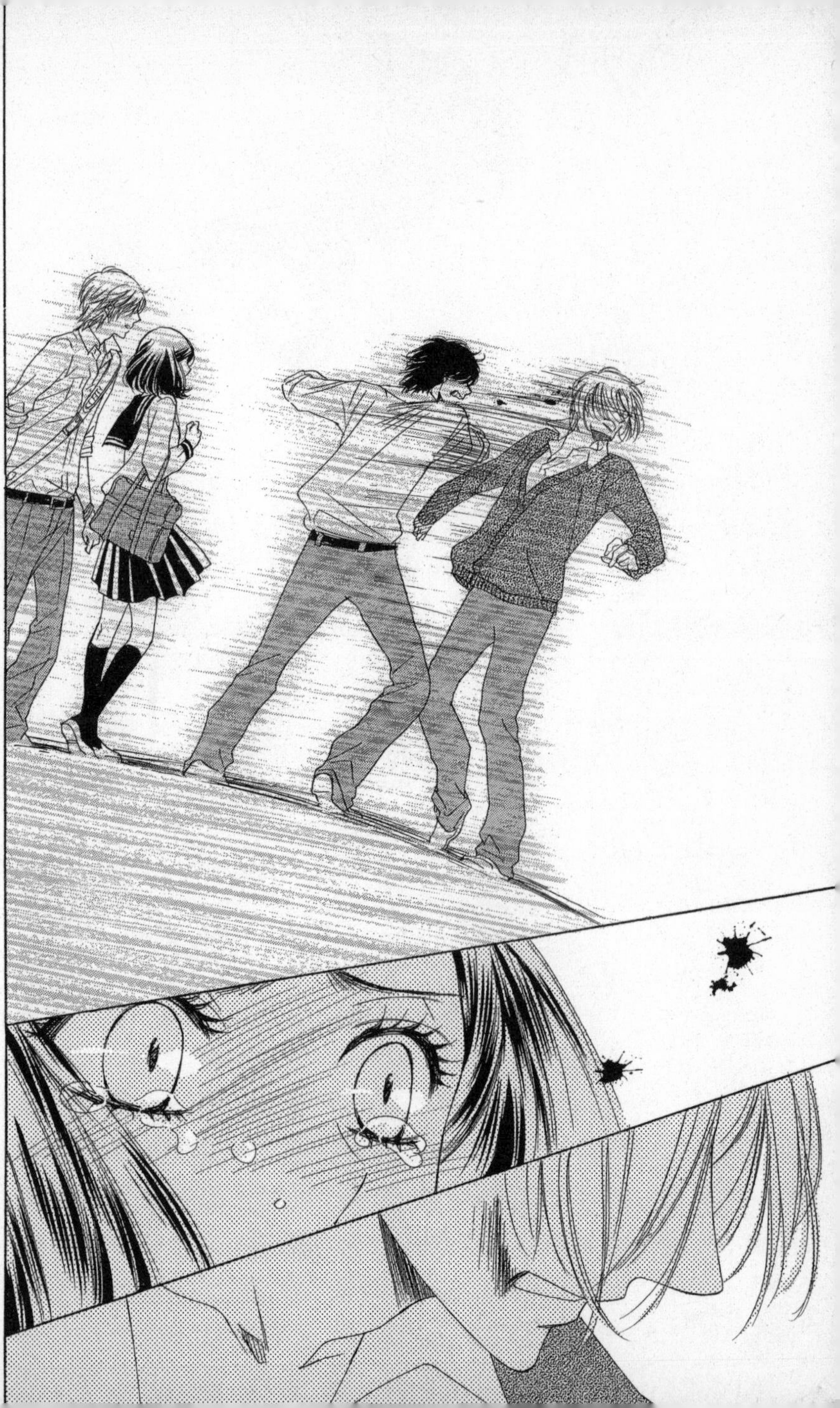

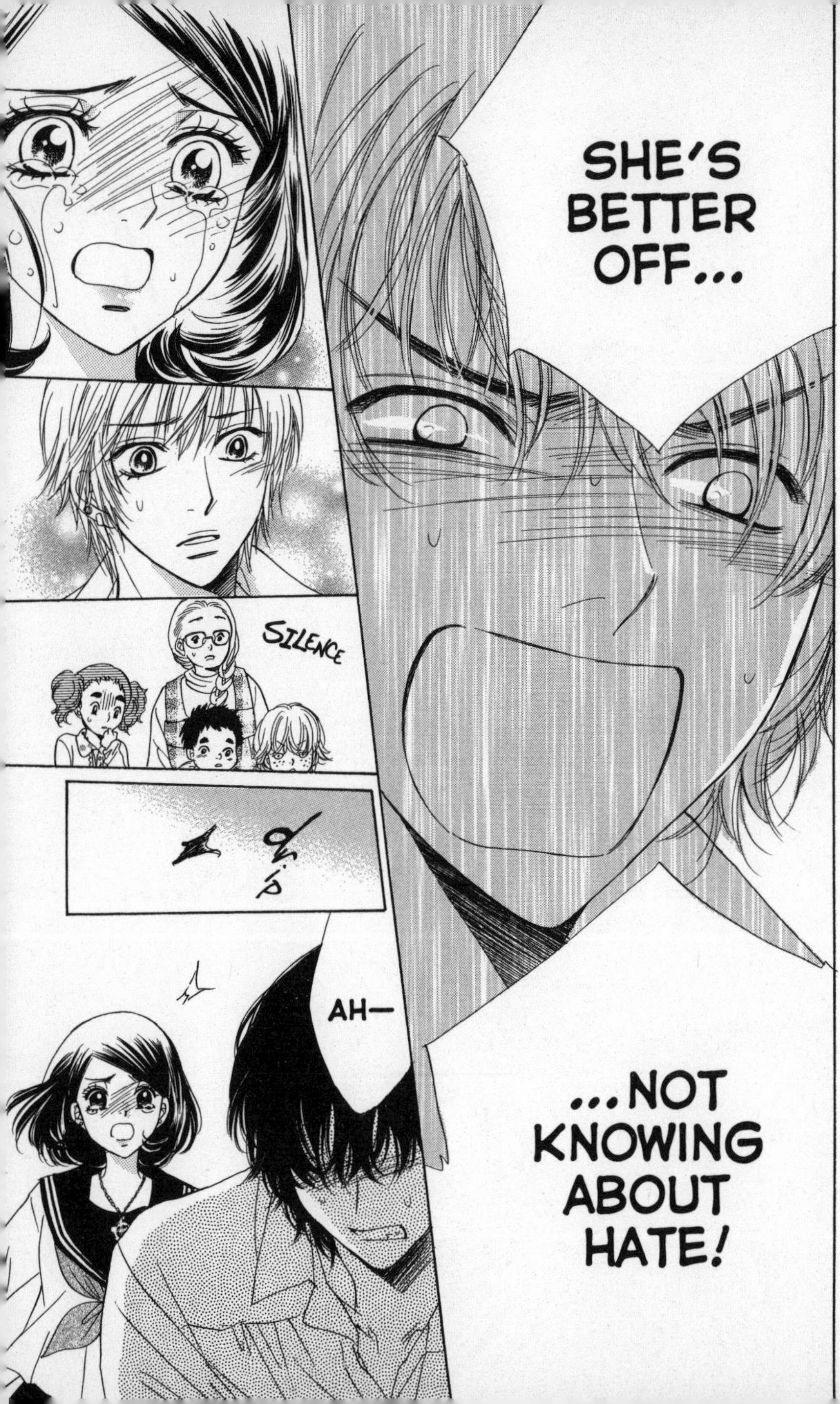
SHE'S BETTER OFF...
...NOT KNOWING ABOUT HATE!
SILENCE
drip
AH—

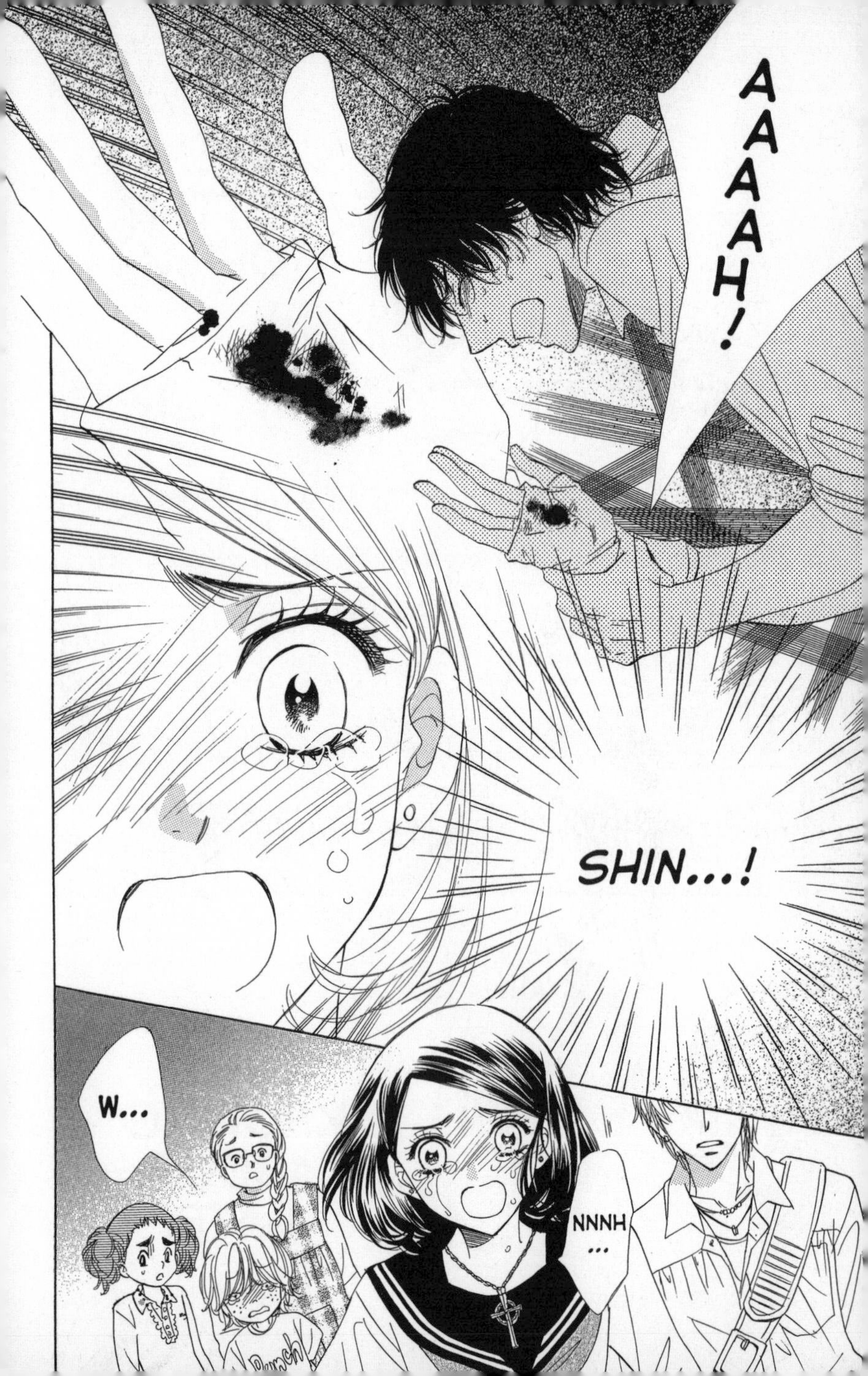
AAAAH!
SHIN...!
NNNH...
W...

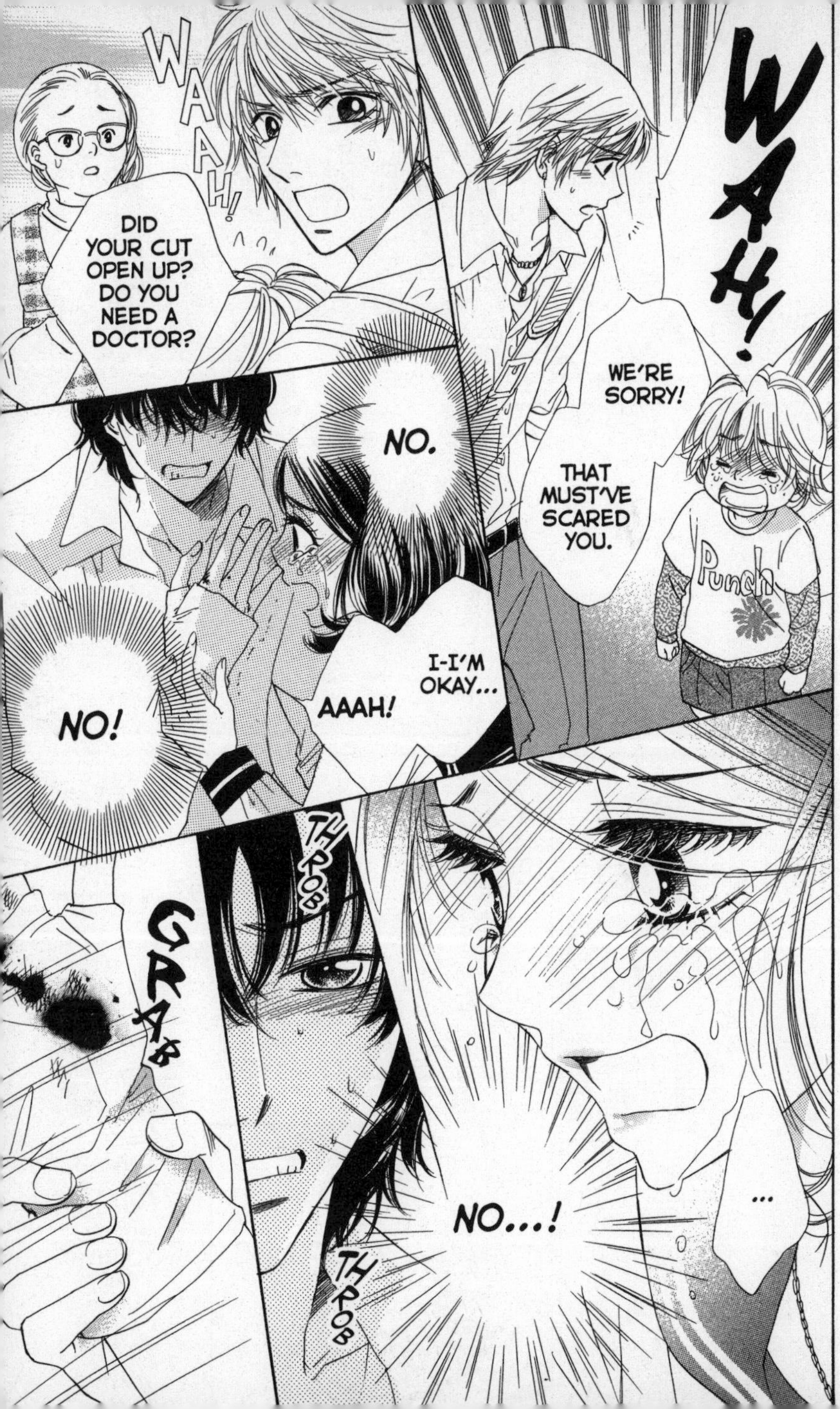
WAH!
WE'RE SORRY!
THAT MUST'VE SCARED YOU.
WAAH!
DID YOUR CUT OPEN UP? DO YOU NEED A DOCTOR?
NO.
I-I'M OKAY...
AAAH!
NO!
...
NO...!
THROB
THROB
GRAB

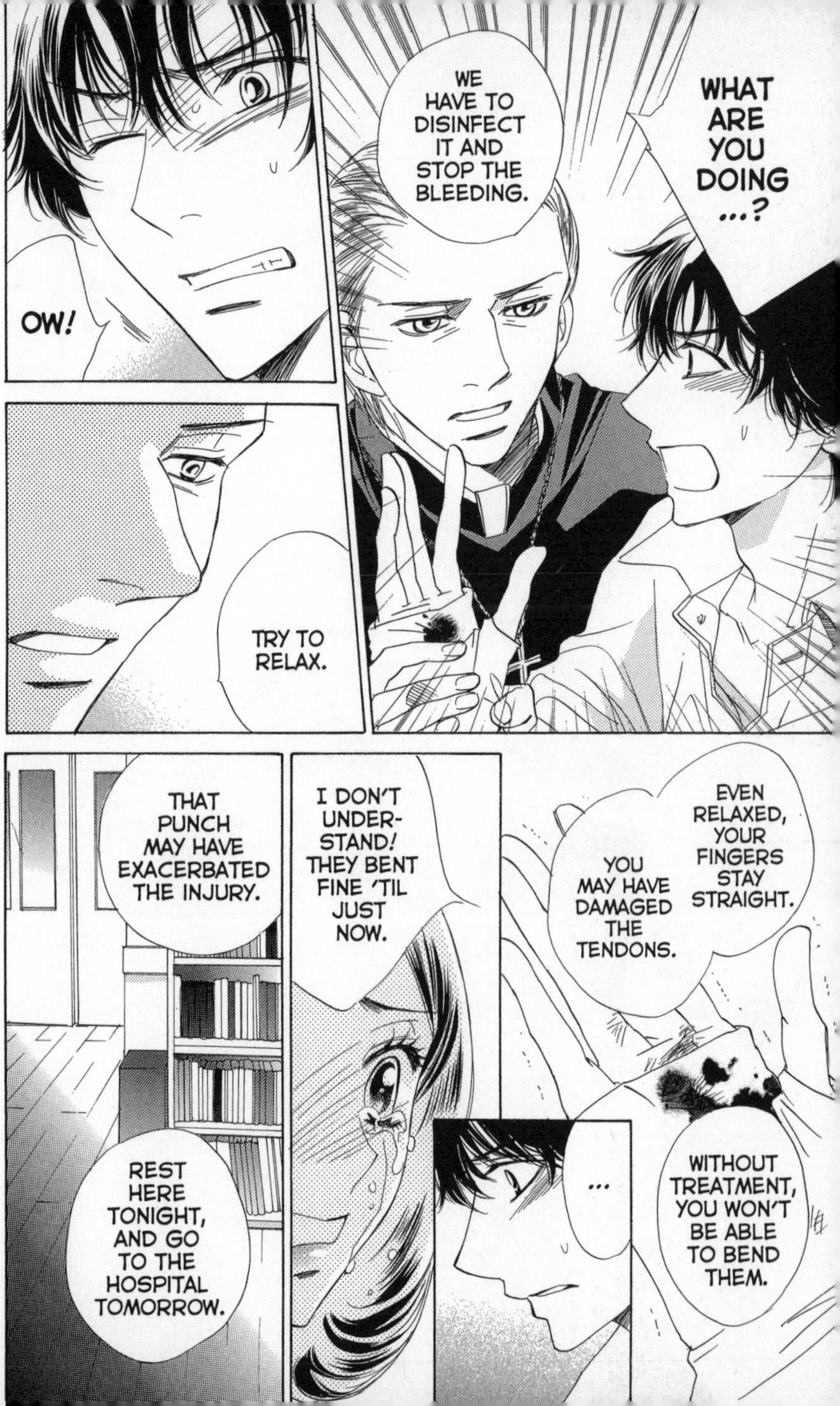
WHAT ARE YOU DOING ...?
WE HAVE TO DISINFECT IT AND STOP THE BLEEDING.
OW!
TRY TO RELAX.
EVEN RELAXED, YOUR FINGERS STAY STRAIGHT.
YOU MAY HAVE DAMAGED THE TENDONS.
WITHOUT TREATMENT, YOU WON'T BE ABLE TO BEND THEM.
...
I DON'T UNDERSTAND! THEY BENT FINE 'TIL JUST NOW.
THAT PUNCH MAY HAVE EXACERBATED THE INJURY.
REST HERE TONIGHT, AND GO TO THE HOSPITAL TOMORROW.

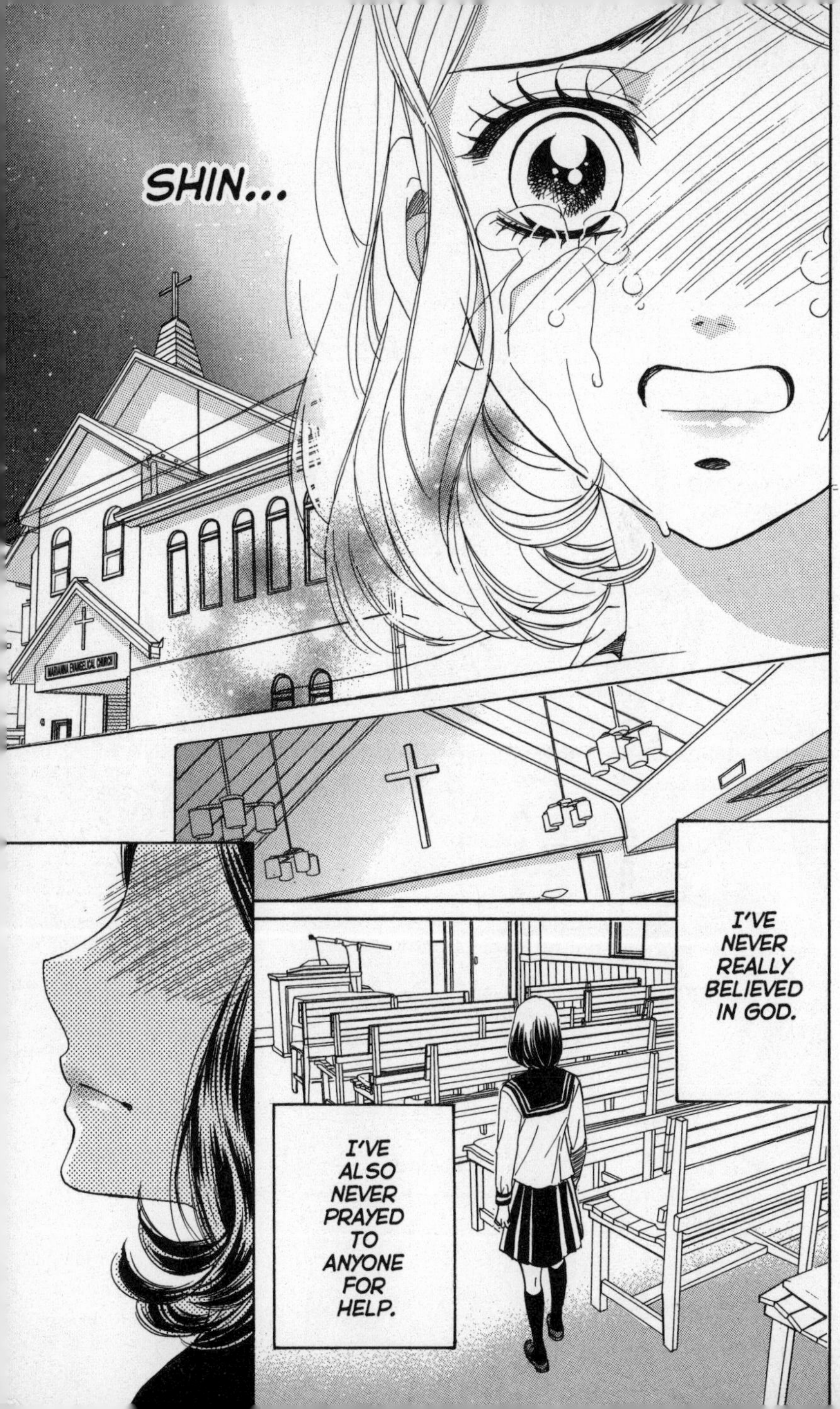
SHIN...
MARIANNA EVANGELICAL CHURCH
I'VE NEVER REALLY BELIEVED IN GOD.
I'VE ALSO NEVER PRAYED TO ANYONE FOR HELP.

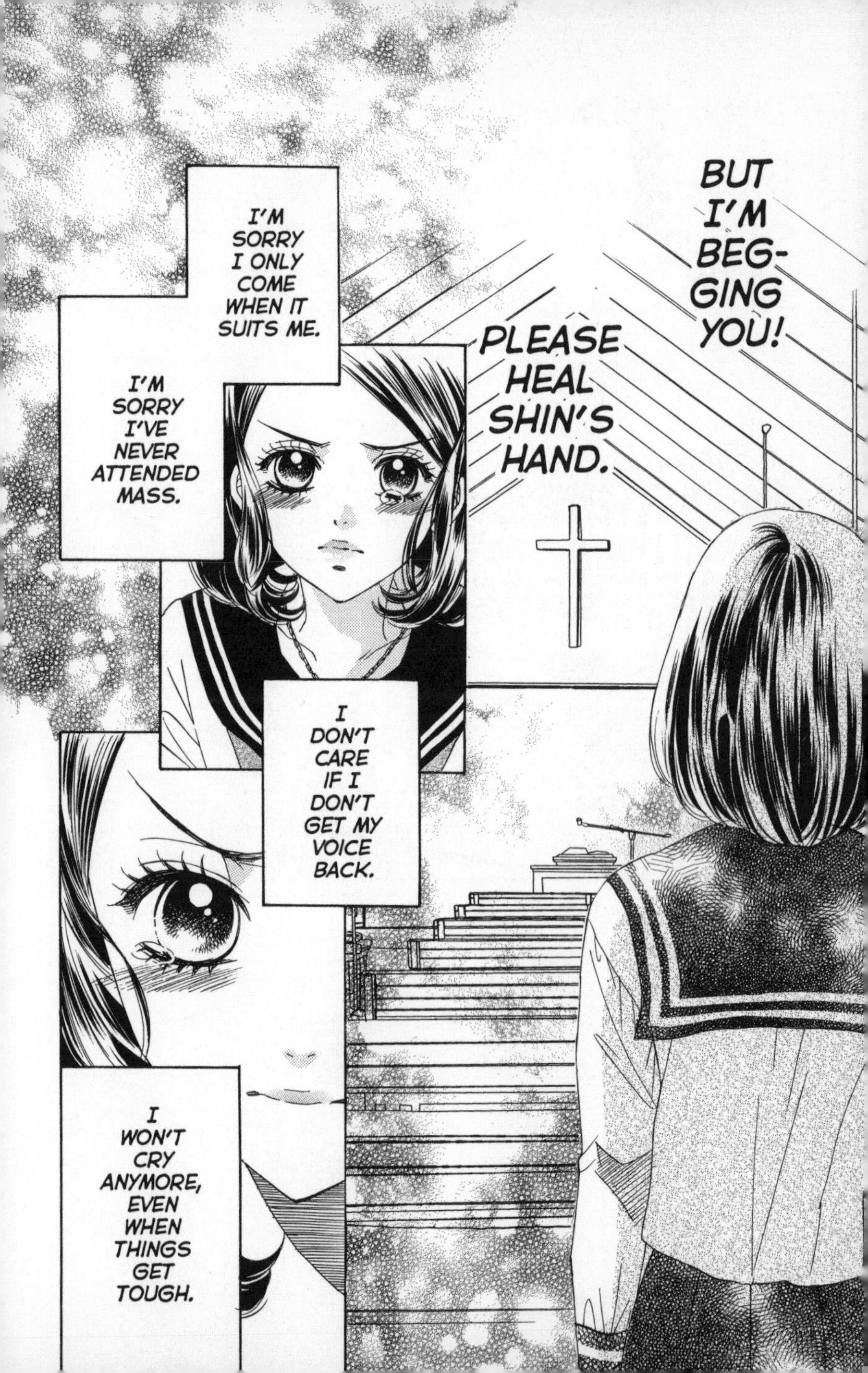
I'M SORRY I ONLY COME WHEN IT SUITS ME.
I'M SORRY I'VE NEVER ATTENDED MASS.
BUT I'M BEG-GING YOU!
PLEASE HEAL SHIN'S HAND.
I DON'T CARE IF I DON'T GET MY VOICE BACK.
I WON'T CRY ANYMORE, EVEN WHEN THINGS GET TOUGH.

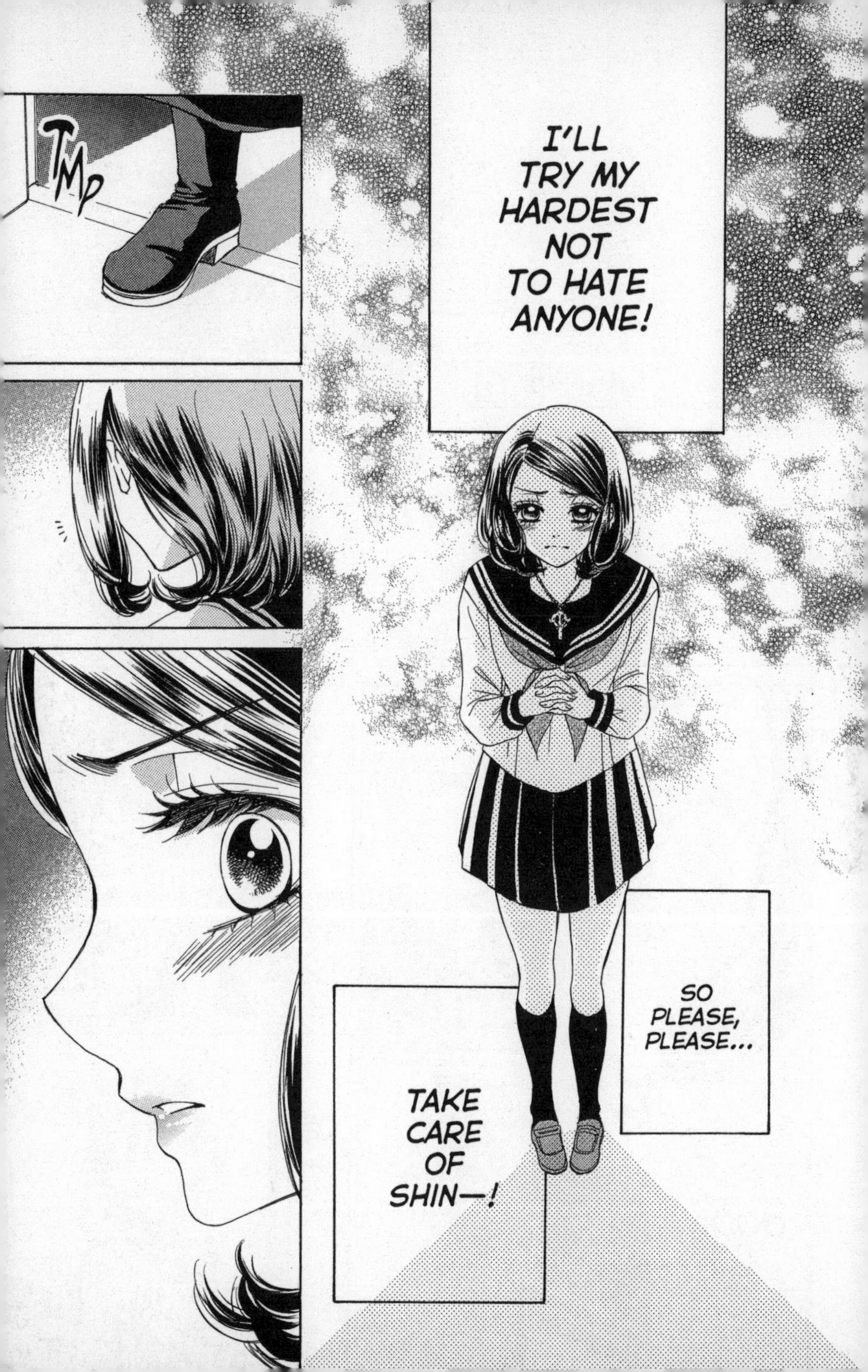
I'LL TRY MY HARDEST NOT TO HATE ANYONE!
SO PLEASE, PLEASE...
TAKE CARE OF SHIN—!
TMP

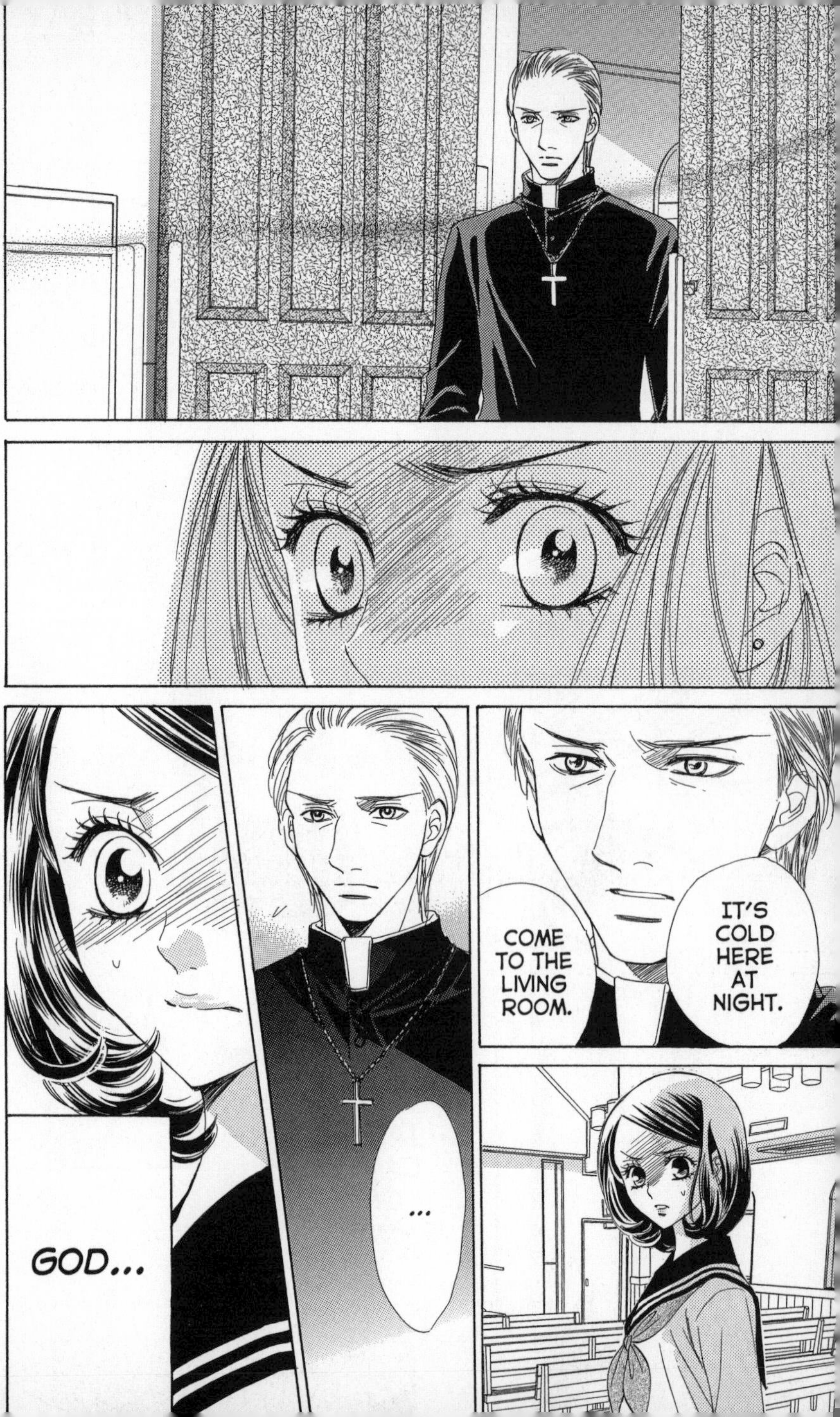
IT'S COLD HERE AT NIGHT.
COME TO THE LIVING ROOM.
...
GOD...

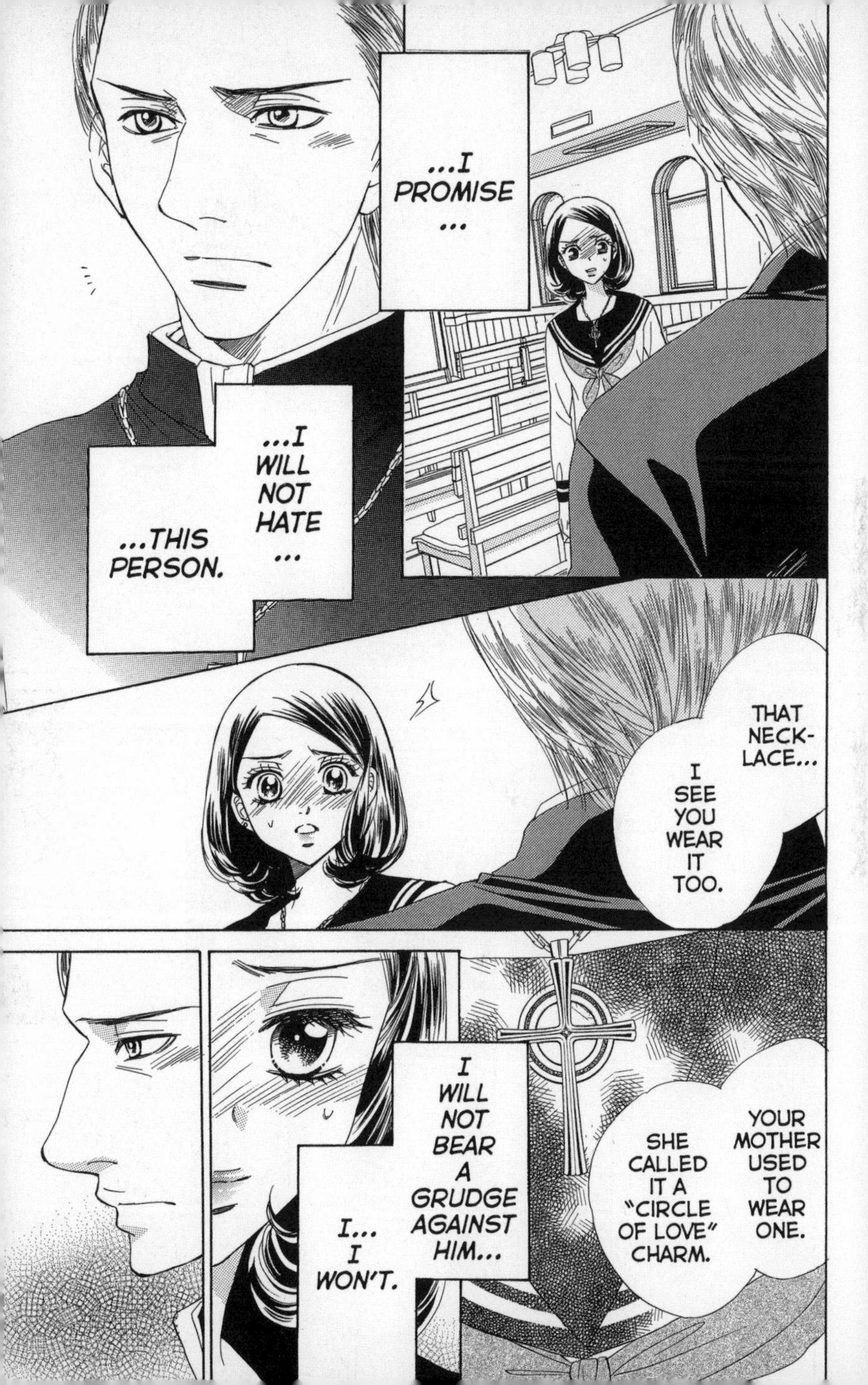
...I PROMISE ...
...I WILL NOT HATE ...
...THIS PERSON.
THAT NECK-LACE...
I SEE YOU WEAR IT TOO.
YOUR MOTHER USED TO WEAR ONE.
SHE CALLED IT A "CIRCLE OF LOVE" CHARM.
I WILL NOT BEAR A GRUDGE AGAINST HIM...
I... I WON'T.

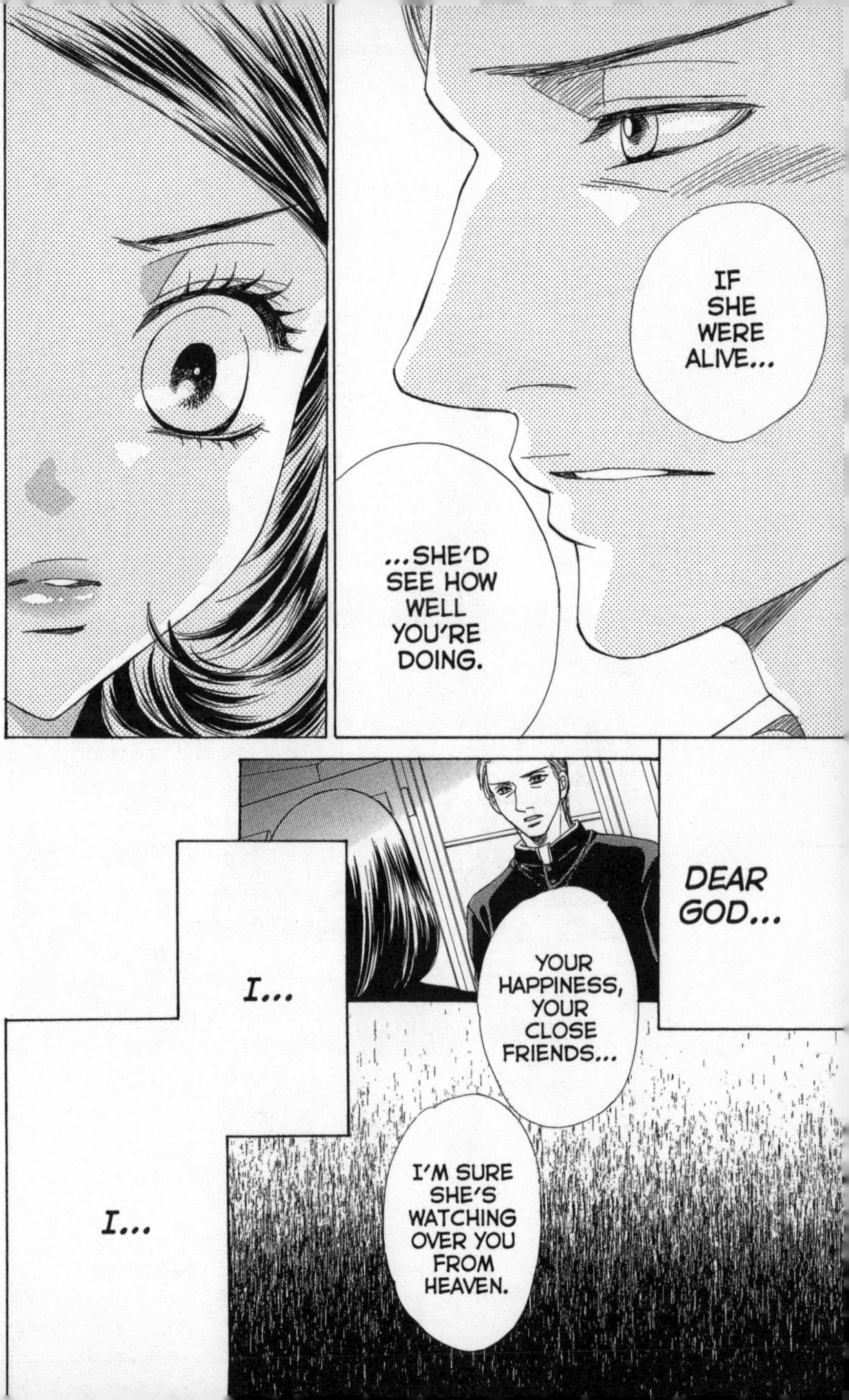
IF SHE WERE ALIVE...
...SHE'D SEE HOW WELL YOU'RE DOING.
DEAR GOD...
YOUR HAPPINESS, YOUR CLOSE FRIENDS...
I'M SURE SHE'S WATCHING OVER YOU FROM HEAVEN.
I...
I...

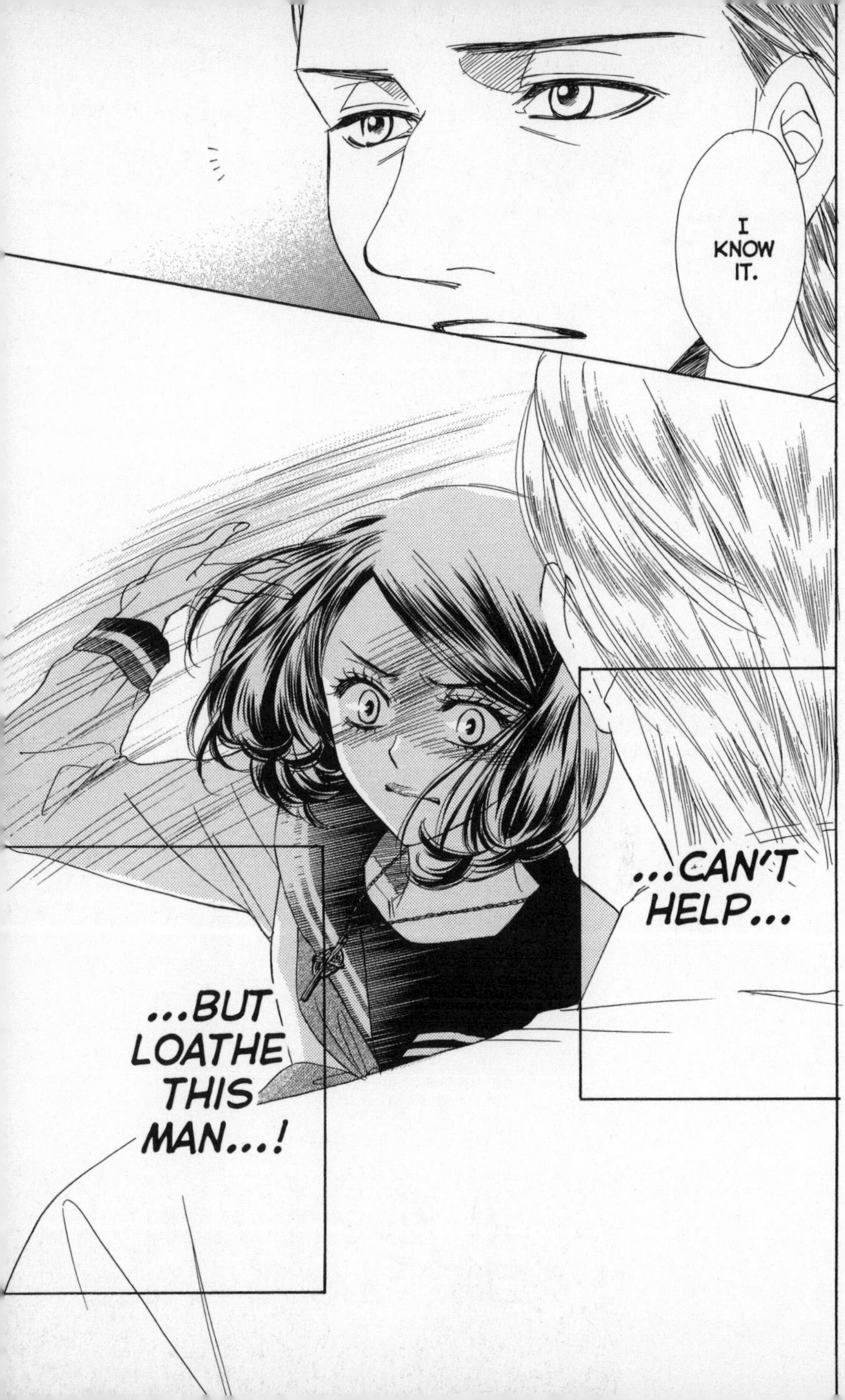
I KNOW IT.
...CAN'T HELP...
...BUT LOATHE THIS MAN...!

A Devil and Her Love Song

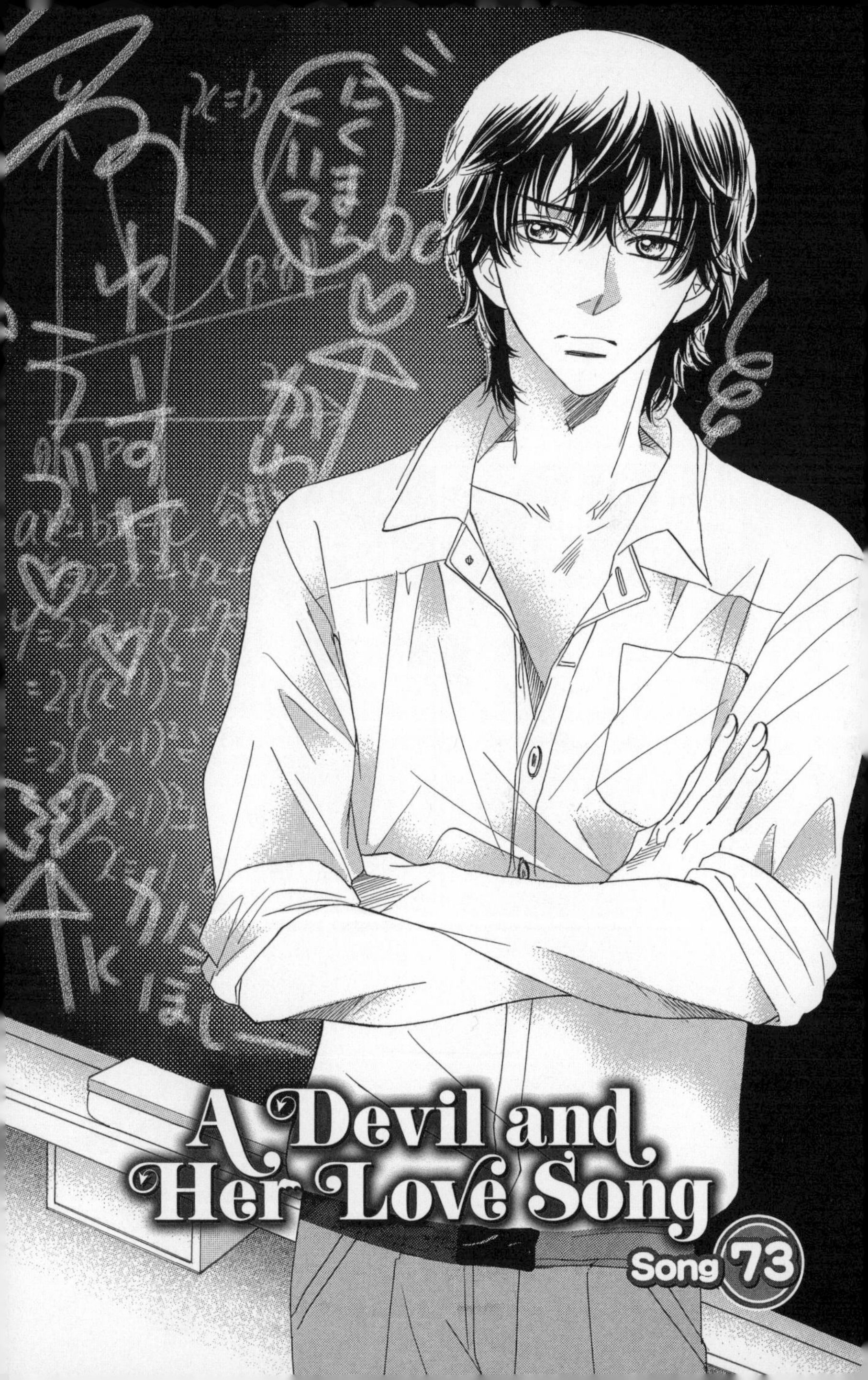
A Devil and Her Love Song
Song 73

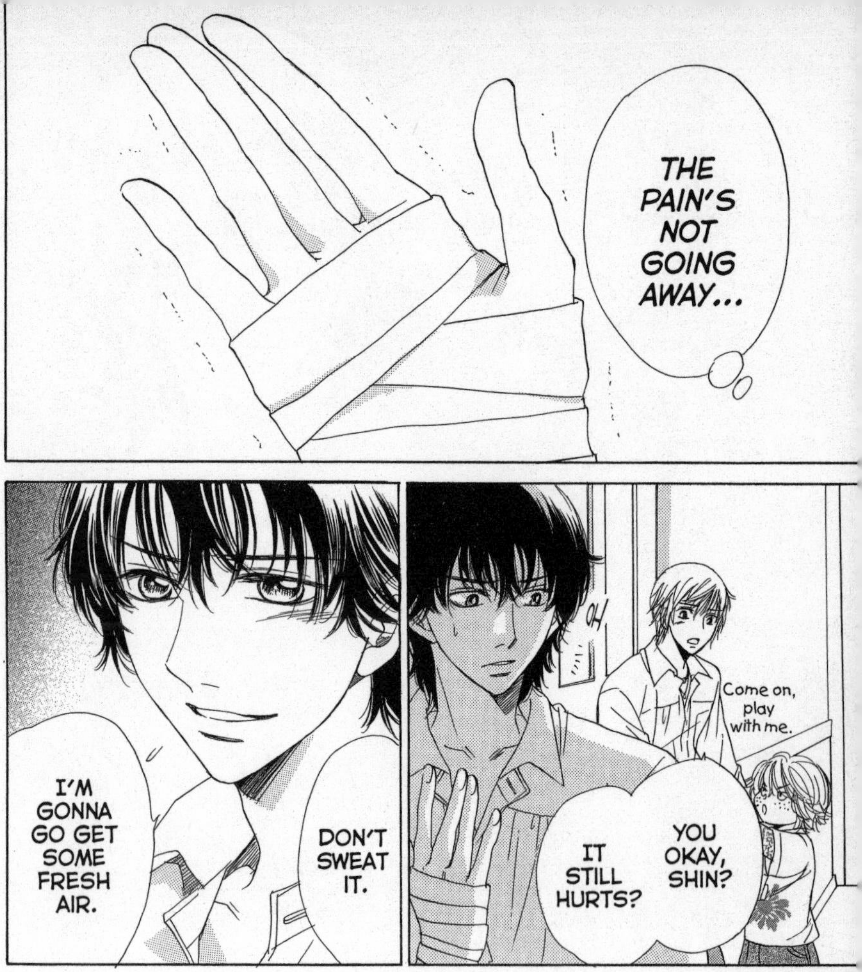
THE PAIN'S NOT GOING AWAY...
OH
Come on, play with me.
YOU OKAY, SHIN?
IT STILL HURTS?
DON'T SWEAT IT.
I'M GONNA GO GET SOME FRESH AIR.

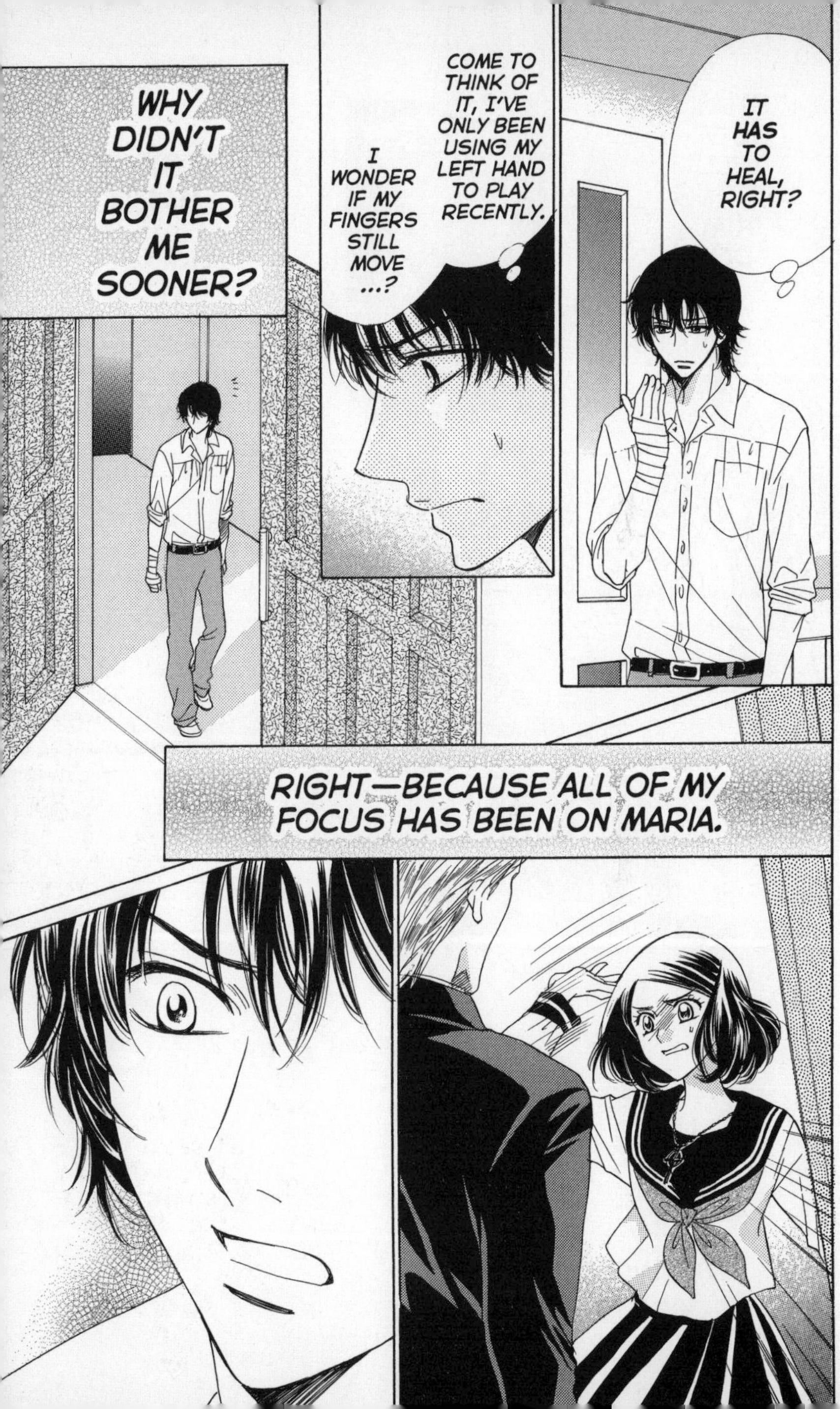
IT HAS TO HEAL, RIGHT?
COME TO THINK OF IT, I'VE ONLY BEEN USING MY LEFT HAND TO PLAY RECENTLY.
I WONDER IF MY FINGERS STILL MOVE ...?
WHY DIDN'T IT BOTHER ME SOONER?
RIGHT—BECAUSE ALL OF MY FOCUS HAS BEEN ON MARIA.

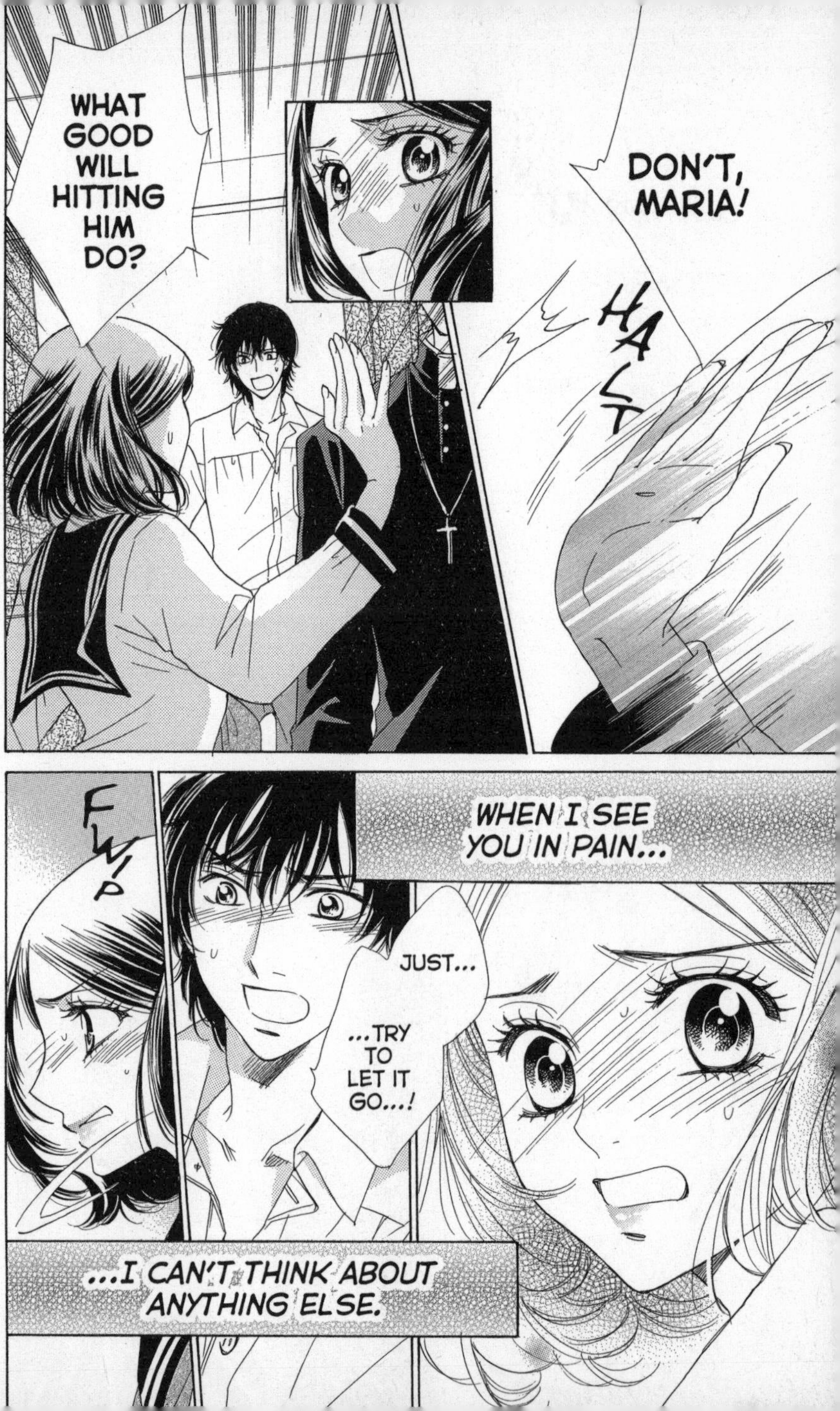
DON'T, MARIA!
HALT
WHAT GOOD WILL HITTING HIM DO?
WHEN I SEE YOU IN PAIN...
JUST...
...TRY TO LET IT GO...!
FWIP
...I CAN'T THINK ABOUT ANYTHING ELSE.

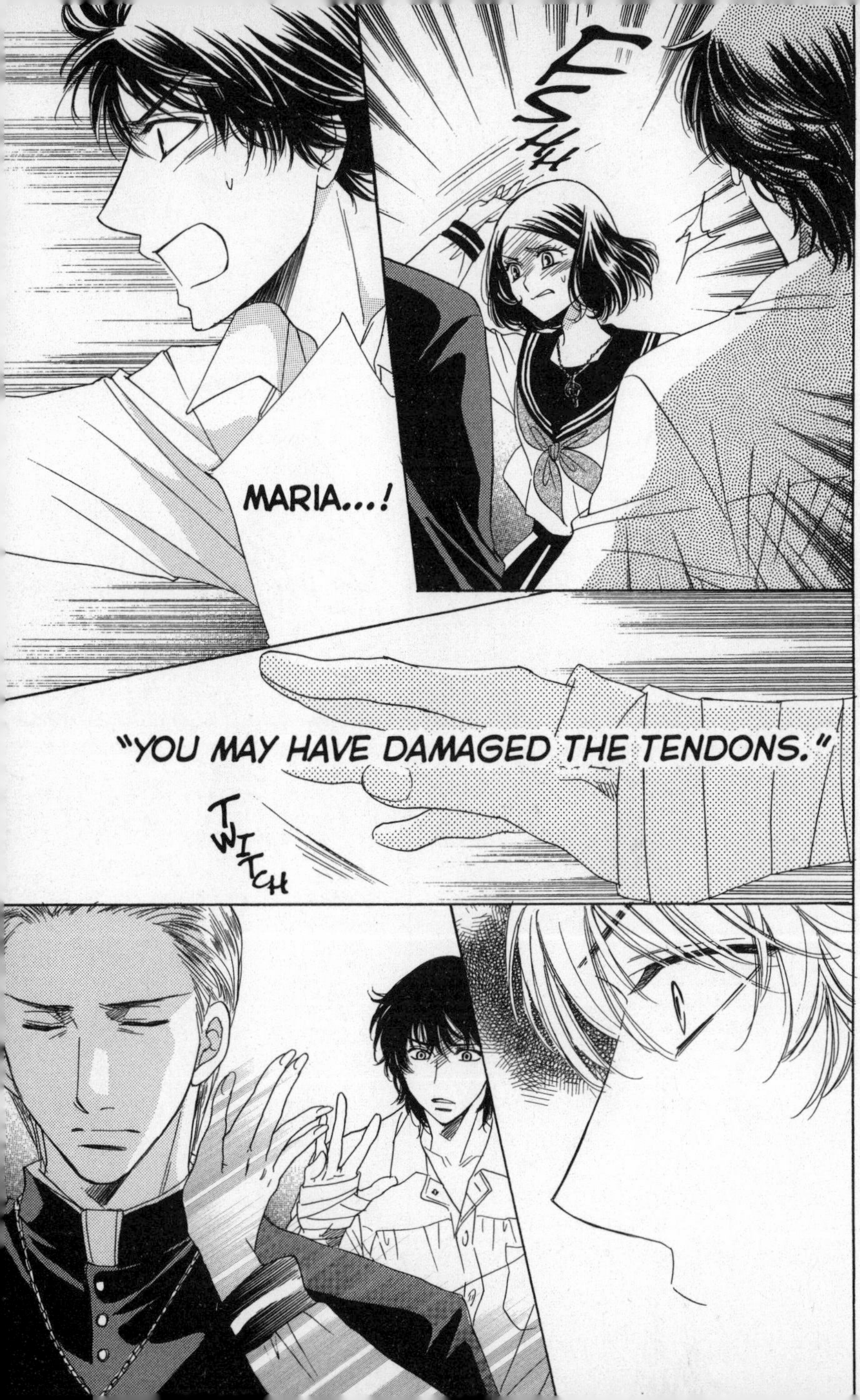
FSHH
MARIA...!
"YOU MAY HAVE DAMAGED THE TENDONS."
TWITCH

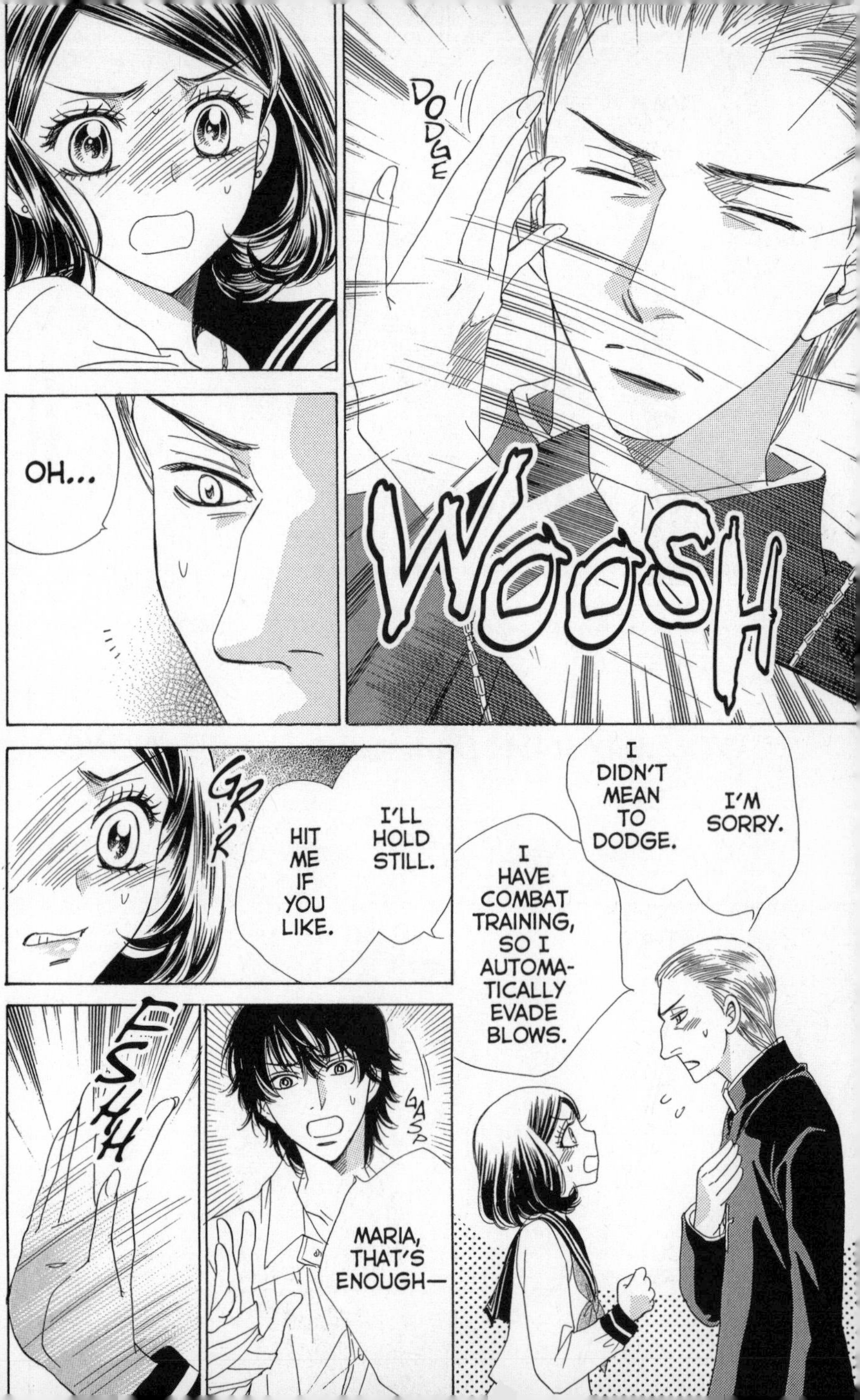
DODGE
WOOSH
OH...
I'M SORRY.
I DIDN'T MEAN TO DODGE.
I HAVE COMBAT TRAINING, SO I AUTOMATICALLY EVADE BLOWS.
GRR
I'LL HOLD STILL.
HIT ME IF YOU LIKE.
GASP
MARIA, THAT'S ENOUGH—
FSHH

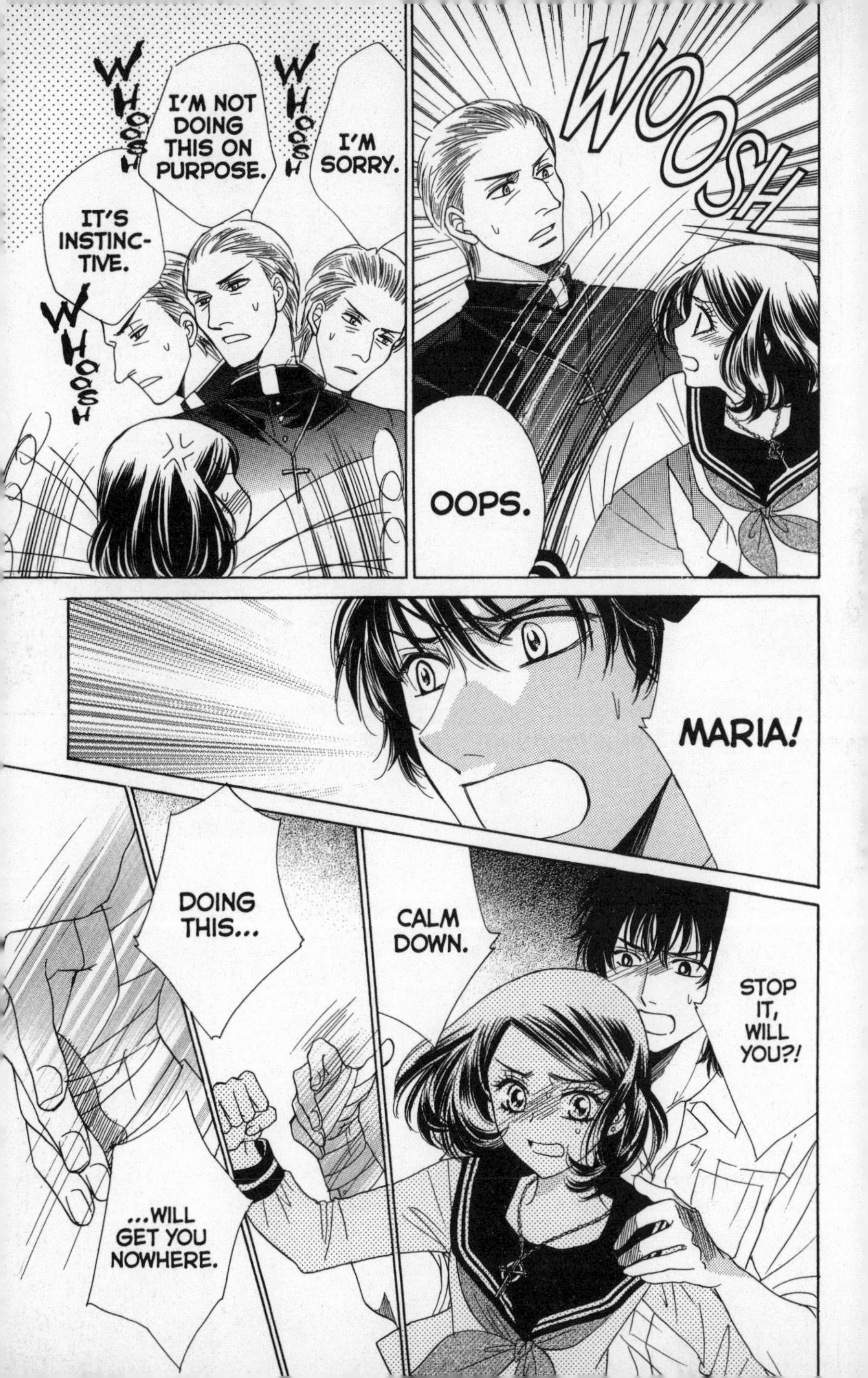
WOOSH
OOPS.
I'M SORRY.
WHOOSH
I'M NOT DOING THIS ON PURPOSE.
WHOOSH
IT'S INSTINC-TIVE.
WHOOSH
MARIA!
STOP IT, WILL YOU?!
CALM DOWN.
DOING THIS...
...WILL GET YOU NOWHERE.

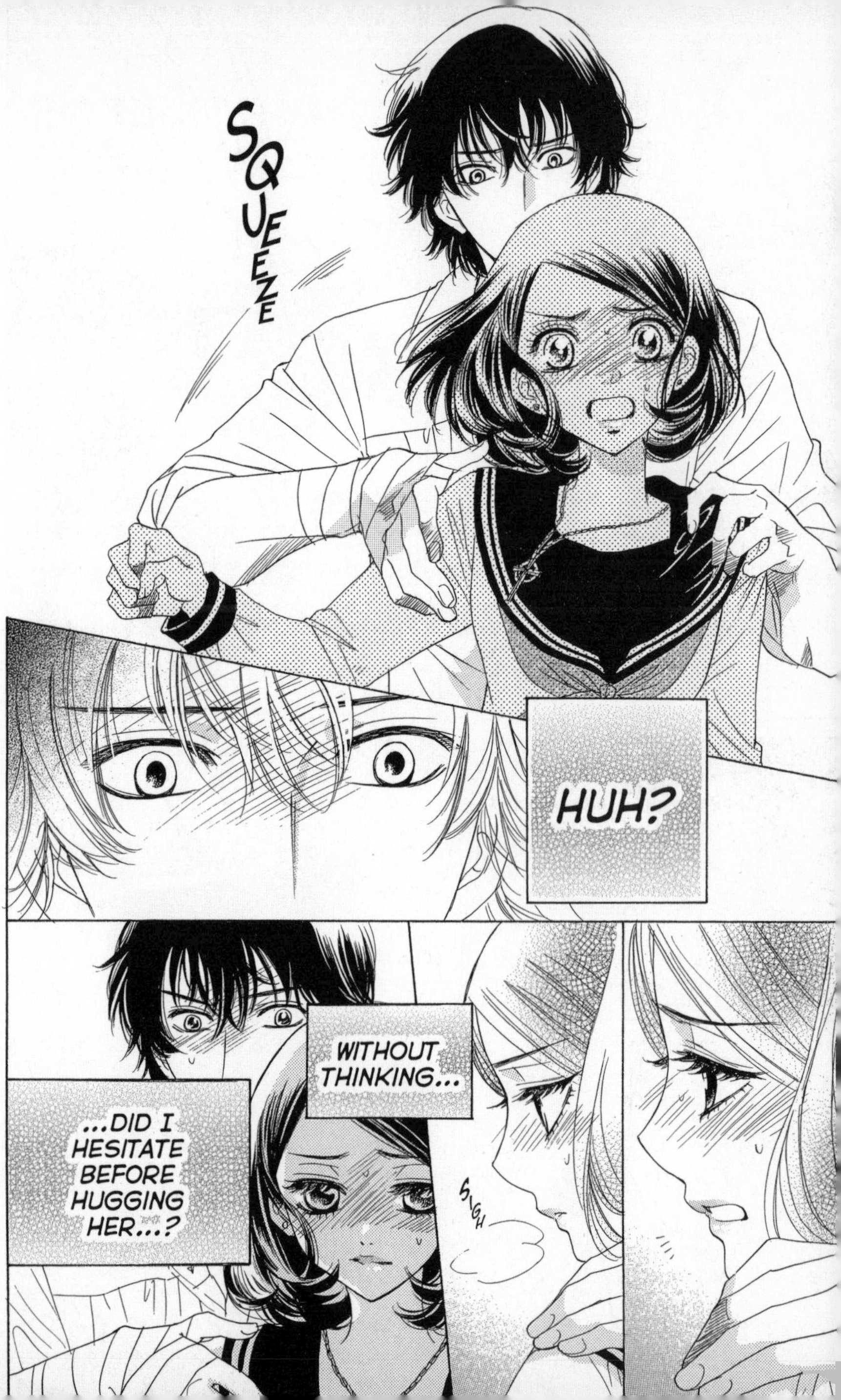
SQUEEZE
HUH?
SIGH
WITHOUT THINKING...
...DID I HESITATE BEFORE HUGGING HER...?

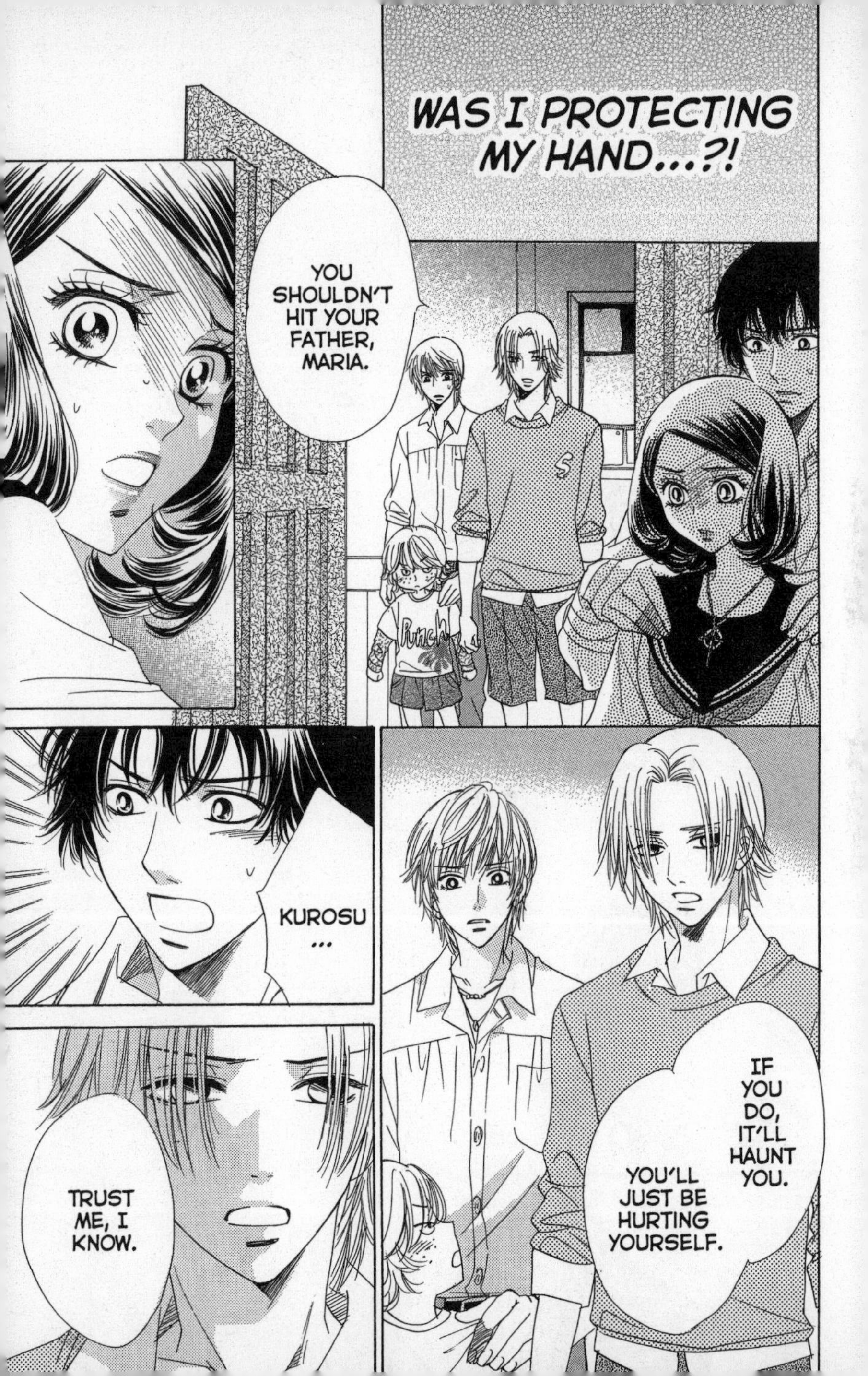
WAS I PROTECTING MY HAND...?!
YOU SHOULDN'T HIT YOUR FATHER, MARIA.
IF YOU DO, IT'LL HAUNT YOU.
YOU'LL JUST BE HURTING YOURSELF.
KUROSU...
TRUST ME, I KNOW.

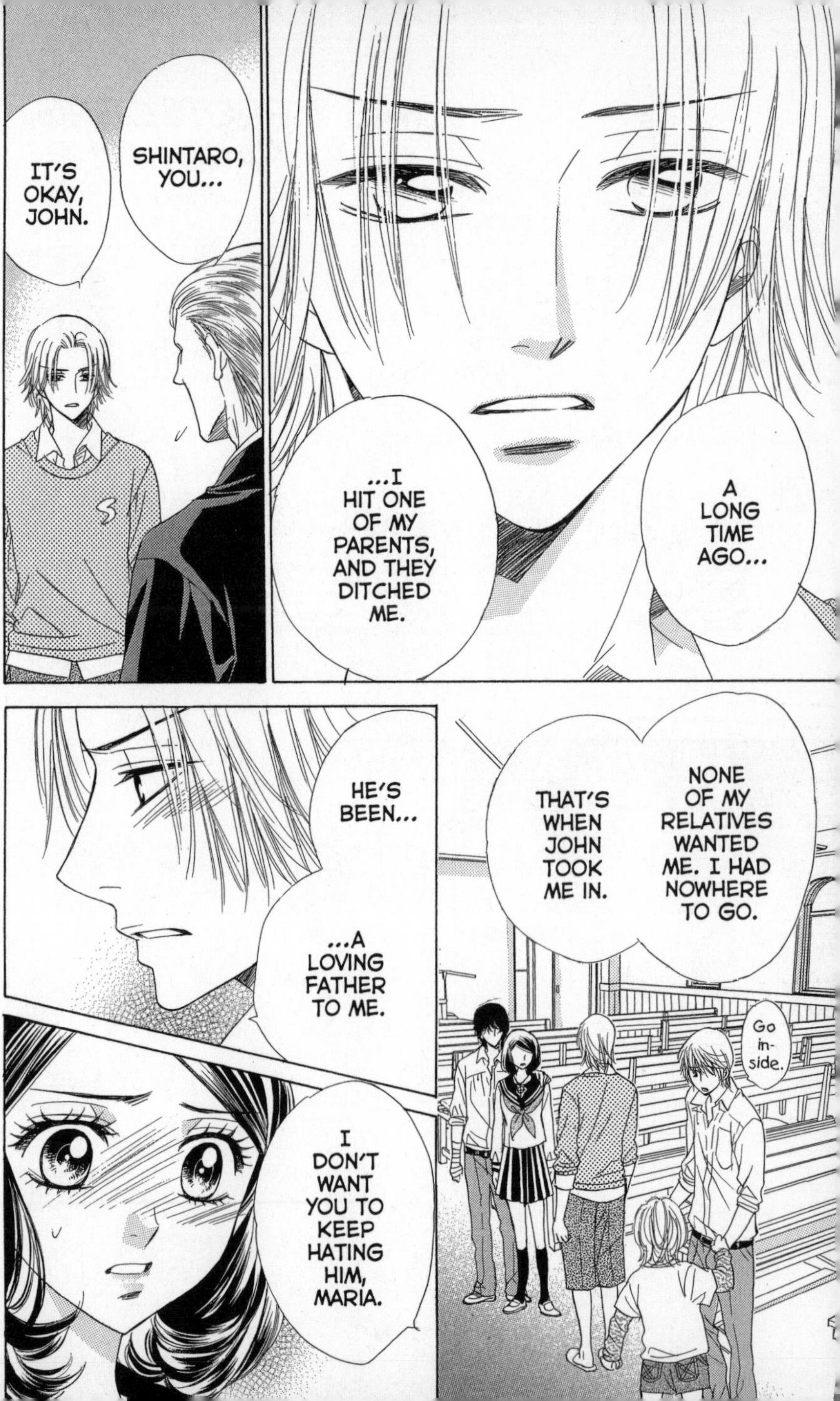
A LONG TIME AGO...
...I HIT ONE OF MY PARENTS, AND THEY DITCHED ME.
SHINTARO, YOU...
IT'S OKAY, JOHN.
NONE OF MY RELATIVES WANTED ME. I HAD NOWHERE TO GO.
THAT'S WHEN JOHN TOOK ME IN.
Go in-side.
HE'S BEEN...
...A LOVING FATHER TO ME.
I DON'T WANT YOU TO KEEP HATING HIM, MARIA.

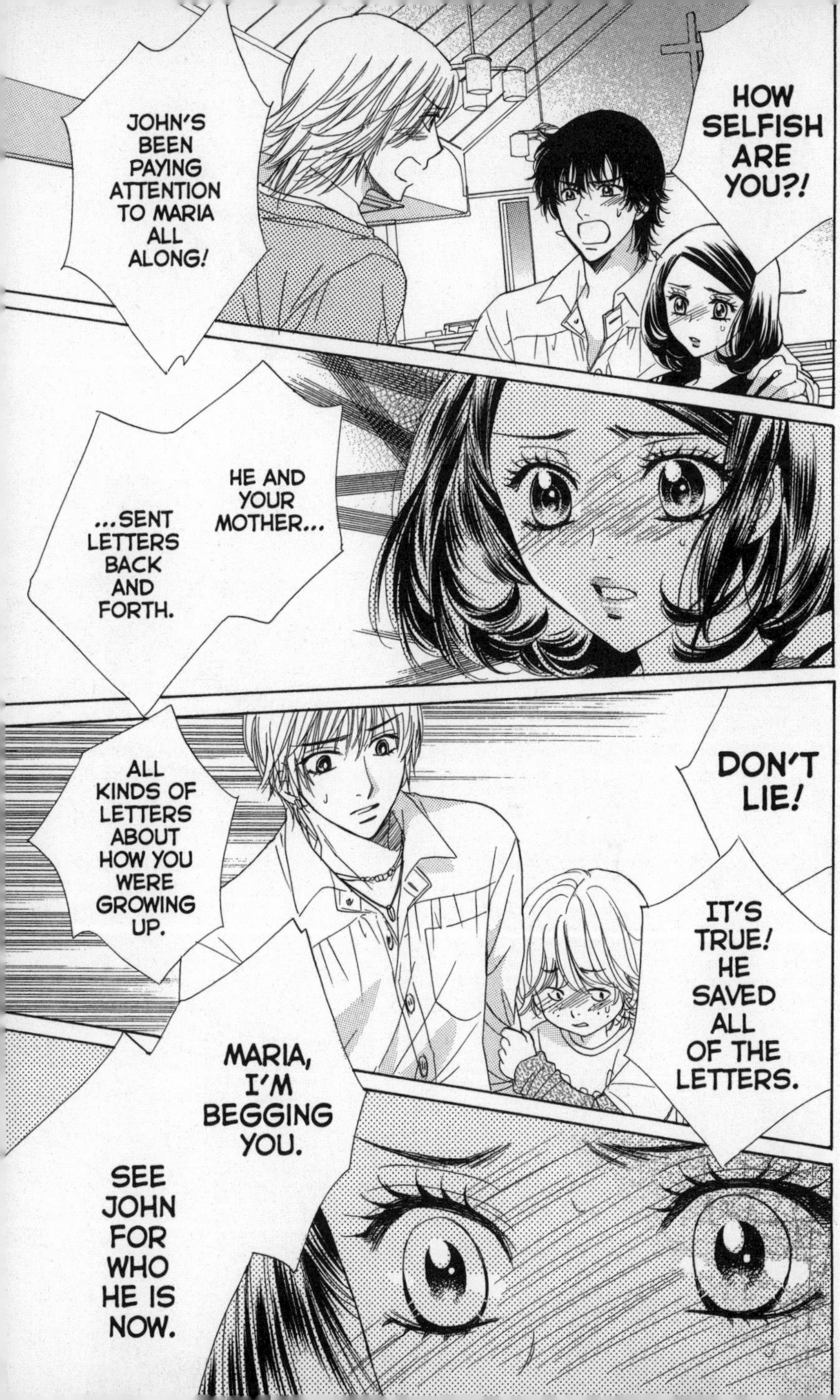
HOW SELFISH ARE YOU?!
JOHN'S BEEN PAYING ATTENTION TO MARIA ALL ALONG!
HE AND YOUR MOTHER...
...SENT LETTERS BACK AND FORTH.
ALL KINDS OF LETTERS ABOUT HOW YOU WERE GROWING UP.
DON'T LIE!
IT'S TRUE! HE SAVED ALL OF THE LETTERS.
MARIA, I'M BEGGING YOU.
SEE JOHN FOR WHO HE IS NOW.

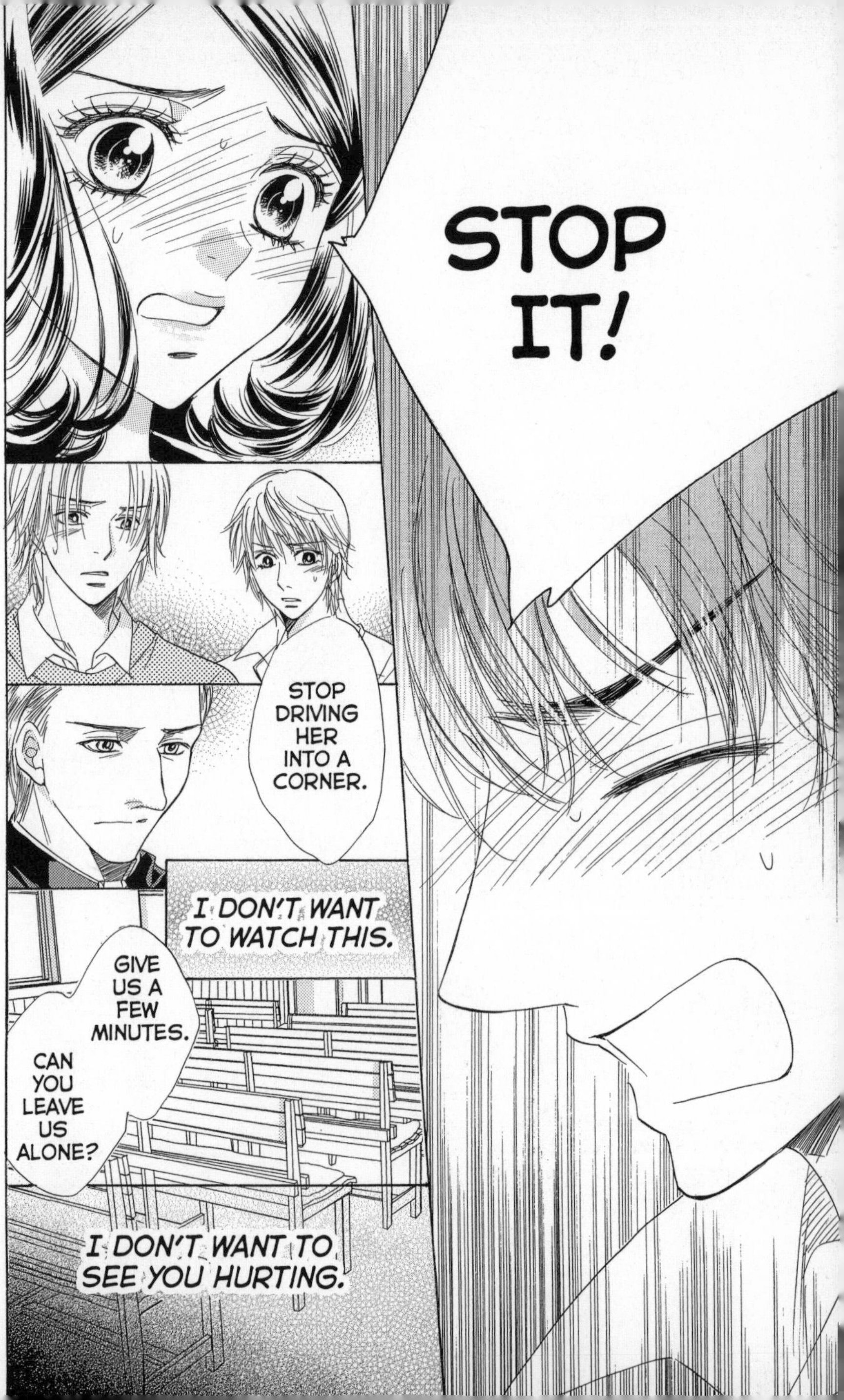
STOP IT!
STOP DRIVING HER INTO A CORNER.
I DON'T WANT TO WATCH THIS.
GIVE US A FEW MINUTES.
CAN YOU LEAVE US ALONE?
I DON'T WANT TO SEE YOU HURTING.

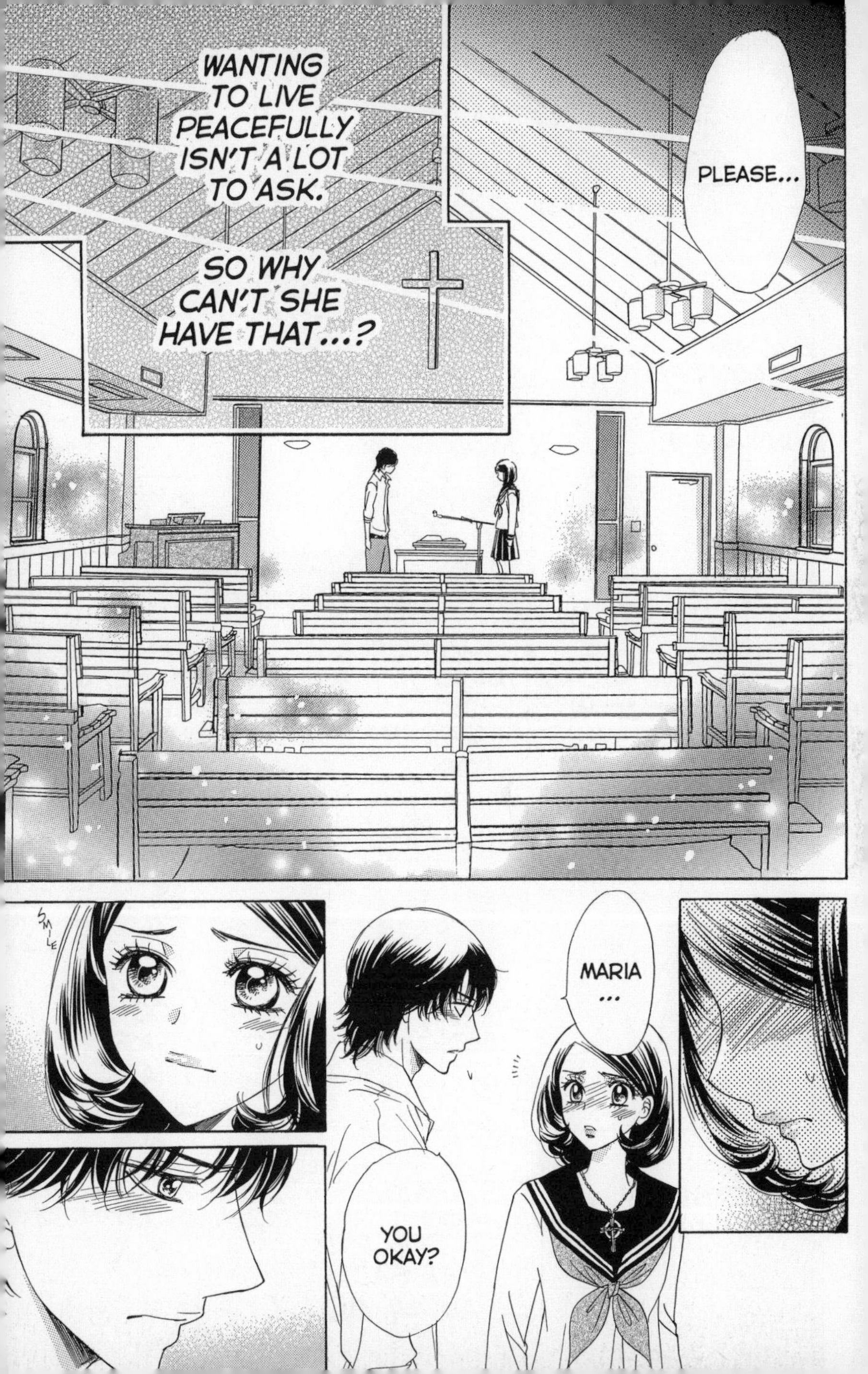
PLEASE...
WANTING TO LIVE PEACEFULLY ISN'T A LOT TO ASK.
SO WHY CAN'T SHE HAVE THAT...?
MARIA...
YOU OKAY?
SMILE

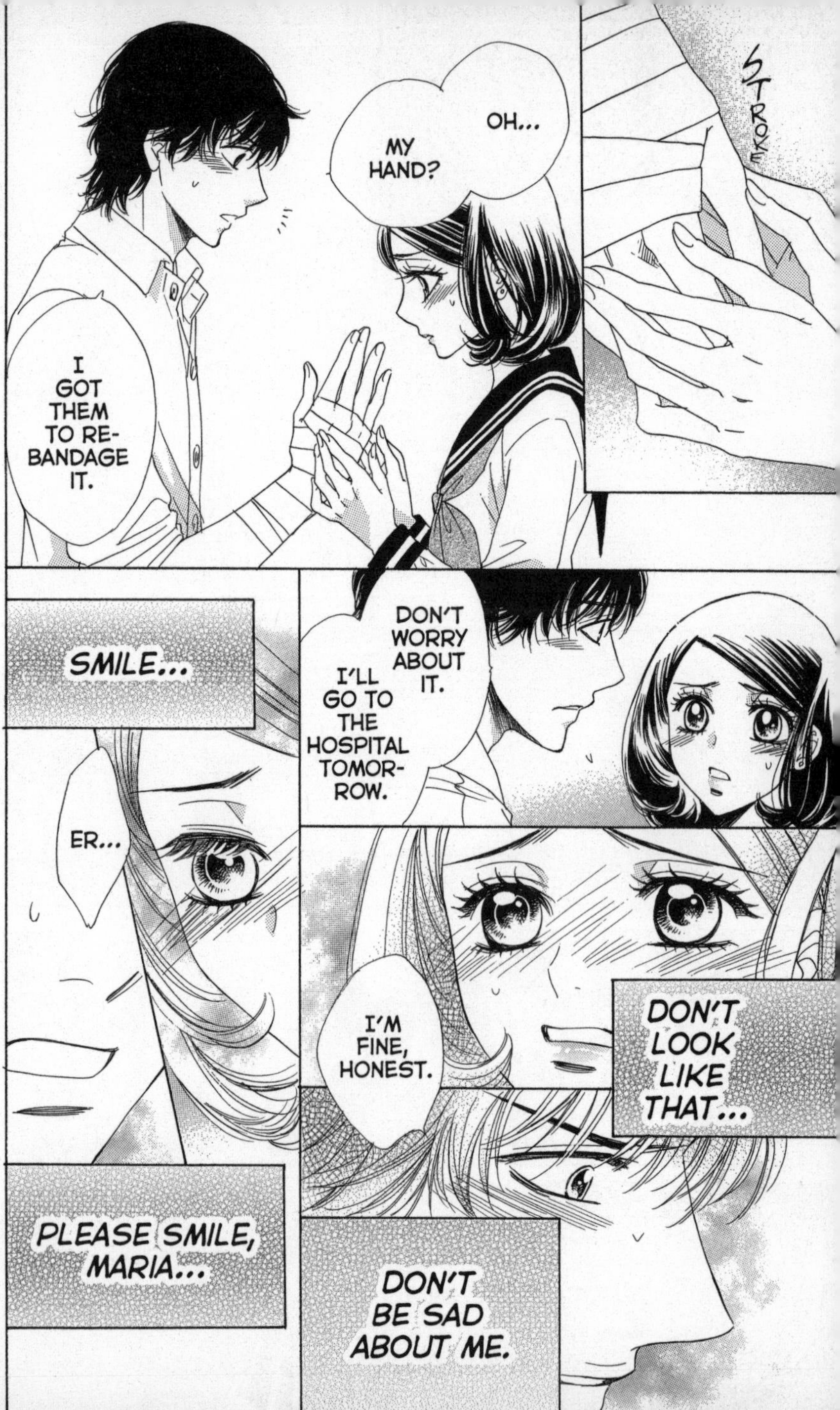
STROKE
OH...
MY HAND?
I GOT THEM TO RE-BANDAGE IT.
DON'T WORRY ABOUT IT.
I'LL GO TO THE HOSPITAL TOMORROW.
DON'T LOOK LIKE THAT...
I'M FINE, HONEST.
DON'T BE SAD ABOUT ME.
SMILE...
ER...
PLEASE SMILE, MARIA...

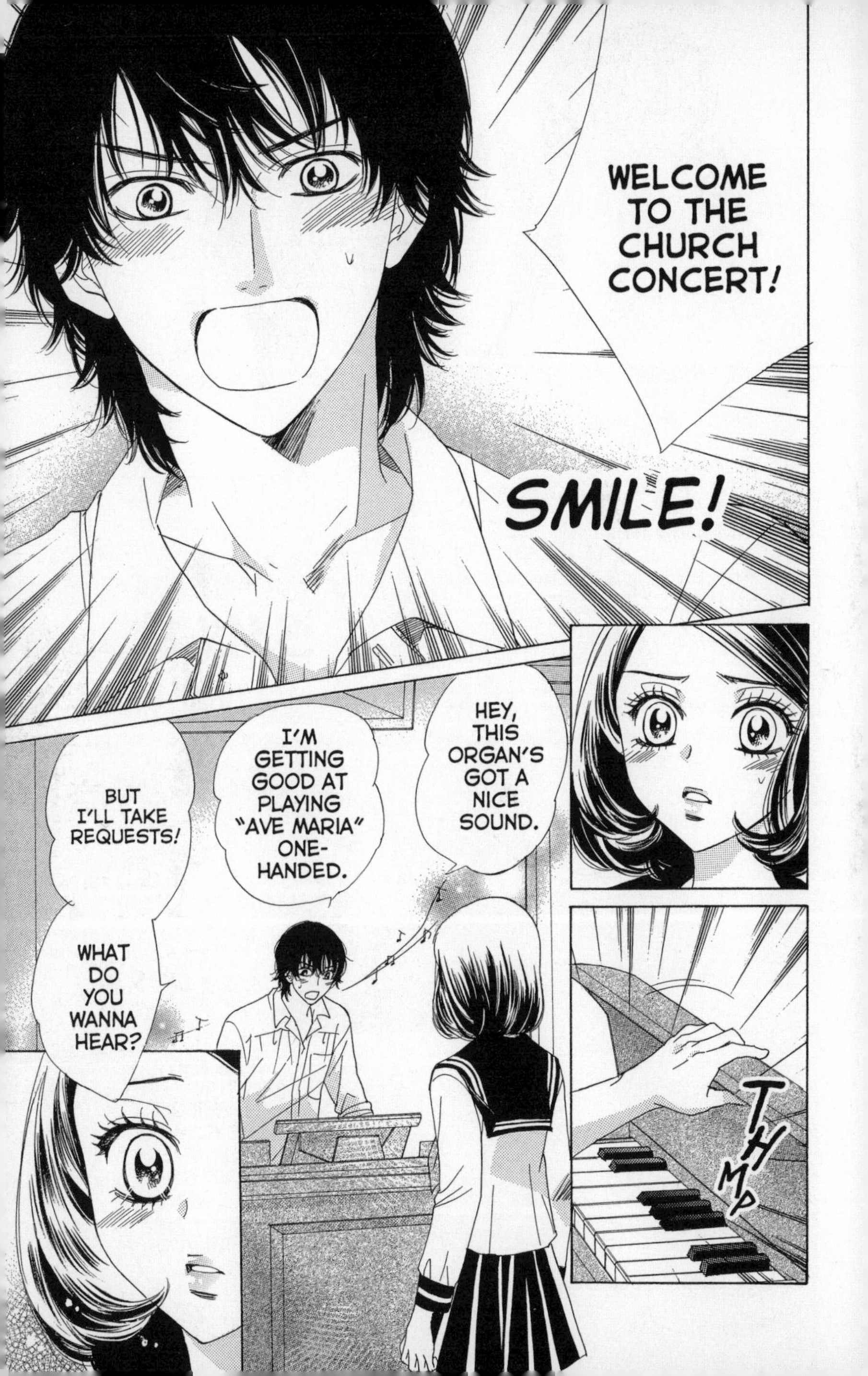
WELCOME TO THE CHURCH CONCERT!
SMILE!
THMP
HEY, THIS ORGAN'S GOT A NICE SOUND.
I'M GETTING GOOD AT PLAYING "AVE MARIA" ONE-HANDED.
BUT I'LL TAKE REQUESTS!
WHAT DO YOU WANNA HEAR?

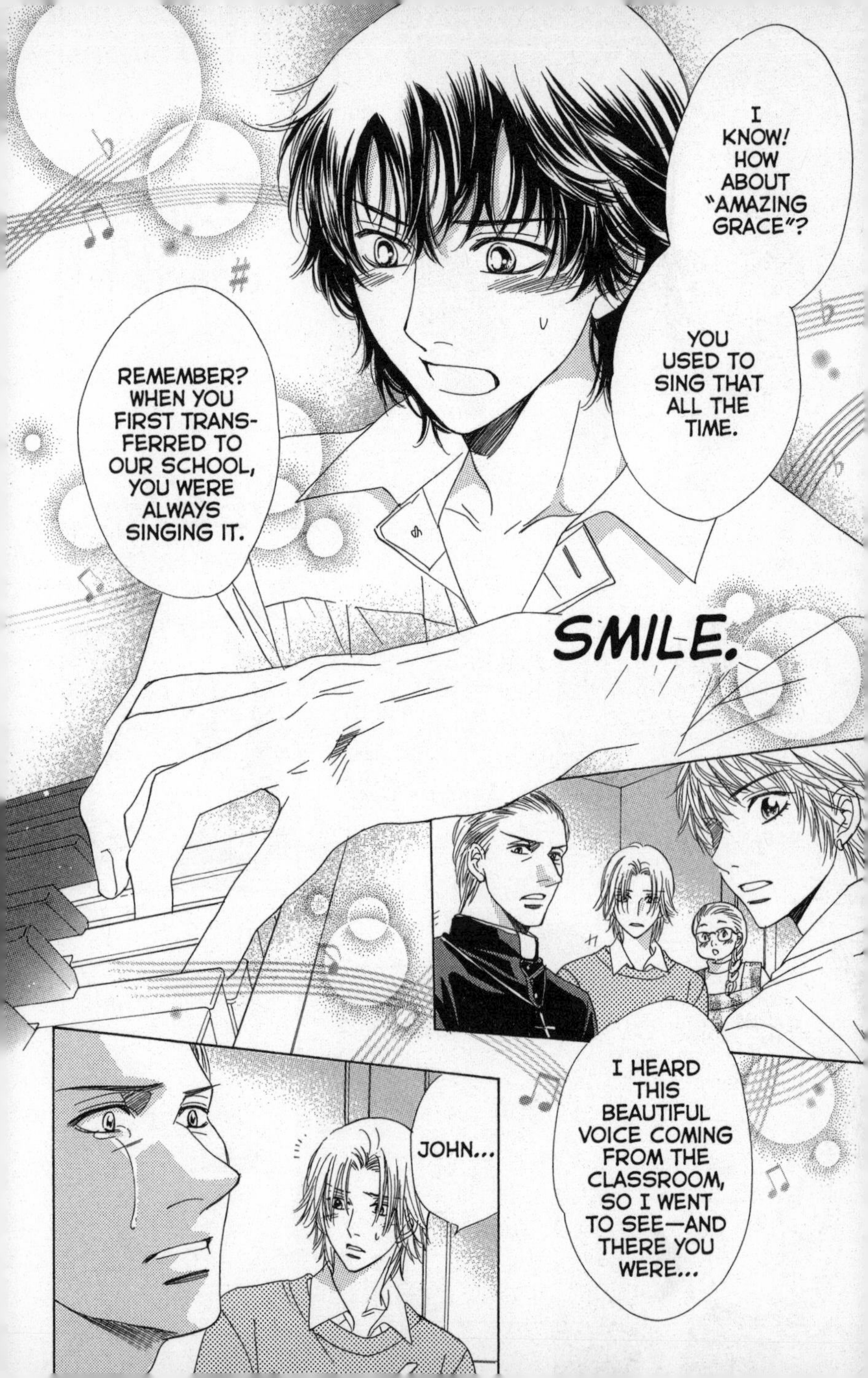

I KNOW! HOW ABOUT "AMAZING GRACE"?
YOU USED TO SING THAT ALL THE TIME.
REMEMBER? WHEN YOU FIRST TRANS-FERRED TO OUR SCHOOL, YOU WERE ALWAYS SINGING IT.
SMILE.
I HEARD THIS BEAUTIFUL VOICE COMING FROM THE CLASSROOM, SO I WENT TO SEE—AND THERE YOU WERE...
JOHN...

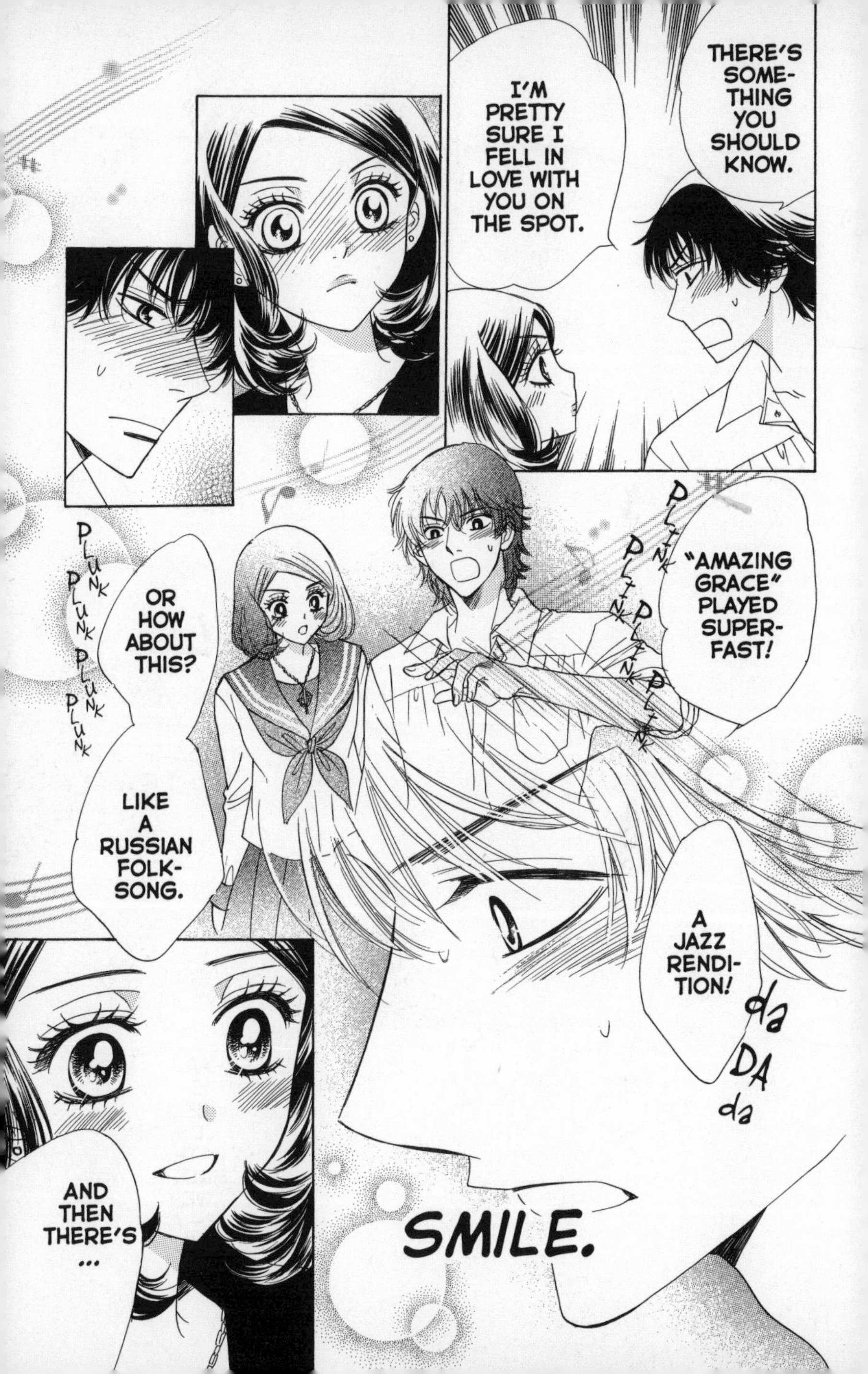
THERE'S SOME-THING YOU SHOULD KNOW.
I'M PRETTY SURE I FELL IN LOVE WITH YOU ON THE SPOT.
PLINK PLINK PLINK PLINK
"AMAZING GRACE" PLAYED SUPER-FAST!
PLUNK PLUNK PLUNK PLUNK
OR HOW ABOUT THIS?
LIKE A RUSSIAN FOLK-SONG.
A JAZZ RENDI-TION!
da DA da
SMILE.
AND THEN THERE'S...

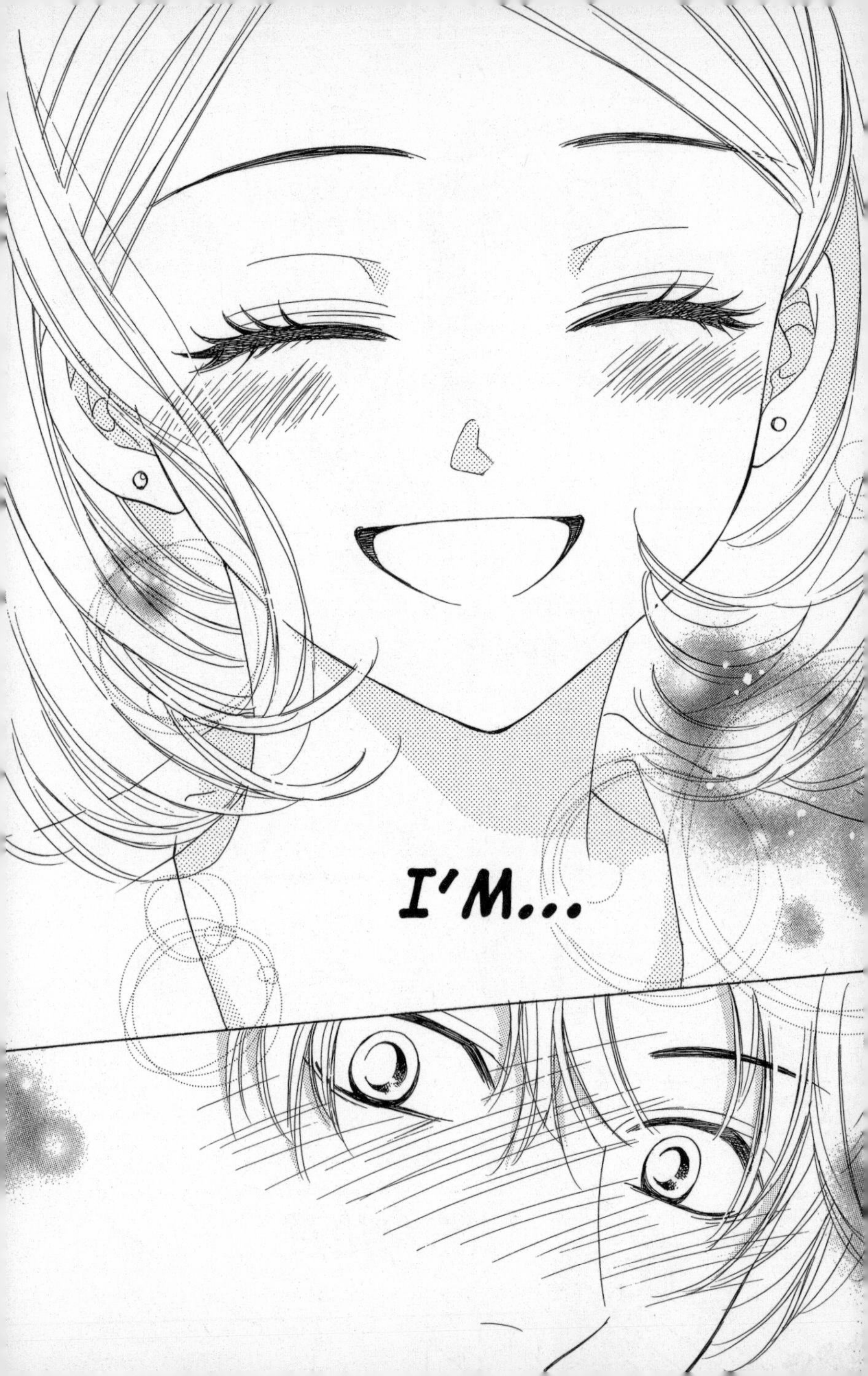
I'M...

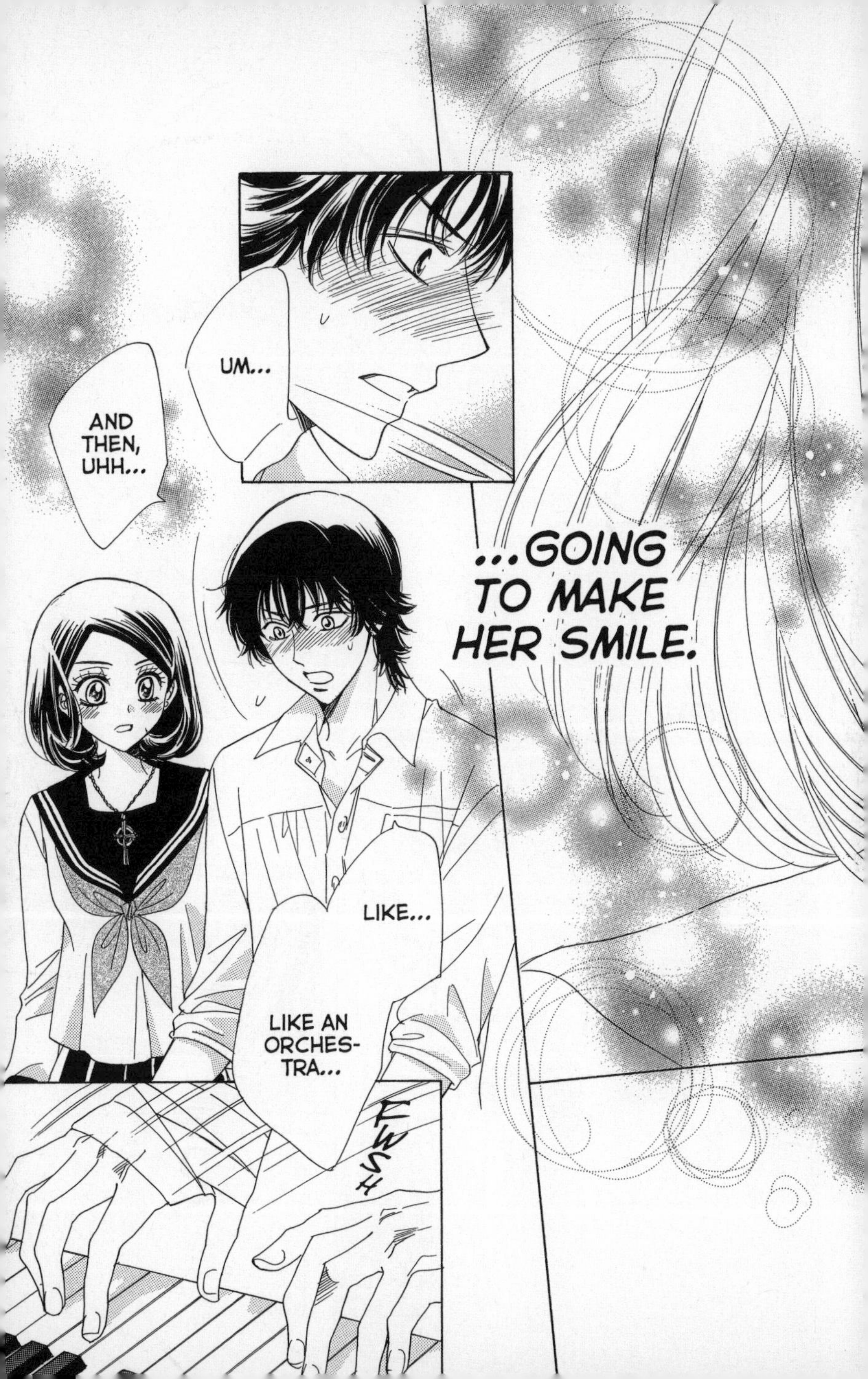
...GOING TO MAKE HER SMILE.
UM...
AND THEN, UHH...
LIKE...
LIKE AN ORCHES-TRA...
FWSH

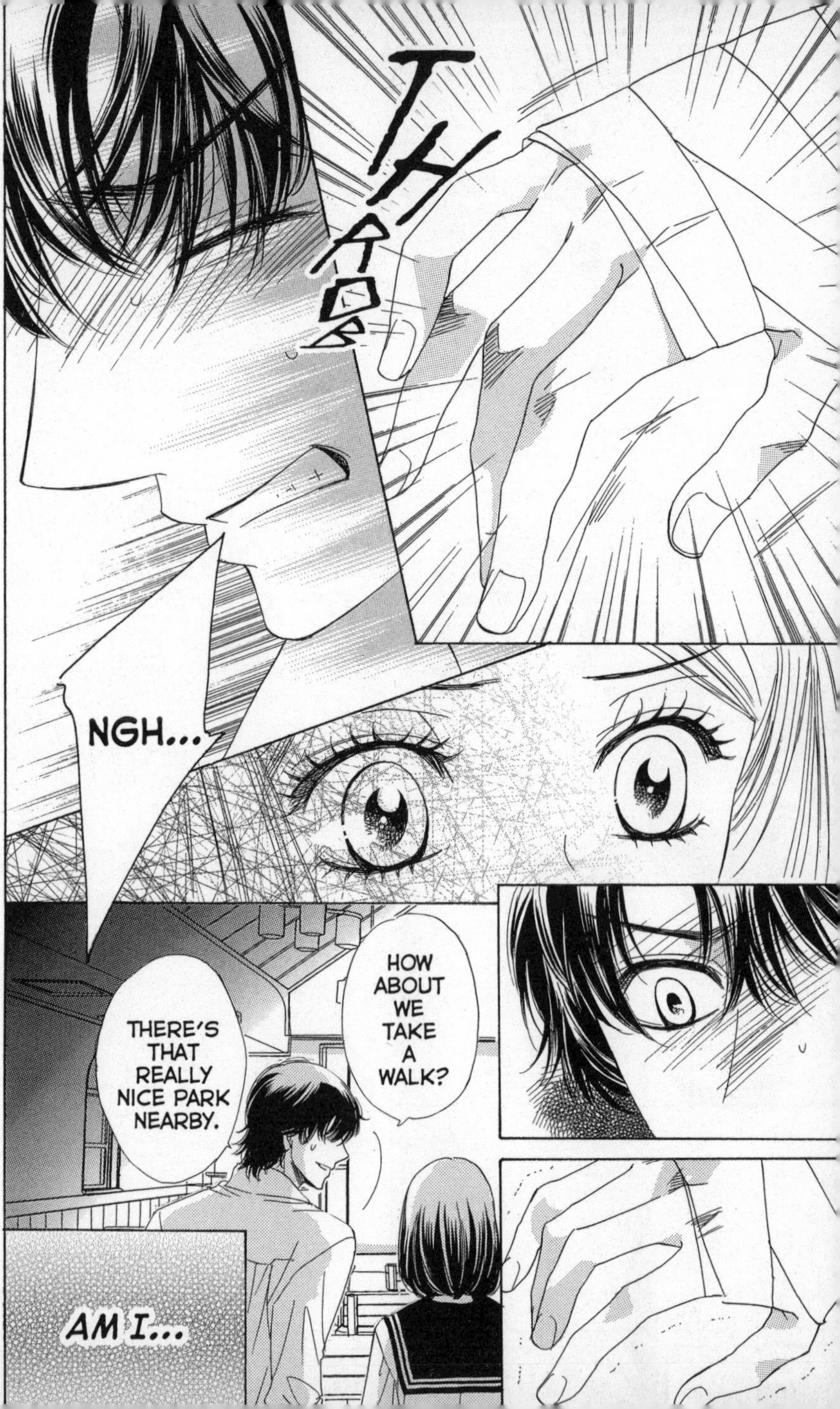
THROB
NGH...
HOW ABOUT WE TAKE A WALK?
THERE'S THAT REALLY NICE PARK NEARBY.
AM I...

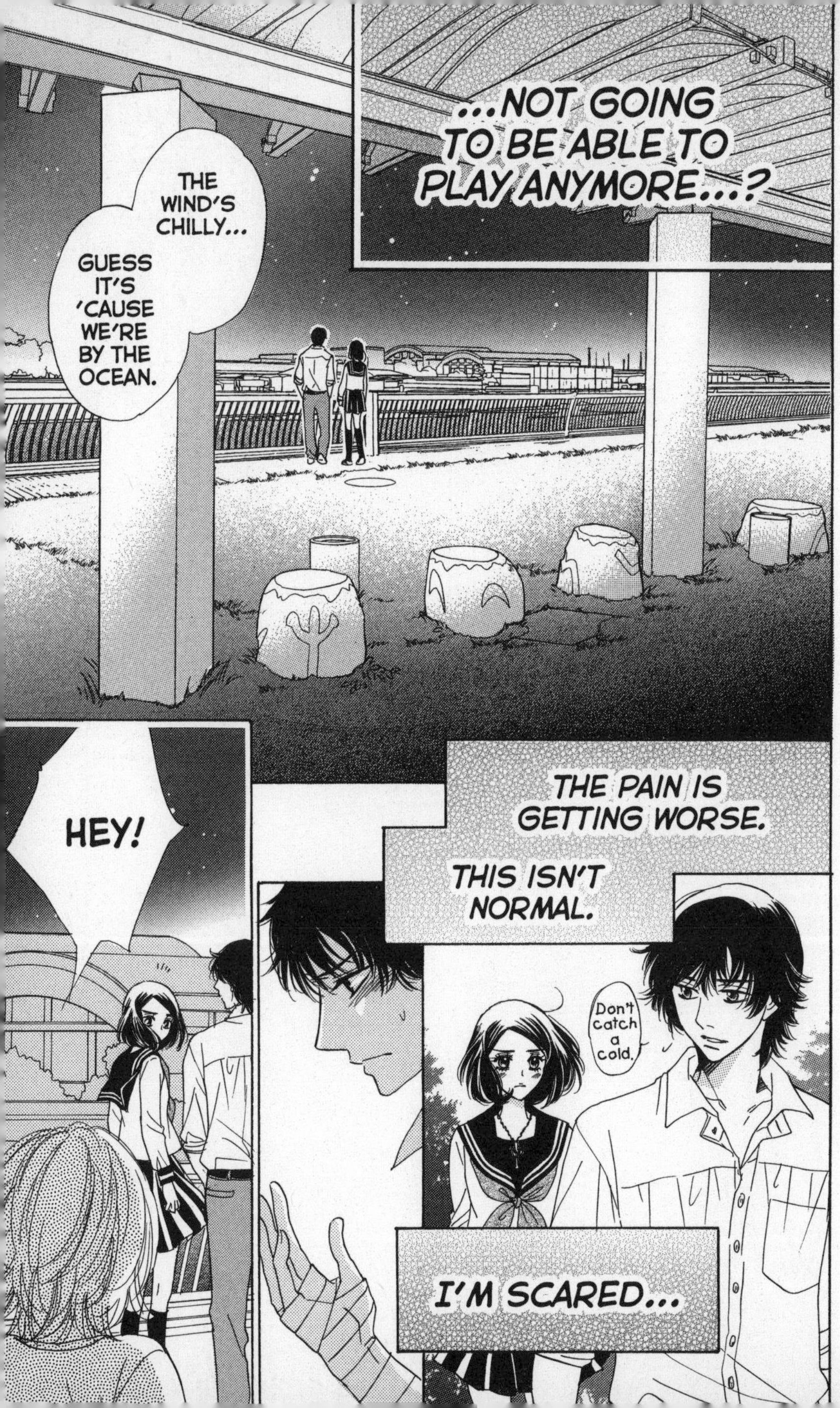
...NOT GOING TO BE ABLE TO PLAY ANYMORE...?
THE WIND'S CHILLY...
GUESS IT'S 'CAUSE WE'RE BY THE OCEAN.
THE PAIN IS GETTING WORSE.
THIS ISN'T NORMAL.
Don't catch a cold.
I'M SCARED...
HEY!

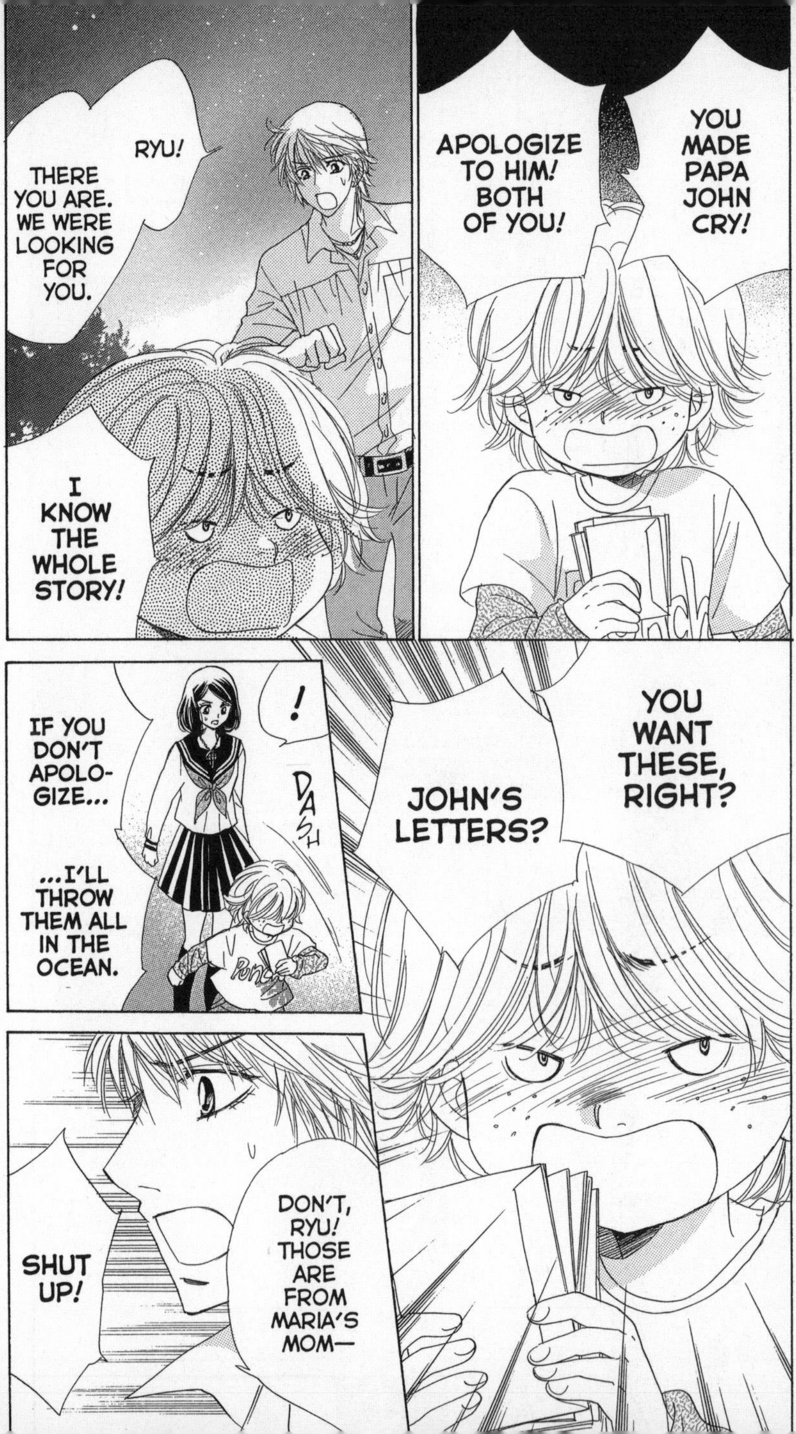
YOU MADE PAPA JOHN CRY!
APOLOGIZE TO HIM! BOTH OF YOU!
RYU!
THERE YOU ARE. WE WERE LOOKING FOR YOU.
I KNOW THE WHOLE STORY!
YOU WANT THESE, RIGHT?
JOHN'S LETTERS?
!
IF YOU DON'T APOLOGIZE...
DASH
...I'LL THROW THEM ALL IN THE OCEAN.
DON'T, RYU! THOSE ARE FROM MARIA'S MOM—
SHUT UP!

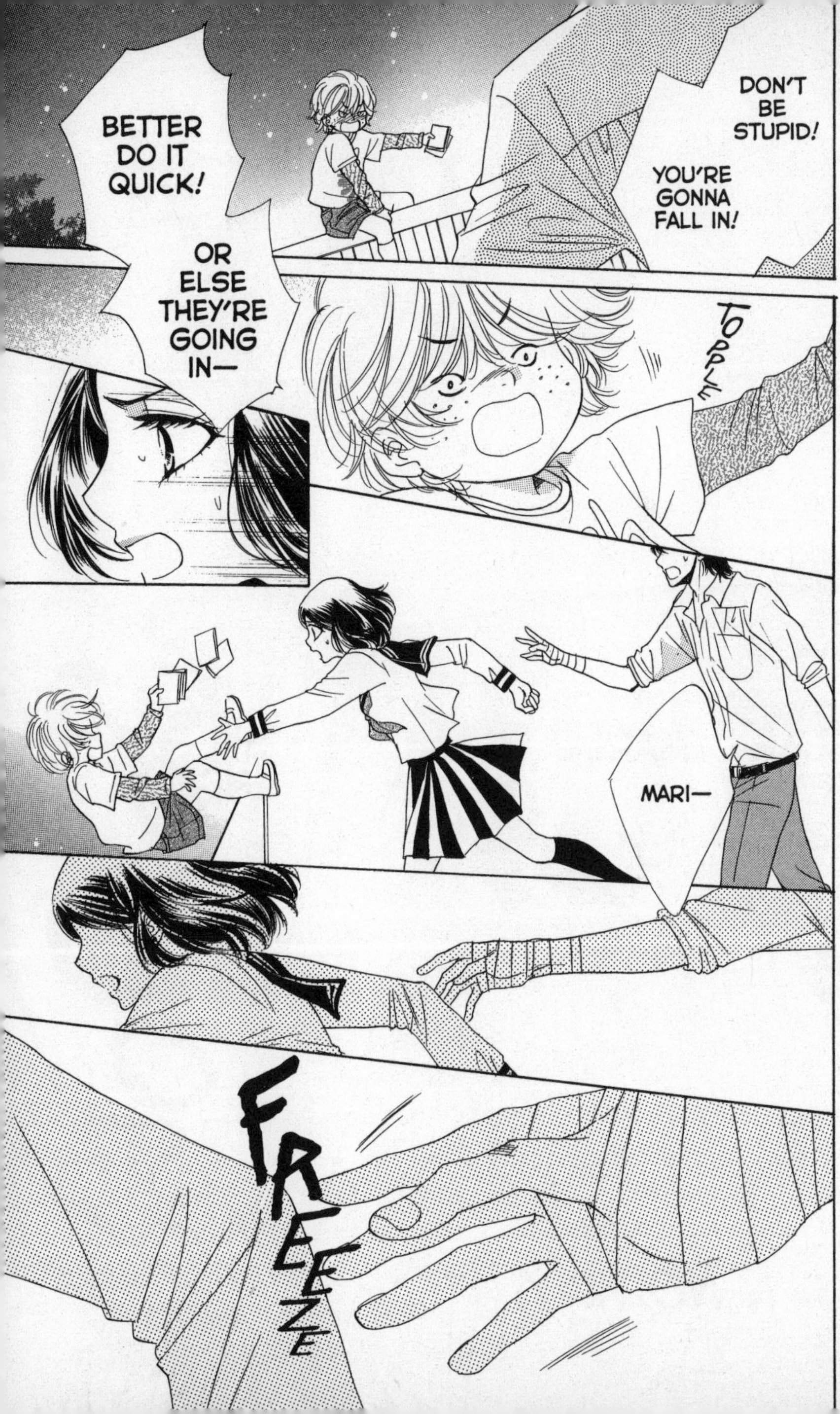
DON'T BE STUPID!
YOU'RE GONNA FALL IN!
BETTER DO IT QUICK!
OR ELSE THEY'RE GOING IN—
TOPPLE
MARI—
FREEZE

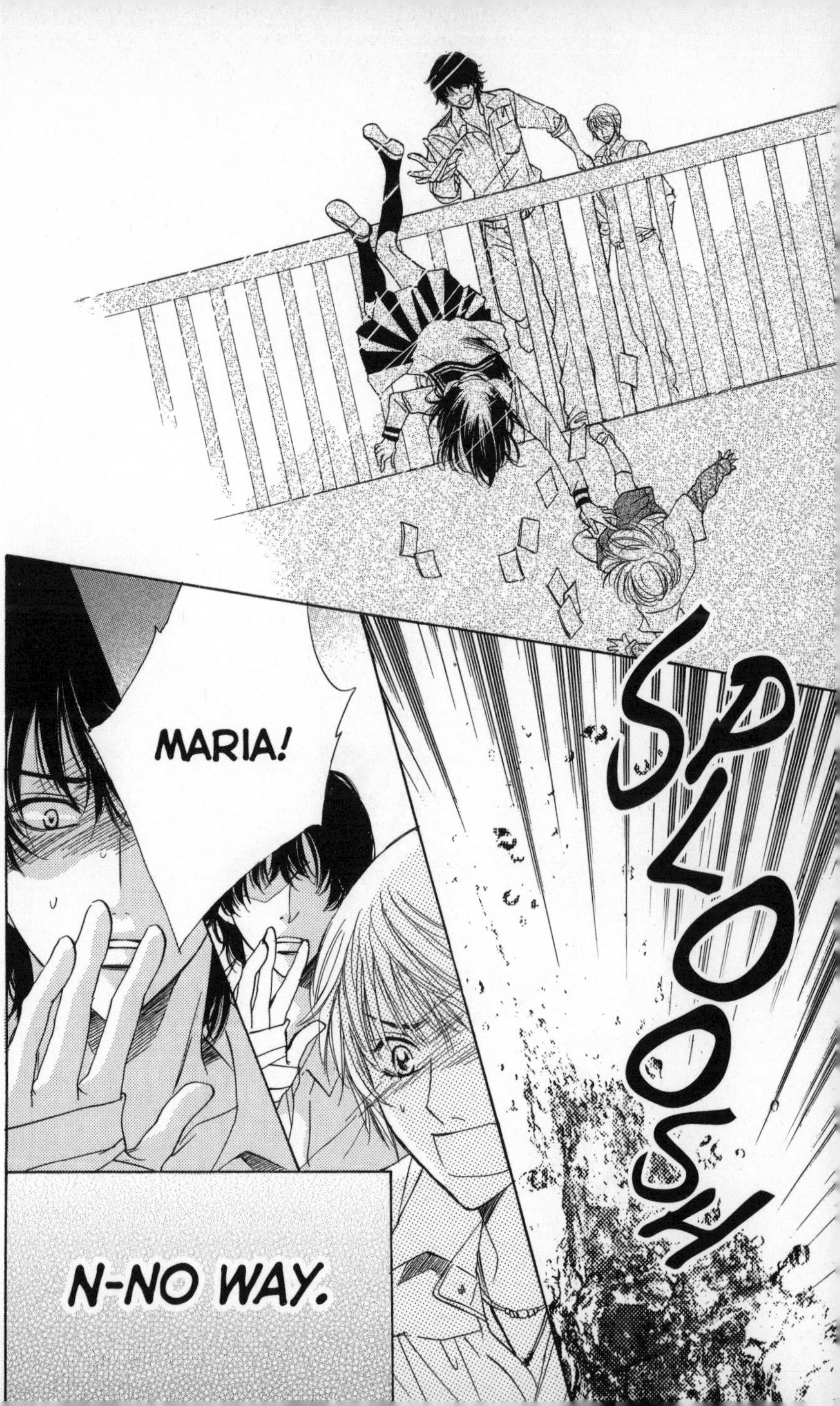
MARIA!
N-NO WAY.

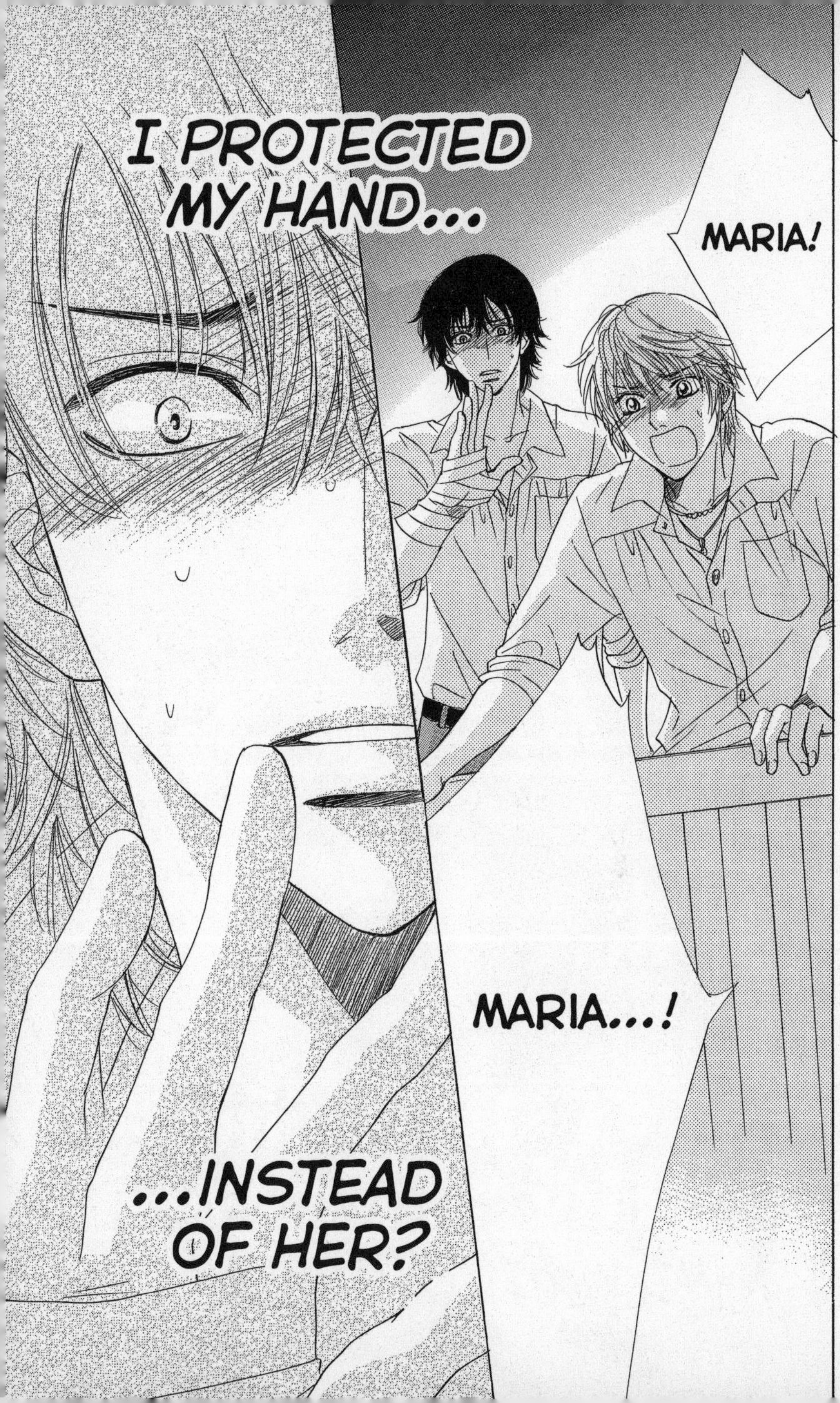
MARIA!
MARIA...!
I PROTECTED MY HAND...
...INSTEAD OF HER?

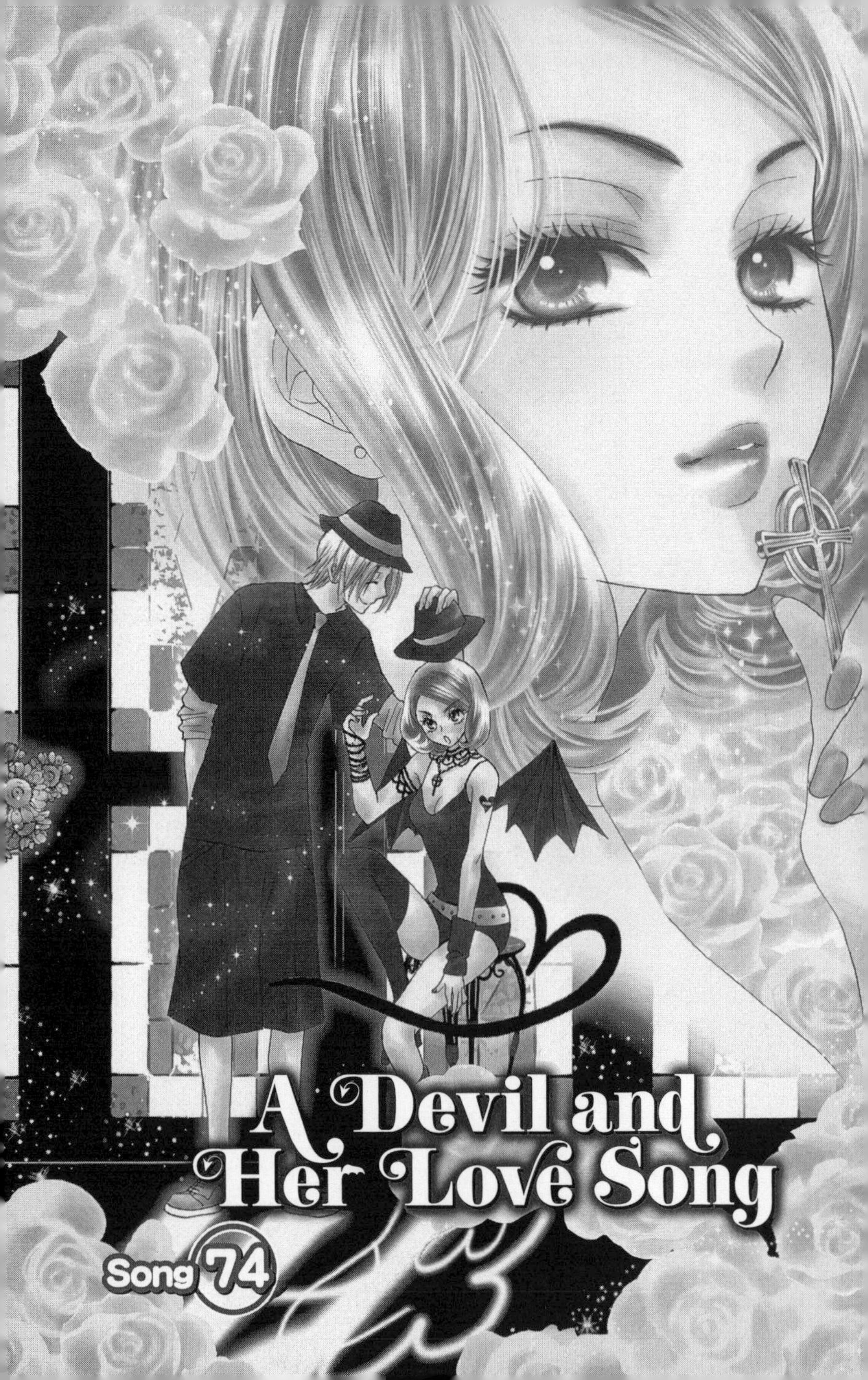
A Devil and Her Love Song
Song 74

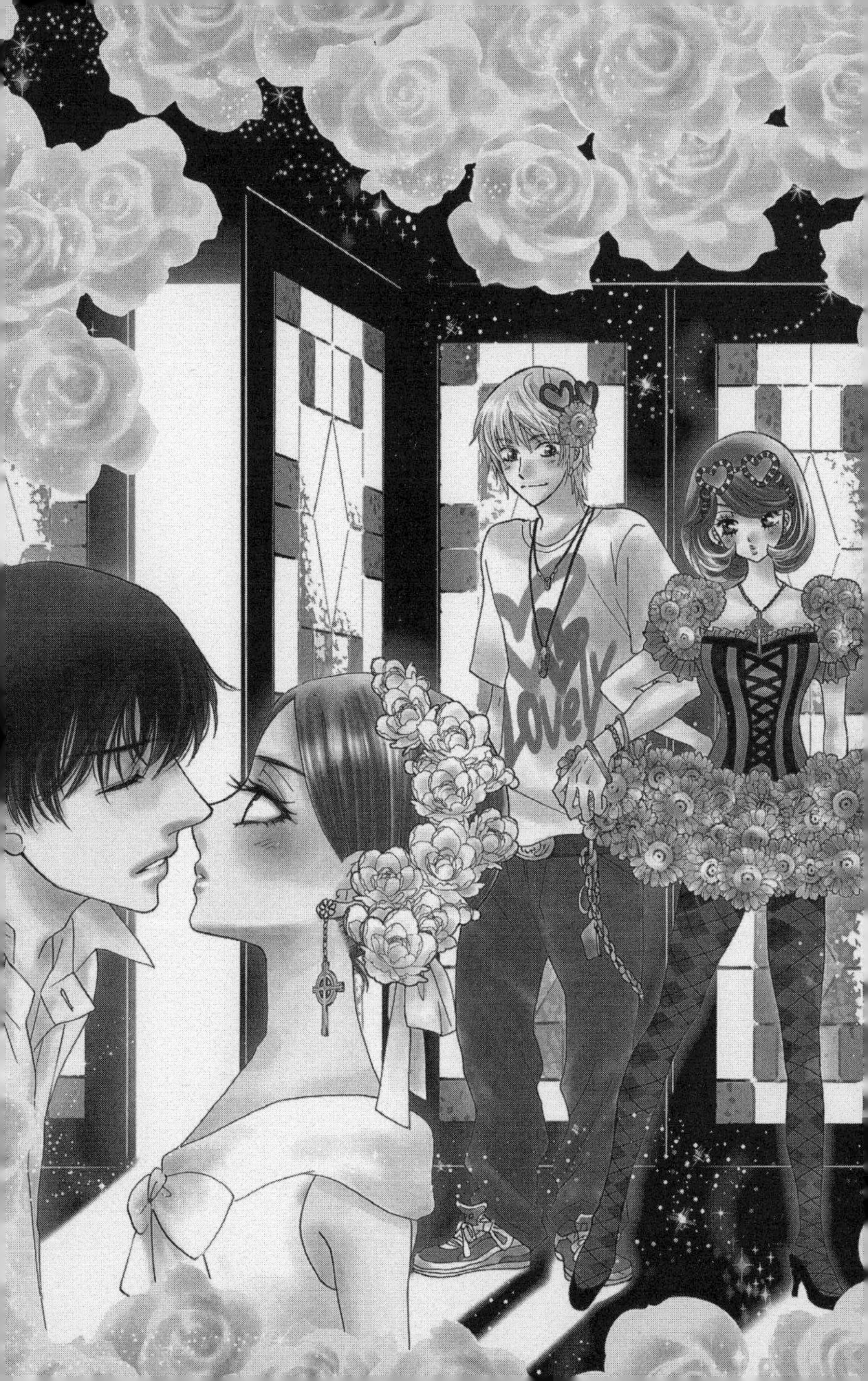

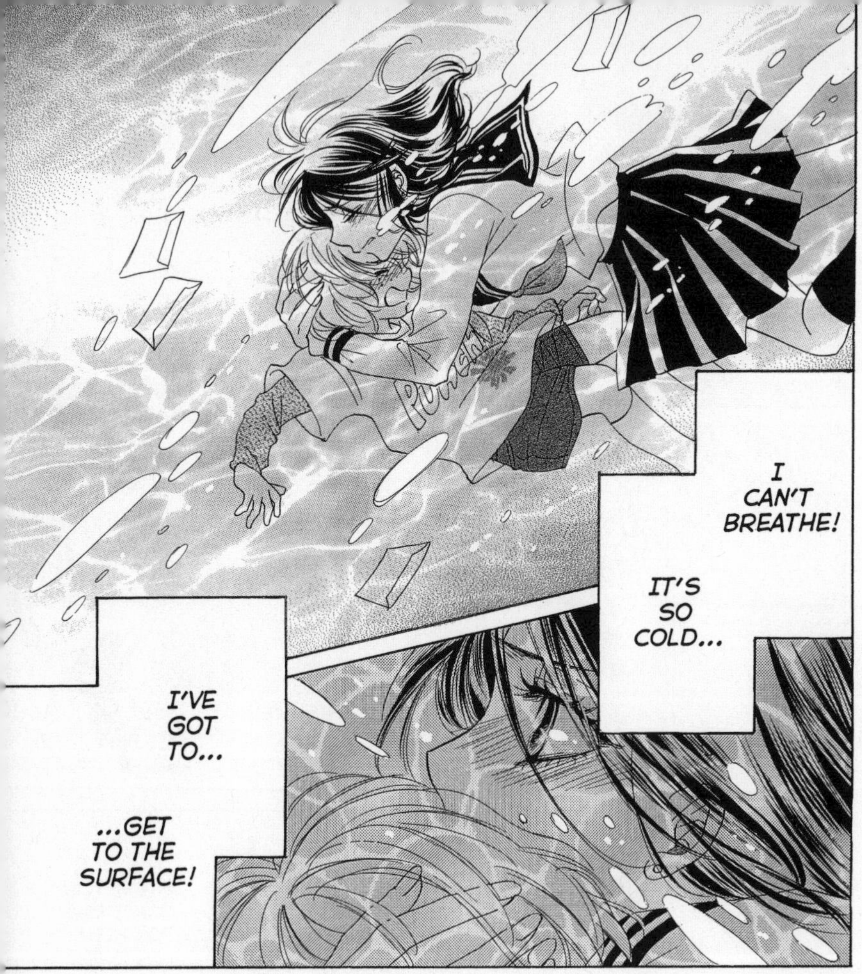
I CAN'T BREATHE!
IT'S SO COLD...
I'VE GOT TO...
...GET TO THE SURFACE!

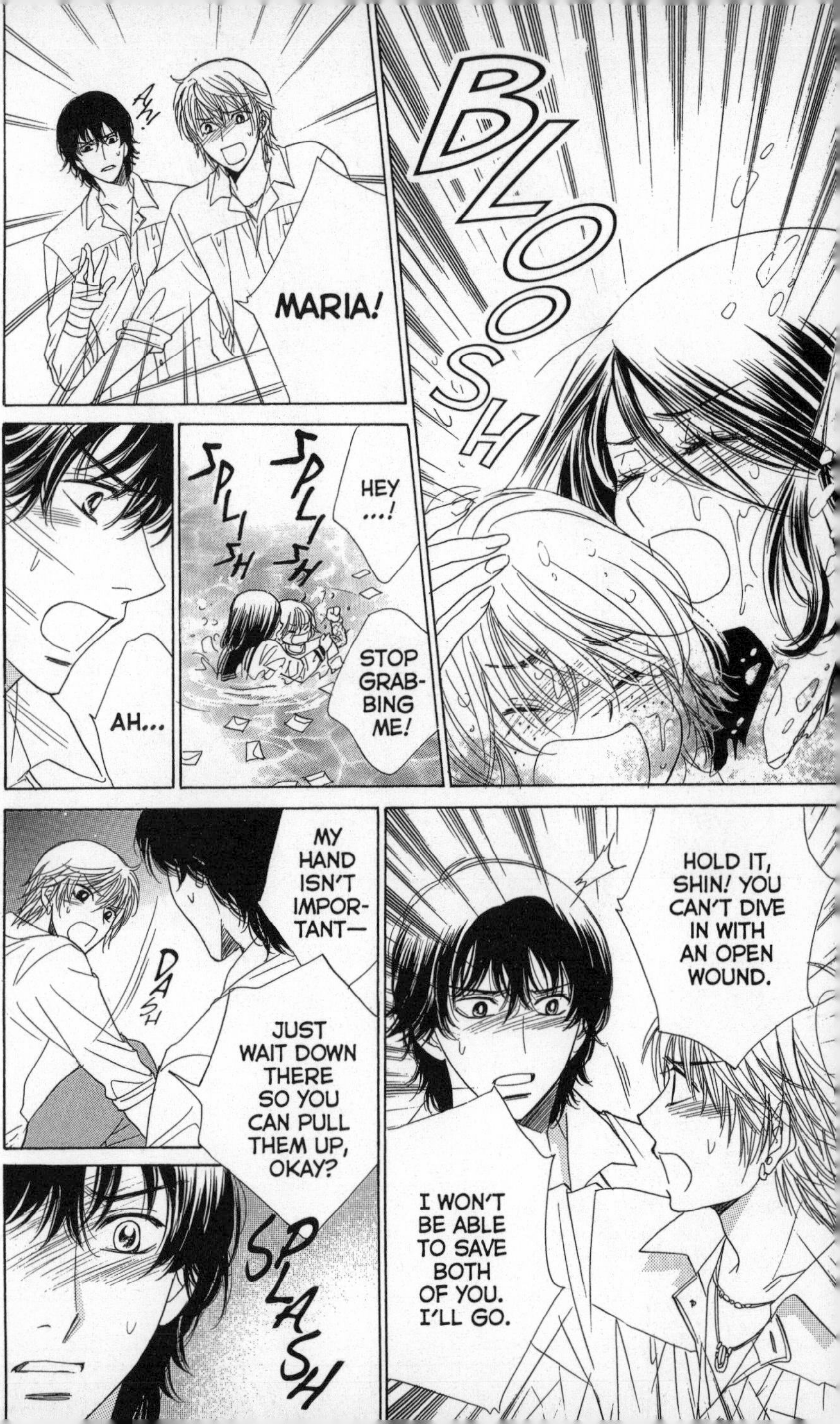
BLOOOSH
MARIA!
AH!
HEY ...!
SPLISH
SPLISH
STOP GRAB-BING ME!
AH...
HOLD IT, SHIN! YOU CAN'T DIVE IN WITH AN OPEN WOUND.
I WON'T BE ABLE TO SAVE BOTH OF YOU. I'LL GO.
MY HAND ISN'T IMPOR-TANT—
JUST WAIT DOWN THERE SO YOU CAN PULL THEM UP, OKAY?
DASH
SPLASH

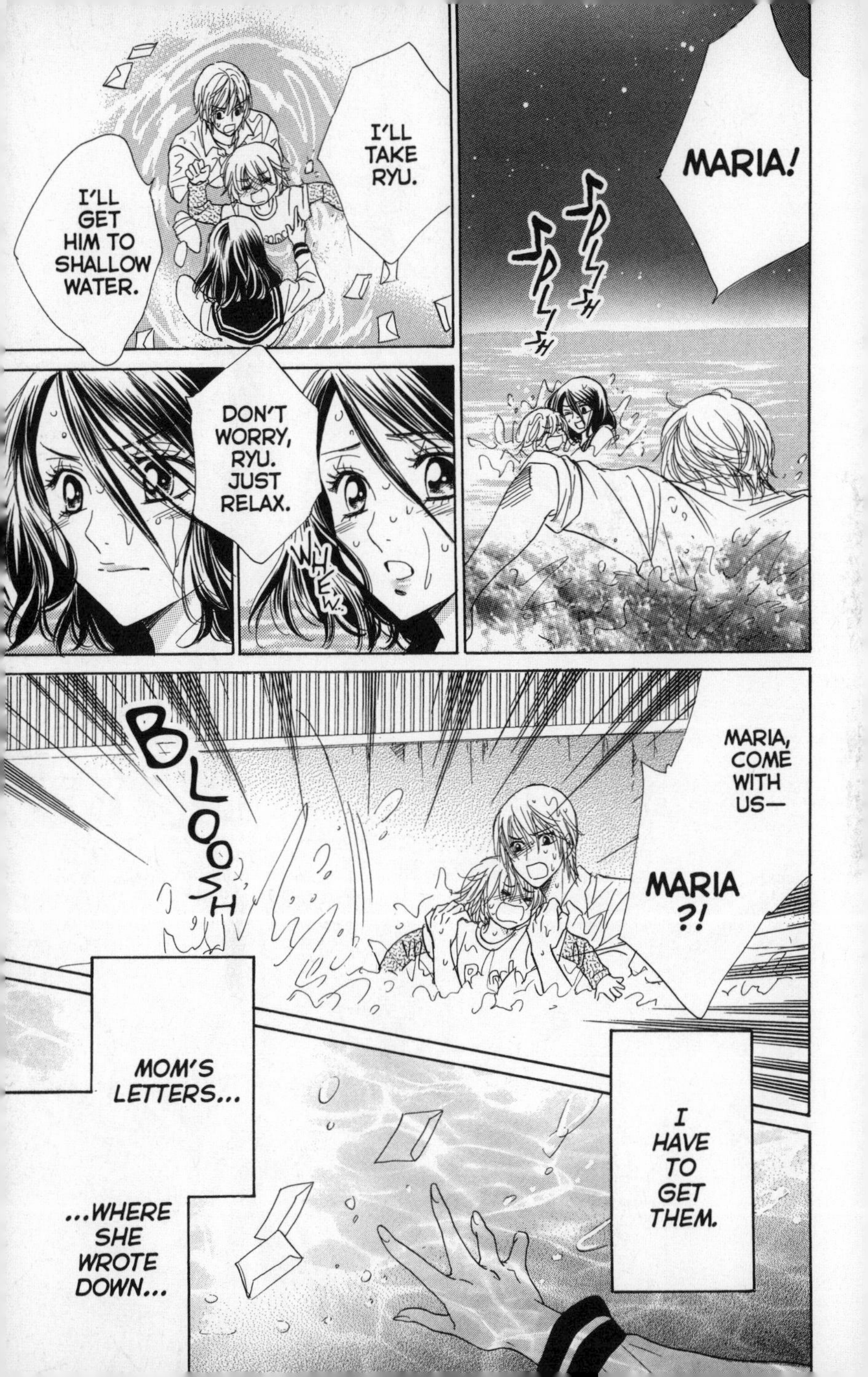
MARIA!
SPLISH
SPLISH
I'LL TAKE RYU.
I'LL GET HIM TO SHALLOW WATER.
DON'T WORRY, RYU. JUST RELAX.
WHEW...
MARIA, COME WITH US—
MARIA?!
BLOOSH
I HAVE TO GET THEM.
MOM'S LETTERS...
...WHERE SHE WROTE DOWN...

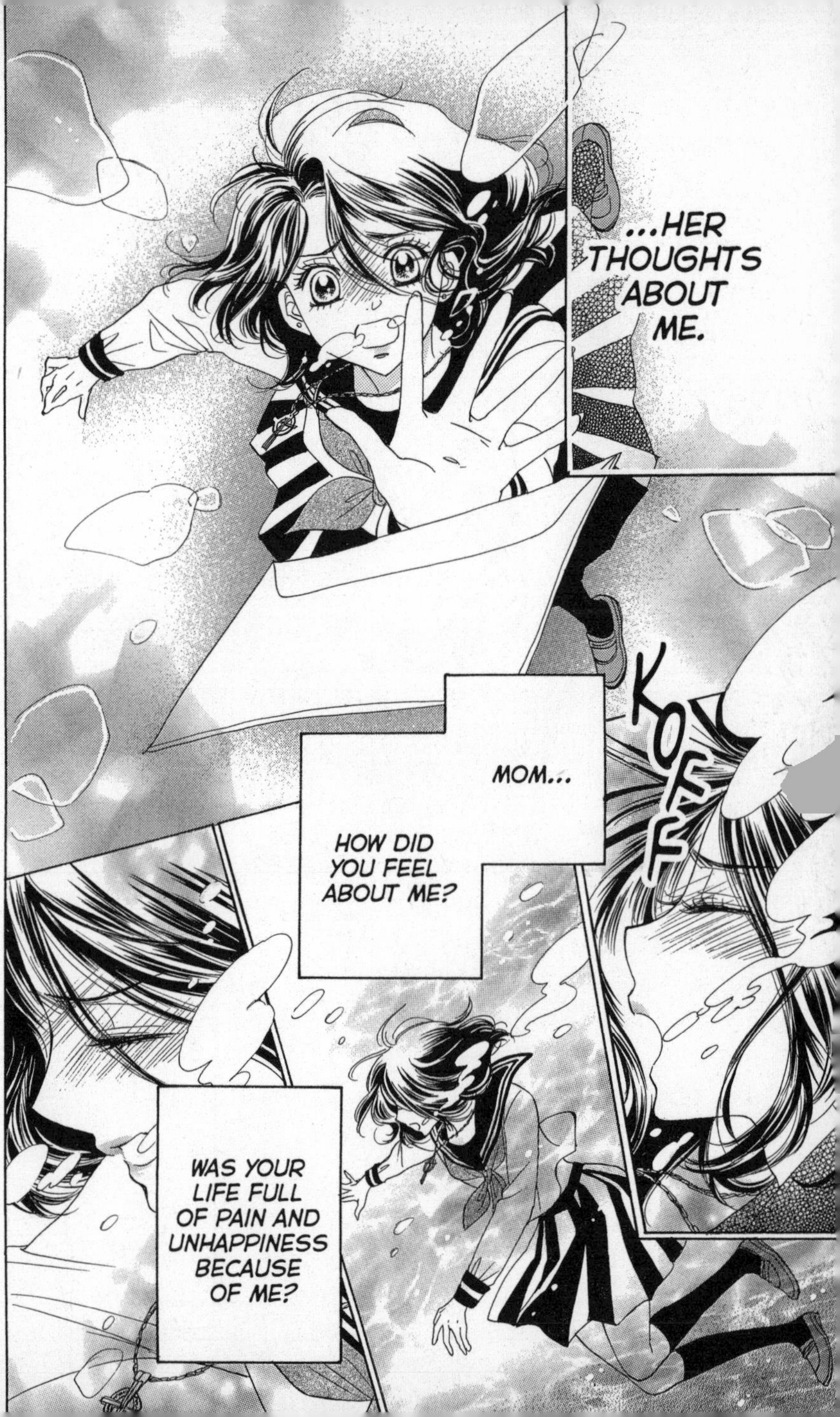
...HER THOUGHTS ABOUT ME.
KOFF
MOM...
HOW DID YOU FEEL ABOUT ME?
WAS YOUR LIFE FULL OF PAIN AND UNHAPPINESS BECAUSE OF ME?

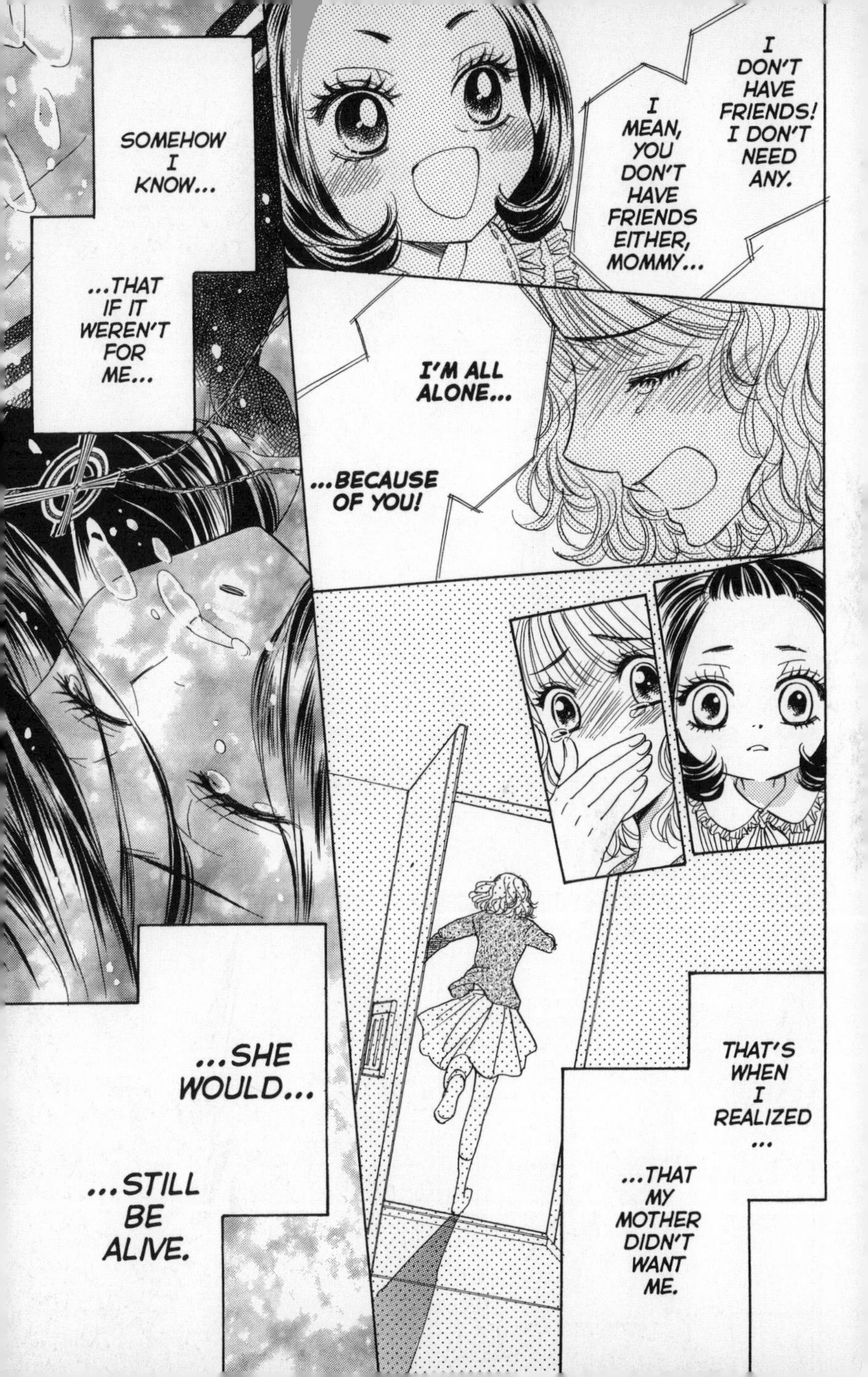
I DON'T HAVE FRIENDS! I DON'T NEED ANY.
I MEAN, YOU DON'T HAVE FRIENDS EITHER, MOMMY...
I'M ALL ALONE...
...BECAUSE OF YOU!
THAT'S WHEN I REALIZED...
...THAT MY MOTHER DIDN'T WANT ME.
SOMEHOW I KNOW...
...THAT IF IT WEREN'T FOR ME...
...SHE WOULD...
...STILL BE ALIVE.

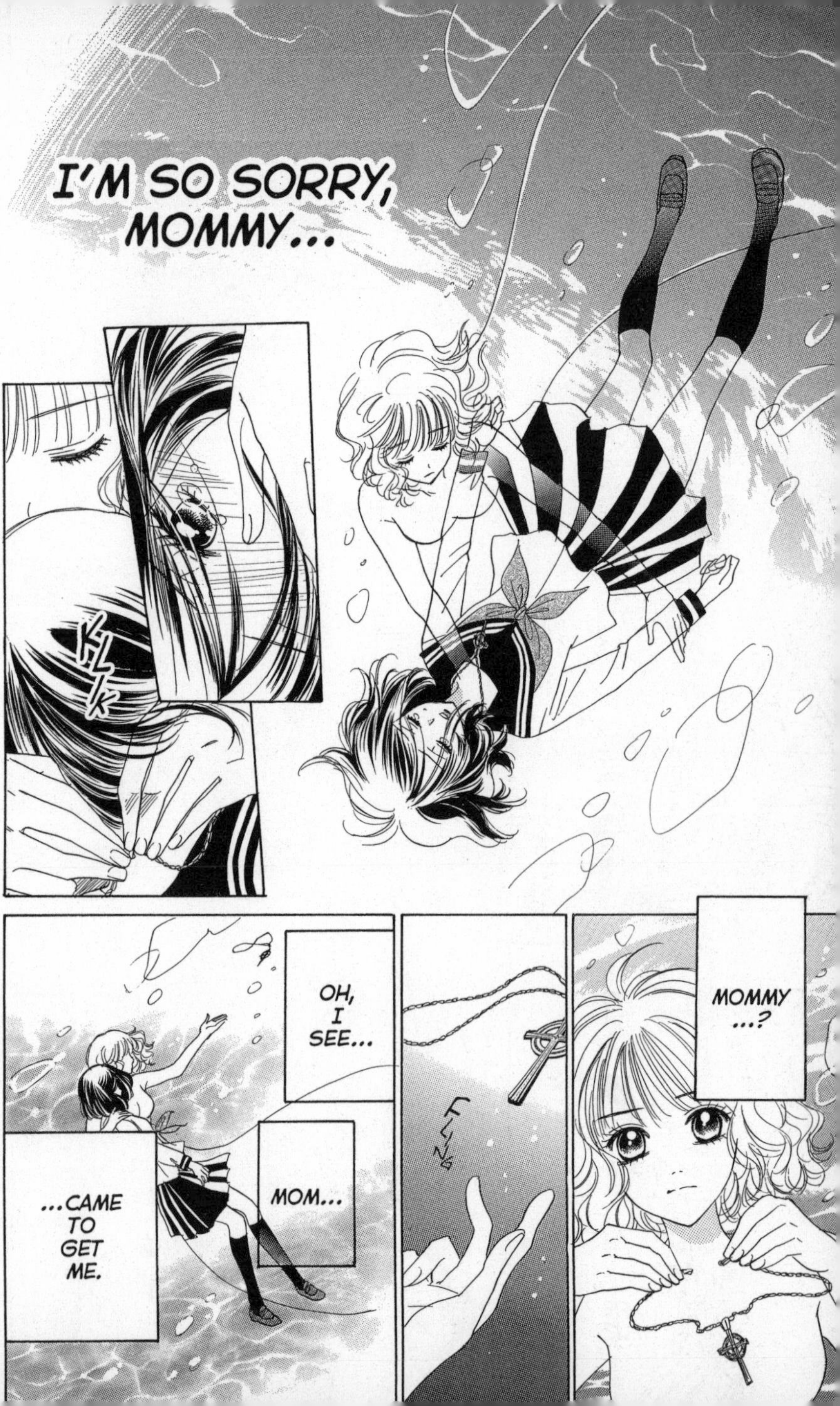
I'M SO SORRY, MOMMY...
KLIK
MOMMY ...?
FLING
OH, I SEE...
MOM...
...CAME TO GET ME.

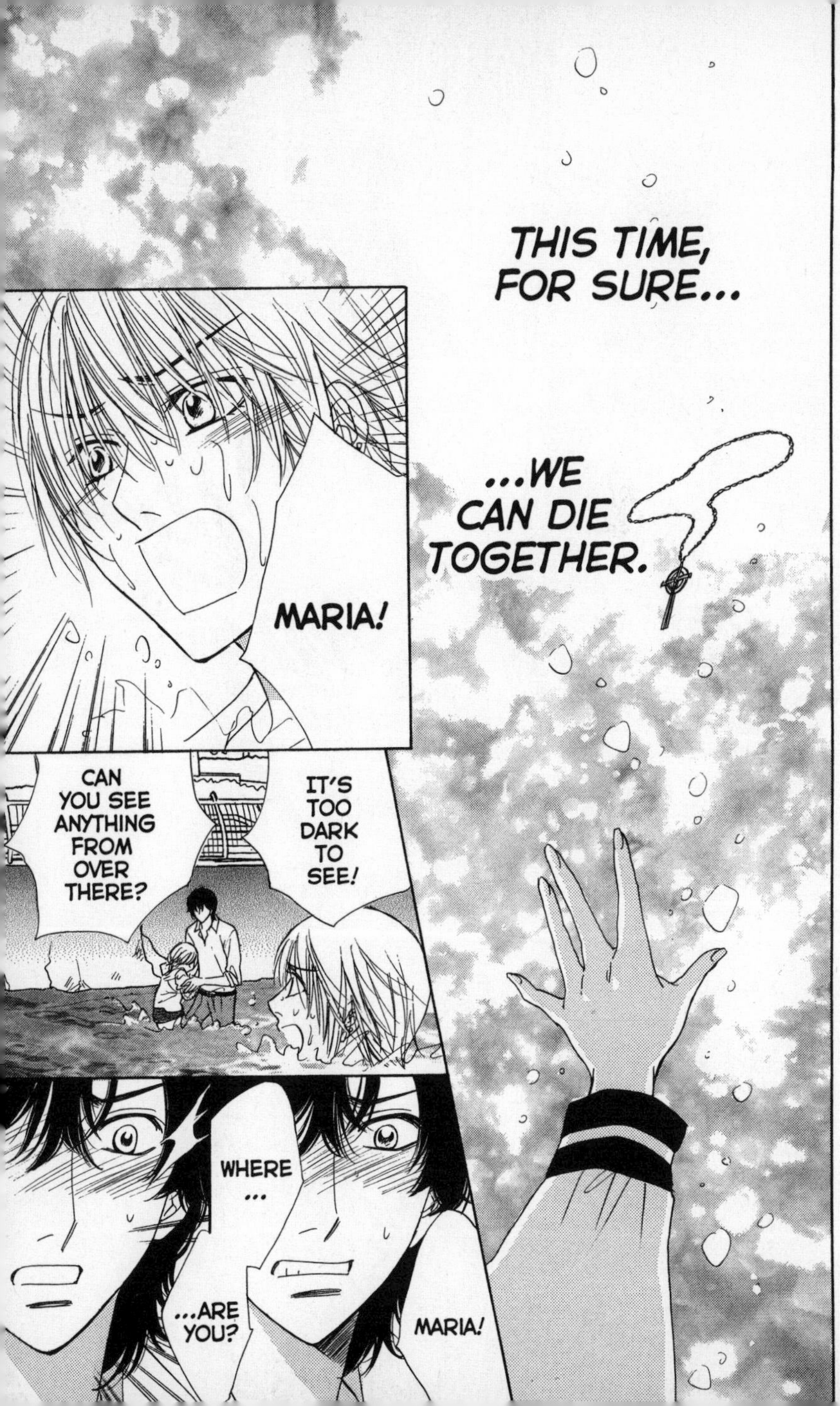
THIS TIME, FOR SURE...
...WE CAN DIE TOGETHER.
MARIA!
CAN YOU SEE ANYTHING FROM OVER THERE?
IT'S TOO DARK TO SEE!
WHERE...
...ARE YOU?
MARIA!

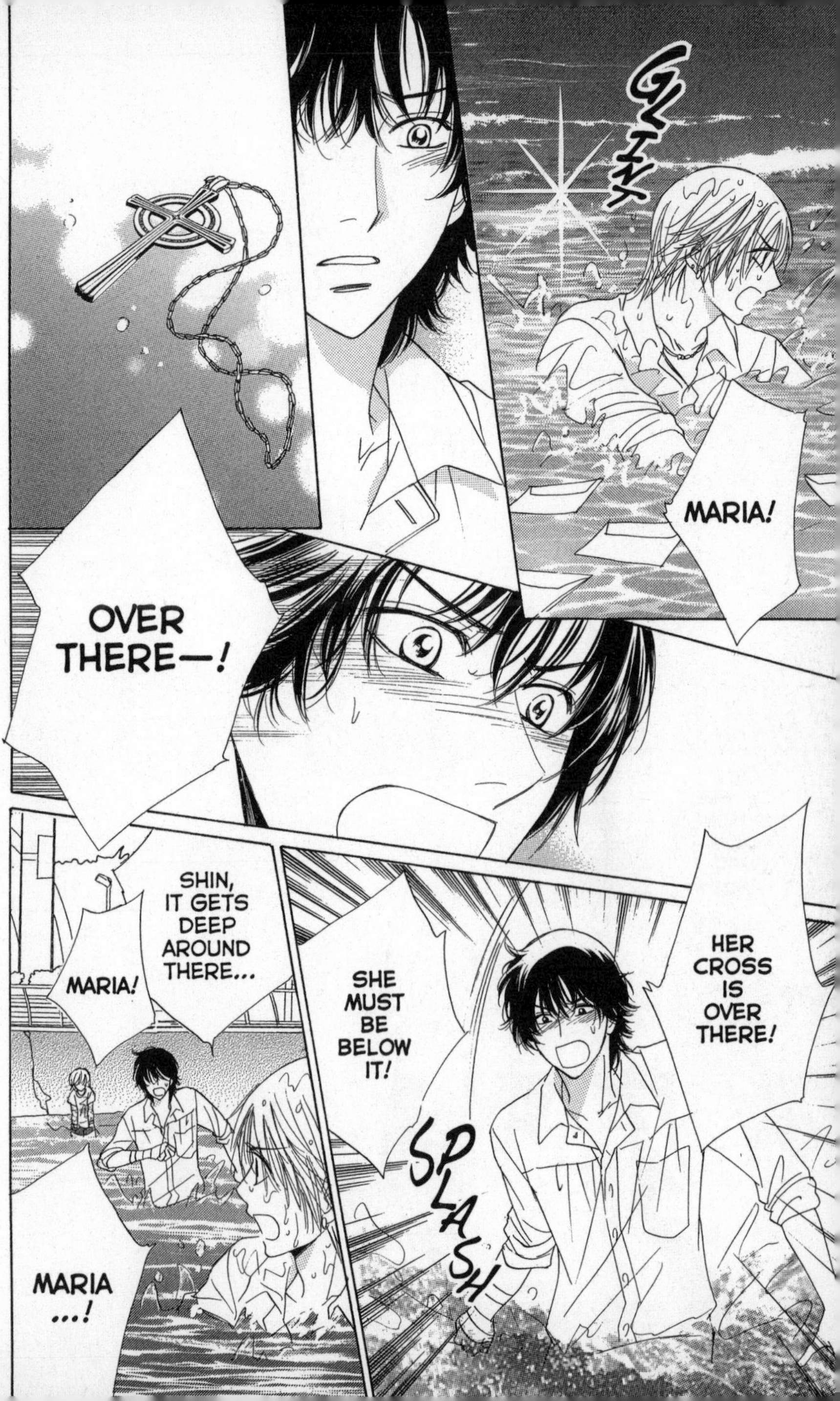
GLINT
MARIA!
OVER THERE—!
HER CROSS IS OVER THERE!
SHE MUST BE BELOW IT!
SPLASH
SHIN, IT GETS DEEP AROUND THERE...
MARIA!
MARIA ...!

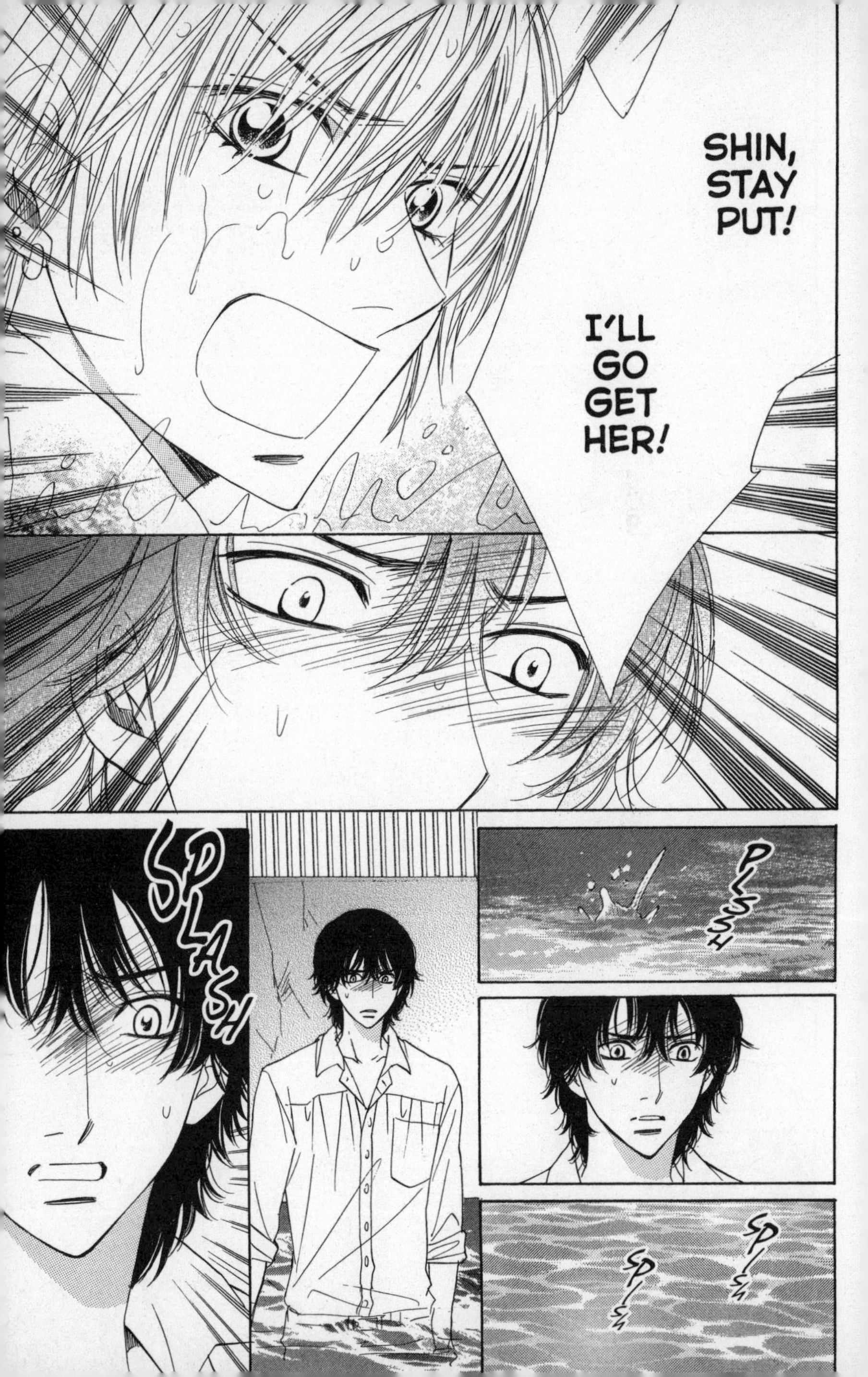
SHIN, STAY PUT!
I'LL GO GET HER!
PLSSH
SPLASH
SPLSH
SPLSH

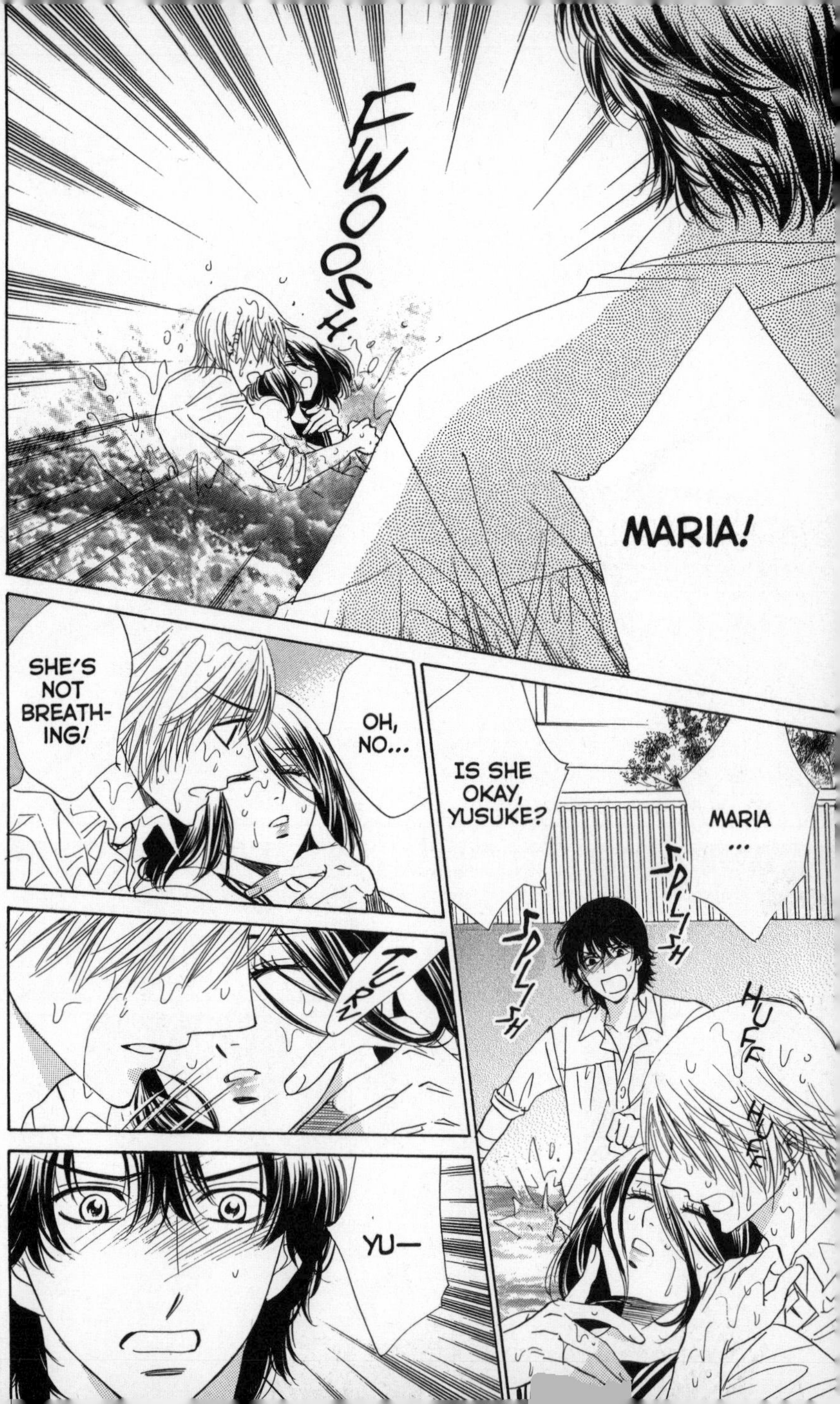
FWOOSH
MARIA!
MARIA ...
IS SHE OKAY, YUSUKE?
SPLISH
SPLISH
HUFF
HUFF
OH, NO...
SHE'S NOT BREATH-ING!
TURN
YU—

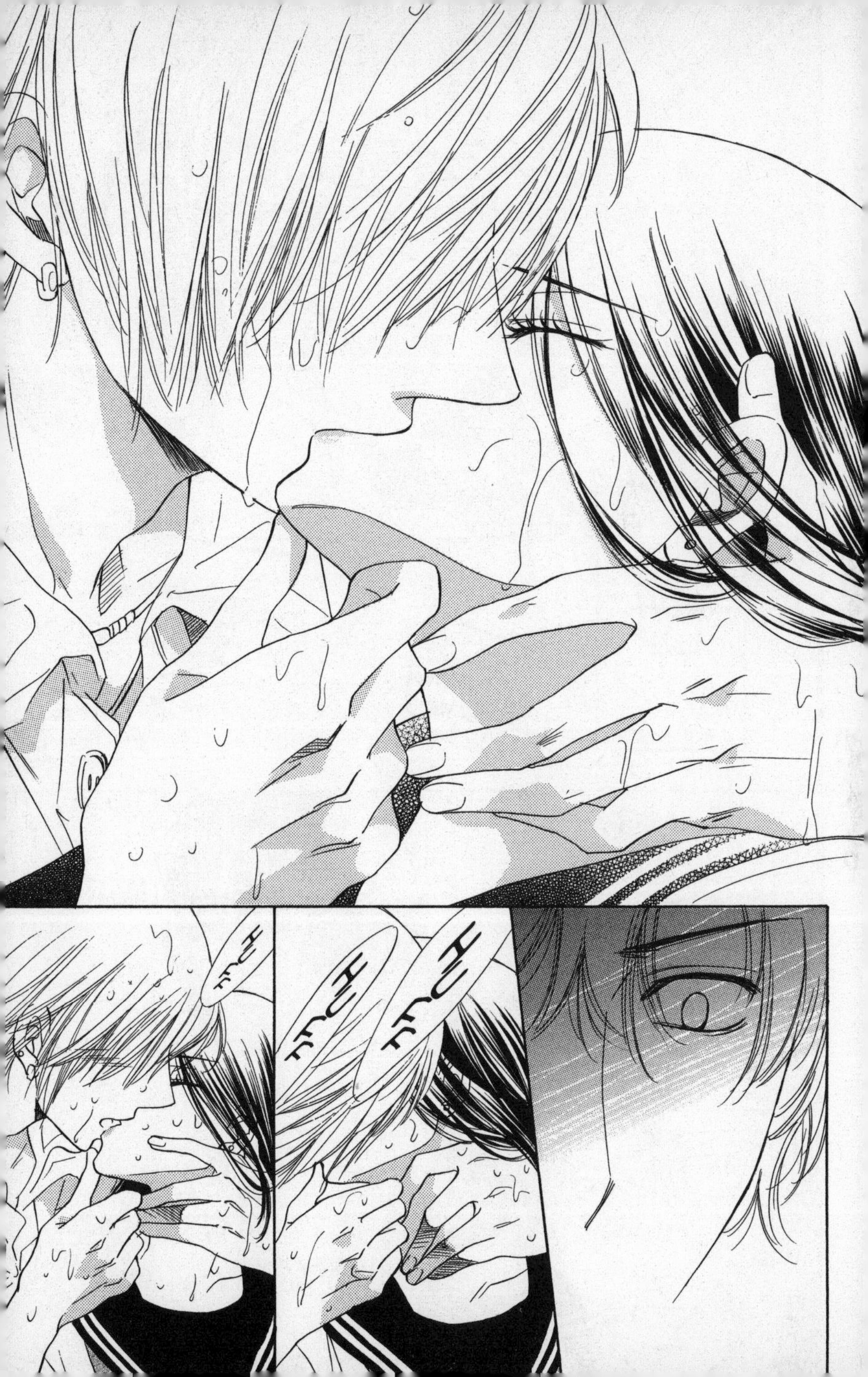
HUFF
HUFF
HUFF

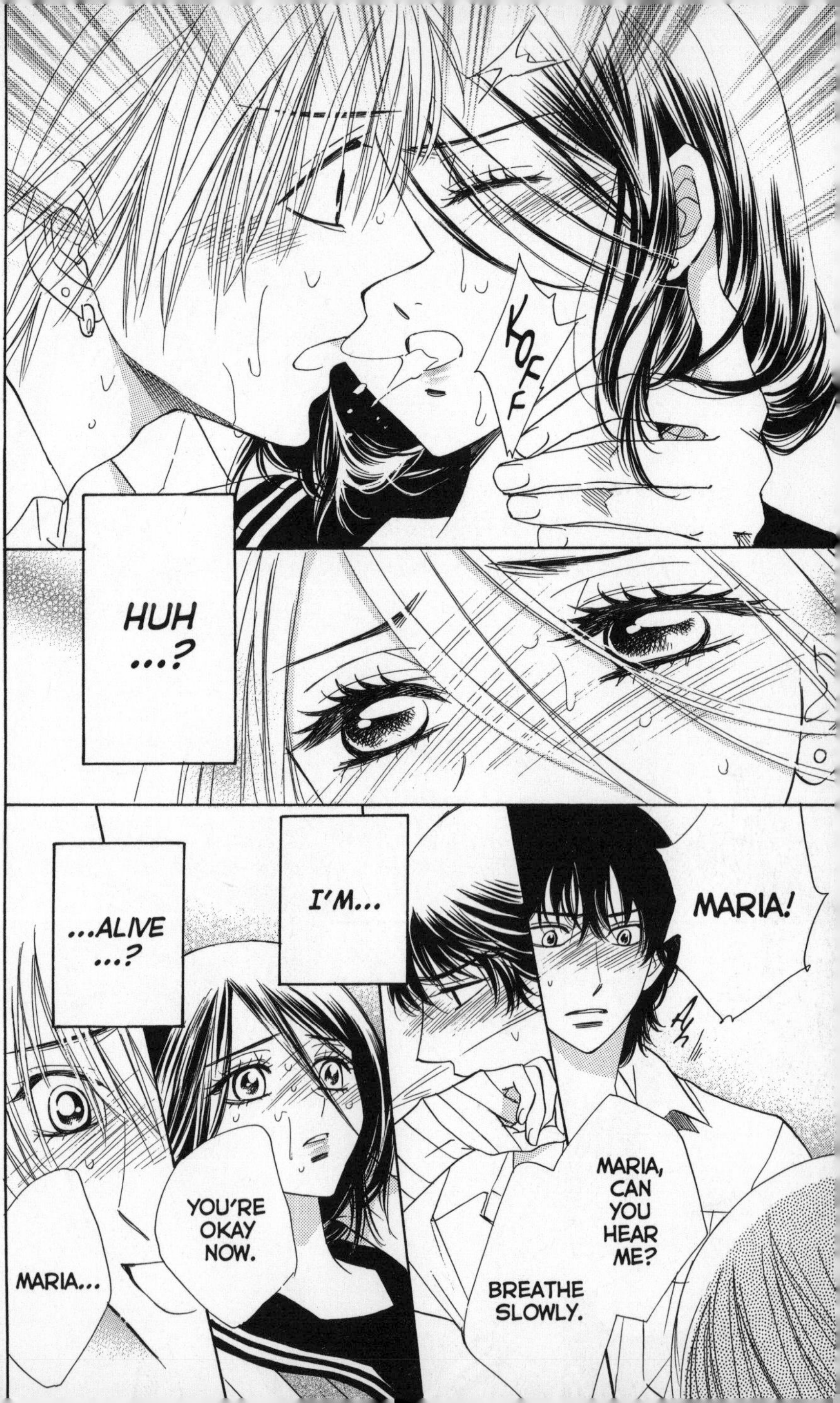
KOFF
HUH ...?
MARIA!
I'M...
...ALIVE ...?
AH
MARIA, CAN YOU HEAR ME?
BREATHE SLOWLY.
YOU'RE OKAY NOW.
MARIA...

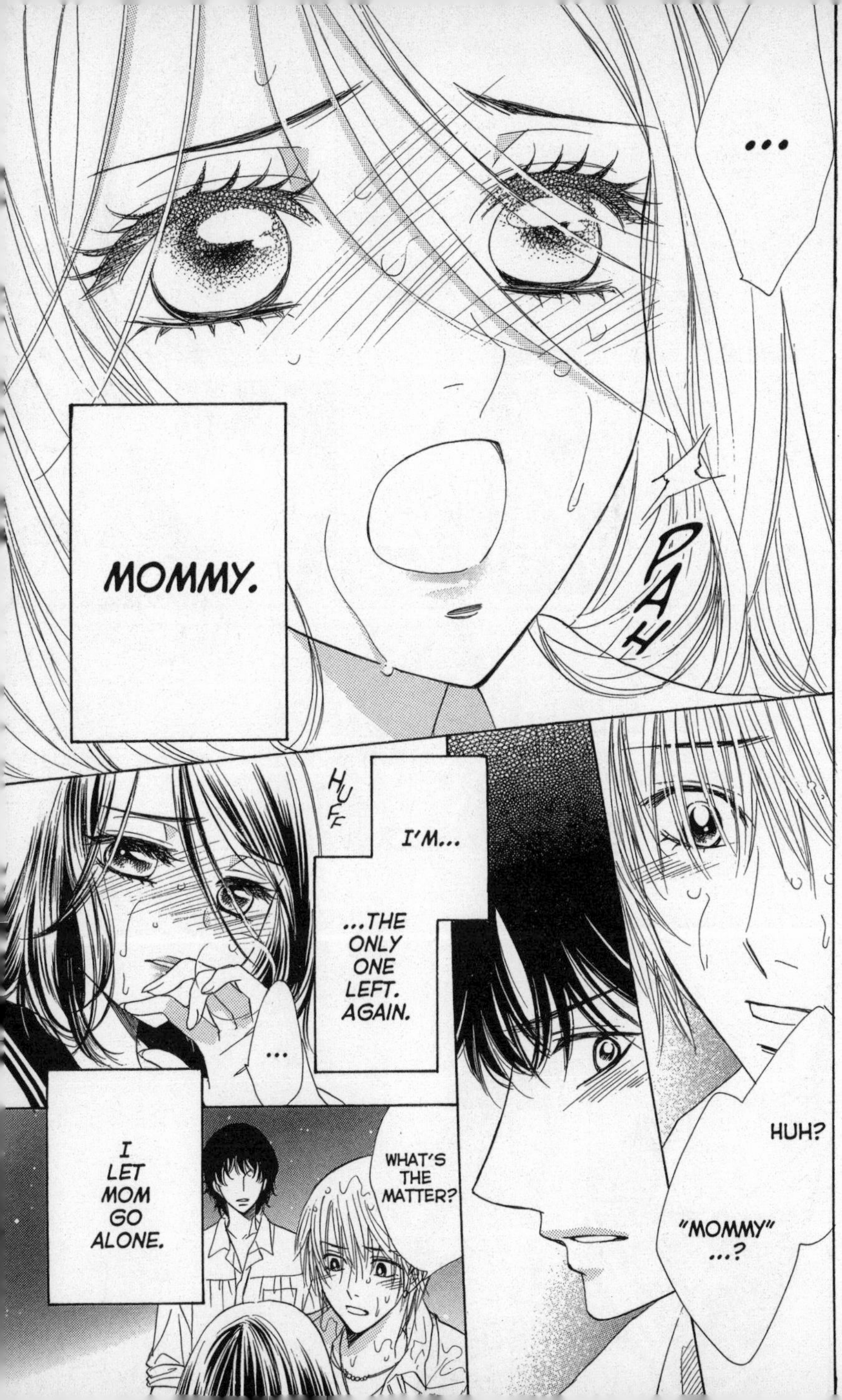
...
PAH
MOMMY.
HUFF
I'M...
...THE ONLY ONE LEFT. AGAIN.
...
HUH?
"MOMMY" ...?
WHAT'S THE MATTER?
I LET MOM GO ALONE.

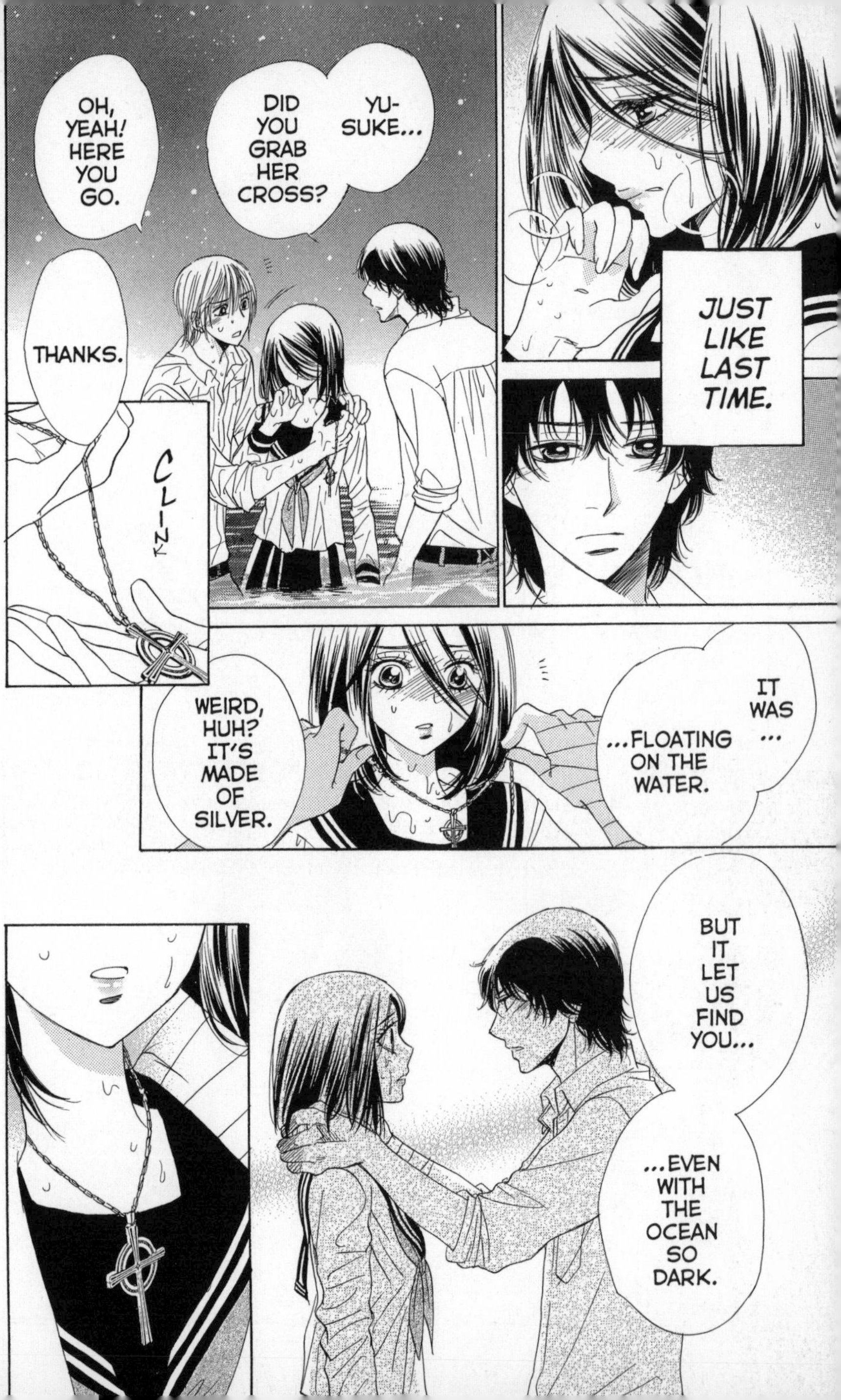
JUST LIKE LAST TIME.
YU-SUKE...
DID YOU GRAB HER CROSS?
OH, YEAH! HERE YOU GO.
THANKS.
CLINK
IT WAS...
...FLOATING ON THE WATER.
WEIRD, HUH? IT'S MADE OF SILVER.
BUT IT LET US FIND YOU...
...EVEN WITH THE OCEAN SO DARK.

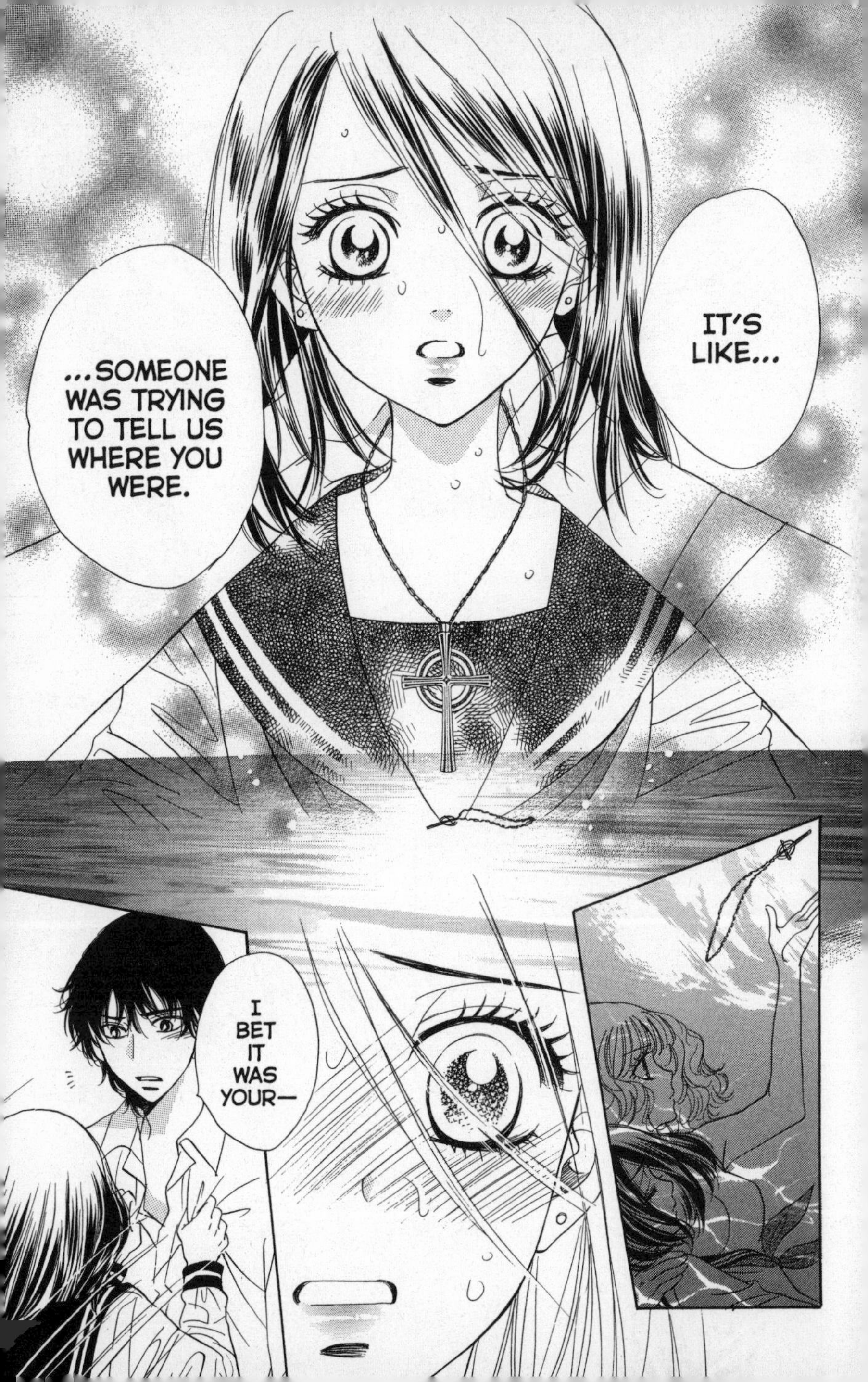
IT'S LIKE...
...SOMEONE WAS TRYING TO TELL US WHERE YOU WERE.
I BET IT WAS YOUR—

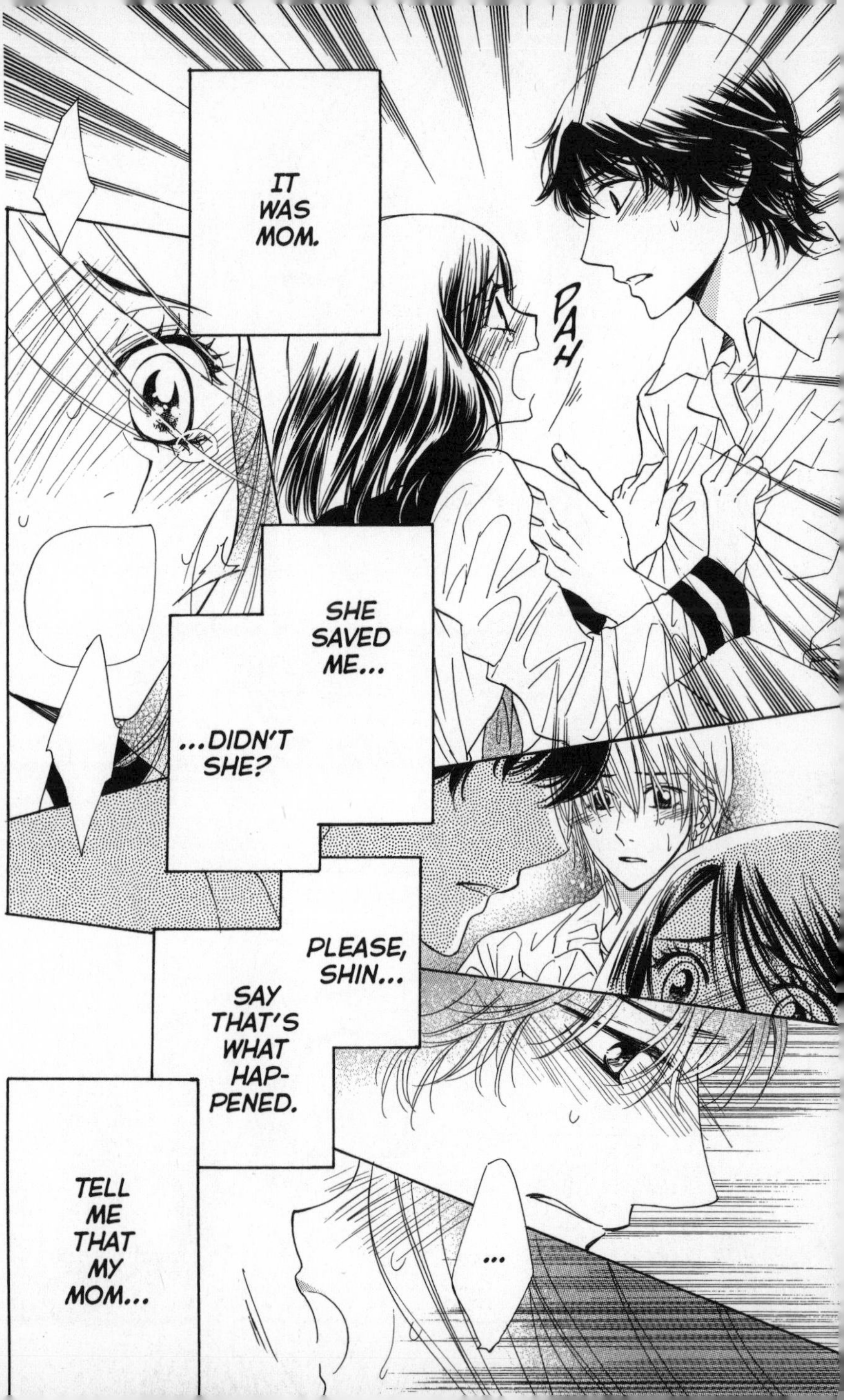
PAH
IT WAS MOM.
SHE SAVED ME...
...DIDN'T SHE?
PLEASE, SHIN...
SAY THAT'S WHAT HAP-PENED.
TELL ME THAT MY MOM...
...

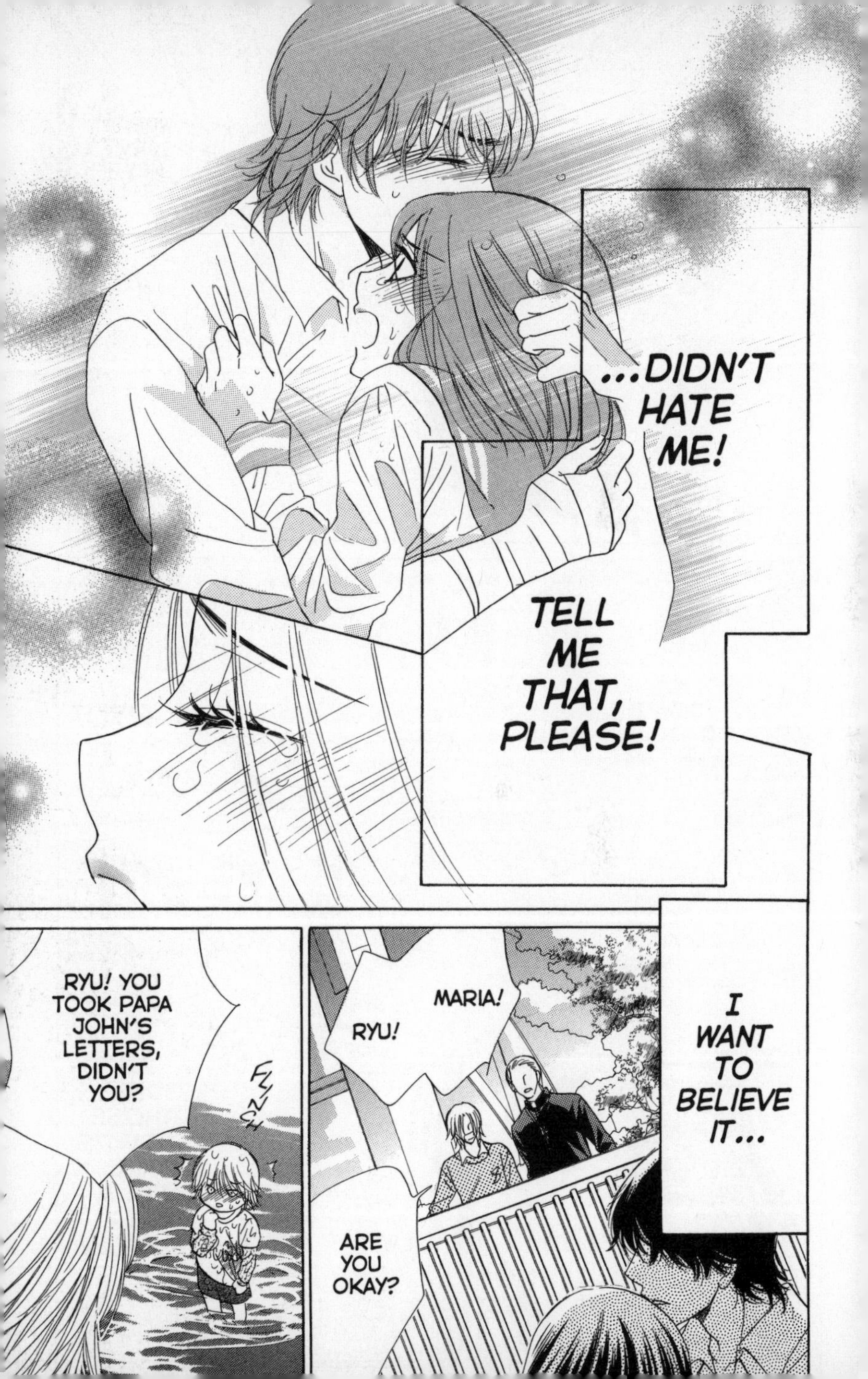
...DIDN'T HATE ME!
TELL ME THAT, PLEASE!
I WANT TO BELIEVE IT...
MARIA!
RYU!
ARE YOU OKAY?
RYU! YOU TOOK PAPA JOHN'S LETTERS, DIDN'T YOU?
FLINCH

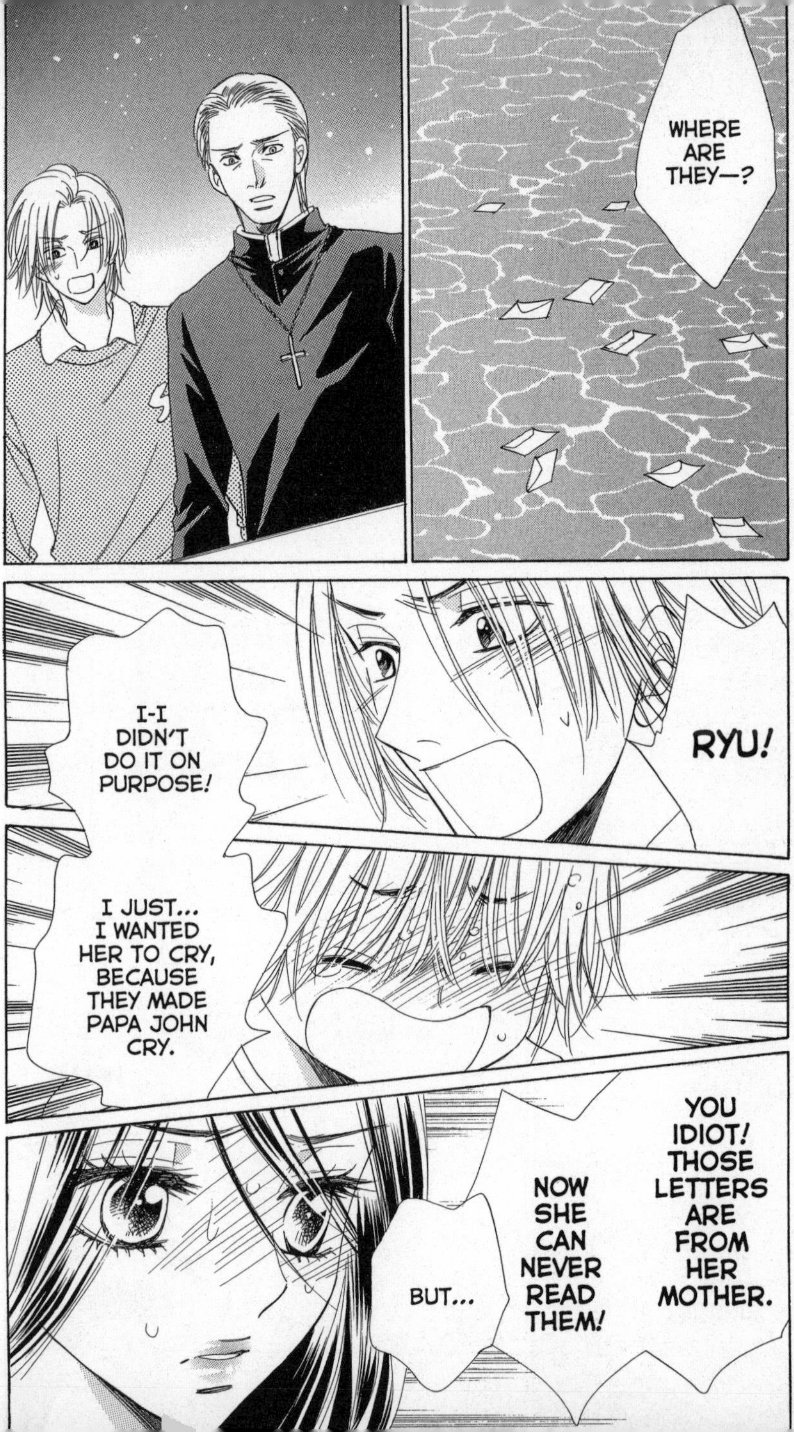
WHERE ARE THEY—?
RYU!
I-I DIDN'T DO IT ON PURPOSE!
I JUST... I WANTED HER TO CRY, BECAUSE THEY MADE PAPA JOHN CRY.
YOU IDIOT! THOSE LETTERS ARE FROM HER MOTHER.
NOW SHE CAN NEVER READ THEM!
BUT...

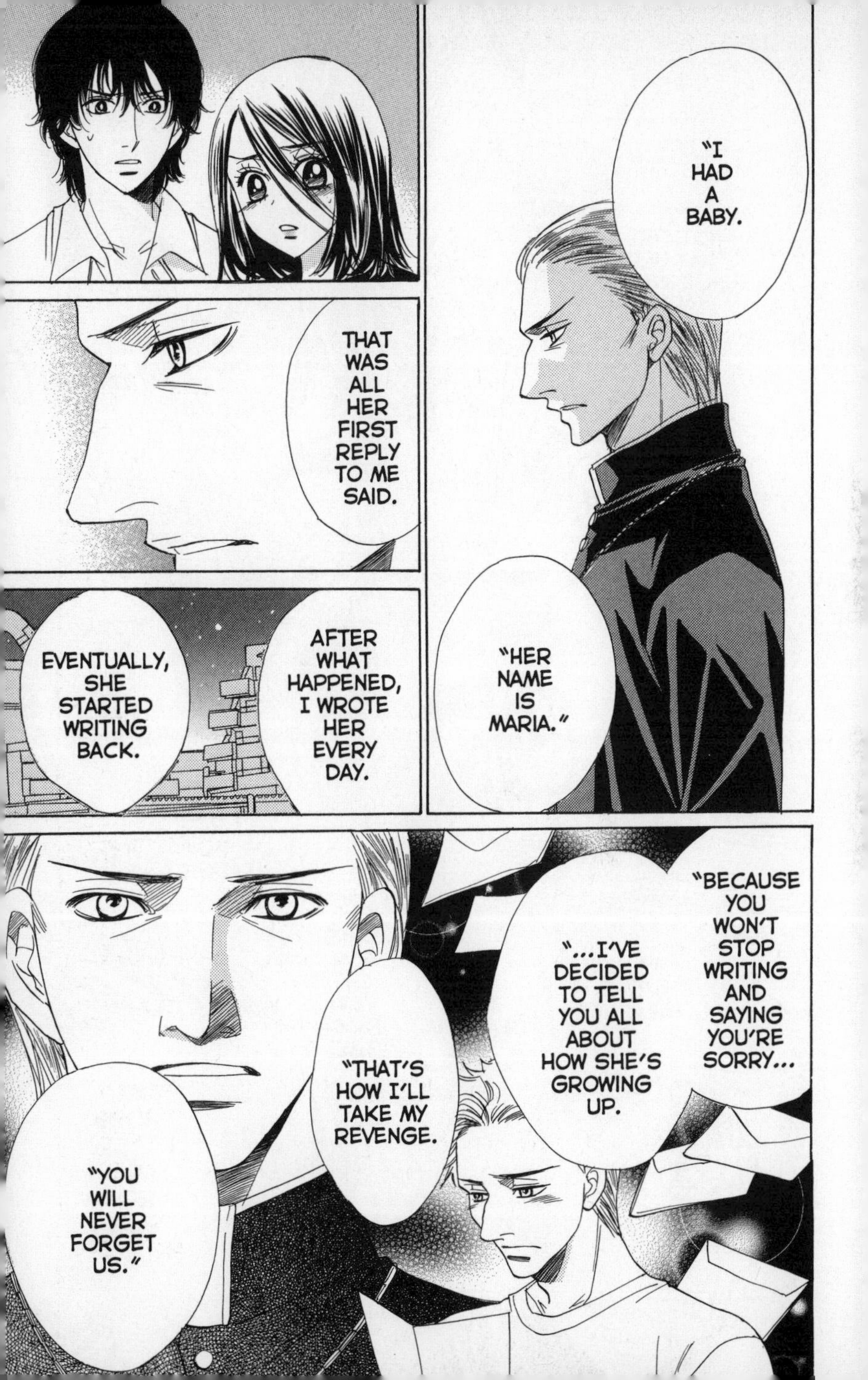
"I HAD A BABY.
"HER NAME IS MARIA."
THAT WAS ALL HER FIRST REPLY TO ME SAID.
AFTER WHAT HAPPENED, I WROTE HER EVERY DAY.
EVENTUALLY, SHE STARTED WRITING BACK.
"BECAUSE YOU WON'T STOP WRITING AND SAYING YOU'RE SORRY...
"...I'VE DECIDED TO TELL YOU ALL ABOUT HOW SHE'S GROWING UP.
"THAT'S HOW I'LL TAKE MY REVENGE.
"YOU WILL NEVER FORGET US."

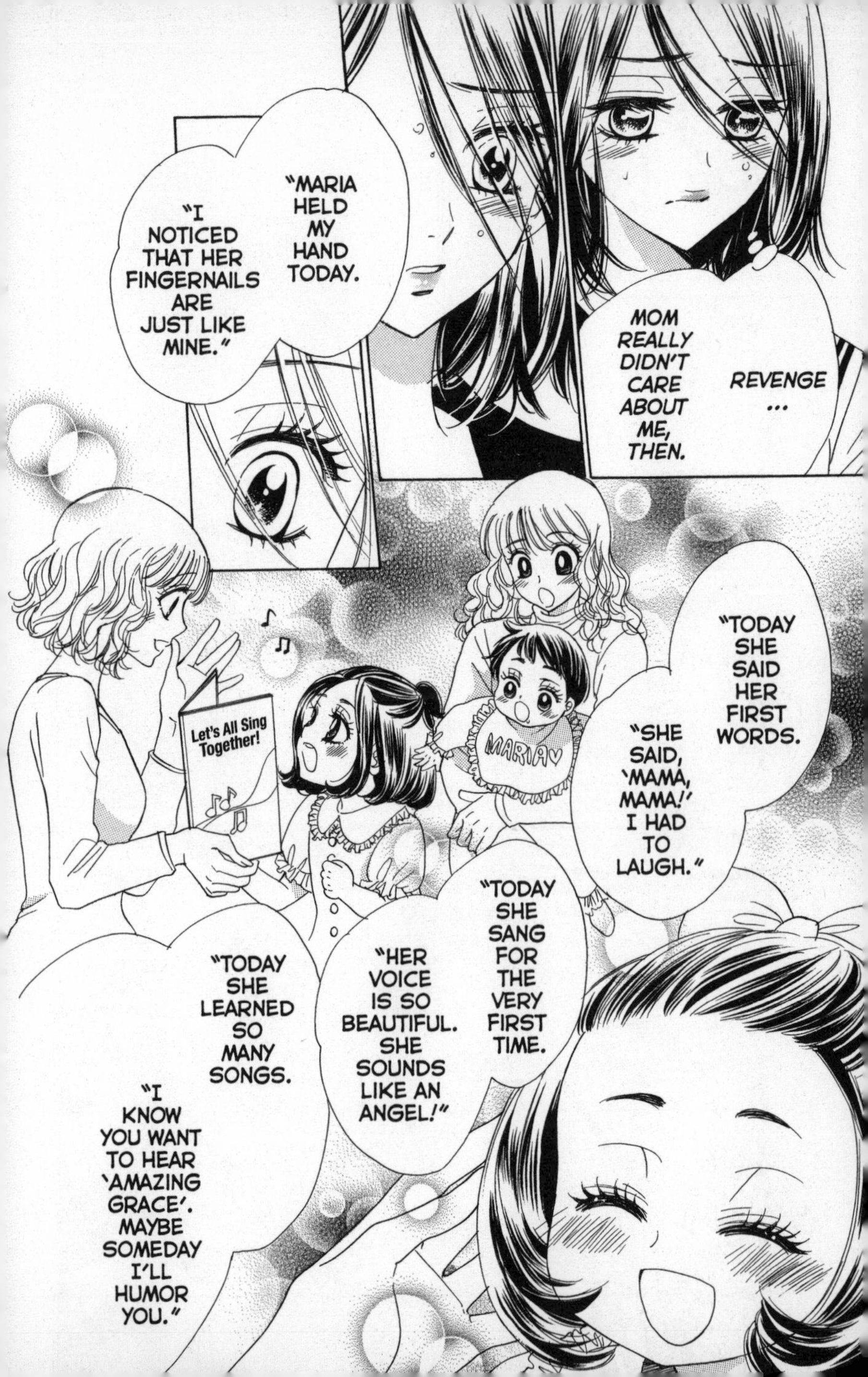
REVENGE...
MOM REALLY DIDN'T CARE ABOUT ME, THEN.
"MARIA HELD MY HAND TODAY.
"I NOTICED THAT HER FINGERNAILS ARE JUST LIKE MINE."
"TODAY SHE SAID HER FIRST WORDS.
"SHE SAID, 'MAMA, MAMA!' I HAD TO LAUGH."
MARIA♥
Let's All Sing Together!
"TODAY SHE SANG FOR THE VERY FIRST TIME.
"HER VOICE IS SO BEAUTIFUL. SHE SOUNDS LIKE AN ANGEL!"
"TODAY SHE LEARNED SO MANY SONGS.
"I KNOW YOU WANT TO HEAR 'AMAZING GRACE'. MAYBE SOMEDAY I'LL HUMOR YOU."

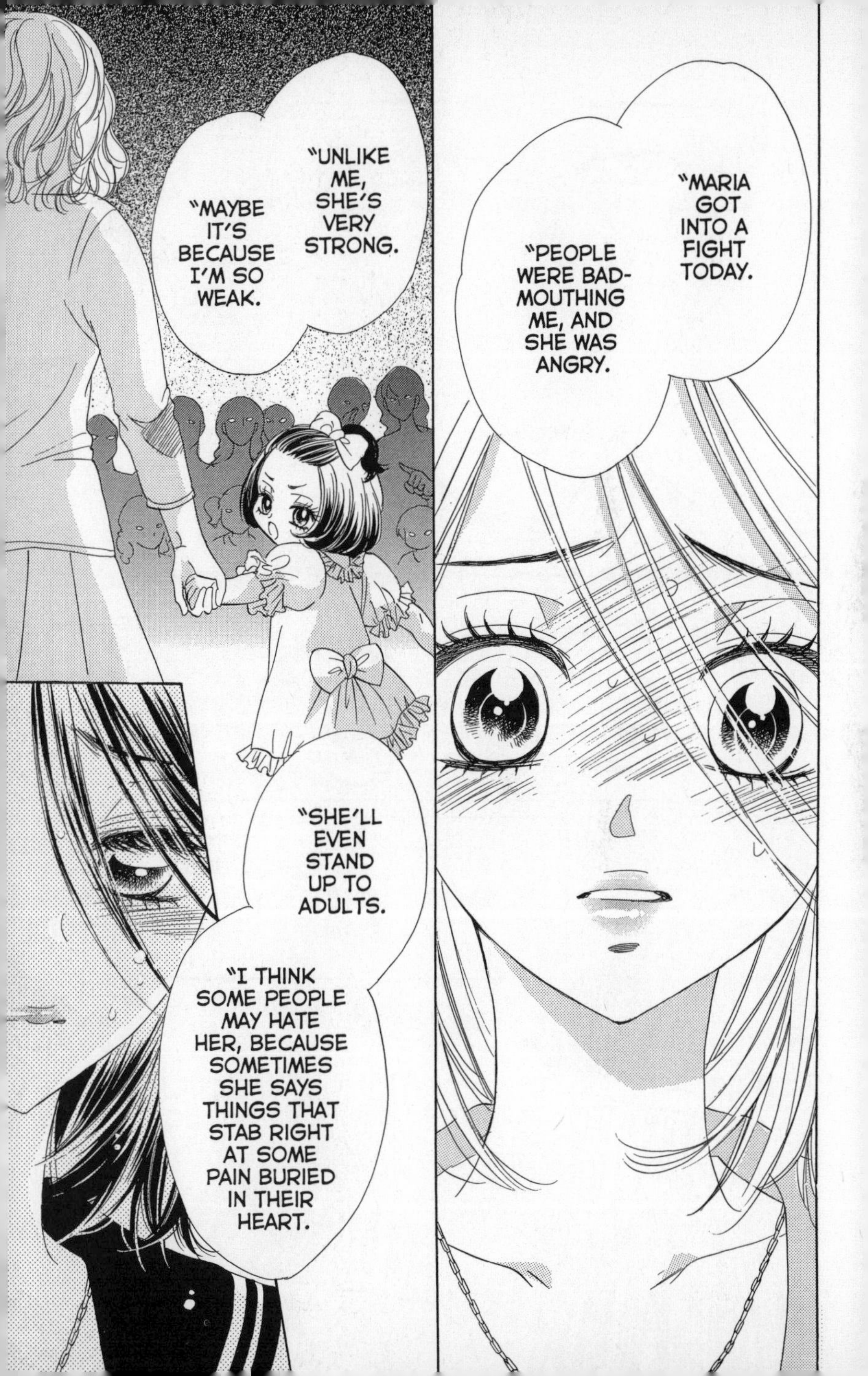
"MARIA GOT INTO A FIGHT TODAY.
"PEOPLE WERE BAD-MOUTHING ME, AND SHE WAS ANGRY.
"UNLIKE ME, SHE'S VERY STRONG.
"MAYBE IT'S BECAUSE I'M SO WEAK.
"SHE'LL EVEN STAND UP TO ADULTS.
"I THINK SOME PEOPLE MAY HATE HER, BECAUSE SOMETIMES SHE SAYS THINGS THAT STAB RIGHT AT SOME PAIN BURIED IN THEIR HEART.

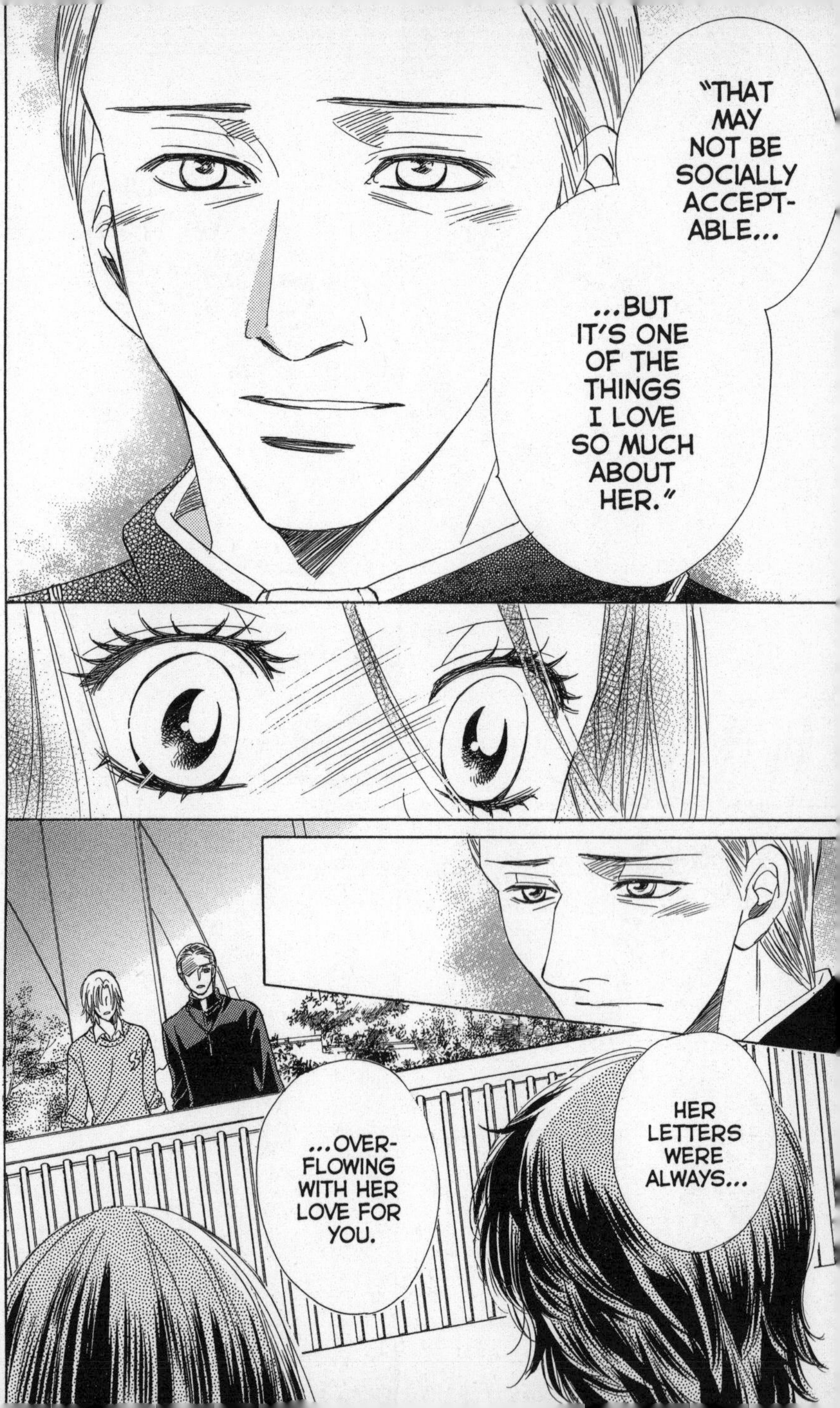
"THAT MAY NOT BE SOCIALLY ACCEPT-ABLE...
...BUT IT'S ONE OF THE THINGS I LOVE SO MUCH ABOUT HER."
HER LETTERS WERE ALWAYS...
...OVER-FLOWING WITH HER LOVE FOR YOU.

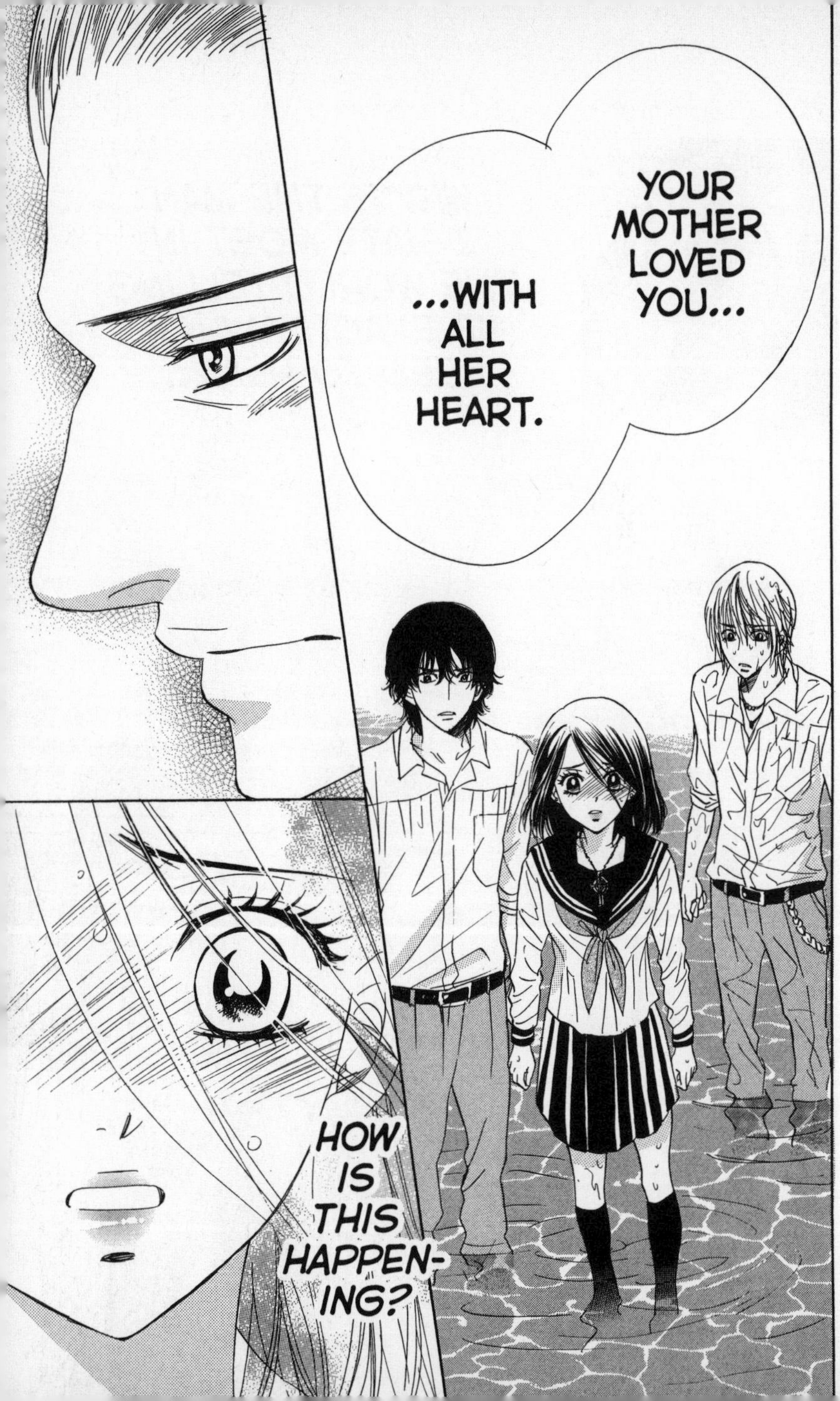
YOUR MOTHER LOVED YOU...
...WITH ALL HER HEART.
HOW IS THIS HAPPEN-ING?

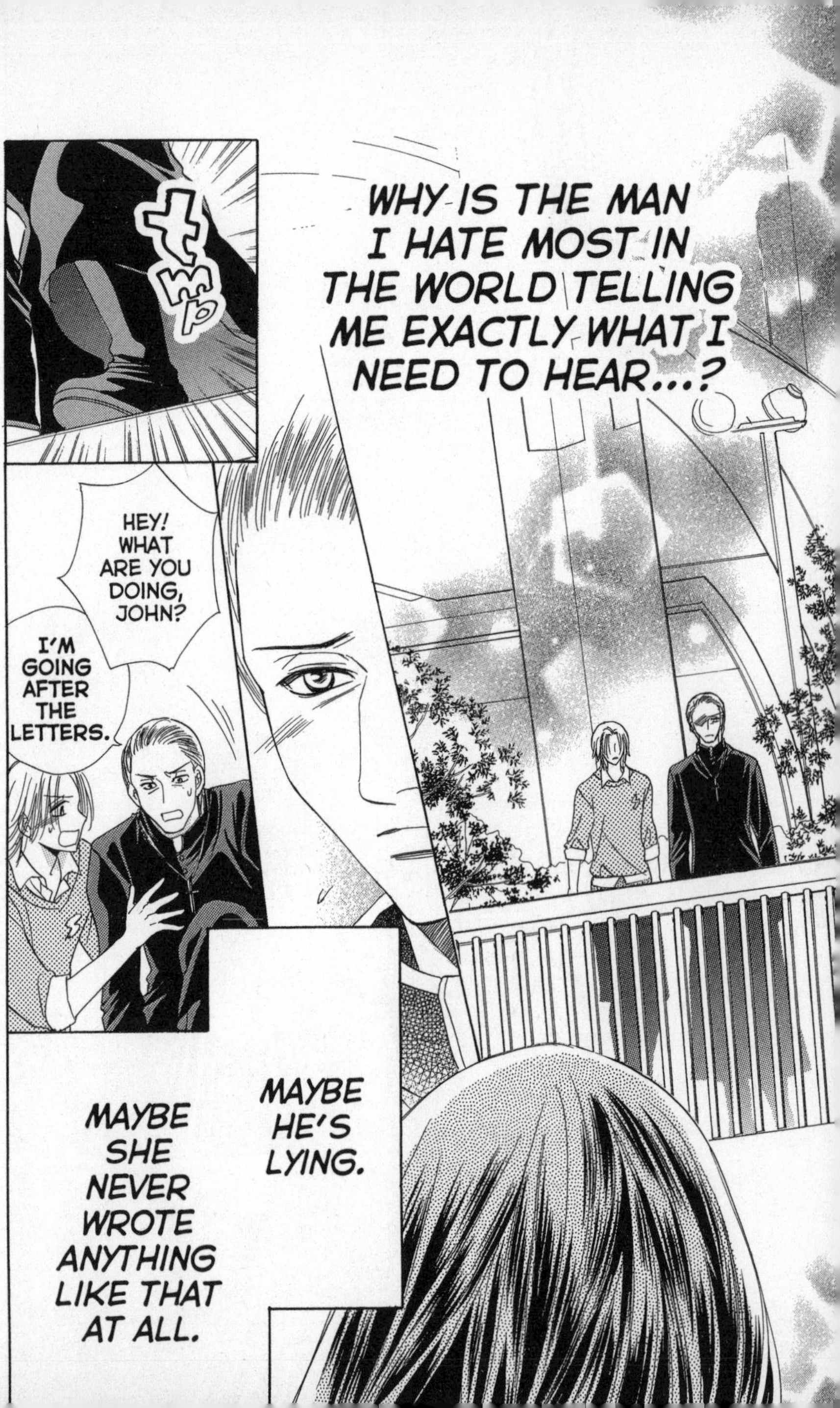
WHY IS THE MAN I HATE MOST IN THE WORLD TELLING ME EXACTLY WHAT I NEED TO HEAR...?
tmp
HEY! WHAT ARE YOU DOING, JOHN?
I'M GOING AFTER THE LETTERS.
MAYBE HE'S LYING.
MAYBE SHE NEVER WROTE ANYTHING LIKE THAT AT ALL.

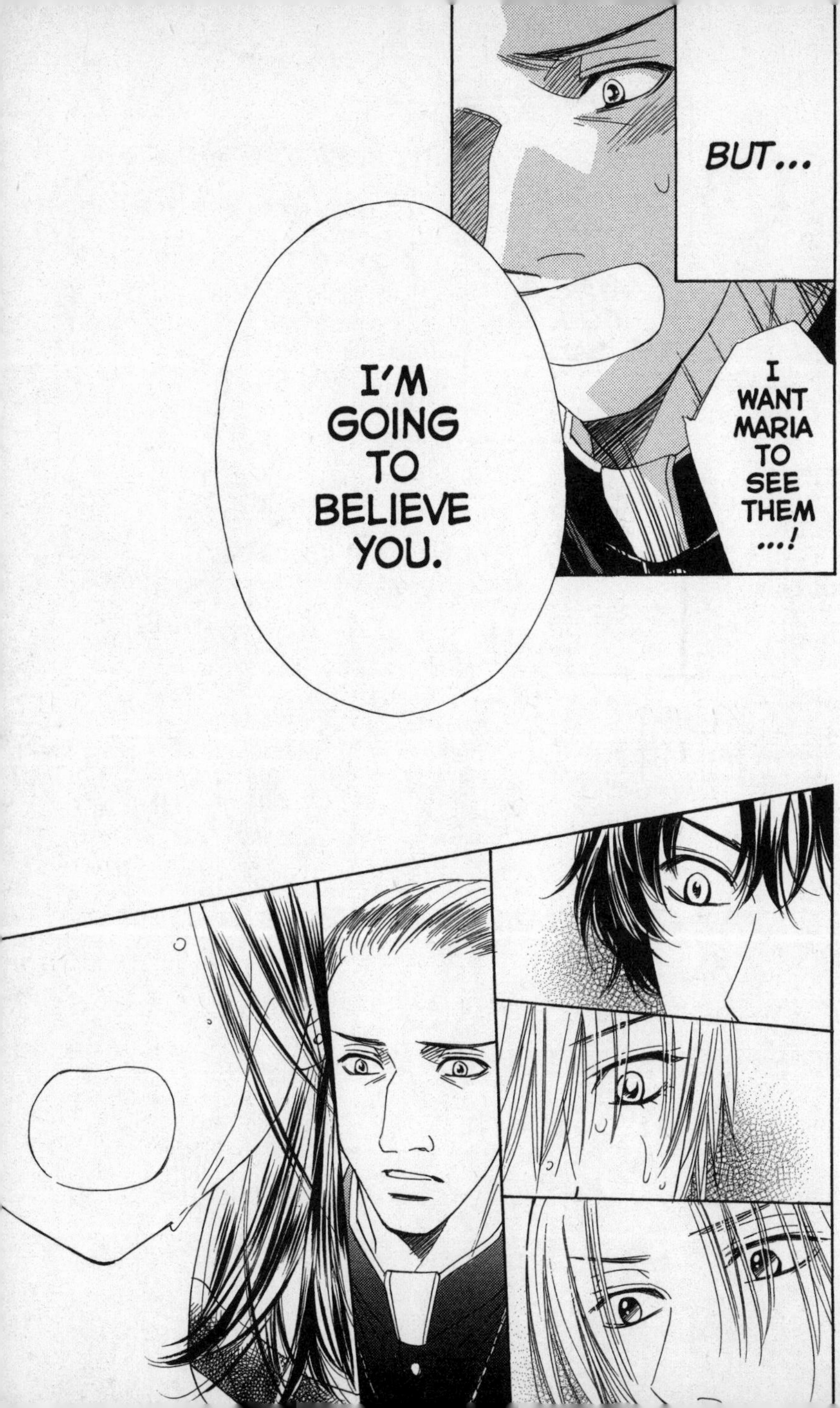
BUT...
I WANT MARIA TO SEE THEM ...!
I'M GOING TO BELIEVE YOU.

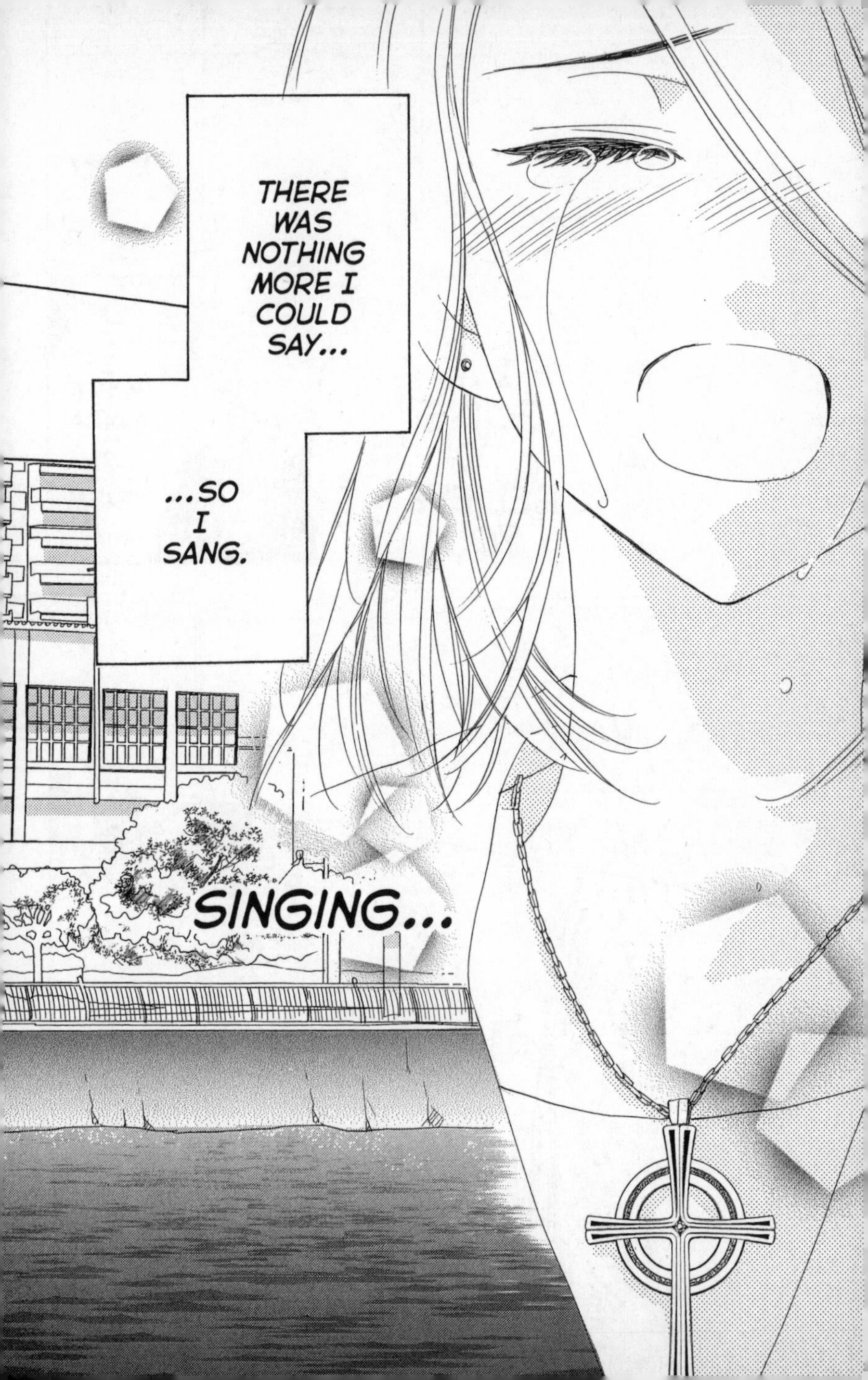
THERE WAS NOTHING MORE I COULD SAY...
...SO I SANG.
SINGING...

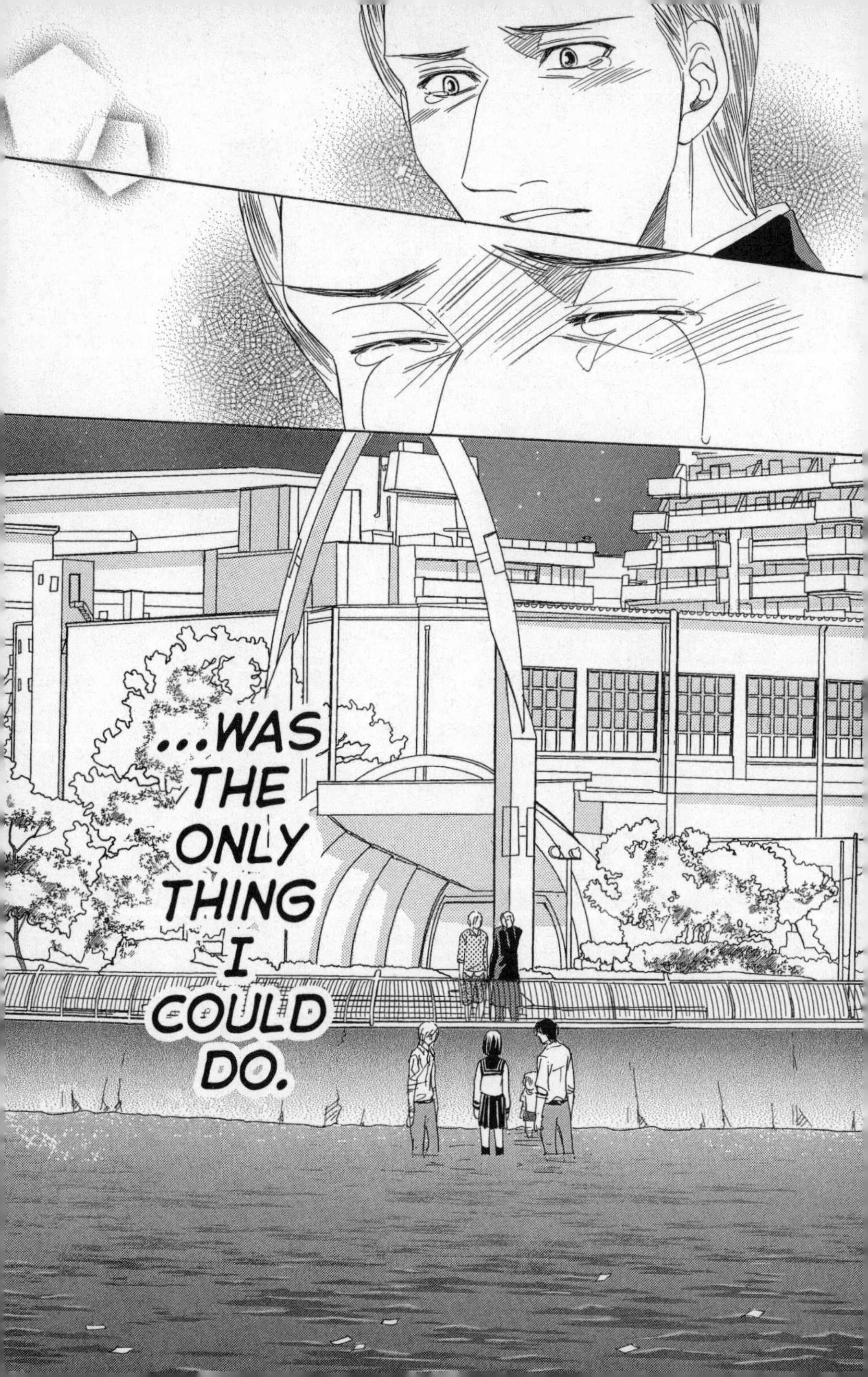
...WAS THE ONLY THING I COULD DO.

A Devil and
Her Love Song

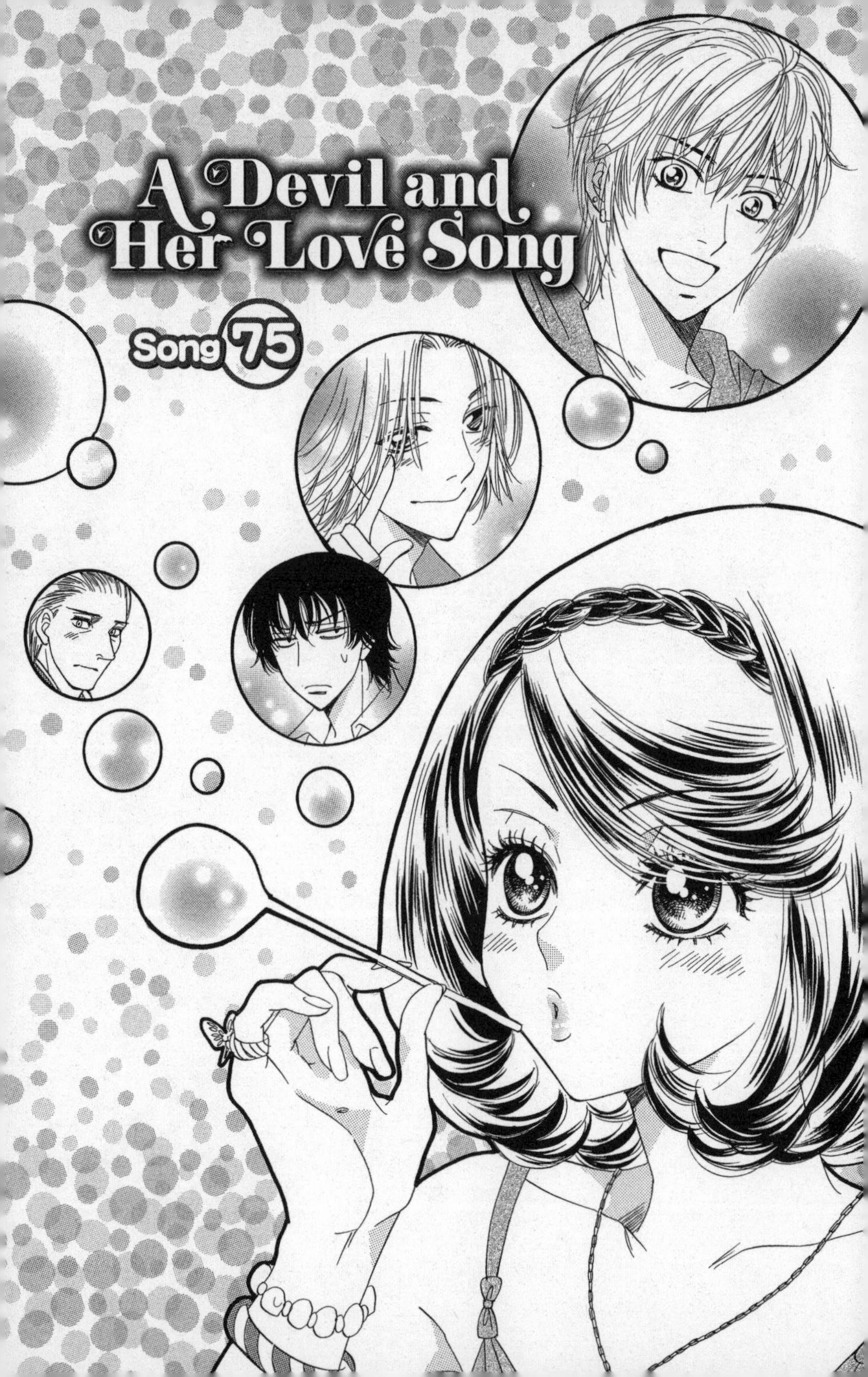
A Devil and Her Love Song
Song 75

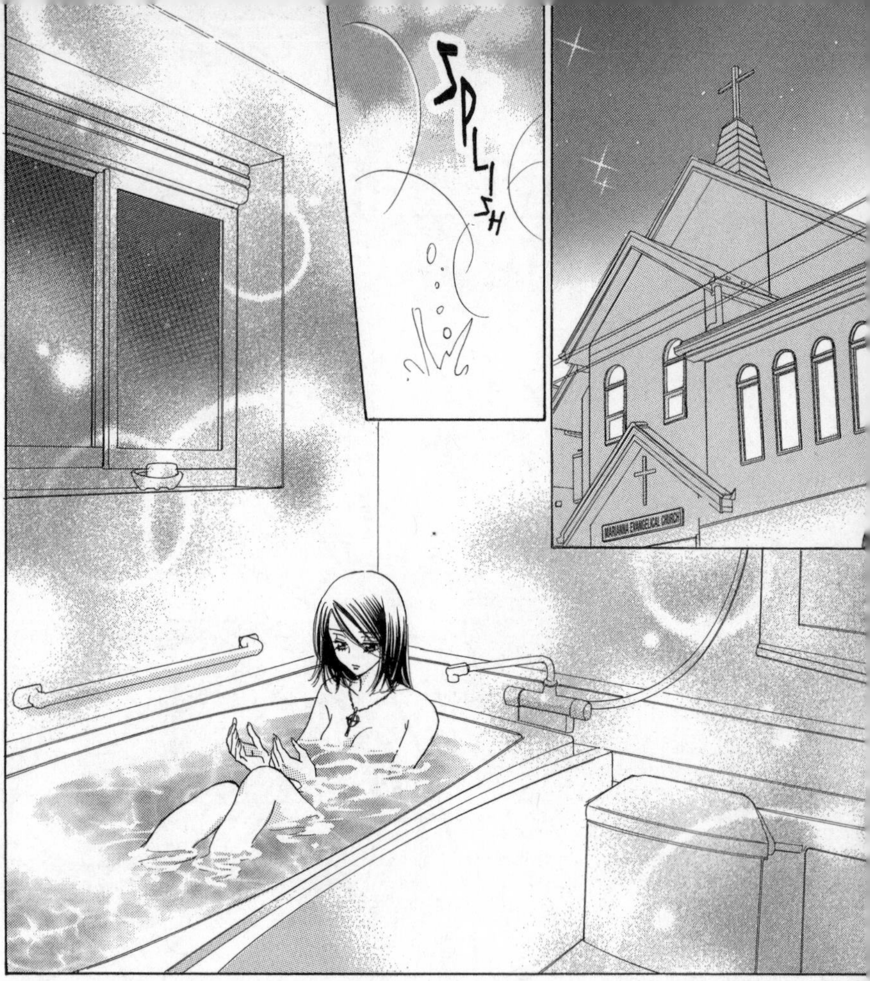
MARIANNA EVANGELICAL CHURCH
SPLISH

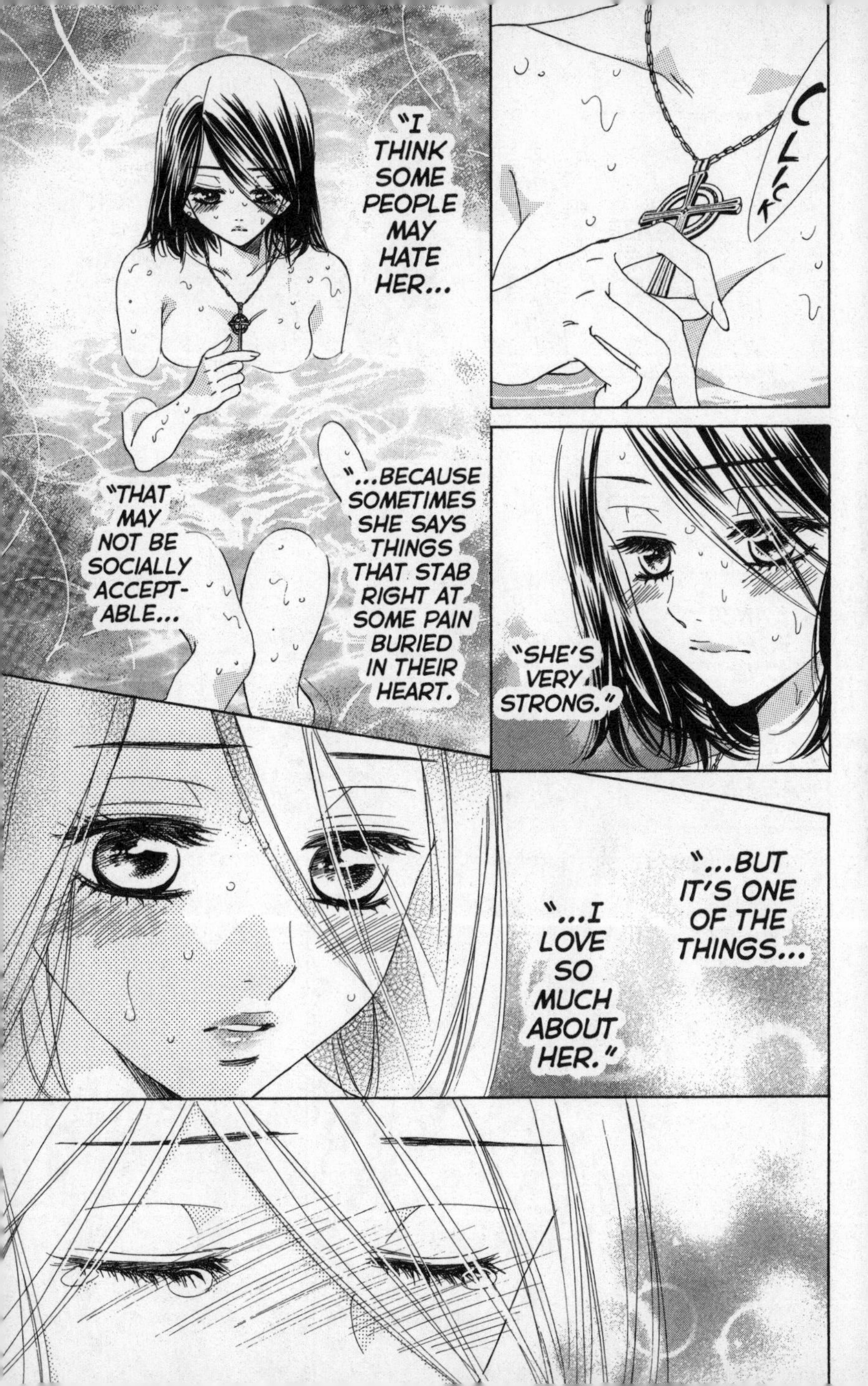
CLICK
"SHE'S VERY STRONG."
"I THINK SOME PEOPLE MAY HATE HER...
"...BECAUSE SOMETIMES SHE SAYS THINGS THAT STAB RIGHT AT SOME PAIN BURIED IN THEIR HEART.
"THAT MAY NOT BE SOCIALLY ACCEPT-ABLE...
"...BUT IT'S ONE OF THE THINGS...
"...I LOVE SO MUCH ABOUT HER."

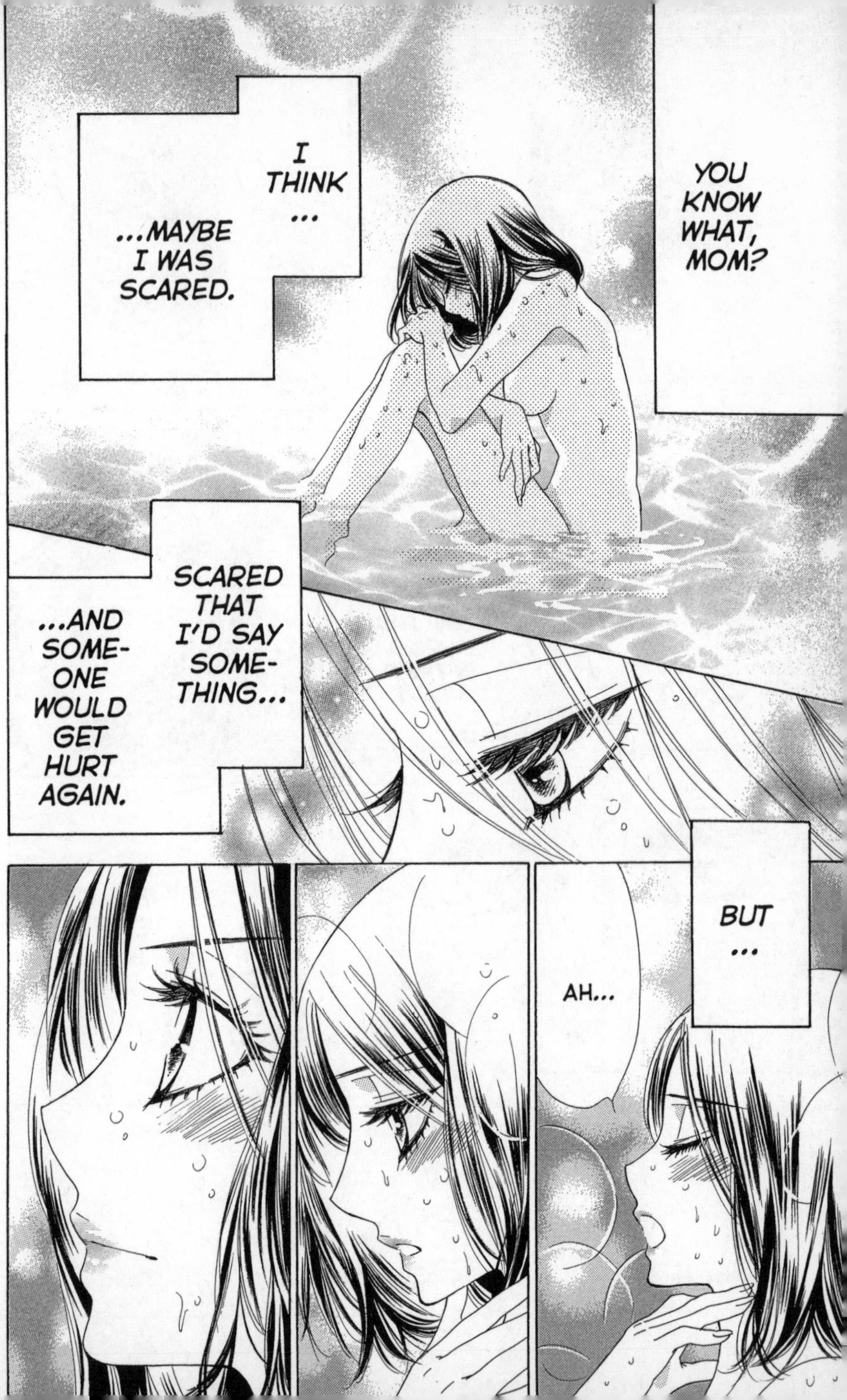
YOU KNOW WHAT, MOM?
I THINK...
...MAYBE I WAS SCARED.
SCARED THAT I'D SAY SOME-THING...
...AND SOME-ONE WOULD GET HURT AGAIN.
BUT...
AH...

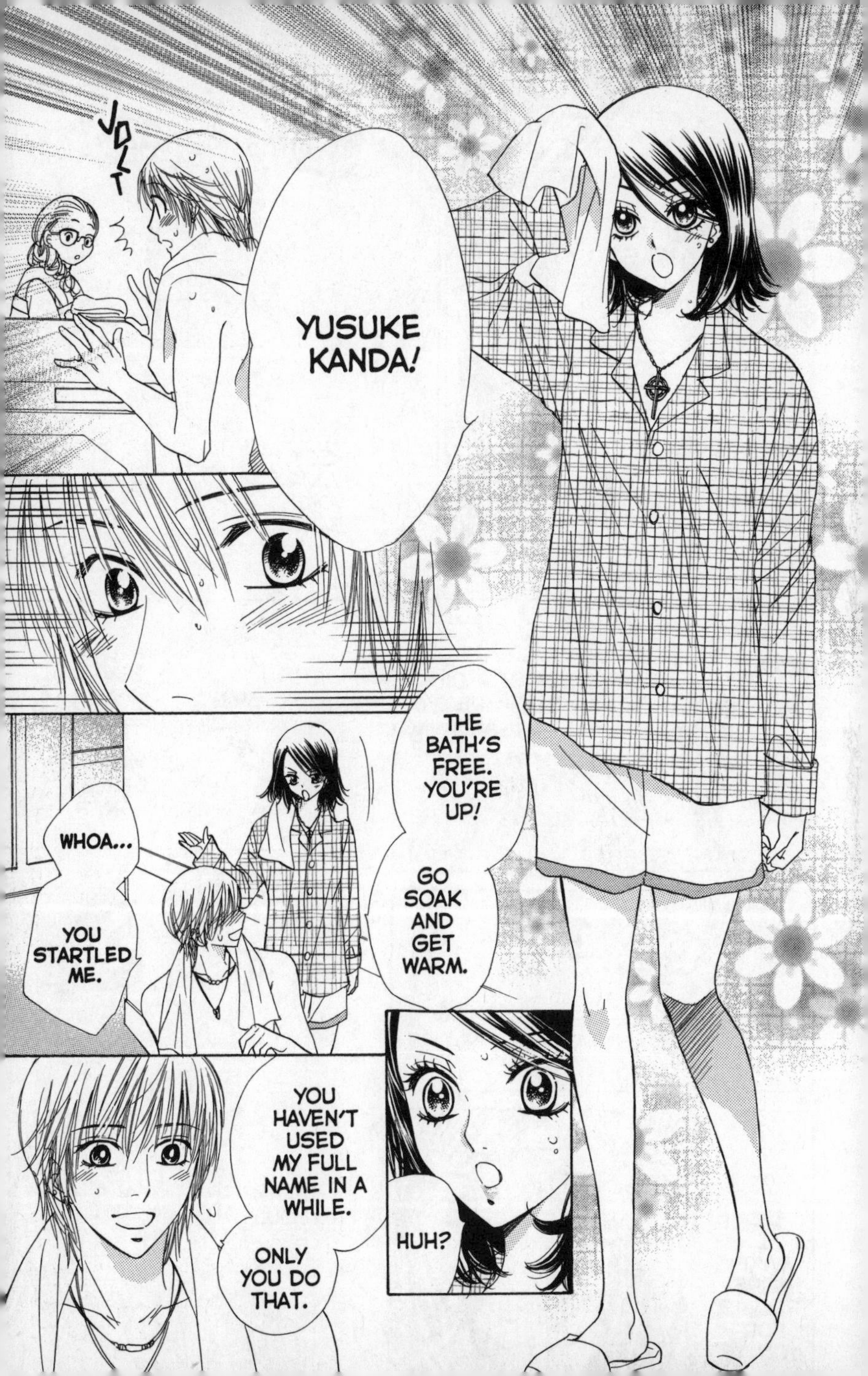
YUSUKE KANDA!
JOLT
THE BATH'S FREE. YOU'RE UP!
GO SOAK AND GET WARM.
WHOA...
YOU STARTLED ME.
HUH?
YOU HAVEN'T USED MY FULL NAME IN A WHILE.
ONLY YOU DO THAT.

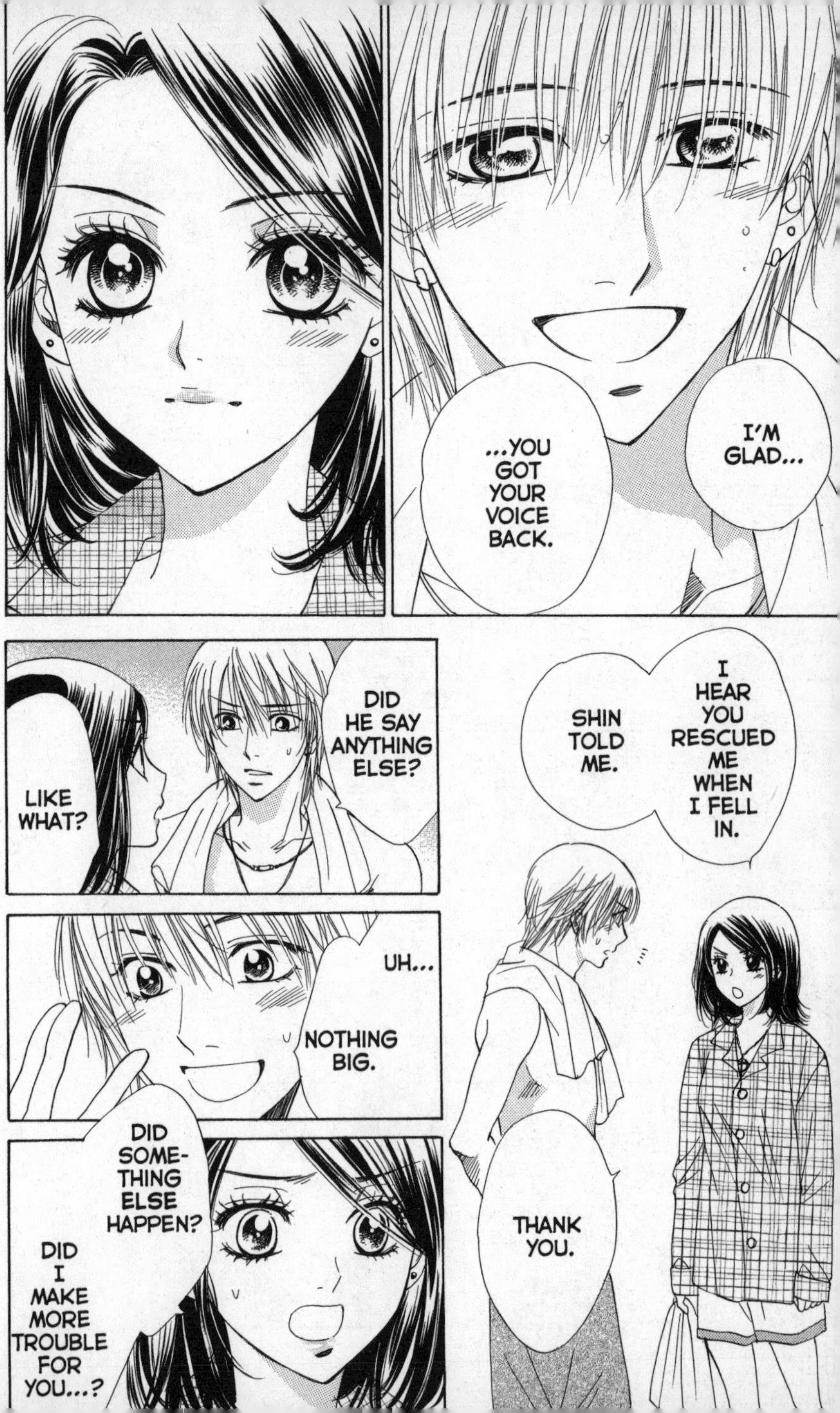
I'M GLAD...
...YOU GOT YOUR VOICE BACK.
I HEAR YOU RESCUED ME WHEN I FELL IN.
SHIN TOLD ME.
THANK YOU.
DID HE SAY ANYTHING ELSE?
LIKE WHAT?
UH...
NOTHING BIG.
DID SOMETHING ELSE HAPPEN?
DID I MAKE MORE TROUBLE FOR YOU...?

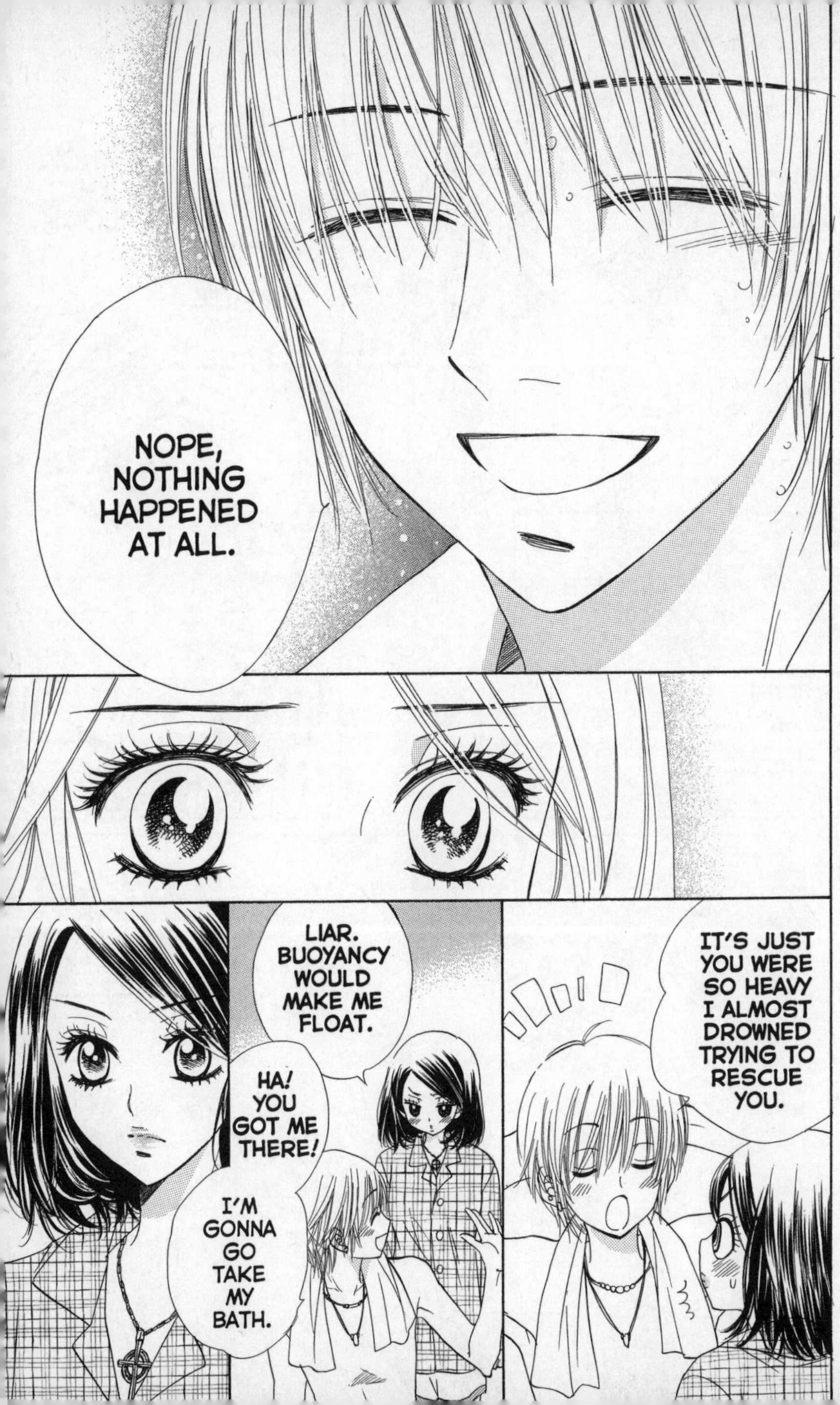
NOPE, NOTHING HAPPENED AT ALL.
IT'S JUST YOU WERE SO HEAVY I ALMOST DROWNED TRYING TO RESCUE YOU.
LIAR. BUOYANCY WOULD MAKE ME FLOAT.
HA! YOU GOT ME THERE!
I'M GONNA GO TAKE MY BATH.

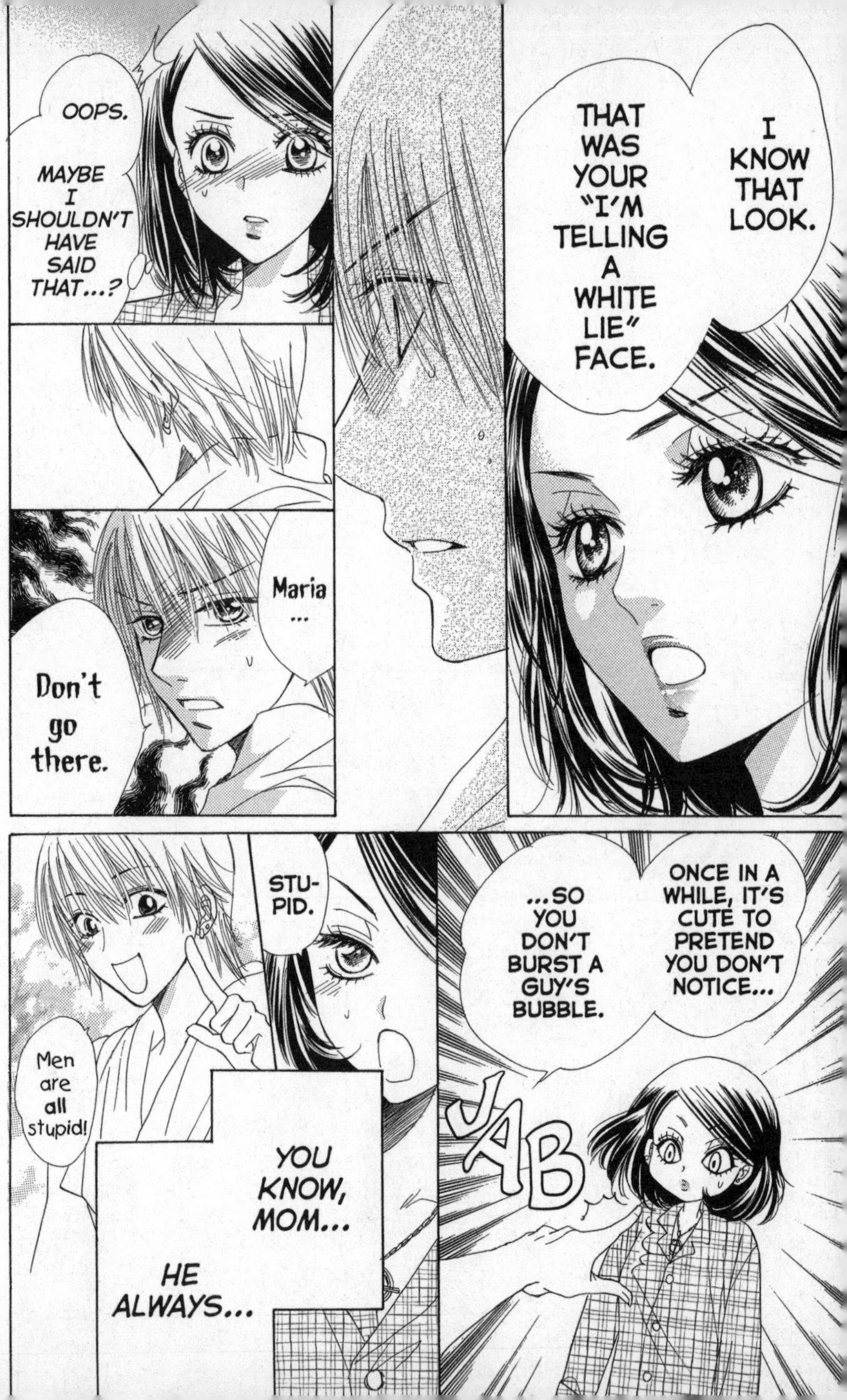
I KNOW THAT LOOK.
THAT WAS YOUR "I'M TELLING A WHITE LIE" FACE.
OOPS.
MAYBE I SHOULDN'T HAVE SAID THAT...?
Maria...
Don't go there.
ONCE IN A WHILE, IT'S CUTE TO PRETEND YOU DON'T NOTICE...
...SO YOU DON'T BURST A GUY'S BUBBLE.
JAB
STU-PID.
Men are all stupid!
YOU KNOW, MOM...
HE ALWAYS...

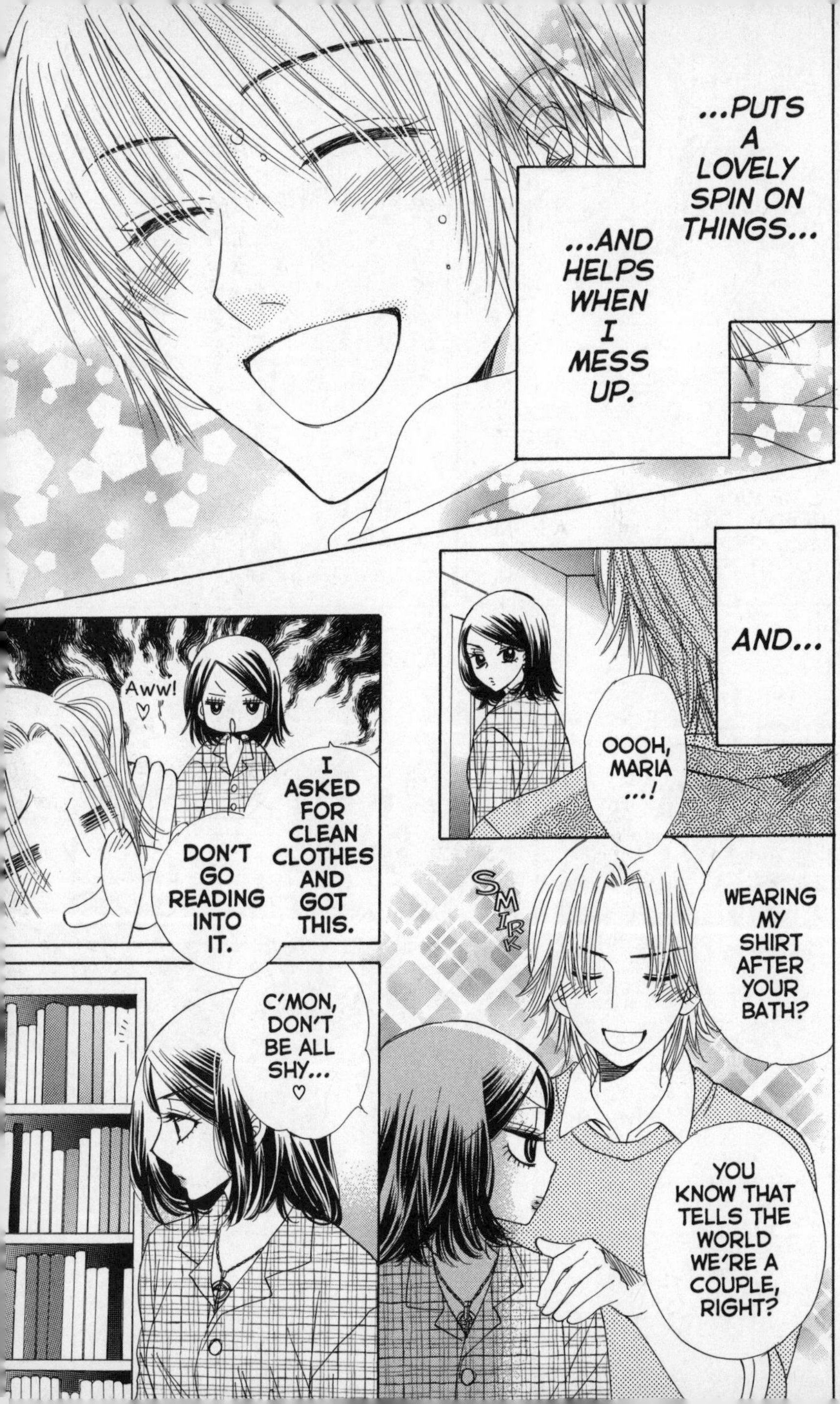
...PUTS A LOVELY SPIN ON THINGS...
...AND HELPS WHEN I MESS UP.
AND...
OOOH, MARIA ...!
SMIRK
WEARING MY SHIRT AFTER YOUR BATH?
YOU KNOW THAT TELLS THE WORLD WE'RE A COUPLE, RIGHT?
I ASKED FOR CLEAN CLOTHES AND GOT THIS.
DON'T GO READING INTO IT.
Aww! ♡
C'MON, DON'T BE ALL SHY... ♡

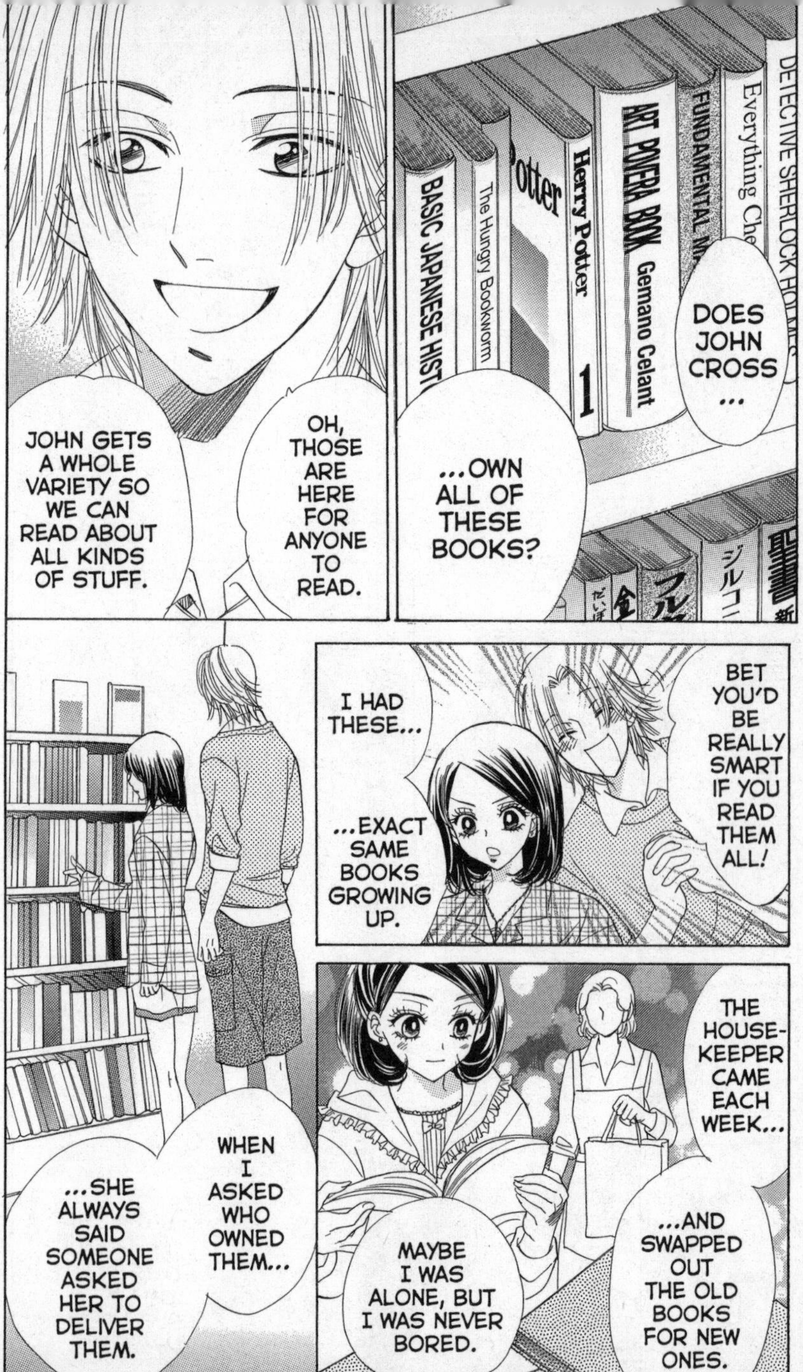

Herry Potter
ART POVERA BOOK
Gemano Celant
The Hungry Bookworm
DOES JOHN CROSS ...
...OWN ALL OF THESE BOOKS?
OH, THOSE ARE HERE FOR ANYONE TO READ.
JOHN GETS A WHOLE VARIETY SO WE CAN READ ABOUT ALL KINDS OF STUFF.
BET YOU'D BE REALLY SMART IF YOU READ THEM ALL!
I HAD THESE...
...EXACT SAME BOOKS GROWING UP.
THE HOUSE-KEEPER CAME EACH WEEK...
...AND SWAPPED OUT THE OLD BOOKS FOR NEW ONES.
MAYBE I WAS ALONE, BUT I WAS NEVER BORED.
WHEN I ASKED WHO OWNED THEM...
...SHE ALWAYS SAID SOMEONE ASKED HER TO DELIVER THEM.

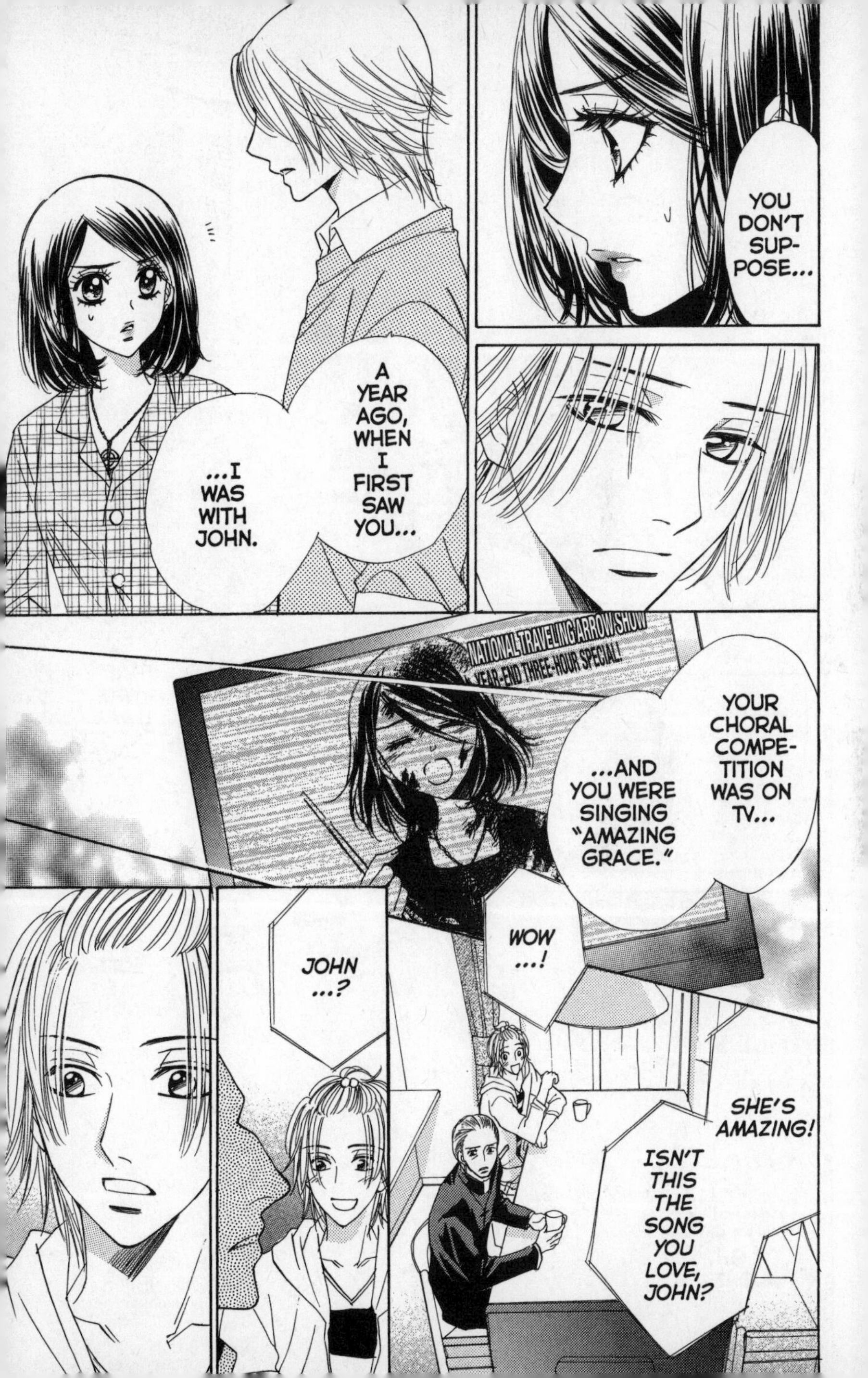
YOU DON'T SUP-POSE...
A YEAR AGO, WHEN I FIRST SAW YOU...
...I WAS WITH JOHN.
NATIONAL TRAVELING ARROW SHOW
YEAR-END THREE-HOUR SPECIAL!
YOUR CHORAL COMPE-TITION WAS ON TV...
...AND YOU WERE SINGING "AMAZING GRACE."
WOW ...!
SHE'S AMAZING!
ISN'T THIS THE SONG YOU LOVE, JOHN?
JOHN ...?

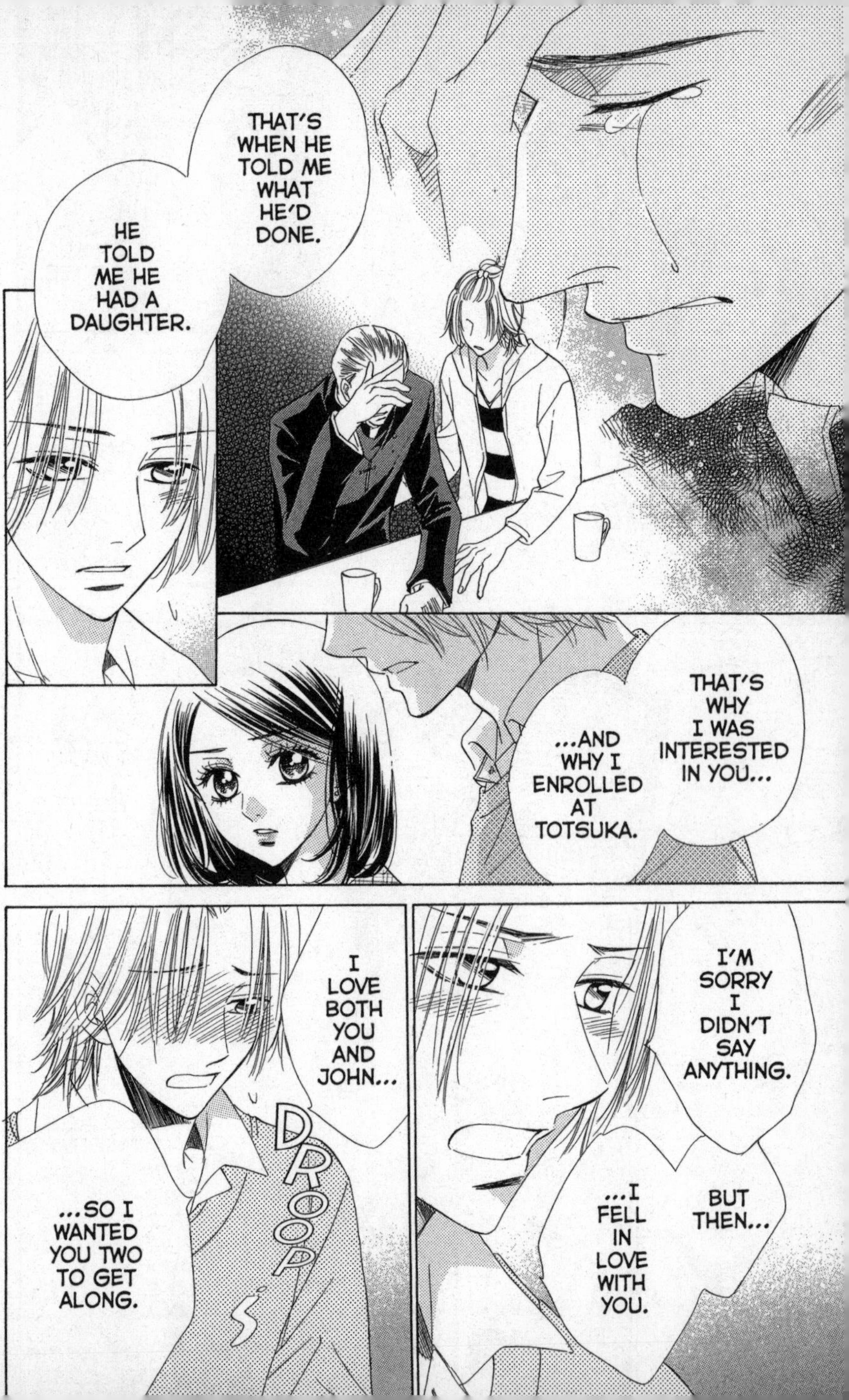
THAT'S WHEN HE TOLD ME WHAT HE'D DONE.
HE TOLD ME HE HAD A DAUGHTER.
THAT'S WHY I WAS INTERESTED IN YOU...
...AND WHY I ENROLLED AT TOTSUKA.
I'M SORRY I DIDN'T SAY ANYTHING.
BUT THEN...
...I FELL IN LOVE WITH YOU.
I LOVE BOTH YOU AND JOHN...
DROOP
...SO I WANTED YOU TWO TO GET ALONG.

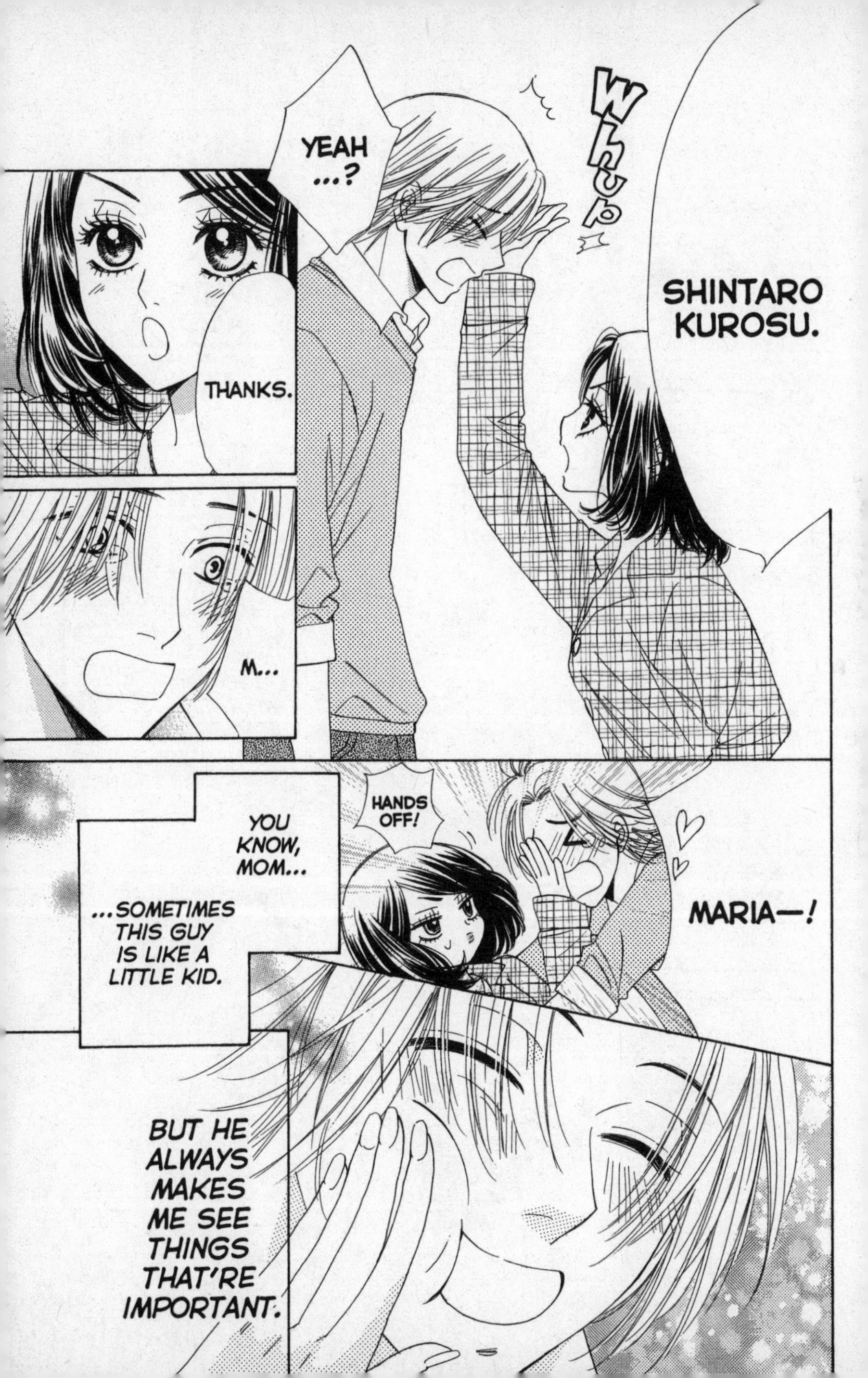
SHINTARO KUROSU.
Whup
YEAH ...?
THANKS.
M...
MARIA—!
HANDS OFF!
YOU KNOW, MOM...
...SOMETIMES THIS GUY IS LIKE A LITTLE KID.
BUT HE ALWAYS MAKES ME SEE THINGS THAT'RE IMPORTANT.

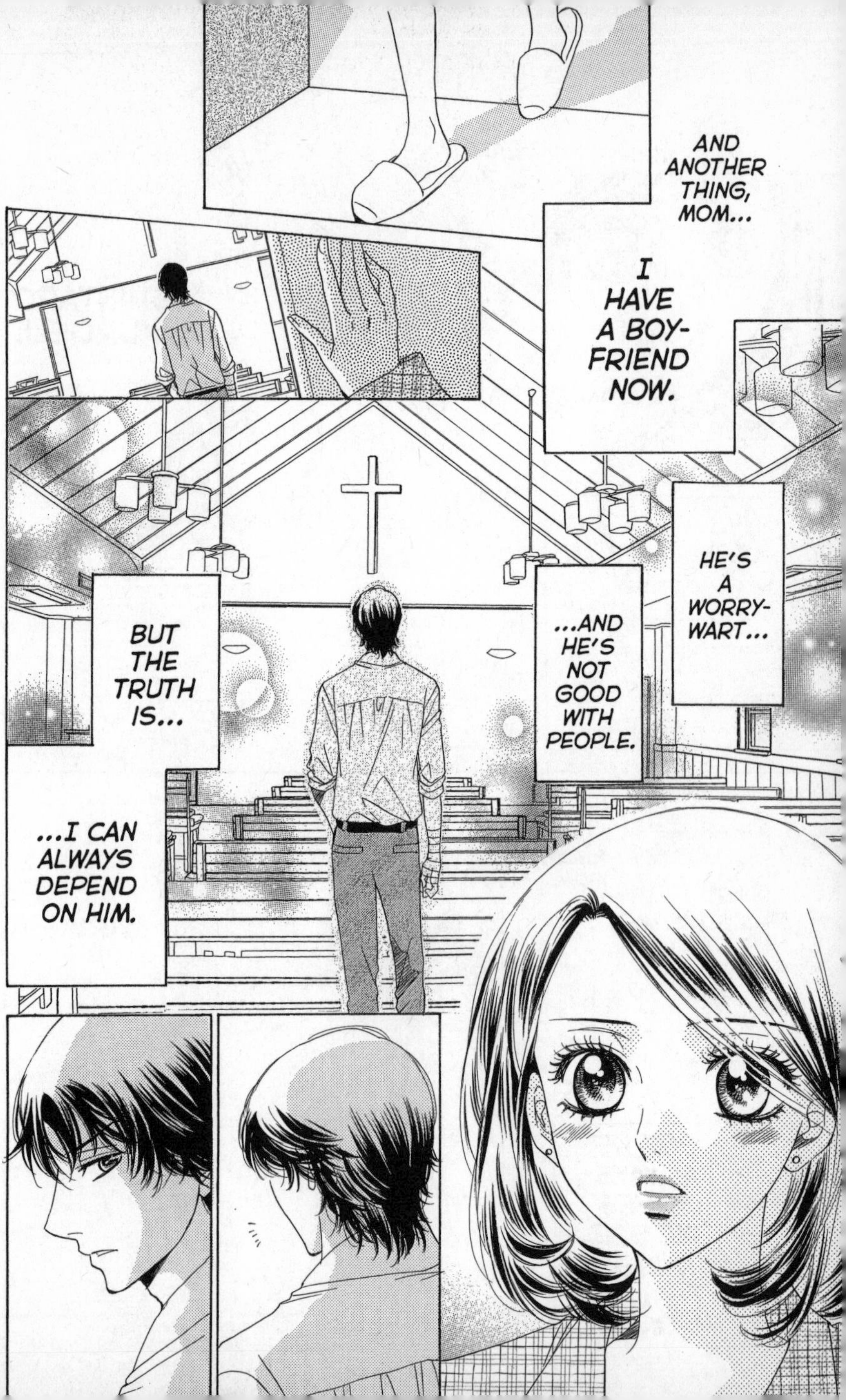
AND ANOTHER THING, MOM...
I HAVE A BOY-FRIEND NOW.
HE'S A WORRY-WART...
...AND HE'S NOT GOOD WITH PEOPLE.
BUT THE TRUTH IS...
...I CAN ALWAYS DEPEND ON HIM.

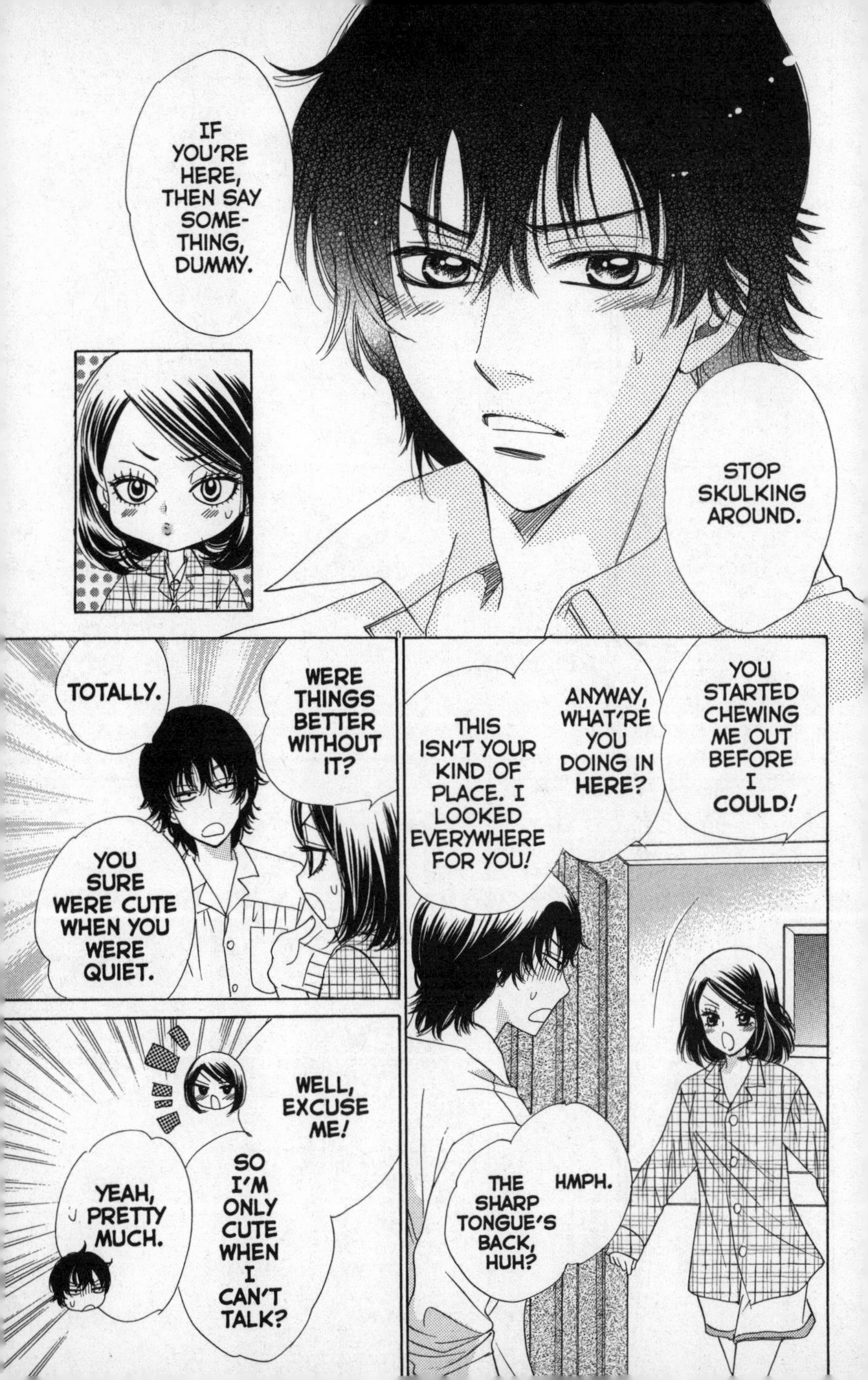
IF YOU'RE HERE, THEN SAY SOME-THING, DUMMY.
STOP SKULKING AROUND.
YOU STARTED CHEWING ME OUT BEFORE I COULD!
ANYWAY, WHAT'RE YOU DOING IN HERE?
THIS ISN'T YOUR KIND OF PLACE. I LOOKED EVERYWHERE FOR YOU!
HMPH.
THE SHARP TONGUE'S BACK, HUH?
WERE THINGS BETTER WITHOUT IT?
TOTALLY.
YOU SURE WERE CUTE WHEN YOU WERE QUIET.
WELL, EXCUSE ME!
SO I'M ONLY CUTE WHEN I CAN'T TALK?
YEAH, PRETTY MUCH.

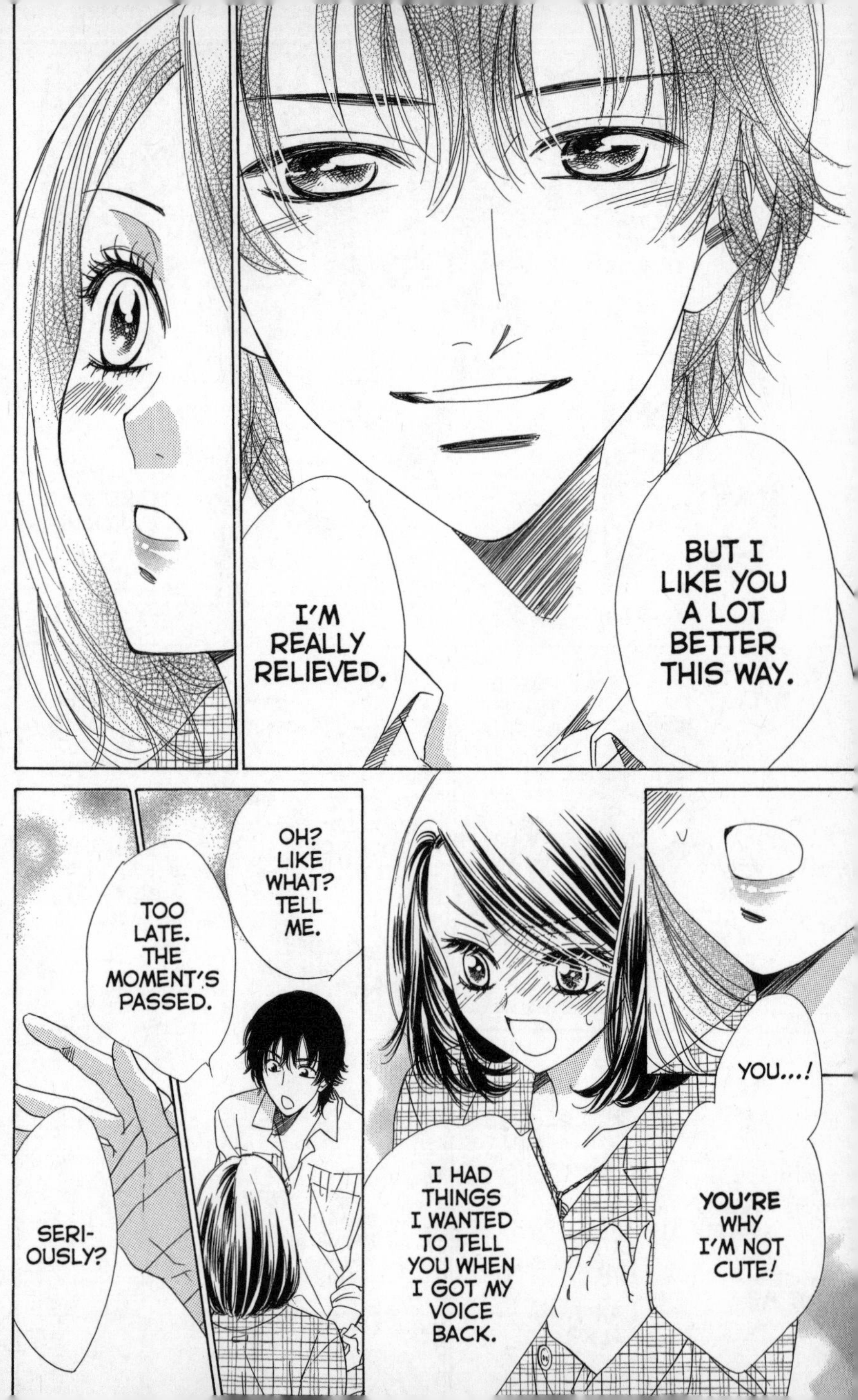
BUT I LIKE YOU A LOT BETTER THIS WAY.
I'M REALLY RELIEVED.
YOU...!
YOU'RE WHY I'M NOT CUTE!
I HAD THINGS I WANTED TO TELL YOU WHEN I GOT MY VOICE BACK.
OH? LIKE WHAT? TELL ME.
TOO LATE. THE MOMENT'S PASSED.
SERI-OUSLY?

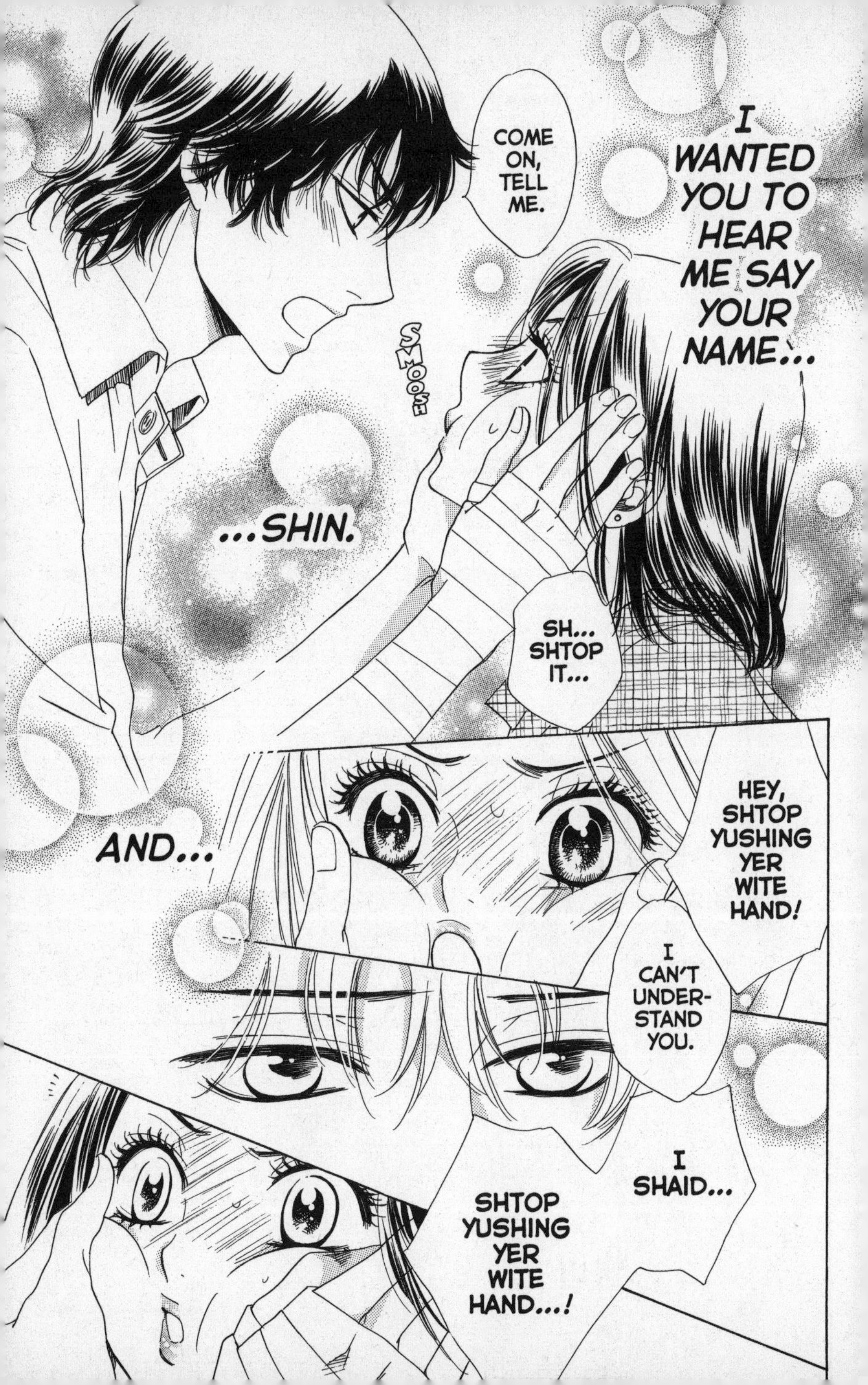
I WANTED YOU TO HEAR ME SAY YOUR NAME...
COME ON, TELL ME.
SMOOSH
...SHIN.
SH... SHTOP IT...
AND...
HEY, SHTOP YUSHING YER WITE HAND!
I CAN'T UNDER-STAND YOU.
I SHAID...
SHTOP YUSHING YER WITE HAND...!

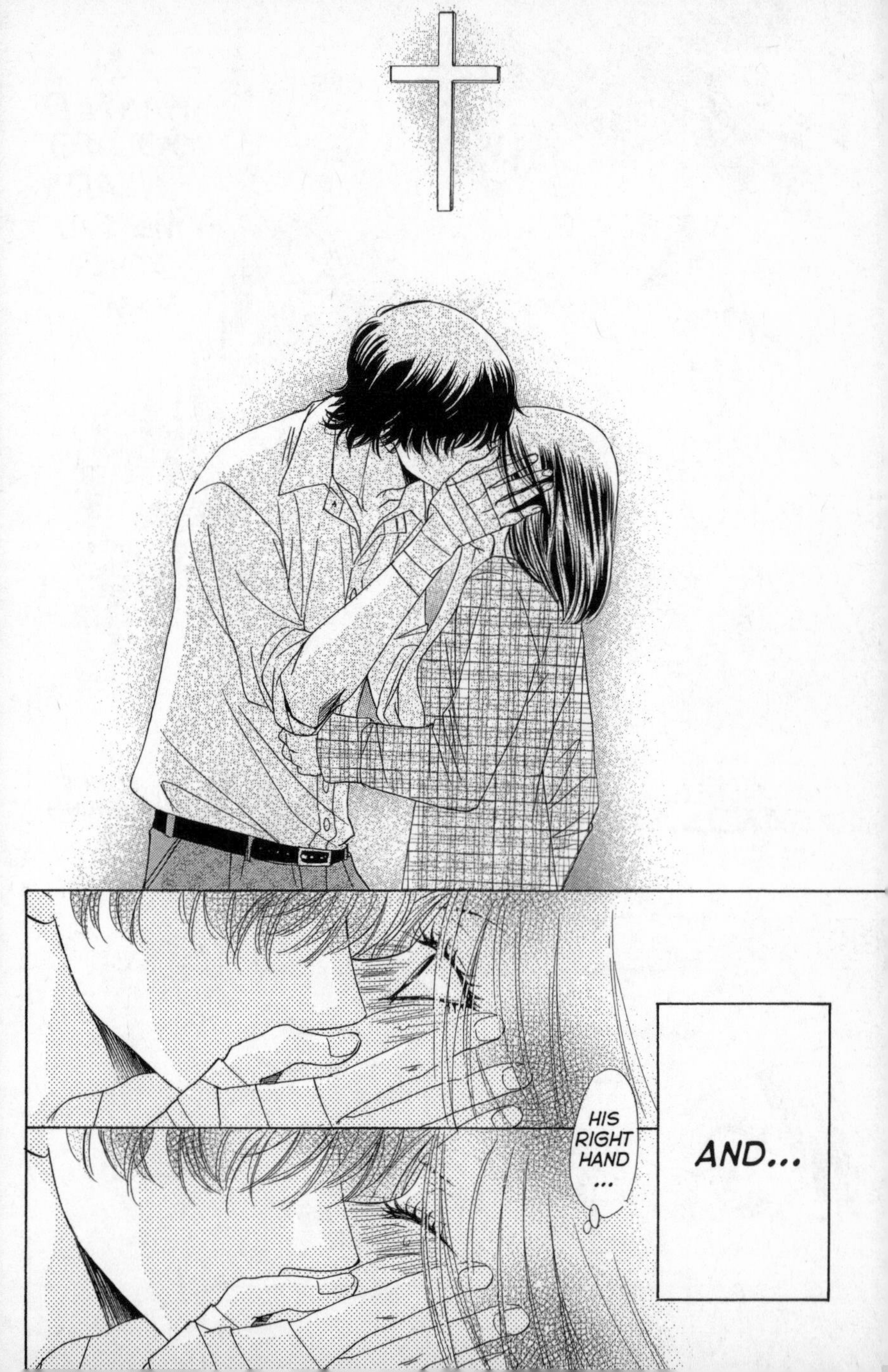
AND...
HIS RIGHT HAND ...

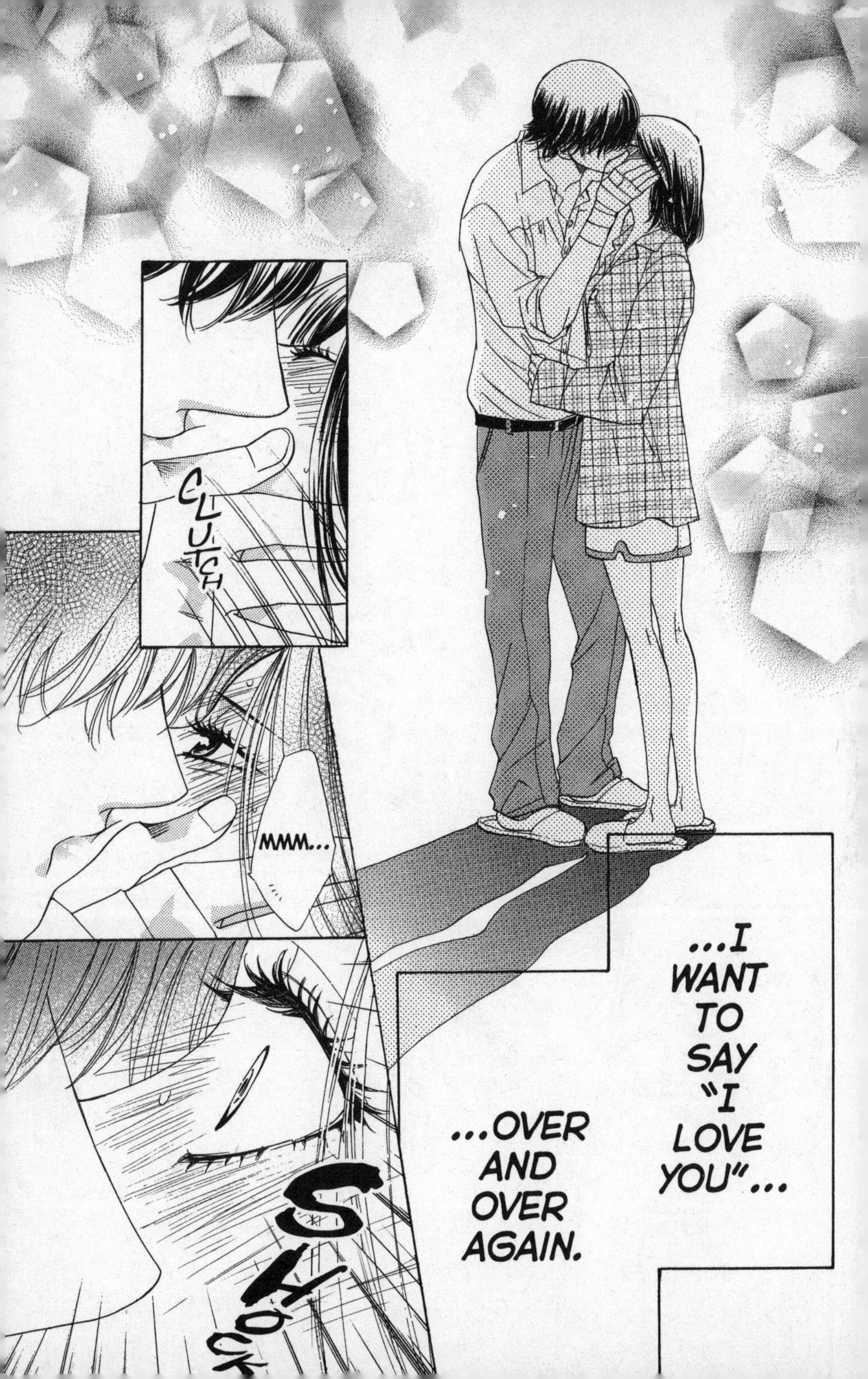
CLUTCH
MMM...
...I WANT TO SAY "I LOVE YOU"...
...OVER AND OVER AGAIN.
SHOCK

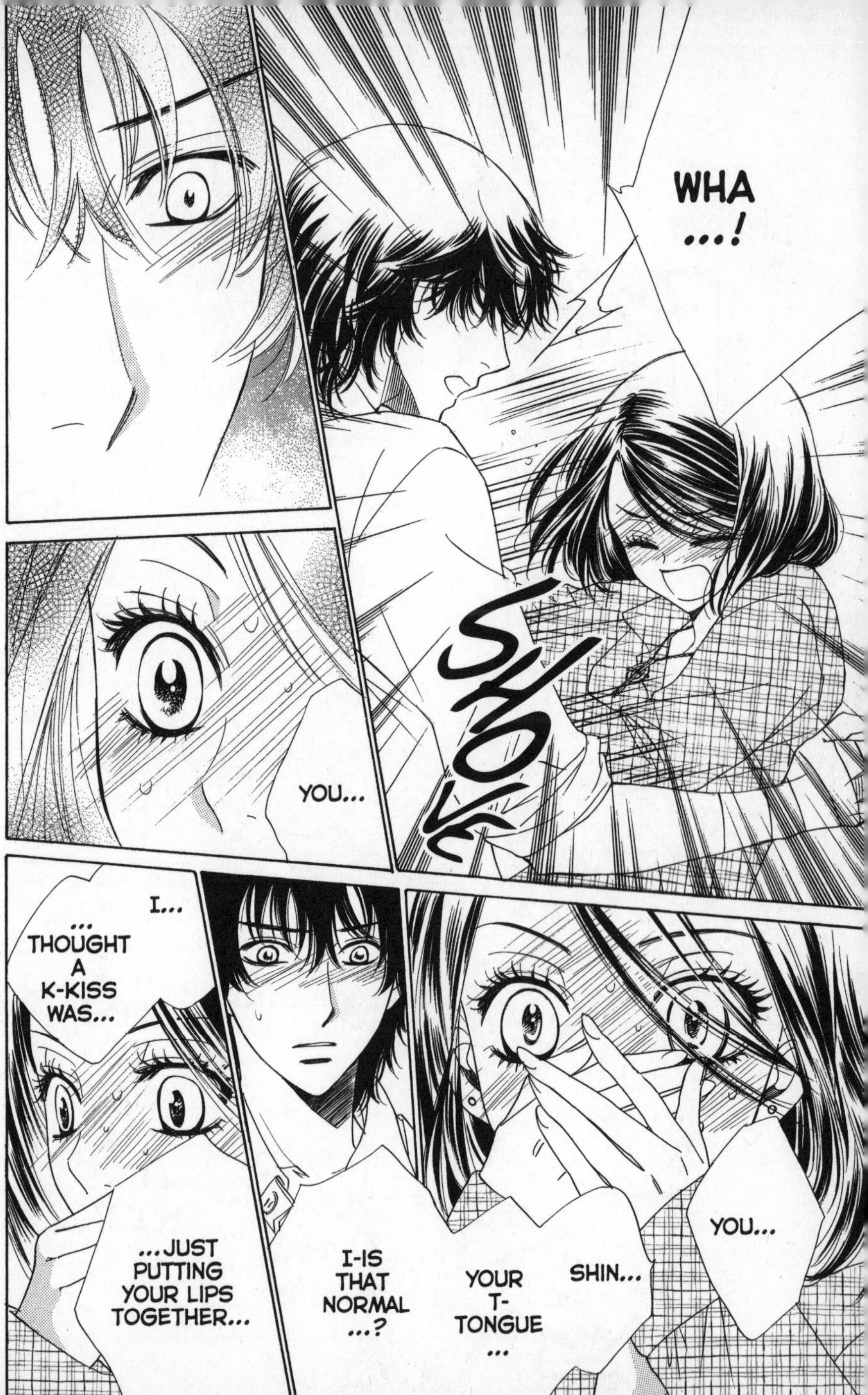
WHA ...!
SHOVE
YOU...
YOU...
SHIN...
YOUR T-TONGUE ...
I-IS THAT NORMAL ...?
I...
... THOUGHT A K-KISS WAS...
...JUST PUTTING YOUR LIPS TOGETHER...

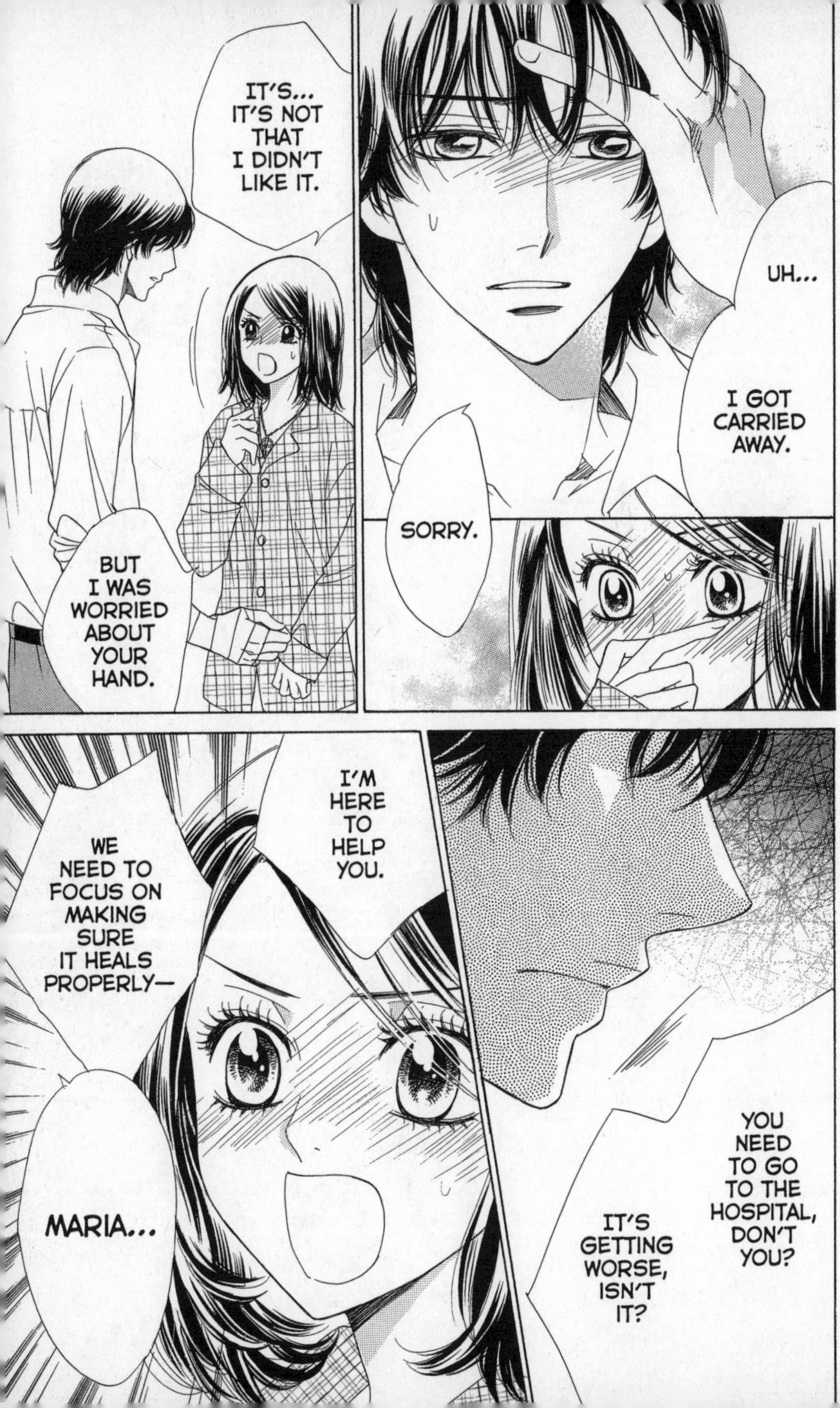
UH...
I GOT CARRIED AWAY.
SORRY.
IT'S... IT'S NOT THAT I DIDN'T LIKE IT.
BUT I WAS WORRIED ABOUT YOUR HAND.
YOU NEED TO GO TO THE HOSPITAL, DON'T YOU?
IT'S GETTING WORSE, ISN'T IT?
I'M HERE TO HELP YOU.
WE NEED TO FOCUS ON MAKING SURE IT HEALS PROPERLY—
MARIA...

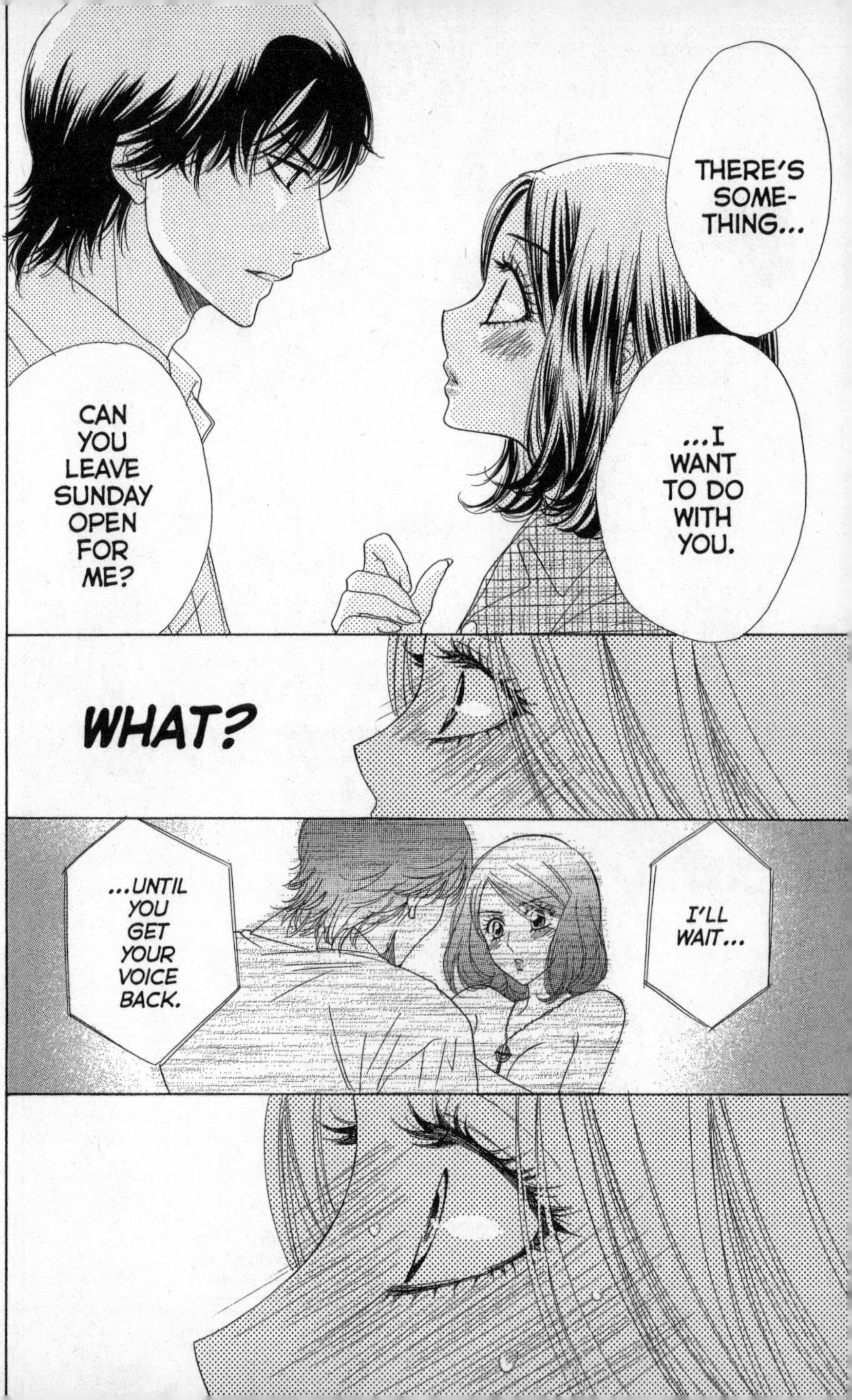
THERE'S SOME-THING...
...I WANT TO DO WITH YOU.
CAN YOU LEAVE SUNDAY OPEN FOR ME?
WHAT?
I'LL WAIT...
...UNTIL YOU GET YOUR VOICE BACK.

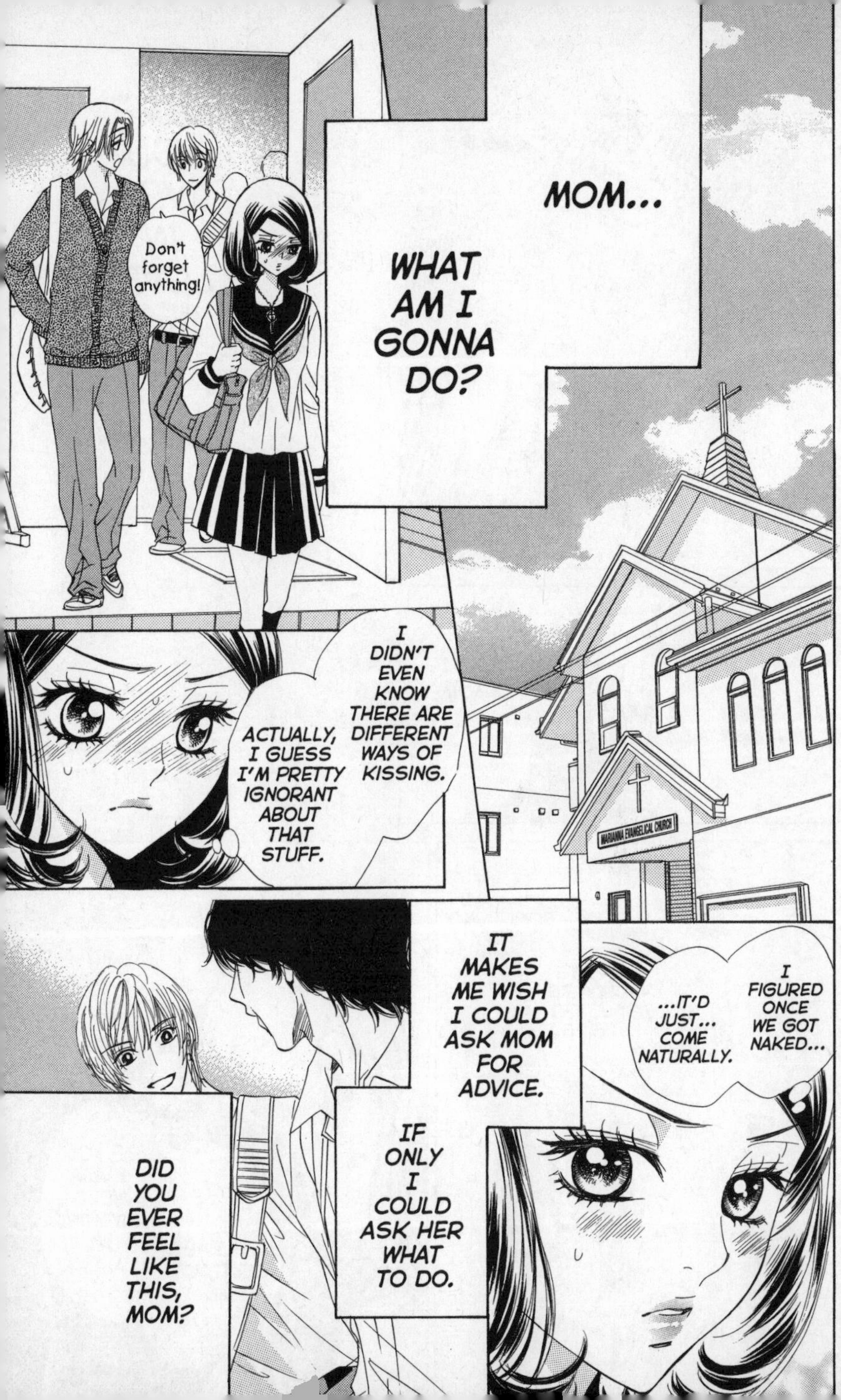
MOM...
WHAT AM I GONNA DO?
MARIANNA EVANGELICAL CHURCH
Don't forget anything!
I DIDN'T EVEN KNOW THERE ARE DIFFERENT WAYS OF KISSING.
ACTUALLY, I GUESS I'M PRETTY IGNORANT ABOUT THAT STUFF.
I FIGURED ONCE WE GOT NAKED...
...IT'D JUST... COME NATURALLY.
IT MAKES ME WISH I COULD ASK MOM FOR ADVICE.
IF ONLY I COULD ASK HER WHAT TO DO.
DID YOU EVER FEEL LIKE THIS, MOM?

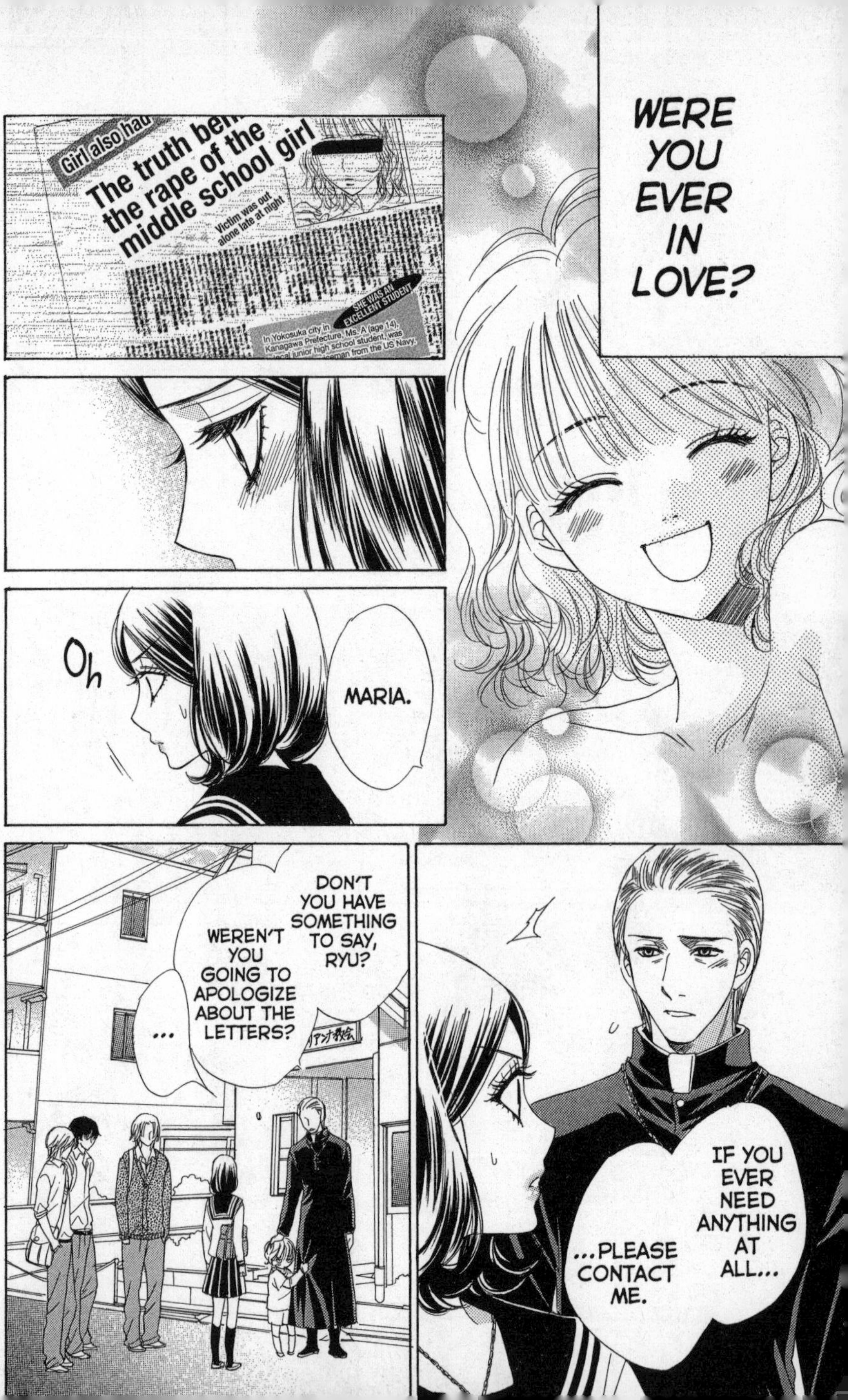
WERE YOU EVER IN LOVE?
Girl also had
The truth beh
the rape of the middle school girl
Victim was out alone late at night
SHE WAS AN EXCELLENT STUDENT
In Yokosuka city in Kanagawa Prefecture, Ms. A (age 14),
Oh
MARIA.
IF YOU EVER NEED ANYTHING AT ALL...
...PLEASE CONTACT ME.
DON'T YOU HAVE SOMETHING TO SAY, RYU?
WEREN'T YOU GOING TO APOLOGIZE ABOUT THE LETTERS?
...

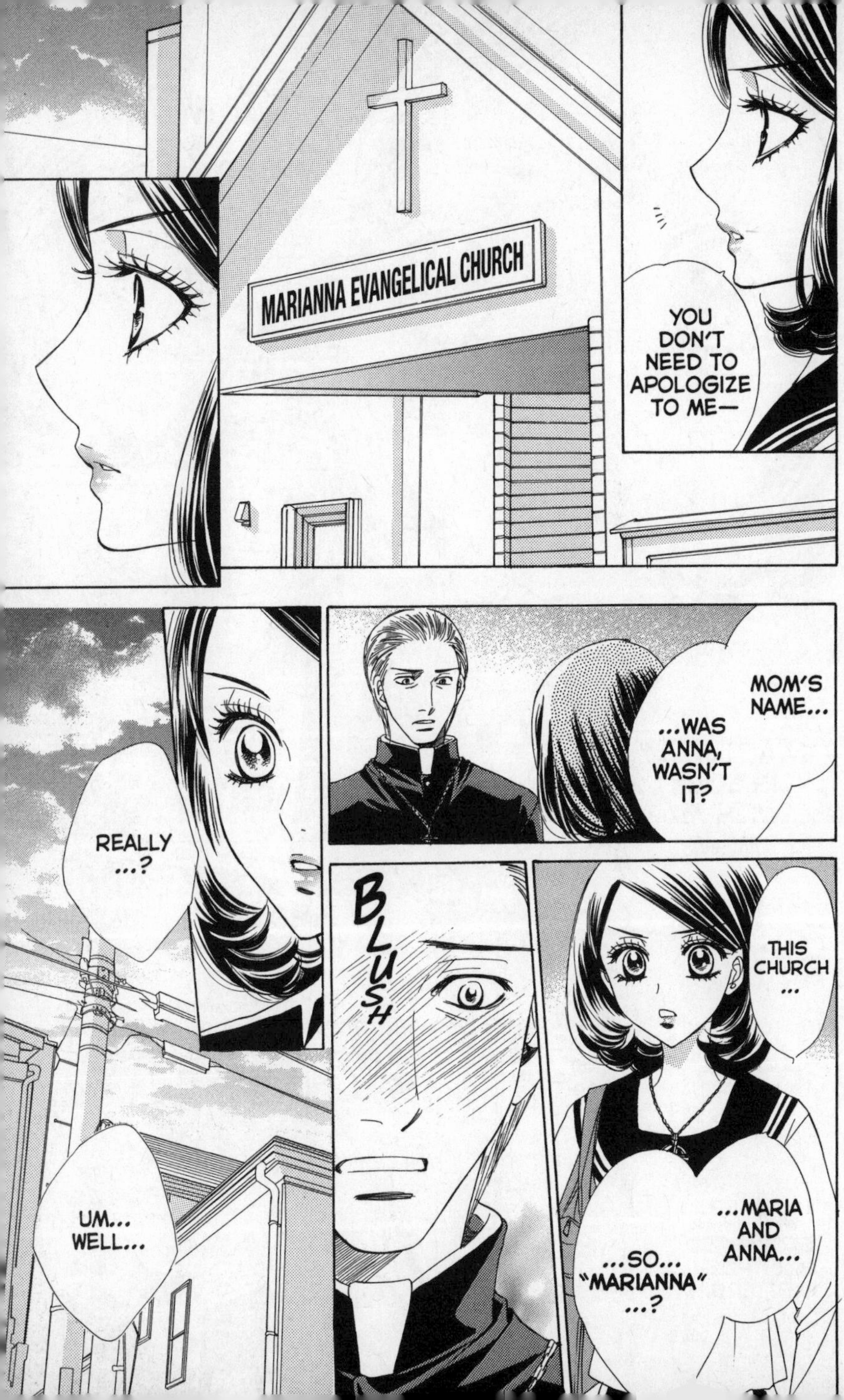
YOU DON'T NEED TO APOLOGIZE TO ME—
MARIANNA EVANGELICAL CHURCH
MOM'S NAME...
...WAS ANNA, WASN'T IT?
THIS CHURCH ...
...MARIA AND ANNA...
...SO... "MARIANNA" ...?
BLUSH
REALLY ...?
UM... WELL...

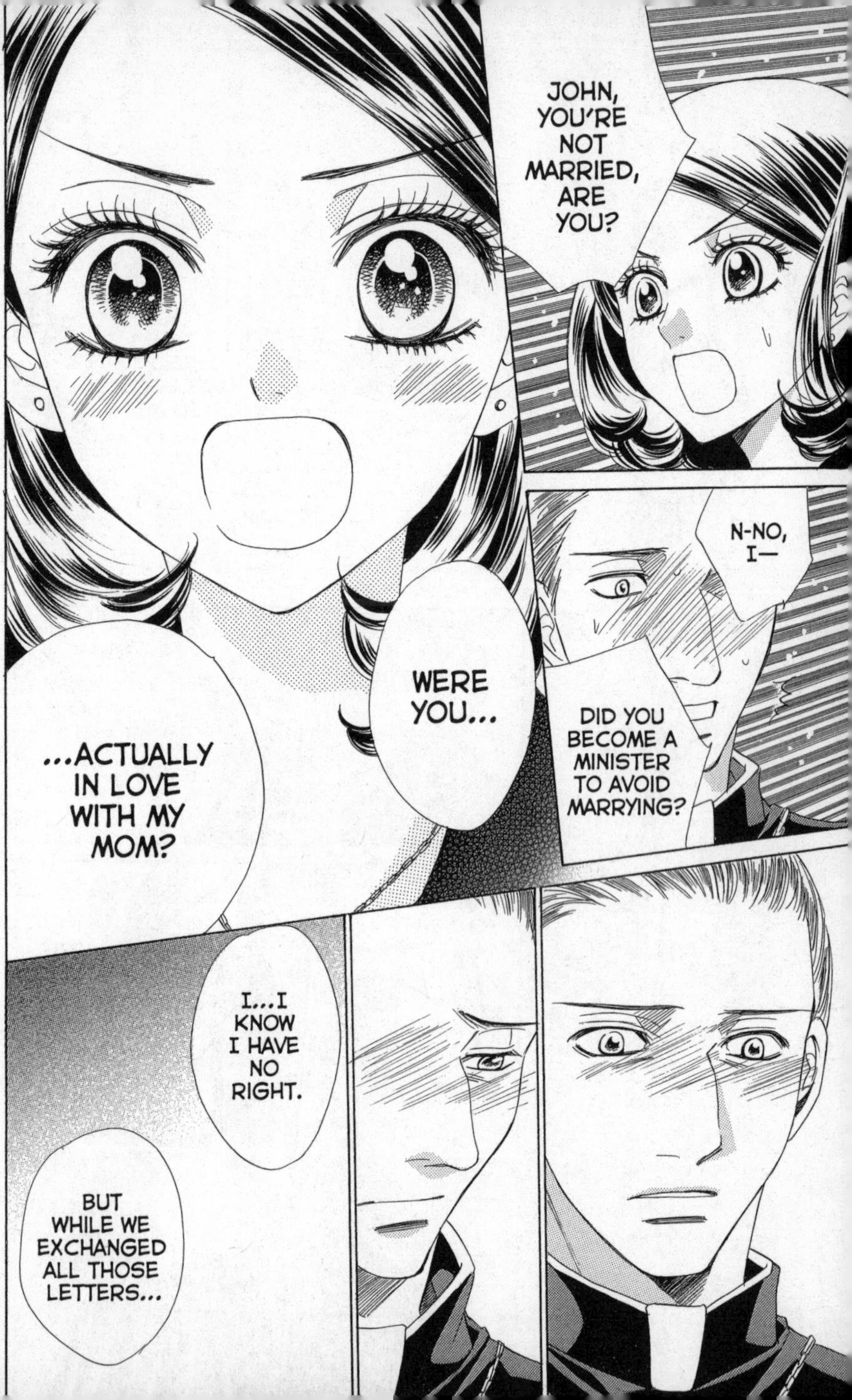
JOHN, YOU'RE NOT MARRIED, ARE YOU?
N-NO, I—
DID YOU BECOME A MINISTER TO AVOID MARRYING?
WERE YOU...
...ACTUALLY IN LOVE WITH MY MOM?
I...I KNOW I HAVE NO RIGHT.
BUT WHILE WE EXCHANGED ALL THOSE LETTERS...

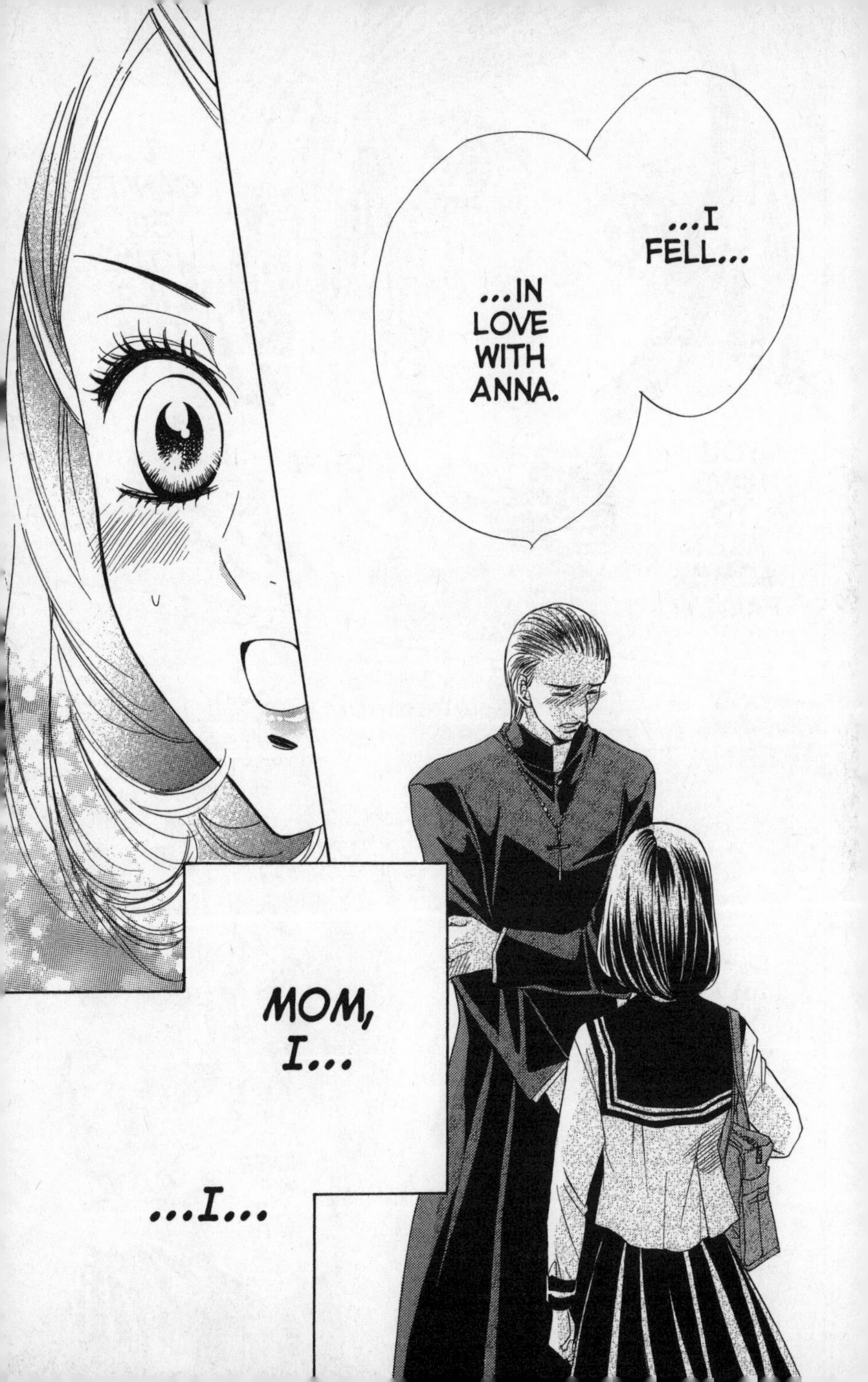
...I FELL...
...IN LOVE WITH ANNA.
MOM, I...
...I...

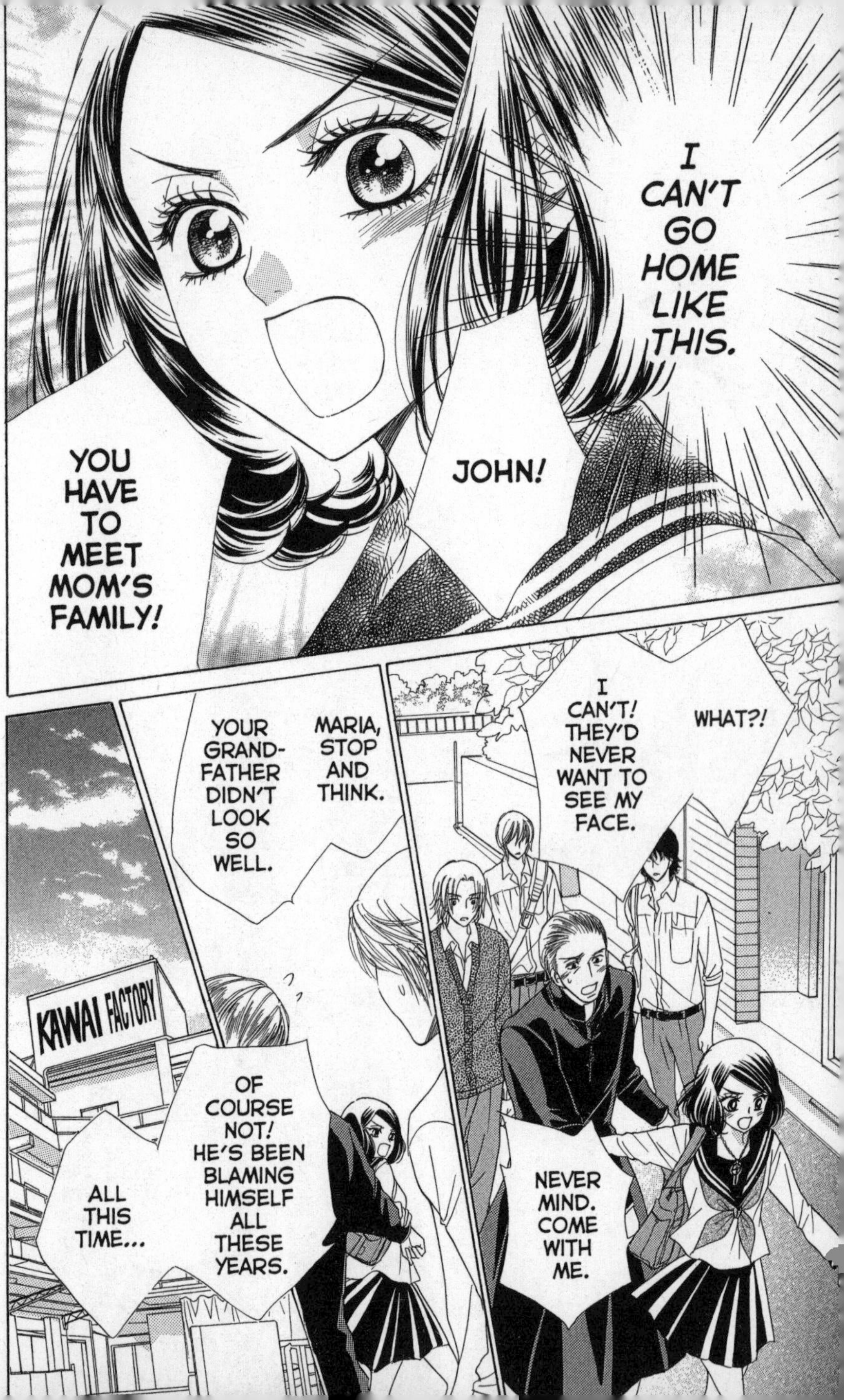
I CAN'T GO HOME LIKE THIS.
JOHN!
YOU HAVE TO MEET MOM'S FAMILY!
WHAT?!
I CAN'T! THEY'D NEVER WANT TO SEE MY FACE.
NEVER MIND. COME WITH ME.
MARIA, STOP AND THINK.
YOUR GRAND-FATHER DIDN'T LOOK SO WELL.
OF COURSE NOT! HE'S BEEN BLAMING HIMSELF ALL THESE YEARS.
ALL THIS TIME...
KAWAI FACTORY

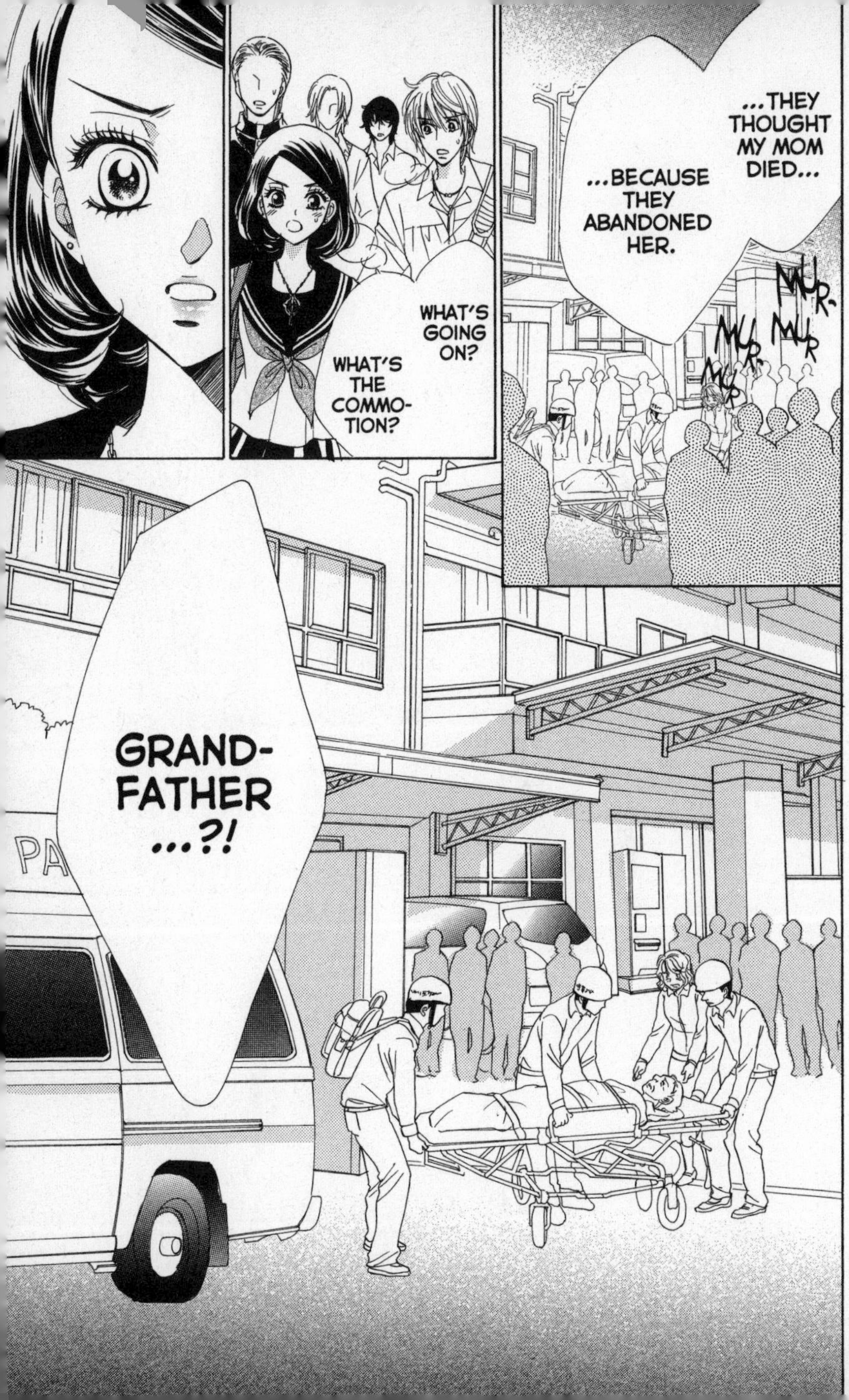
...THEY THOUGHT MY MOM DIED...
...BECAUSE THEY ABANDONED HER.
MUR-MUR
MUR-MUR
WHAT'S GOING ON?
WHAT'S THE COMMOTION?
GRAND-FATHER ...?!
PA

A Devil and
Her Love Song

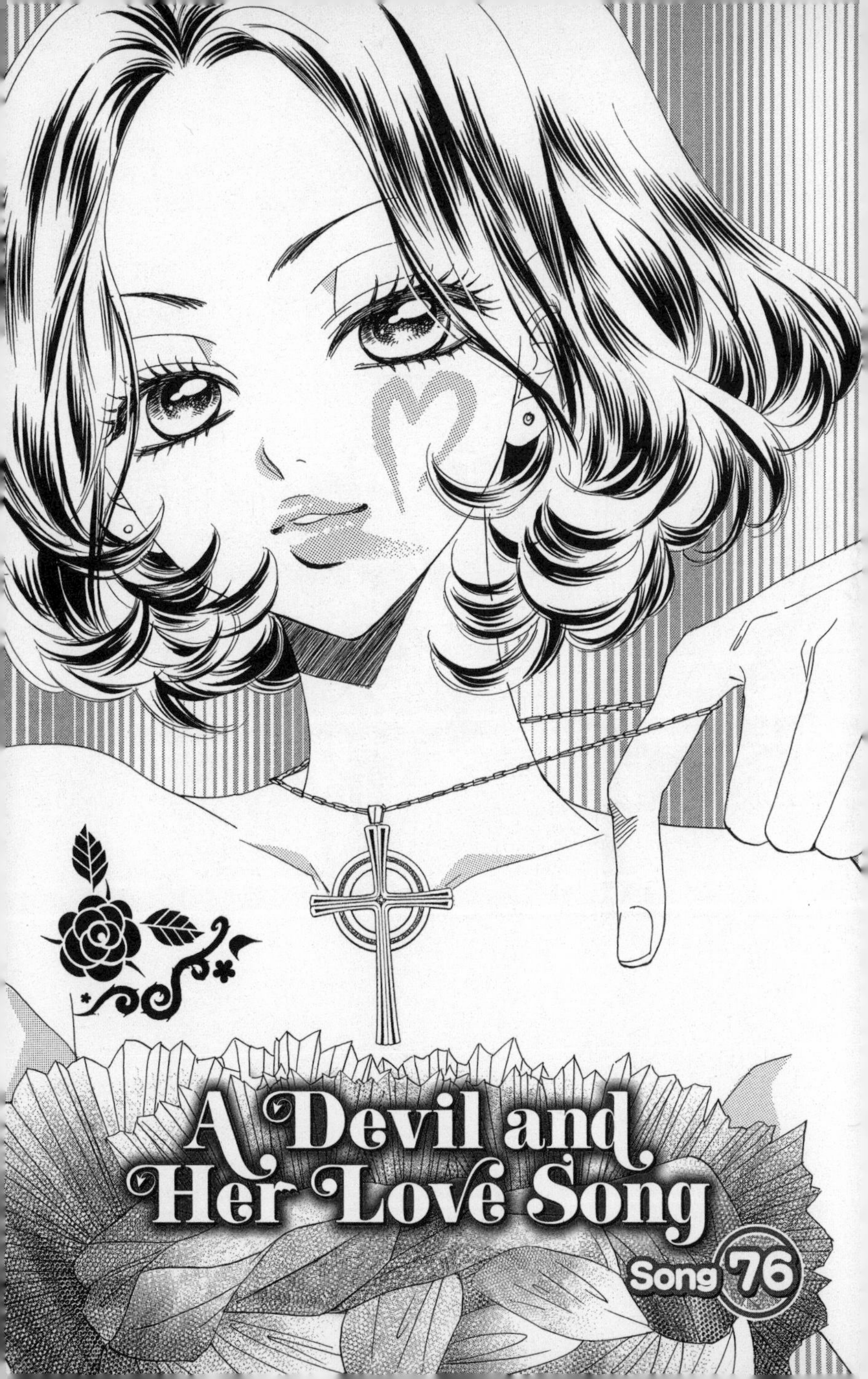
A Devil and
Her Love Song
Song 76

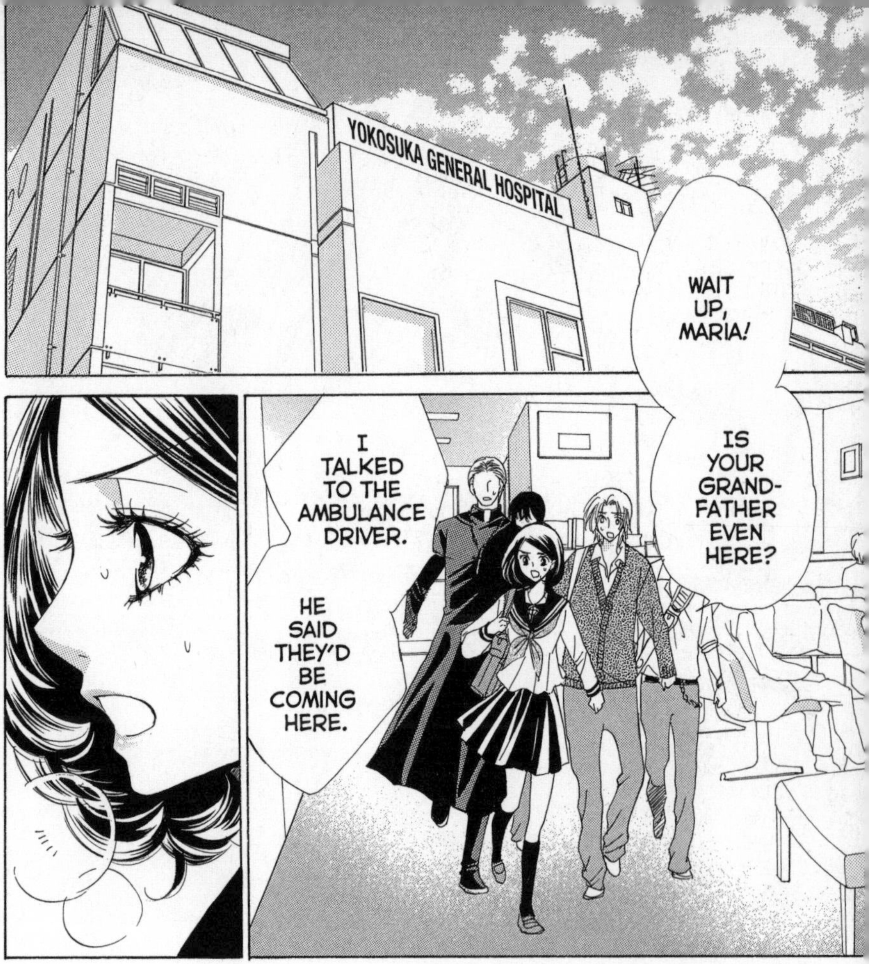
YOKOSUKA GENERAL HOSPITAL
WAIT UP, MARIA!
IS YOUR GRANDFATHER EVEN HERE?
I TALKED TO THE AMBULANCE DRIVER.
HE SAID THEY'D BE COMING HERE.

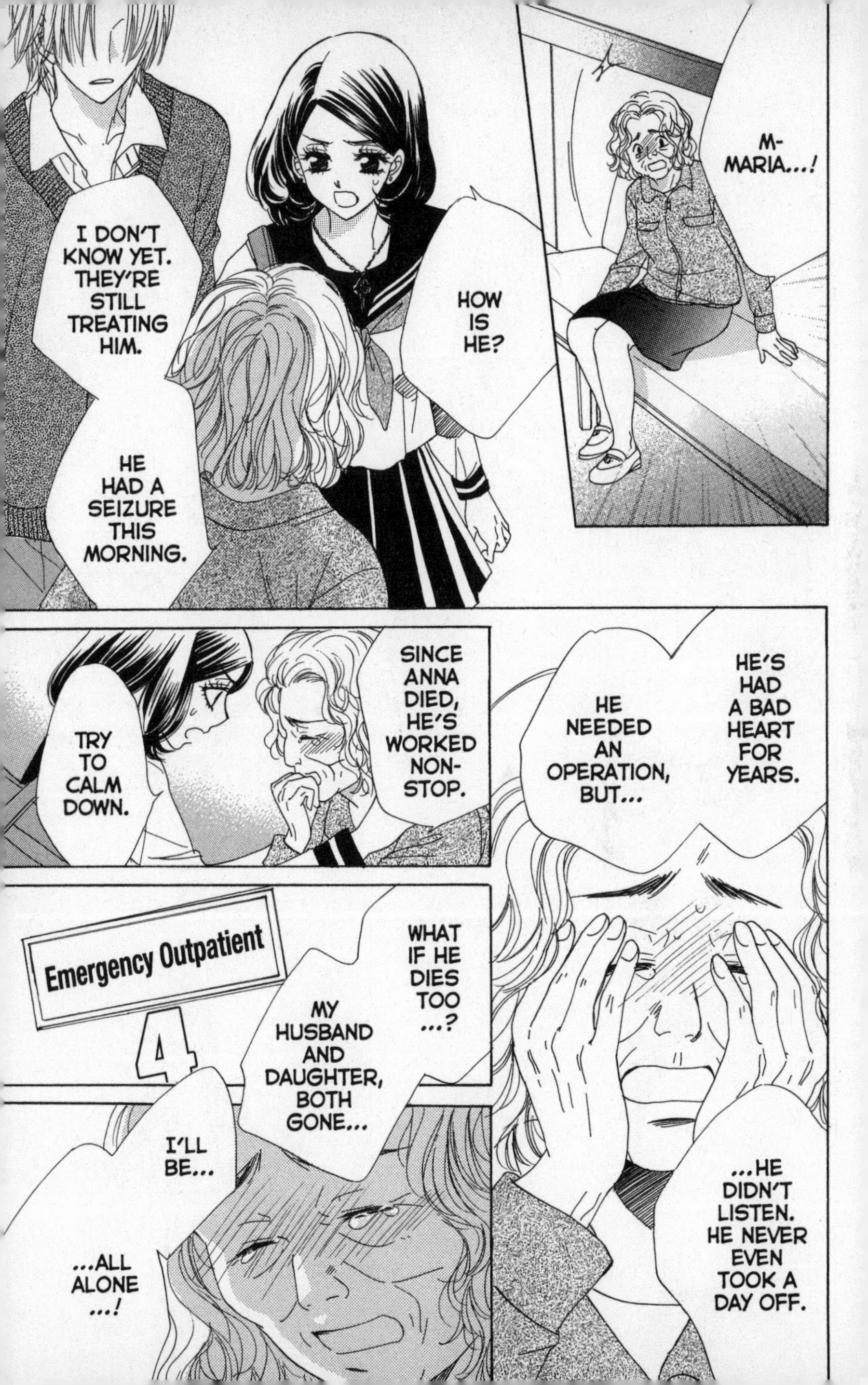
M-MARIA...!
HOW IS HE?
I DON'T KNOW YET. THEY'RE STILL TREATING HIM.
HE HAD A SEIZURE THIS MORNING.
HE'S HAD A BAD HEART FOR YEARS.
HE NEEDED AN OPERATION, BUT...
...HE DIDN'T LISTEN. HE NEVER EVEN TOOK A DAY OFF.
SINCE ANNA DIED, HE'S WORKED NON-STOP.
TRY TO CALM DOWN.
WHAT IF HE DIES TOO...?
MY HUSBAND AND DAUGHTER, BOTH GONE...
Emergency Outpatient
4
I'LL BE...
...ALL ALONE...!

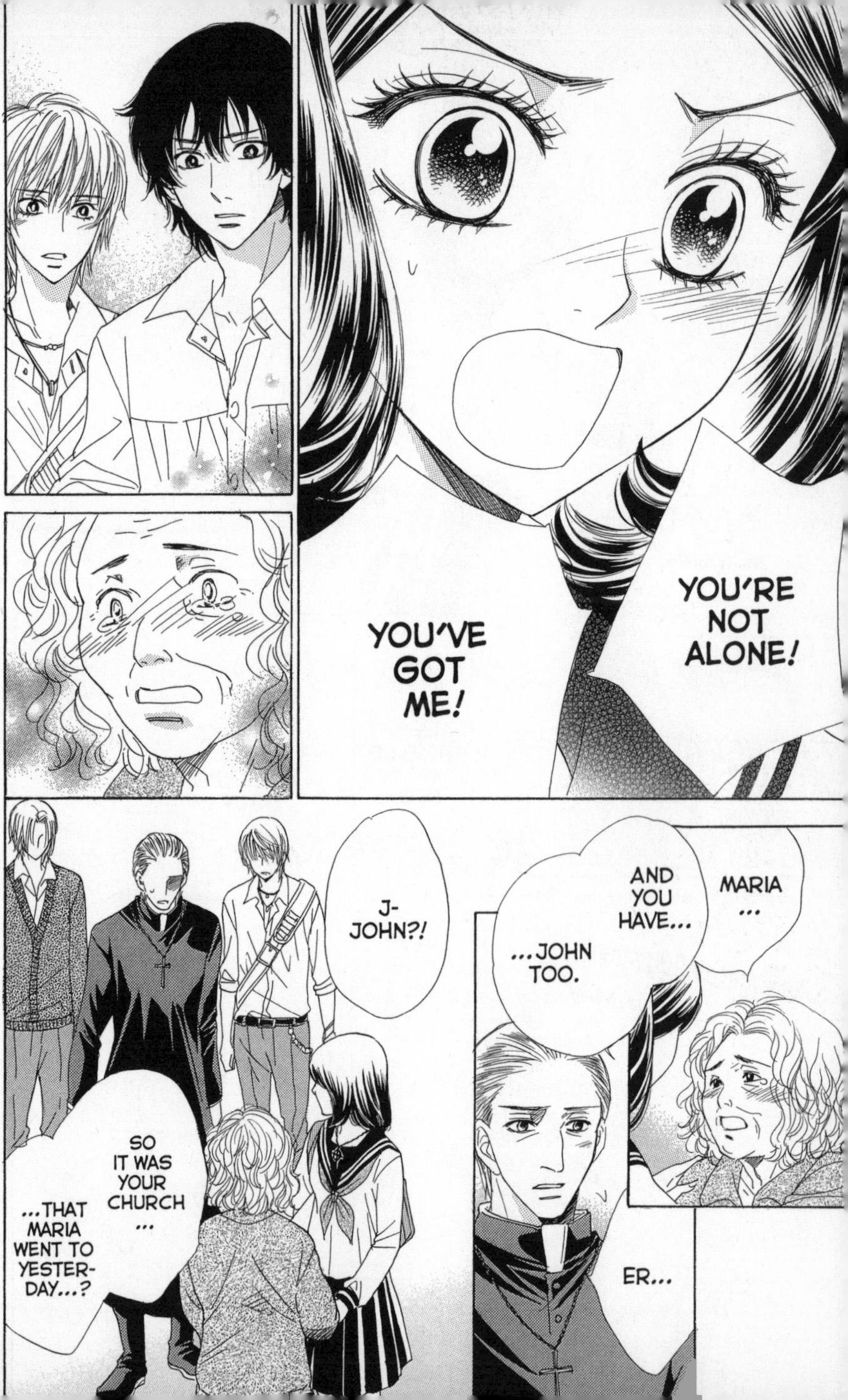
YOU'RE NOT ALONE!
YOU'VE GOT ME!
MARIA ...
AND YOU HAVE...
...JOHN TOO.
ER...
J- JOHN?!
SO IT WAS YOUR CHURCH ...
...THAT MARIA WENT TO YESTER- DAY...?

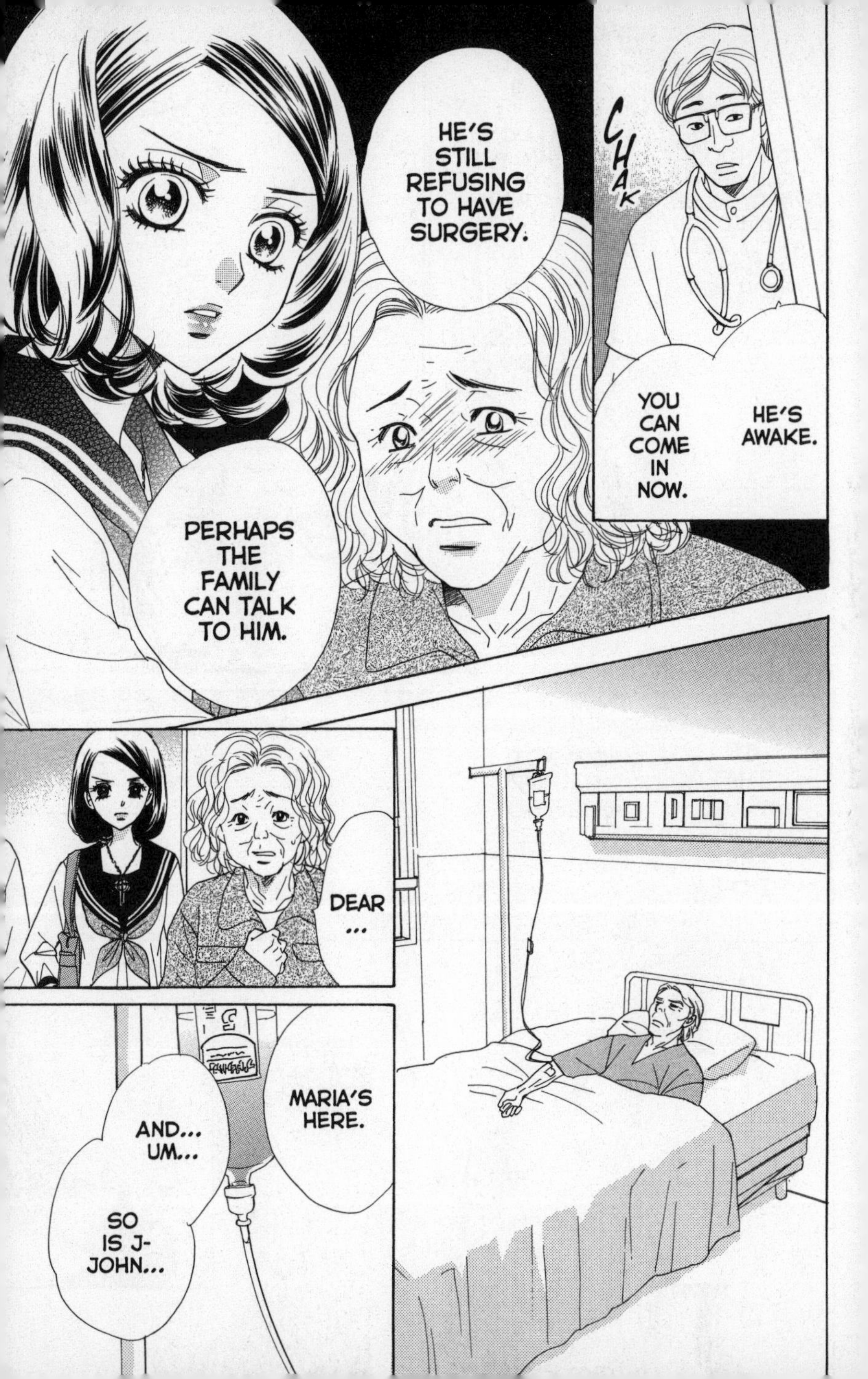
CHAK
HE'S AWAKE.
YOU CAN COME IN NOW.
HE'S STILL REFUSING TO HAVE SURGERY.
PERHAPS THE FAMILY CAN TALK TO HIM.
DEAR...
MARIA'S HERE.
AND... UM...
SO IS J-JOHN...

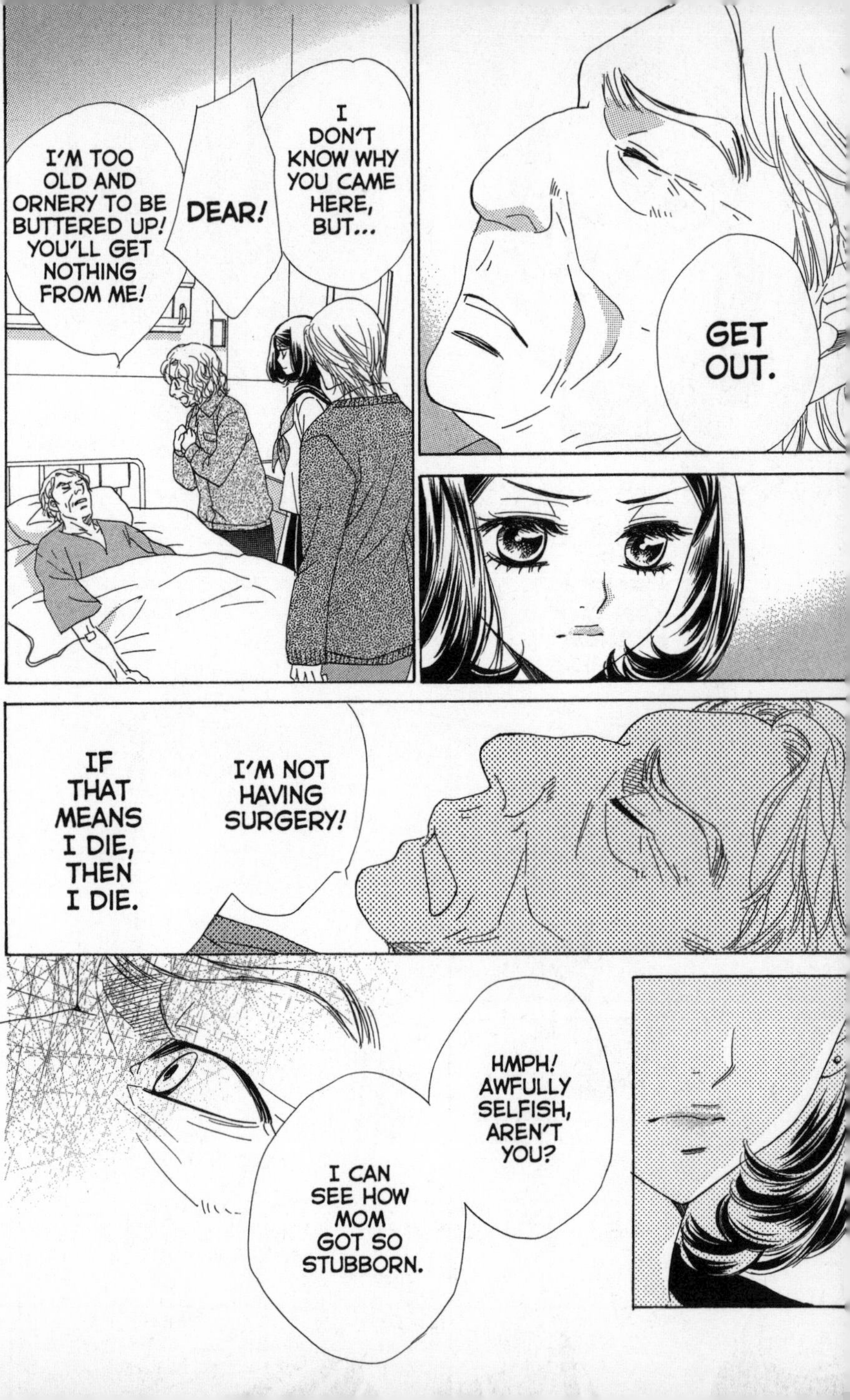
GET OUT.
I DON'T KNOW WHY YOU CAME HERE, BUT...
DEAR!
I'M TOO OLD AND ORNERY TO BE BUTTERED UP! YOU'LL GET NOTHING FROM ME!
I'M NOT HAVING SURGERY!
IF THAT MEANS I DIE, THEN I DIE.
HMPH! AWFULLY SELFISH, AREN'T YOU?
I CAN SEE HOW MOM GOT SO STUBBORN.

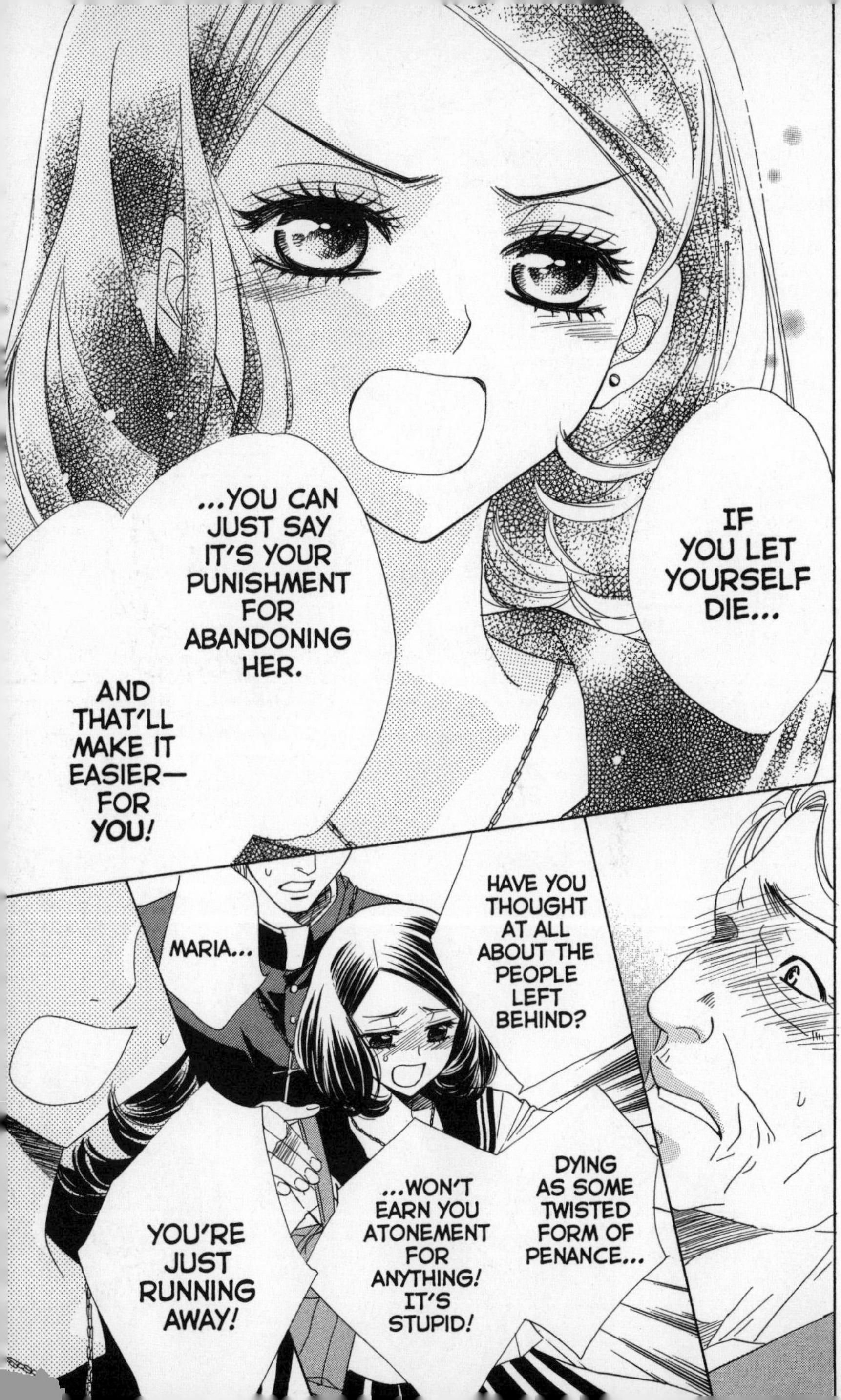
IF YOU LET YOURSELF DIE...
...YOU CAN JUST SAY IT'S YOUR PUNISHMENT FOR ABANDONING HER.
AND THAT'LL MAKE IT EASIER— FOR YOU!
HAVE YOU THOUGHT AT ALL ABOUT THE PEOPLE LEFT BEHIND?
MARIA...
DYING AS SOME TWISTED FORM OF PENANCE...
...WON'T EARN YOU ATONEMENT FOR ANYTHING! IT'S STUPID!
YOU'RE JUST RUNNING AWAY!

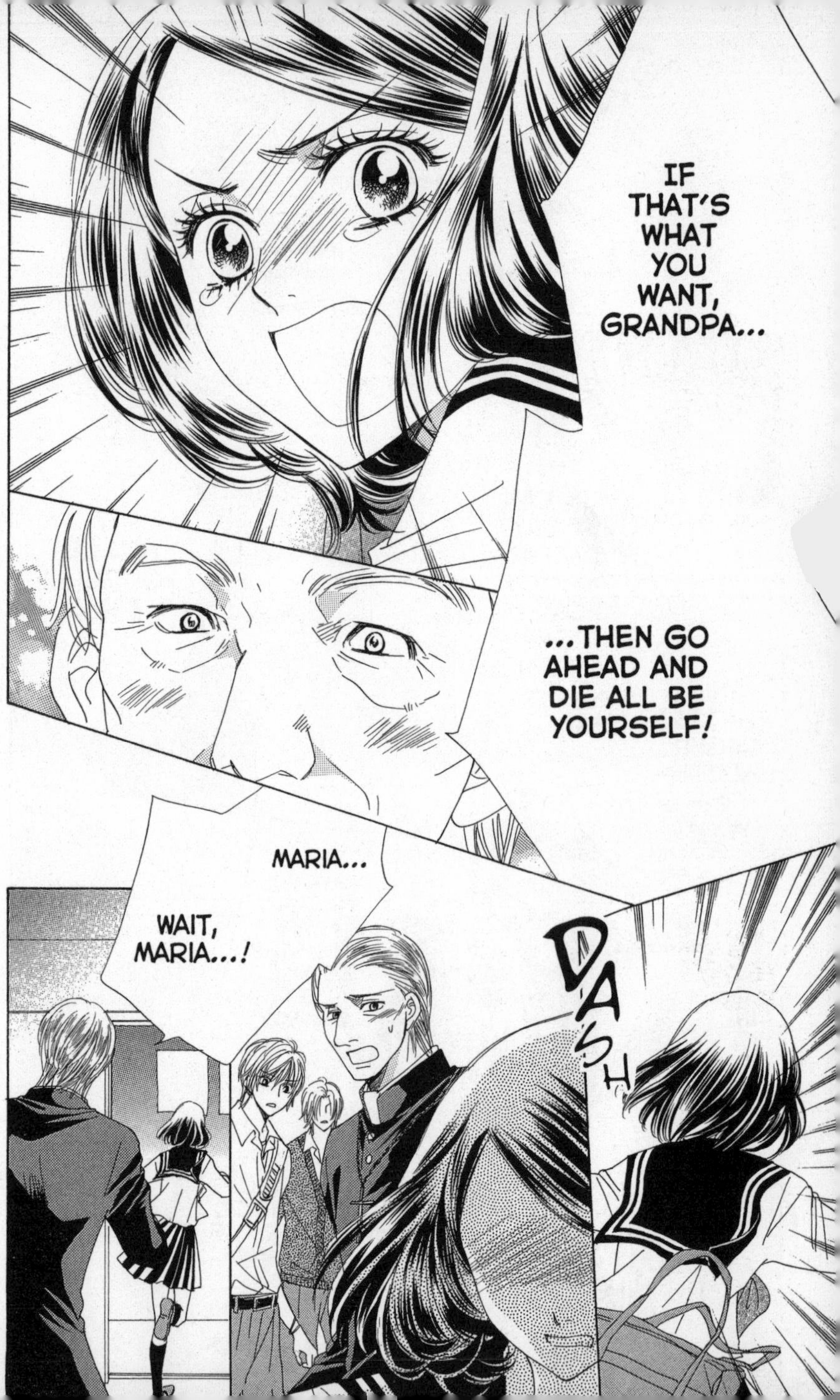
IF THAT'S WHAT YOU WANT, GRANDPA...
...THEN GO AHEAD AND DIE ALL BE YOURSELF!
MARIA...
DASH
WAIT, MARIA...!

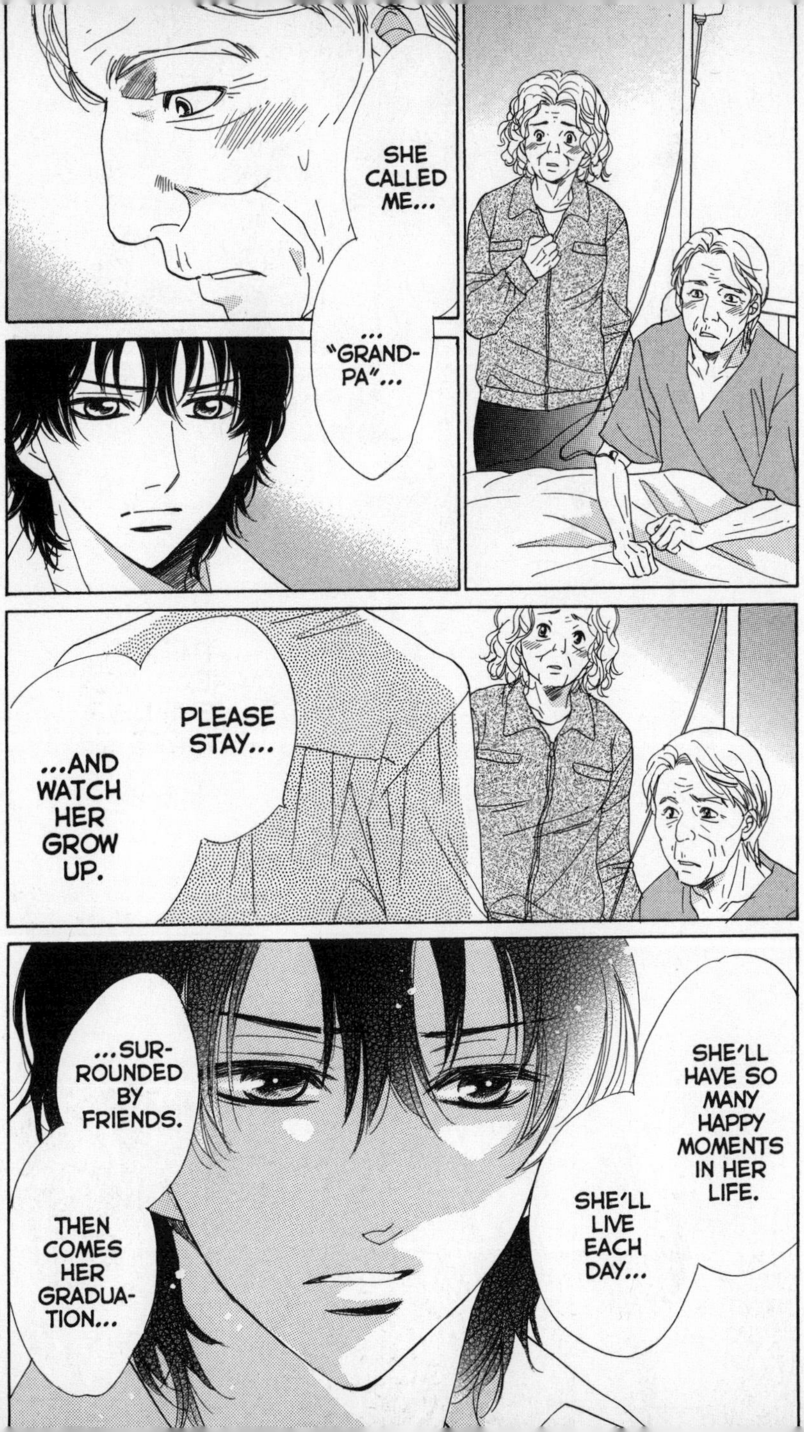
SHE CALLED ME...
..."GRAND-PA"...
PLEASE STAY...
...AND WATCH HER GROW UP.
SHE'LL HAVE SO MANY HAPPY MOMENTS IN HER LIFE.
SHE'LL LIVE EACH DAY...
...SUR-ROUNDED BY FRIENDS.
THEN COMES HER GRADUA-TION...

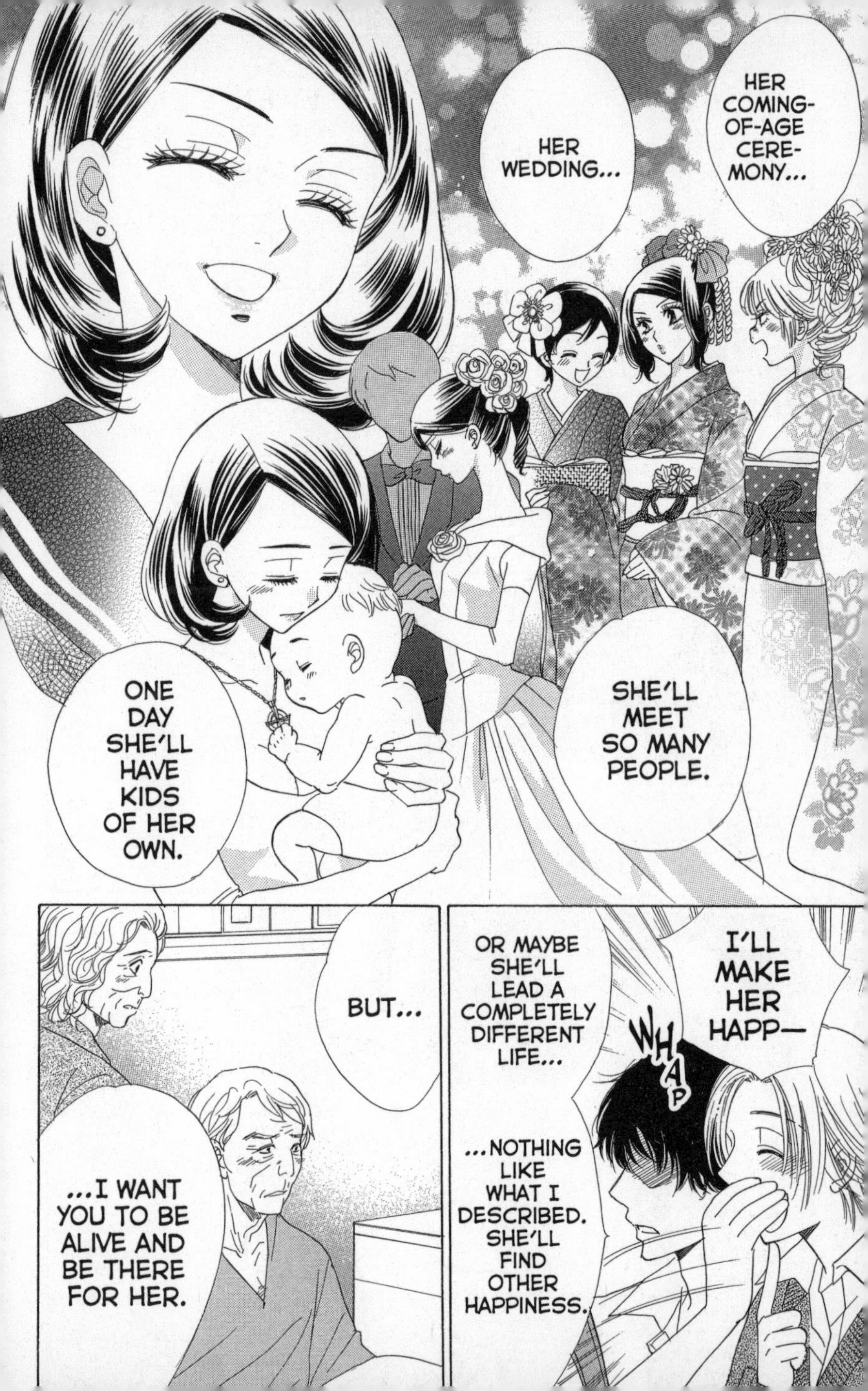
HER COMING-OF-AGE CEREMONY...
HER WEDDING...
SHE'LL MEET SO MANY PEOPLE.
ONE DAY SHE'LL HAVE KIDS OF HER OWN.
I'LL MAKE HER HAPP—
WHAP
OR MAYBE SHE'LL LEAD A COMPLETELY DIFFERENT LIFE...
...NOTHING LIKE WHAT I DESCRIBED. SHE'LL FIND OTHER HAPPINESS.
BUT...
...I WANT YOU TO BE ALIVE AND BE THERE FOR HER.

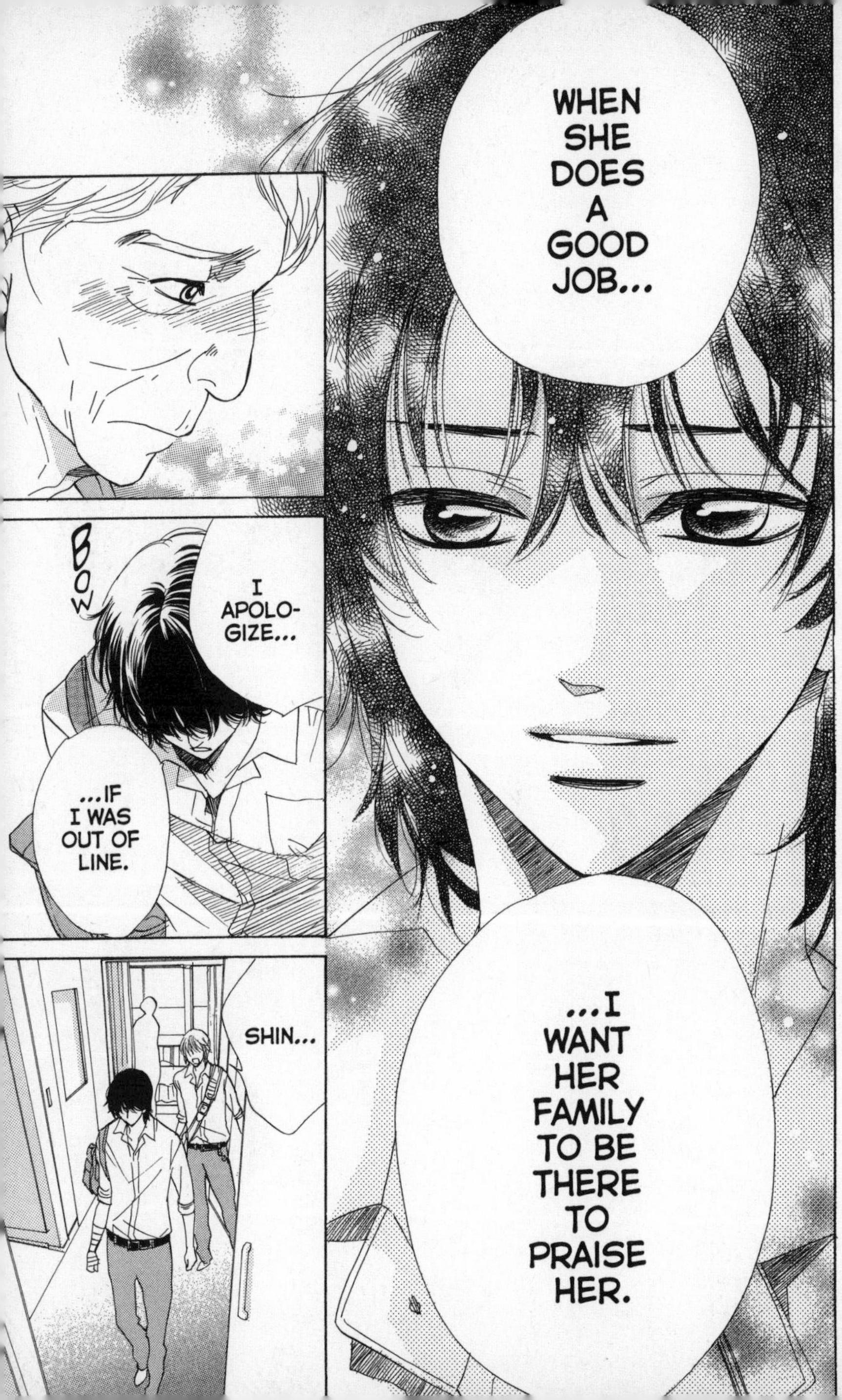
WHEN SHE DOES A GOOD JOB...
...I WANT HER FAMILY TO BE THERE TO PRAISE HER.
BOW
I APOLOGIZE...
...IF I WAS OUT OF LINE.
SHIN...

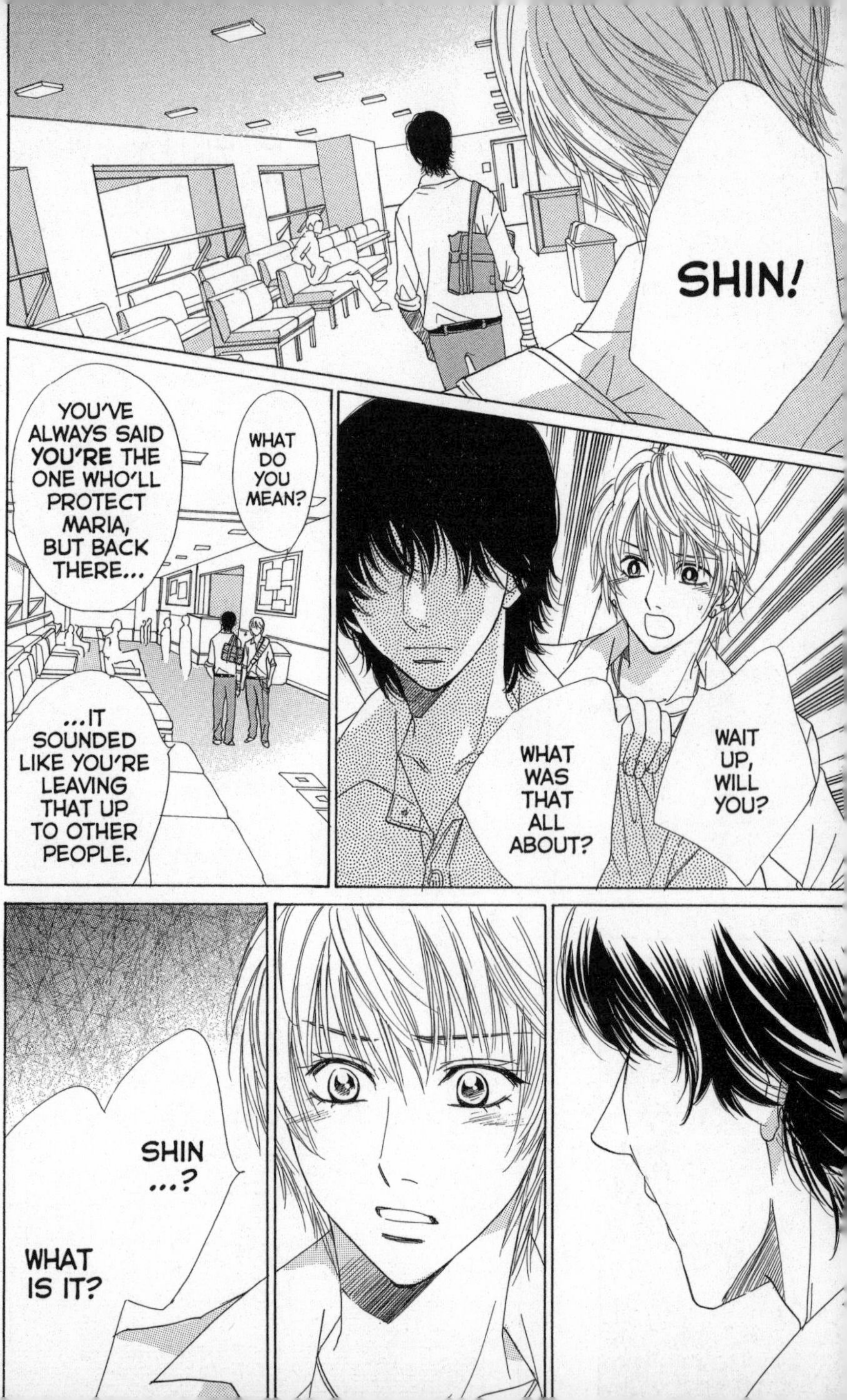
SHIN!
WAIT UP, WILL YOU?
WHAT WAS THAT ALL ABOUT?
WHAT DO YOU MEAN?
YOU'VE ALWAYS SAID YOU'RE THE ONE WHO'LL PROTECT MARIA, BUT BACK THERE...
...IT SOUNDED LIKE YOU'RE LEAVING THAT UP TO OTHER PEOPLE.
SHIN ...?
WHAT IS IT?

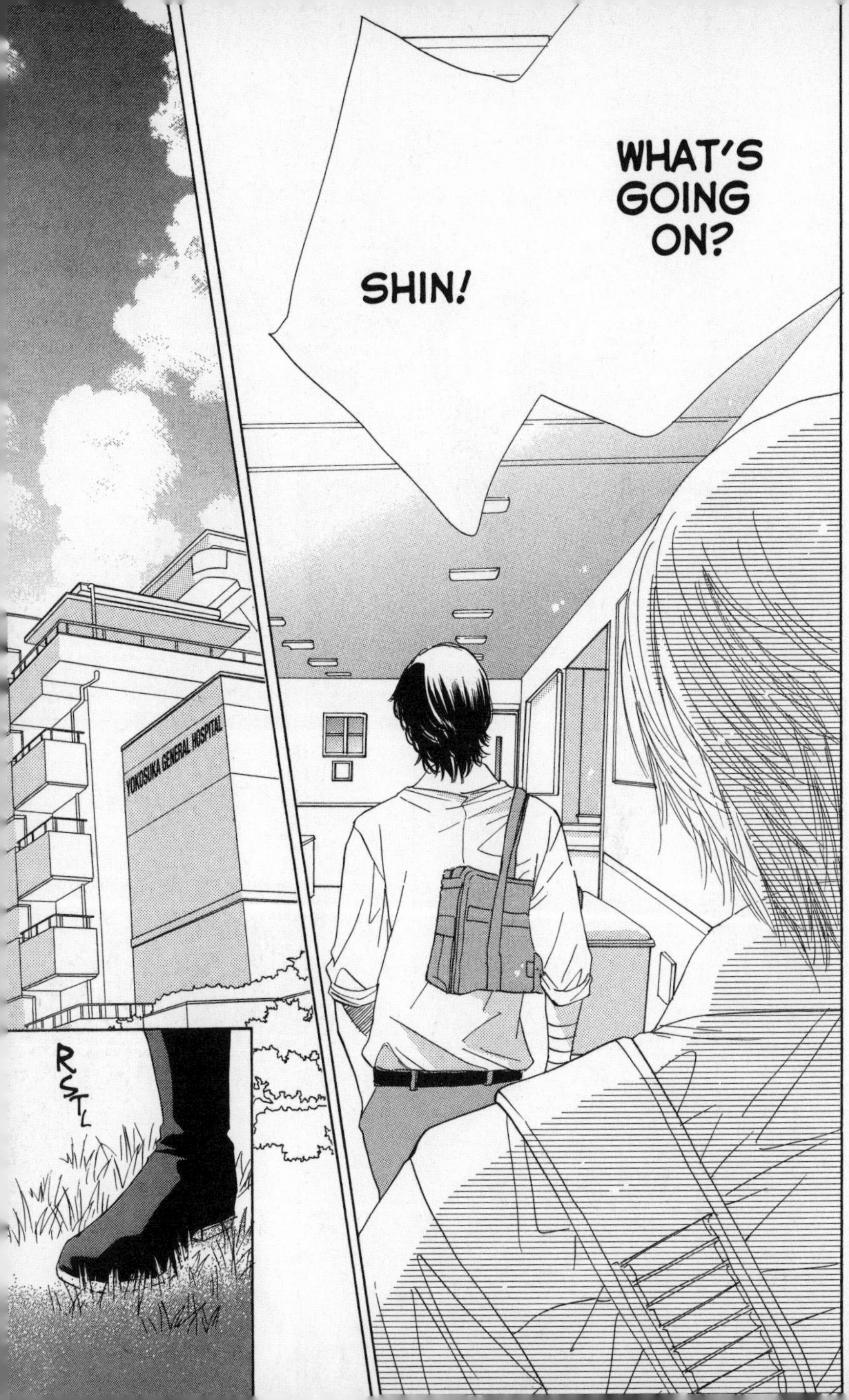
WHAT'S GOING ON?
SHIN!
YOKOSUKA GENERAL HOSPITAL
RSTL

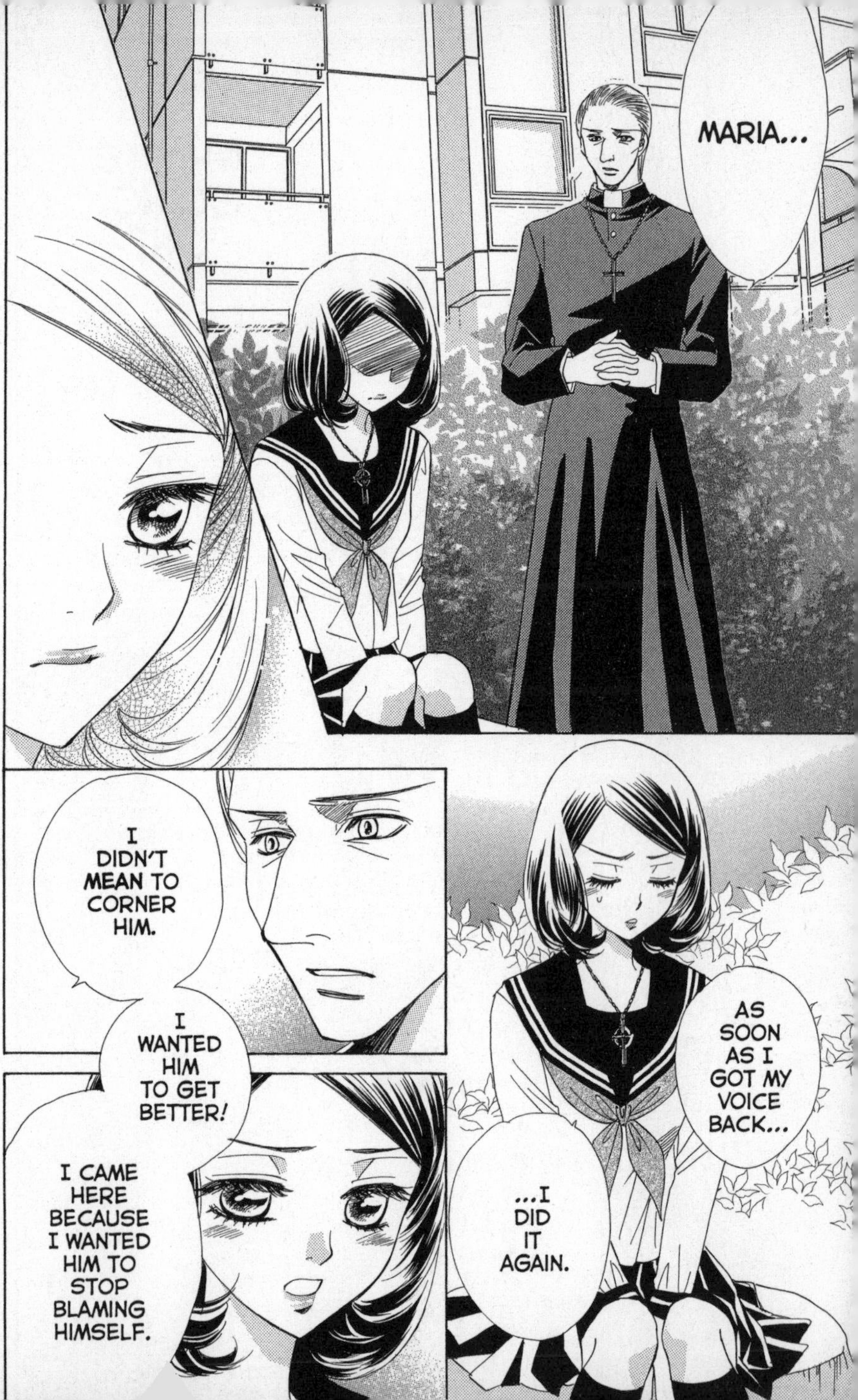
MARIA...
AS SOON AS I GOT MY VOICE BACK...
...I DID IT AGAIN.
I DIDN'T MEAN TO CORNER HIM.
I WANTED HIM TO GET BETTER!
I CAME HERE BECAUSE I WANTED HIM TO STOP BLAMING HIMSELF.

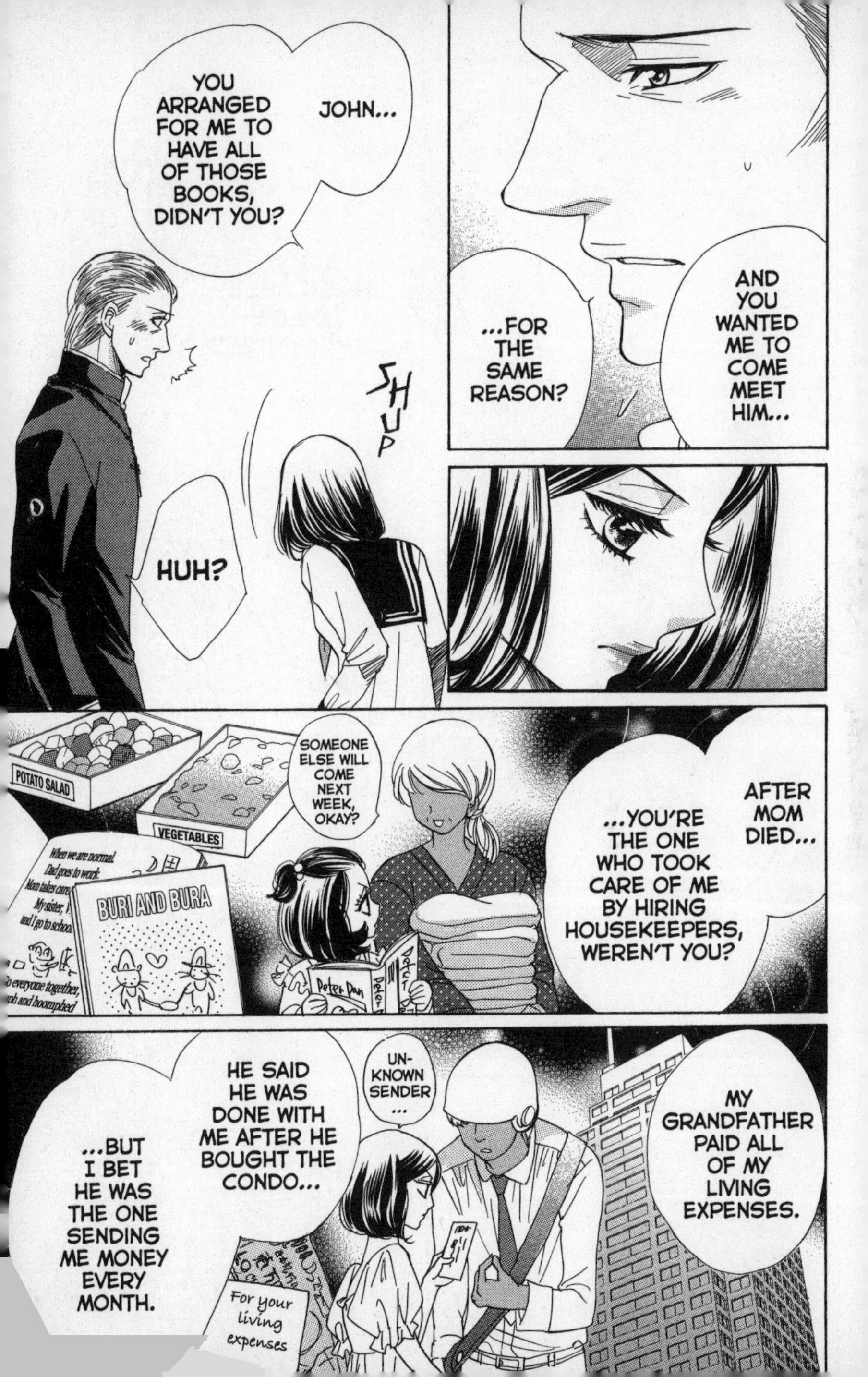
AND YOU WANTED ME TO COME MEET HIM...
...FOR THE SAME REASON?
JOHN...
YOU ARRANGED FOR ME TO HAVE ALL OF THOSE BOOKS, DIDN'T YOU?
SHUP
HUH?
AFTER MOM DIED...
...YOU'RE THE ONE WHO TOOK CARE OF ME BY HIRING HOUSEKEEPERS, WEREN'T YOU?
SOMEONE ELSE WILL COME NEXT WEEK, OKAY?
POTATO SALAD
VEGETABLES
When we are normal
Dad goes to work
BURI AND BURA
Peter Pan
MY GRANDFATHER PAID ALL OF MY LIVING EXPENSES.
UN-KNOWN SENDER ...
HE SAID HE WAS DONE WITH ME AFTER HE BOUGHT THE CONDO...
...BUT I BET HE WAS THE ONE SENDING ME MONEY EVERY MONTH.
For your living expenses

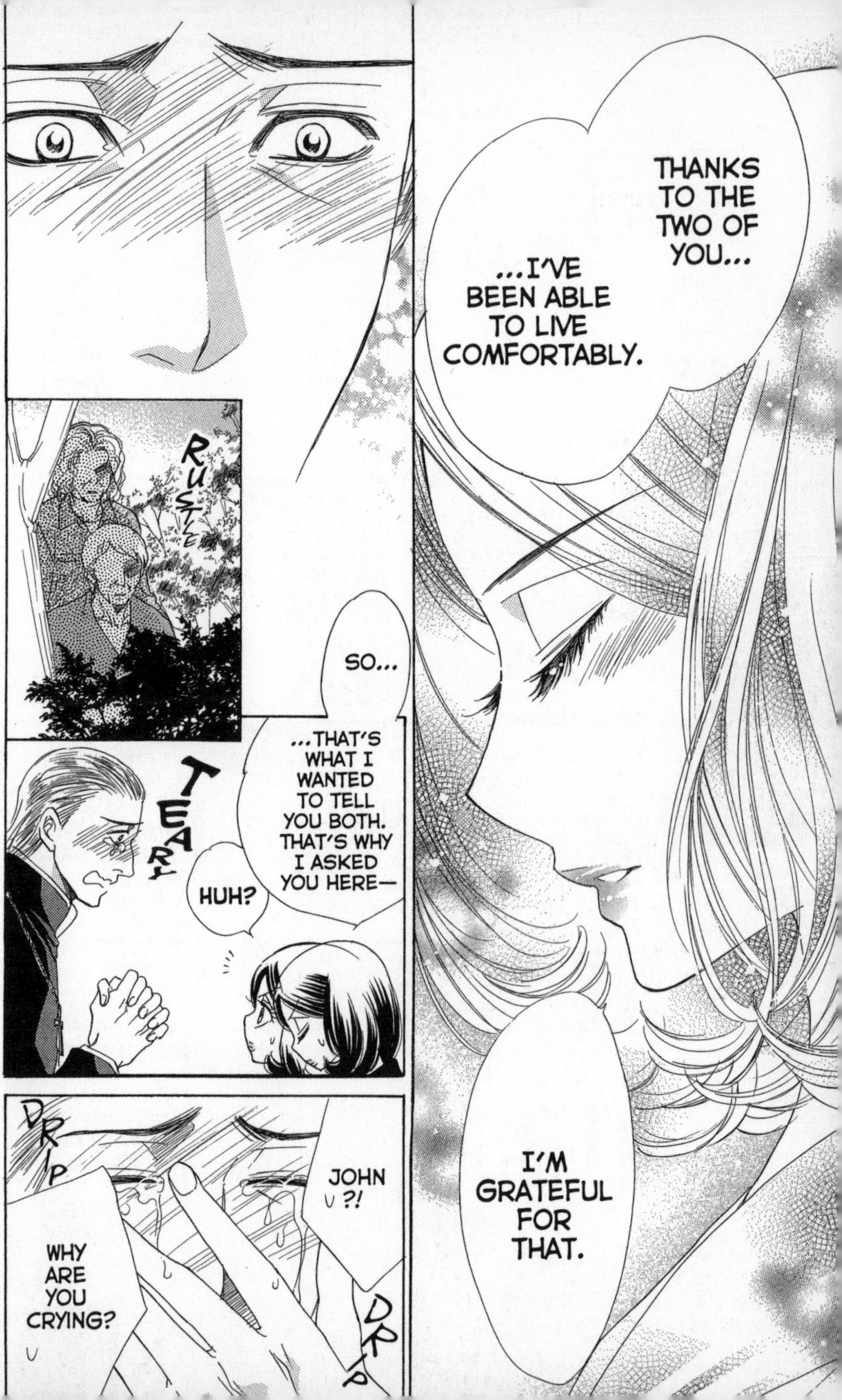
THANKS TO THE TWO OF YOU...
...I'VE BEEN ABLE TO LIVE COMFORTABLY.
I'M GRATEFUL FOR THAT.
RUSTLE
SO...
...THAT'S WHAT I WANTED TO TELL YOU BOTH. THAT'S WHY I ASKED YOU HERE—
TEAR
HUH?
JOHN?!
DRIP
WHY ARE YOU CRYING?
DRIP

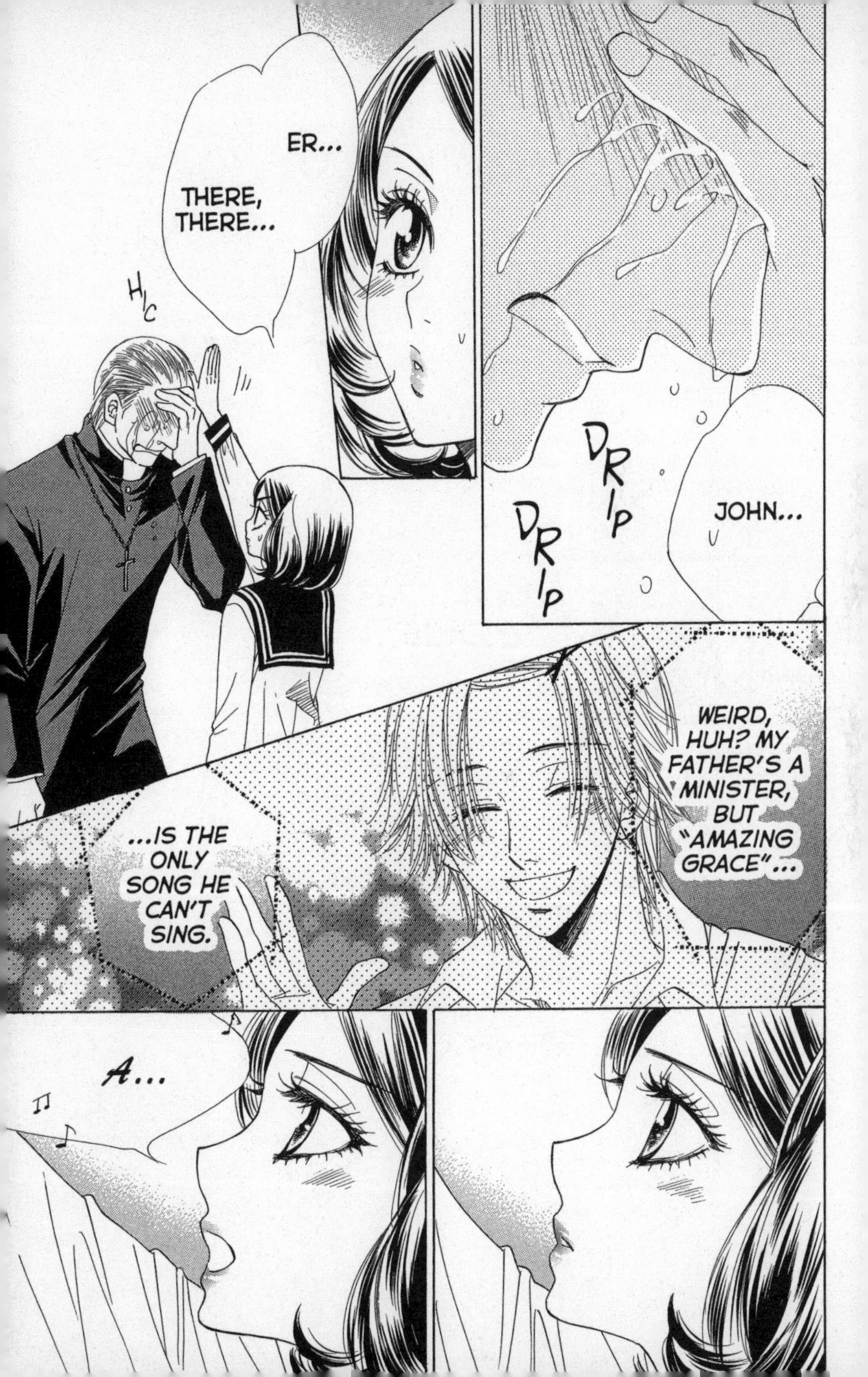
JOHN...
DRIP
DRIP
ER...
THERE, THERE...
HIC
WEIRD, HUH? MY FATHER'S A MINISTER, BUT "AMAZING GRACE"...
...IS THE ONLY SONG HE CAN'T SING.
A...

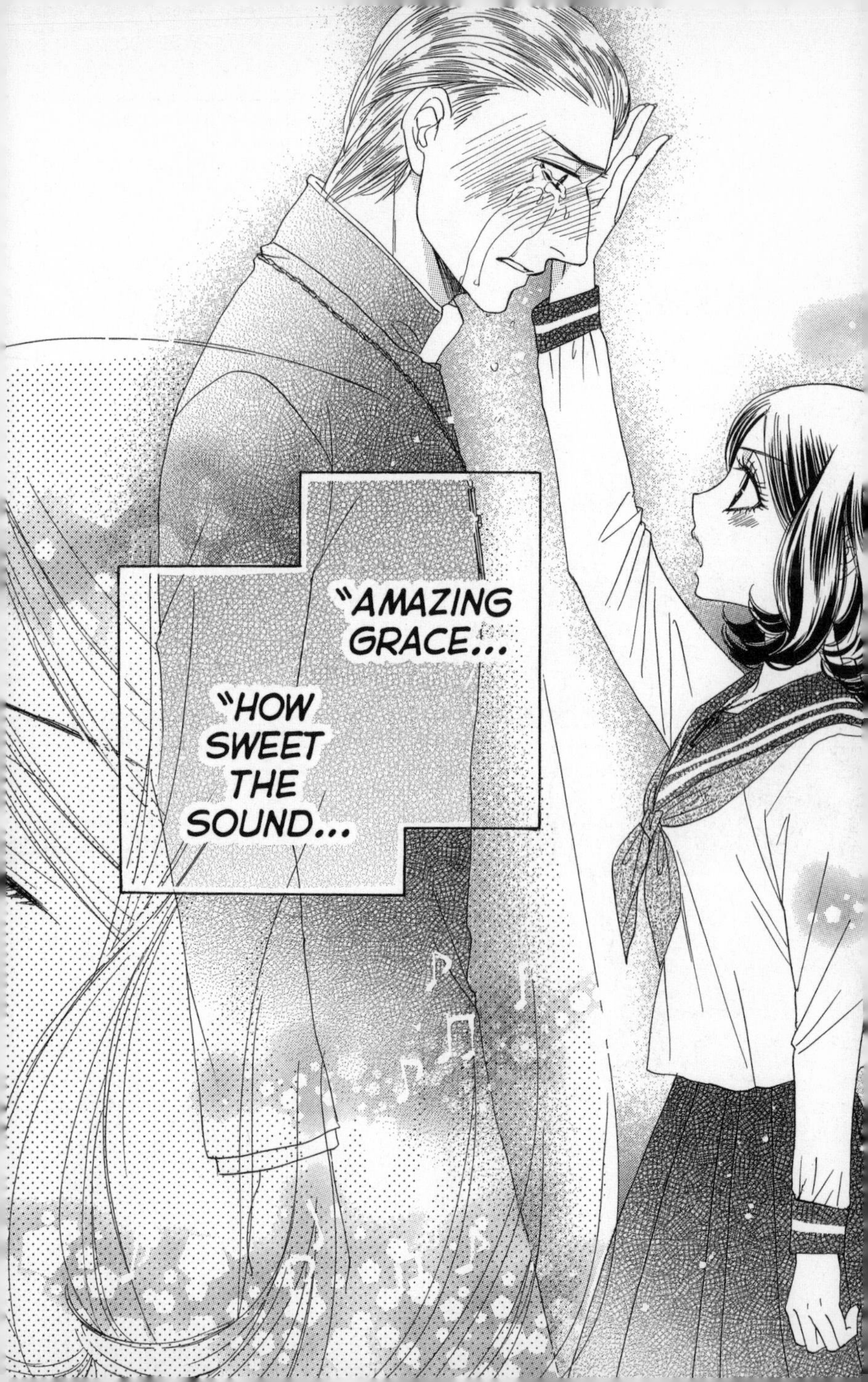
"AMAZING GRACE...
"HOW SWEET THE SOUND...

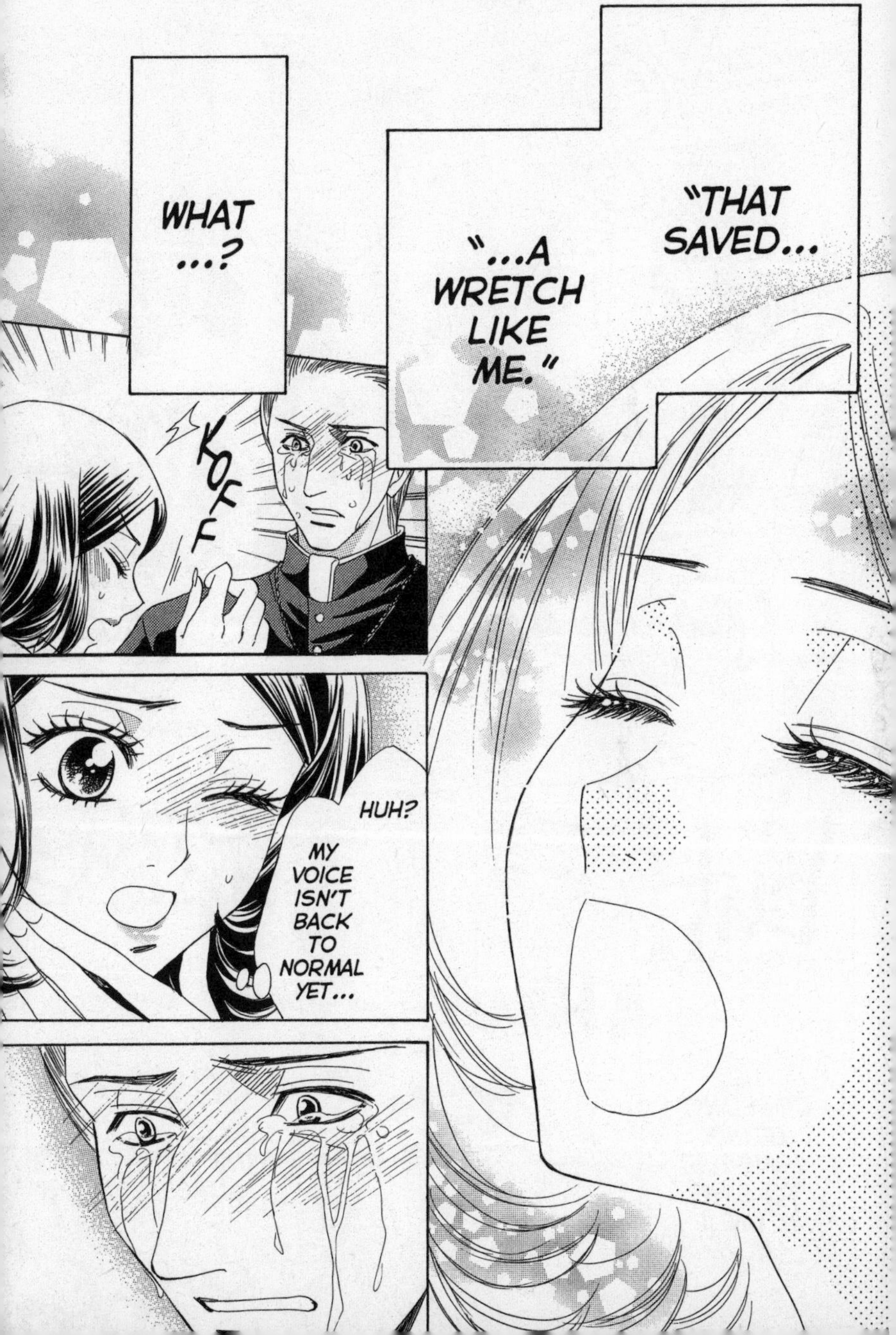
"THAT SAVED...
"...A WRETCH LIKE ME."
WHAT ...?
KOFF
HUH?
MY VOICE ISN'T BACK TO NORMAL YET...

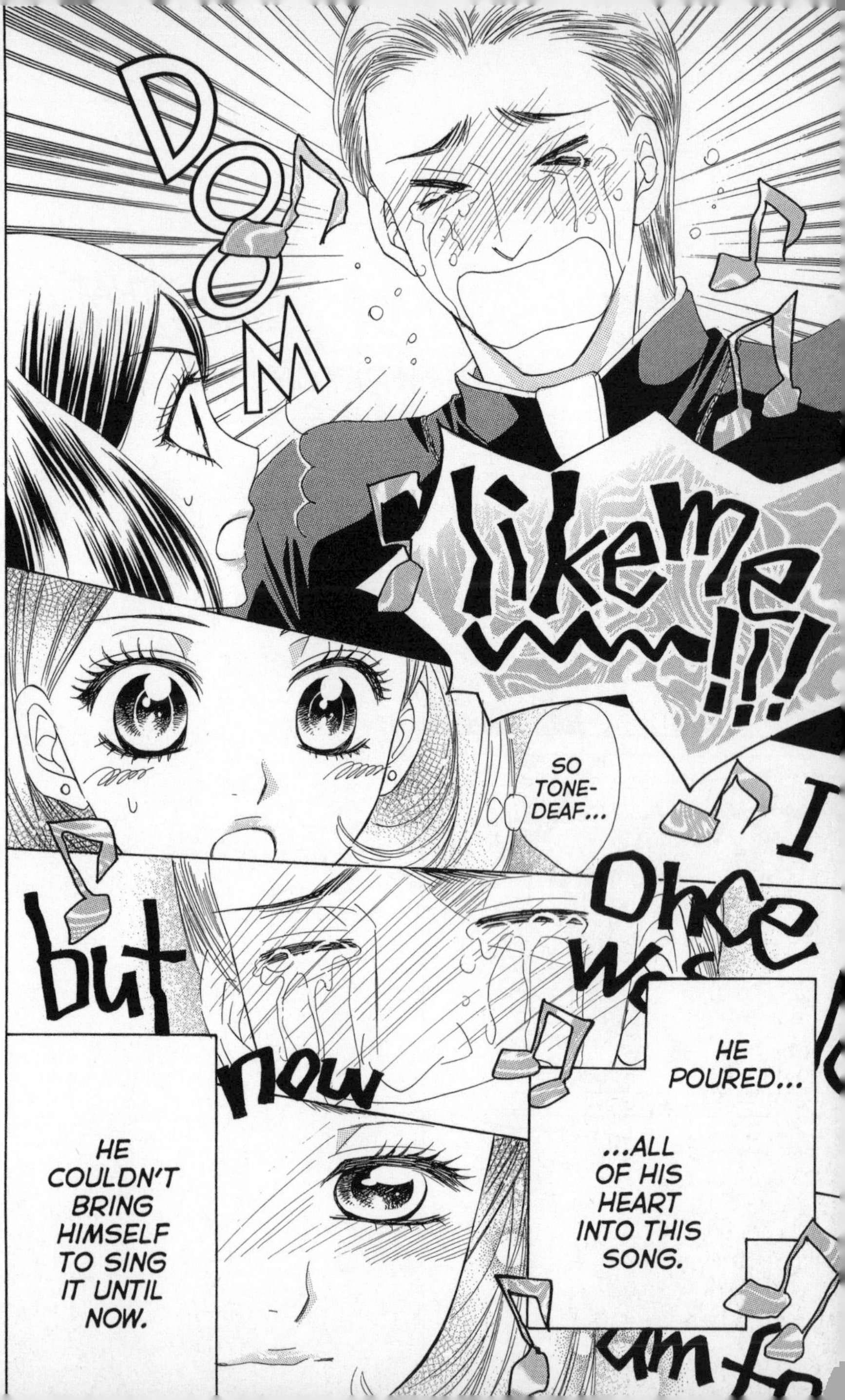
like me!!!
DOOM
SO TONE-DEAF...
I Once
but now
HE POURED...
...ALL OF HIS HEART INTO THIS SONG.
HE COULDN'T BRING HIMSELF TO SING IT UNTIL NOW.

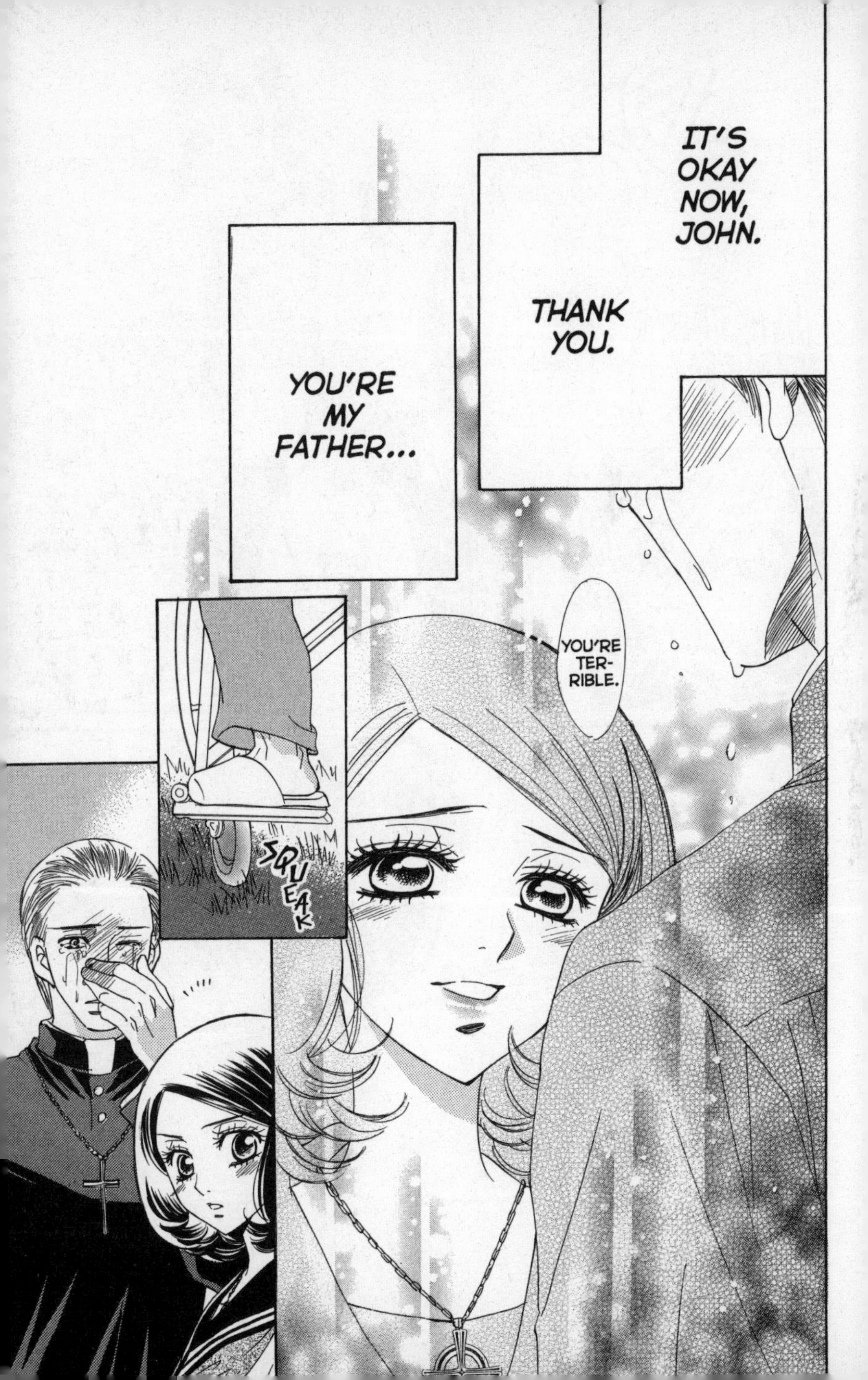
IT'S OKAY NOW, JOHN.
THANK YOU.
YOU'RE MY FATHER...
YOU'RE TER-RIBLE.
SQUEAK

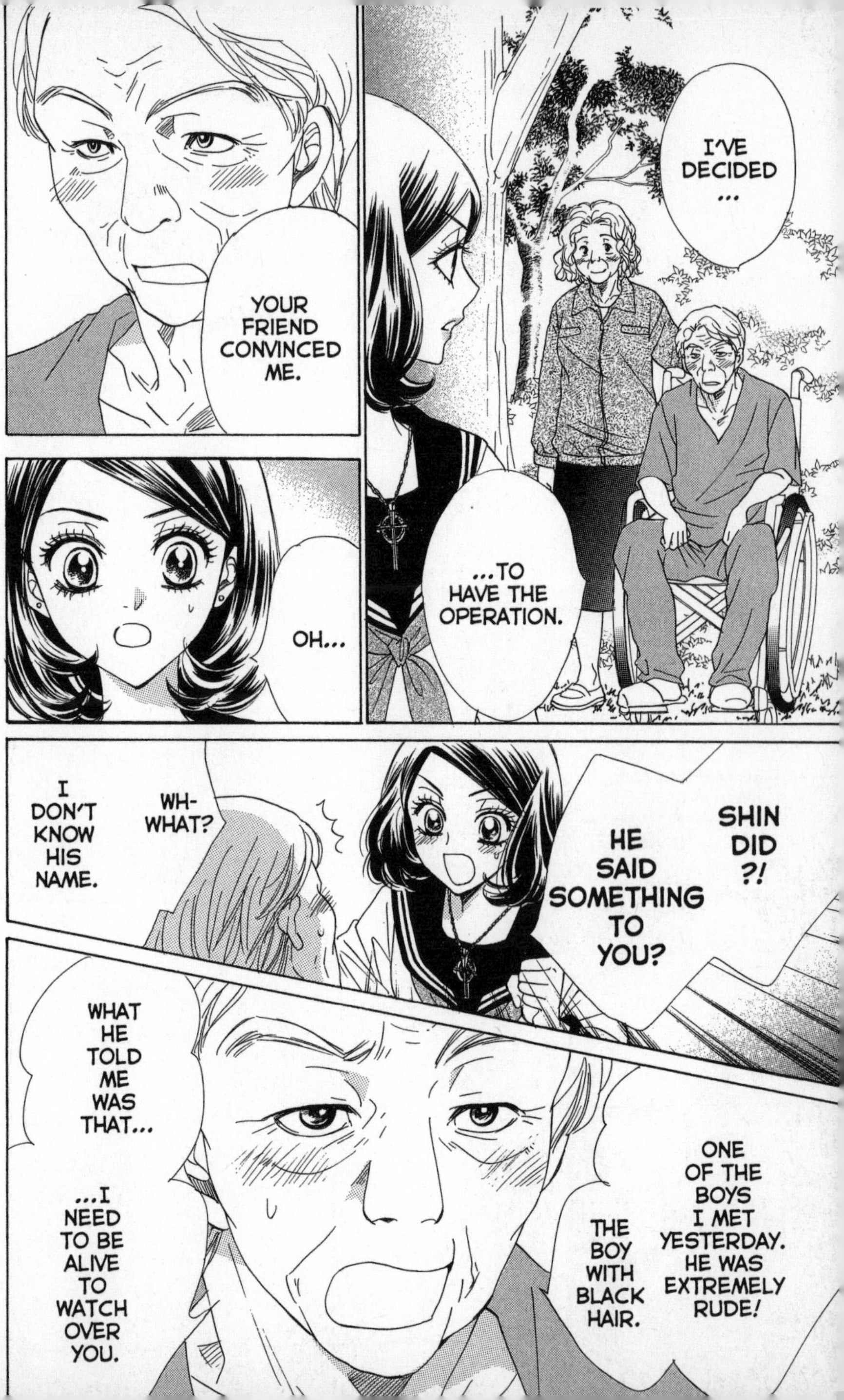
I'VE DECIDED ...
...TO HAVE THE OPERATION.
YOUR FRIEND CONVINCED ME.
OH...
SHIN DID ?!
HE SAID SOMETHING TO YOU?
WH- WHAT?
I DON'T KNOW HIS NAME.
ONE OF THE BOYS I MET YESTERDAY. HE WAS EXTREMELY RUDE!
THE BOY WITH BLACK HAIR.
WHAT HE TOLD ME WAS THAT...
...I NEED TO BE ALIVE TO WATCH OVER YOU.

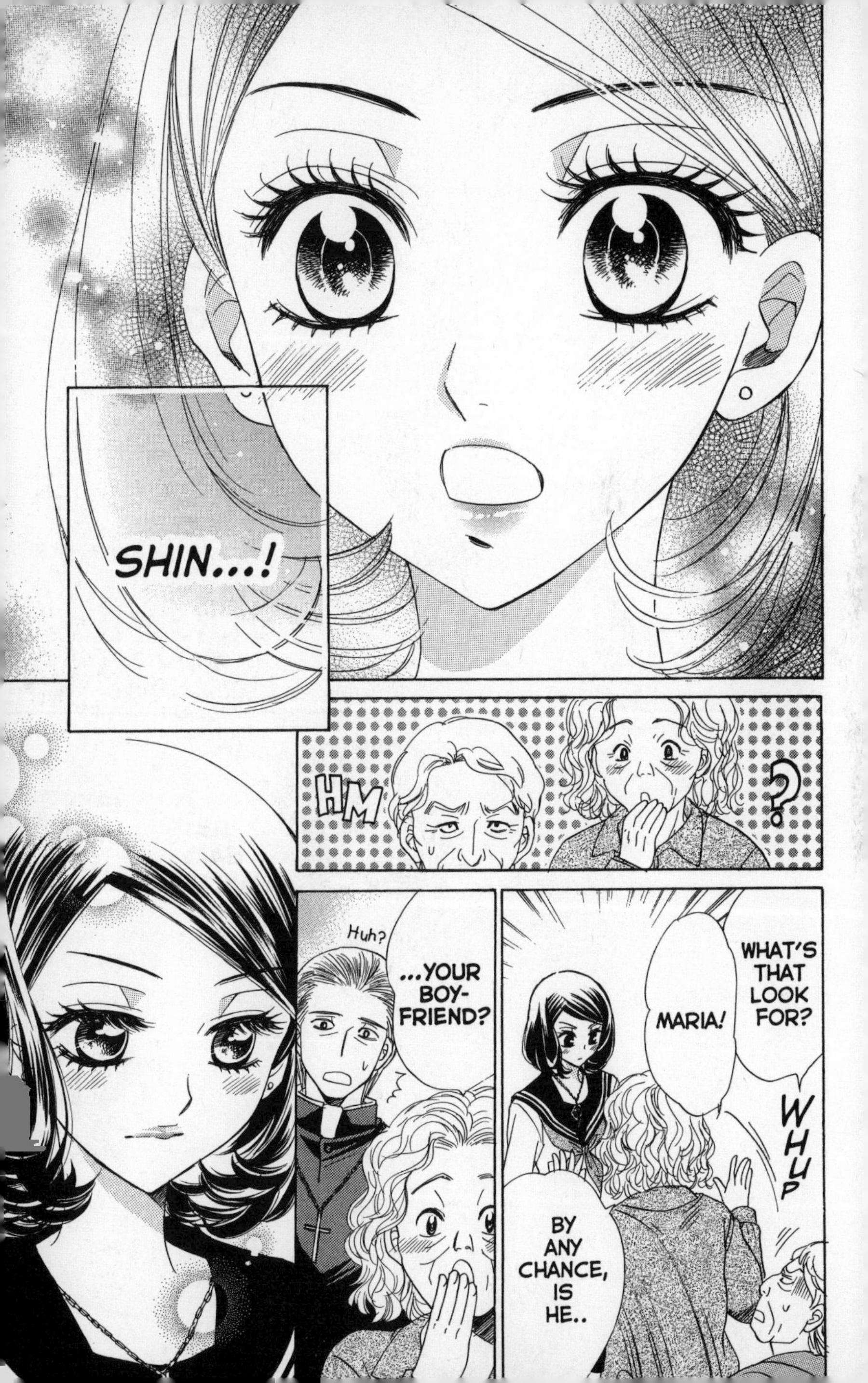
SHIN...!
?
HM
WHAT'S THAT LOOK FOR?
MARIA!
WHUP
BY ANY CHANCE, IS HE..
...YOUR BOY-FRIEND?
Huh?

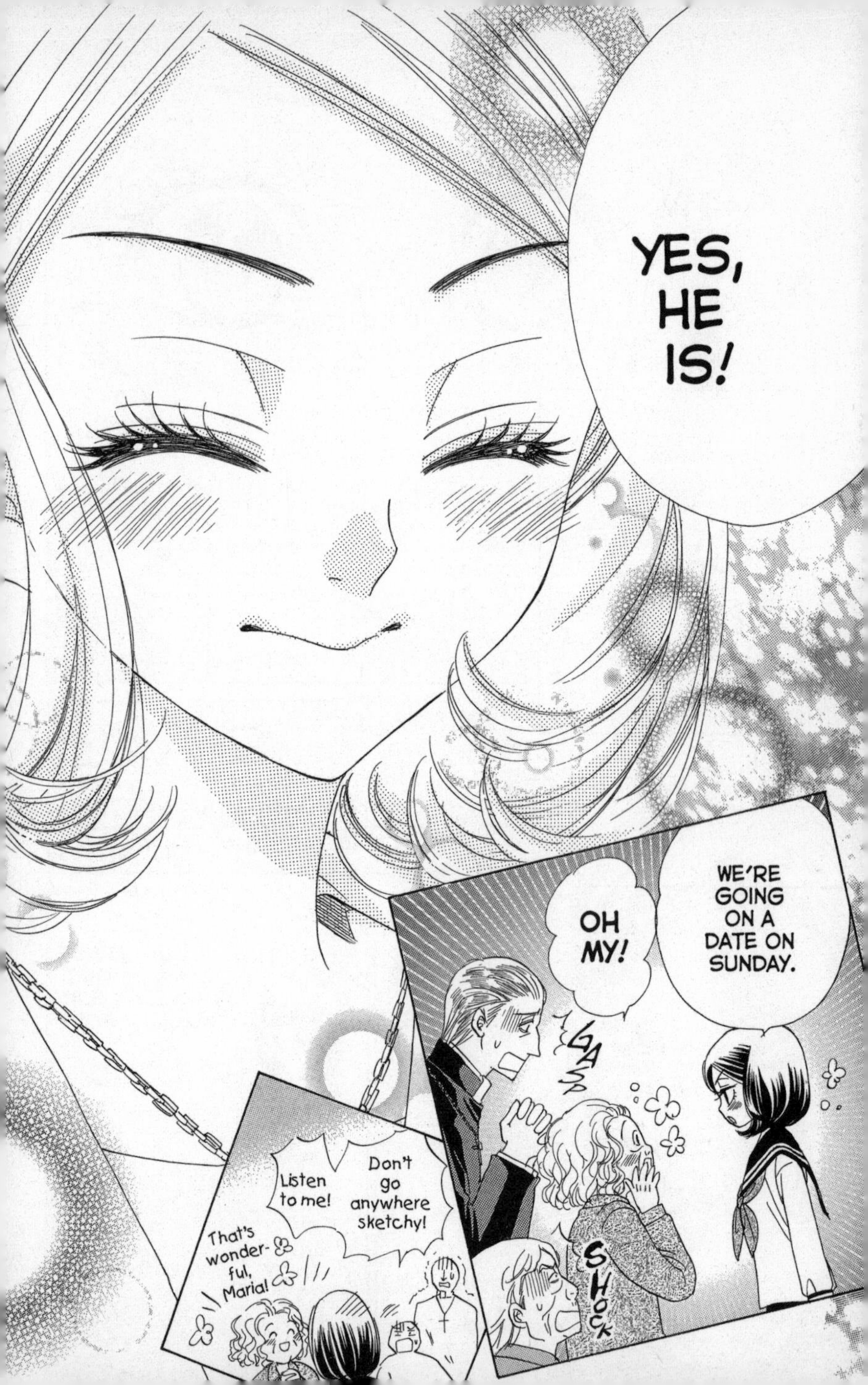
YES, HE IS!
WE'RE GOING ON A DATE ON SUNDAY.
OH MY!
GASP
SHOCK
Don't go anywhere sketchy!
Listen to me!
That's wonder-ful, Maria!

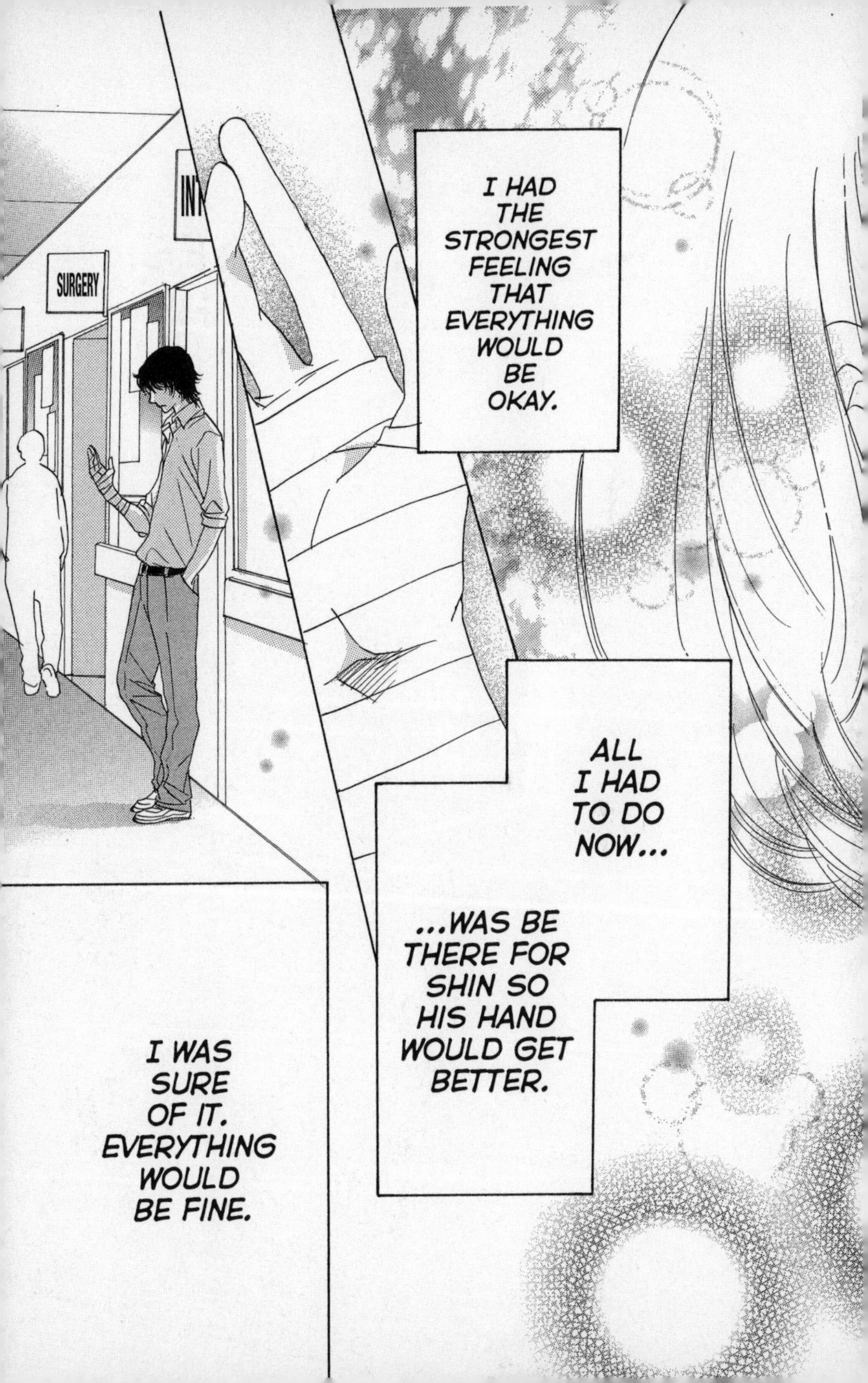
I HAD THE STRONGEST FEELING THAT EVERYTHING WOULD BE OKAY.
ALL I HAD TO DO NOW...
...WAS BE THERE FOR SHIN SO HIS HAND WOULD GET BETTER.
SURGERY
I WAS SURE OF IT. EVERYTHING WOULD BE FINE.

Continued
in
volume 12

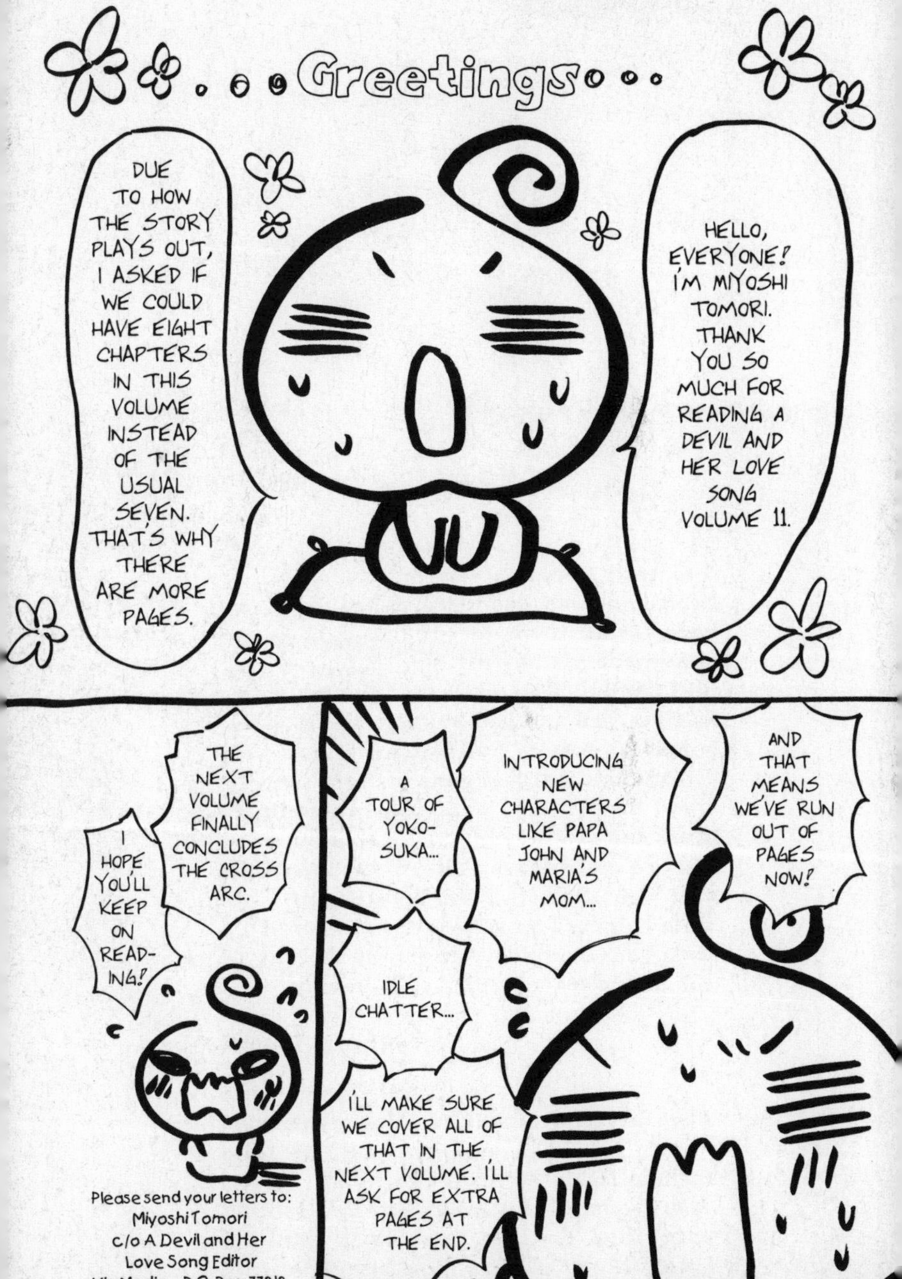
Greetings
HELLO, EVERYONE! I'M MIYOSHI TOMORI. THANK YOU SO MUCH FOR READING A DEVIL AND HER LOVE SONG VOLUME 11.
DUE TO HOW THE STORY PLAYS OUT, I ASKED IF WE COULD HAVE EIGHT CHAPTERS IN THIS VOLUME INSTEAD OF THE USUAL SEVEN. THAT'S WHY THERE ARE MORE PAGES.
AND THAT MEANS WE'VE RUN OUT OF PAGES NOW!
INTRODUCING NEW CHARACTERS LIKE PAPA JOHN AND MARIA'S MOM...
A TOUR OF YOKO-SUKA...
IDLE CHATTER...
I'LL MAKE SURE WE COVER ALL OF THAT IN THE NEXT VOLUME. I'LL ASK FOR EXTRA PAGES AT THE END.
THE NEXT VOLUME FINALLY CONCLUDES THE CROSS ARC.
I HOPE YOU'LL KEEP ON READ-ING!
Please send your letters to:
Miyoshi Tomori
c/o A Devil and Her
Love Song Editor
Viz Media P.O. Box 77010
San Francisco, CA 94107

I recently bought a new cell phone to replace the old one that I've had for many years. It was love at first sight that made me buy my old cell phone, so I continued to use it even though it was cracked and had buttons falling off, a bulging battery, and text messaging capabilities that had gone haywire. One day, I happened to walk into a Docomo store and saw a cell phone with a flower pattern on it. Once again, it was love at first sight. So here I am, polishing my little baby as I gaze lovingly at it every day. (I realize this might not be the way the phone was intended to be used.)

–Miyoshi Tomori

Miyoshi Tomori made her debut as a manga creator in 2001, and her previous titles include *Hatsukare* (First Boyfriend), *Tongari Root* (Square Root), and *Brass Love!!* In her spare time she likes listening to music in the bath and playing musical instruments.

A DEVIL AND HER LOVE SONG
Volume 11
Shojo Beat Edition

STORY AND ART BY
MIYOSHI TOMORI

English Adaptation/Ysabet MacFarlane
Translation/JN Productions
Touch-up Art & Lettering/Monalisa de Asis
Design/Courtney Utt
Editor/Amy Yu

AKUMA TO LOVE SONG © 2006 by Miyoshi Tomori
All rights reserved. First published in Japan in 2006
by SHUEISHA Inc., Tokyo.
English translation rights arranged
by SHUEISHA Inc.

Printed in the U.S.A.

Published by VIZ Media, LLC
P.O. Box 77010
San Francisco, CA 94107

10 9 8 7 6 5 4 3 2 1
First printing, October 2013

www.viz.com   www.shojobeat.com

Surprise!

You may be reading the wrong way!

It's true: In keeping with the original Japanese comic format, this book reads from right to left—so action, sound effects, and word balloons are completely reversed. This preserves the orientation of the original artwork—plus, it's fun! Check out the diagram shown here to get the hang of things, and then turn to the other side of the book to get started!

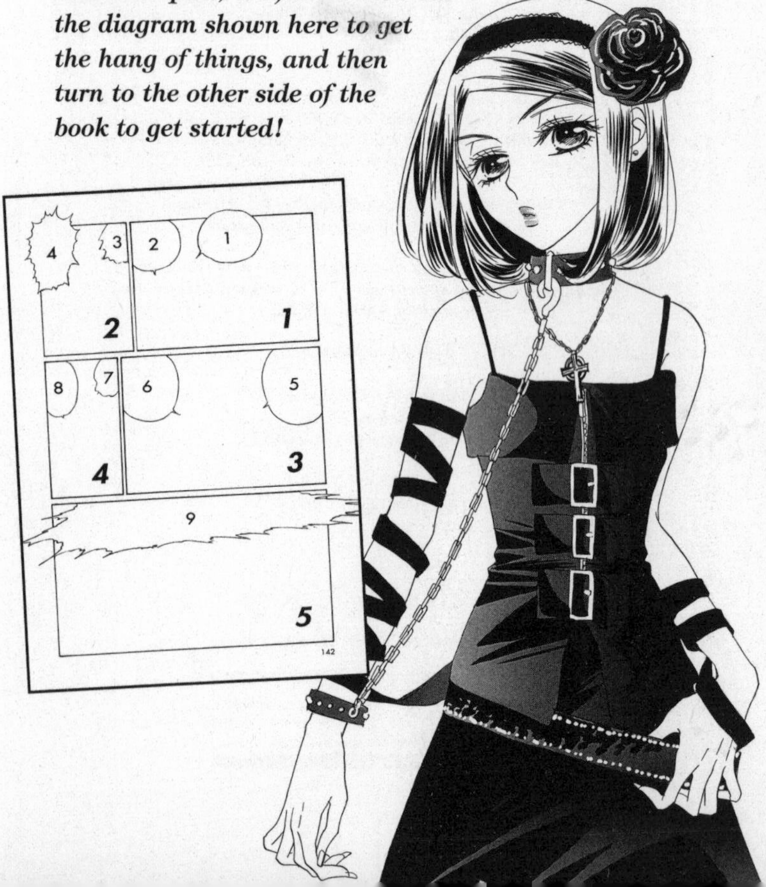
1
2
3
4
1
2
5
6
7
8
3
4
9
5
142